Muslim and Christian Understanding

Theory and Application of "A Common Word"

Muslim and Christian Understanding

Theory and Application of "A Common Word"

Edited by

Waleed El-Ansary and David K. Linnan

palgrave
macmillan

MUSLIM AND CHRISTIAN UNDERSTANDING

First published in 2010 by
PALGRAVE MACMILLAN®
in the United States—a division of St. Martin's Press LLC,
175 Fifth Avenue, New York, NY 10010.

Where this book is distributed in the UK, Europe and the rest of the world, this is by Palgrave Macmillan, a division of Macmillan Publishers Limited, registered in England, company number 785998, of Houndmills, Basingstoke, Hampshire RG21 6XS.

Palgrave Macmillan is the global academic imprint of the above companies and has companies and representatives throughout the world.

Palgrave® and Macmillan® are registered trademarks in the United States, the United Kingdom, Europe and other countries.

ISBN: 978–0–230–10370–2 (hardback)
ISBN: 978–0–230–10442–6 (paperback)

Library of Congress Cataloging-in-Publication Data

Muslim and Christian understanding : theory and application of a common word / edited by Waleed El-Ansary and David K. Linnan.
p. cm.
ISBN 978–0–230–10370–2 (hardback)
1. Islam—Relations—Christianity. 2. Christianity and other religions—Islam. 3. Dialogue—Religious aspects—Islam. 4. Dialogue—Religious aspects—Christianity. I. El-Ansary, Waleed Adel. II. Linnan, David K., 1953–

BP172.M796 2010
297.2′83—dc22 2010016025

A catalogue record of the book is available from the British Library.

Design by Newgen Imaging Systems (P) Ltd., Chennai, India.

First edition: October 2010

10 9 8 7 6 5 4 3 2 1

Printed in the United States of America.

Contents

C. Metaphysics

Part II Applications

A. Environment and Climate Change

B. Human Rights and Ethics

C. Development

Illustrations

Map

Figures

Table

Foreword

This work represents the latest fruit of *A Common Word Between Us and You* (http://www. acommonword.com), a high-level Christian-Muslim dialogue that provides the focus of our exploration of commonalities, differences, and shared interests between the Western and Islamic worlds. We would like to thank the chief architect of the "Common Word" initiative, HRH Prince Ghazi bin Muhammad, for his encouragement in exploring the initiative's wide-ranging implications in an academic setting. His leadership in promoting interfaith relations has been both visionary and inspirational.

We are also grateful to Zayed University in the United Arab Emirates for its support in bringing together senior Muslim and Christian figures from throughout the Middle East to discuss various themes of the book, which have enriched it greatly. In particular, we would like to thank HE Shaykh Nahayan Mabarak Al Nahayan, UAE Minister of Higher Education and Scientific Research, and President of Zayed University, for his support. We are also grateful to HE Shaykh Ali Gomaʿa, the Grand Mufti of Egypt, who not only contributed an essay to the volume, but was a catalyst for the book itself. Finally, we would like to thank Dr. Sulaiman Al Jassim, Vice President of Zayed University, Dr. Nasr Arif, Professor of Political Science of Zayed University, and Ms. Marlys Berg, Director, Administration of Zayed University, for all their encouragement and efforts.

On the Christian side, we are most grateful to Rudolph C. Barnes, Jr., whose family endowed the Barnes Symposium at the University of South Carolina that provided a forum to engage in serious academic inquiry on pressing issues of law and morality understood in the broadest sense. His commitment to interfaith dialogue between Christianity and Islam helped make this book possible. We also wish to thank the Right Reverend William O. Gregg, Episcopal Bishop of Charlotte, for his warm engagement. Once your appetite is whetted by this book, the reader can watch more at http://www.lfip.org/barnes/2009/videopage.htm.

We thank, of course, our families (especially Eman) for patience during all the late nights involved in producing scholarship, and to whom this work is dedicated. We also acknowledge our colleagues and contributors in Indonesia and elsewhere, who spent their own late nights on the work. We close by thanking God, for by grace everything fell into place so well in our efforts that it all seemed preordained, and, on a human level, thanks to the people of good will who thought it was high time to do something. Hopefully things continue.

July, 2010 CE; Sha‘bān, 1431 AH

Waleed El-Ansary, Cairo
David K. Linnan, Columbia

1

Narrative Introduction

Waleed El-Ansary and David K. Linnan

In October 2007, 138 leading Muslim scholars and intellectuals from all corners of the globe representing every Islamic denomination and school of thought—including such figures as the Grand Muftis of Egypt, Syria, Jordan, Oman, Bosnia, Russia, and Istanbul—issued an open letter to leaders of Christian churches and denominations throughout the world entitled "A Common Word Between Us and You." The initiative brings to the fore, in the interest of developing a meaningful peace, how the Muslim and Christian communities representing well over half of the world's population might agree on love of God and love of neighbor as common beliefs. How did this all come about?

The title of the initiative itself derives from a Qur'ānic verse that enjoins Muslims to issue the following call to Christians (and to Jews—the "People of Scripture," as they are known in the Qur'ān): "Say: 'O People of Scripture! Come to a common word between us and you: that we shall worship none but God, and that we shall ascribe no partner unto Him, and that none of us shall take others for lords beside God'" (Q 3:64). In fact, this initiative followed another open letter exactly one year earlier addressed to His Holiness Pope Benedict XVI that was designed to point out politely factual mistakes in the Pope's controversial 2006 Regensburg lecture perceived from differing viewpoints as an attack on Islam itself as a religion condoning violence, versus a call to control all religious intolerance.[1]

The response to "A Common Word" has been profound, finding resonance in the senior levels of Catholic, Protestant and Orthodox branches of Christianity.[2] It is now the most important theological exchange between Christianity and Islam in the world, and provides a framework to address the most pressing issues between the two world communities. The original initiative and profound response thus grew in part out of a sense at the highest level of religious communities that something was wrong that had to be addressed and, ultimately, changed.

What Is the Islamic World?

As a point of departure, we need first to explain what the Islamic world is. Many Westerners equate Islam and Islamic civilization with the Arab zone of the Islamic world, since this was the birthplace of Islam and was for centuries the only part of the Islamic world that the West knew. But only 20% of Muslims today are Arab, as the accompanying map illustrates. The Arab world as the initial zone of Islamic

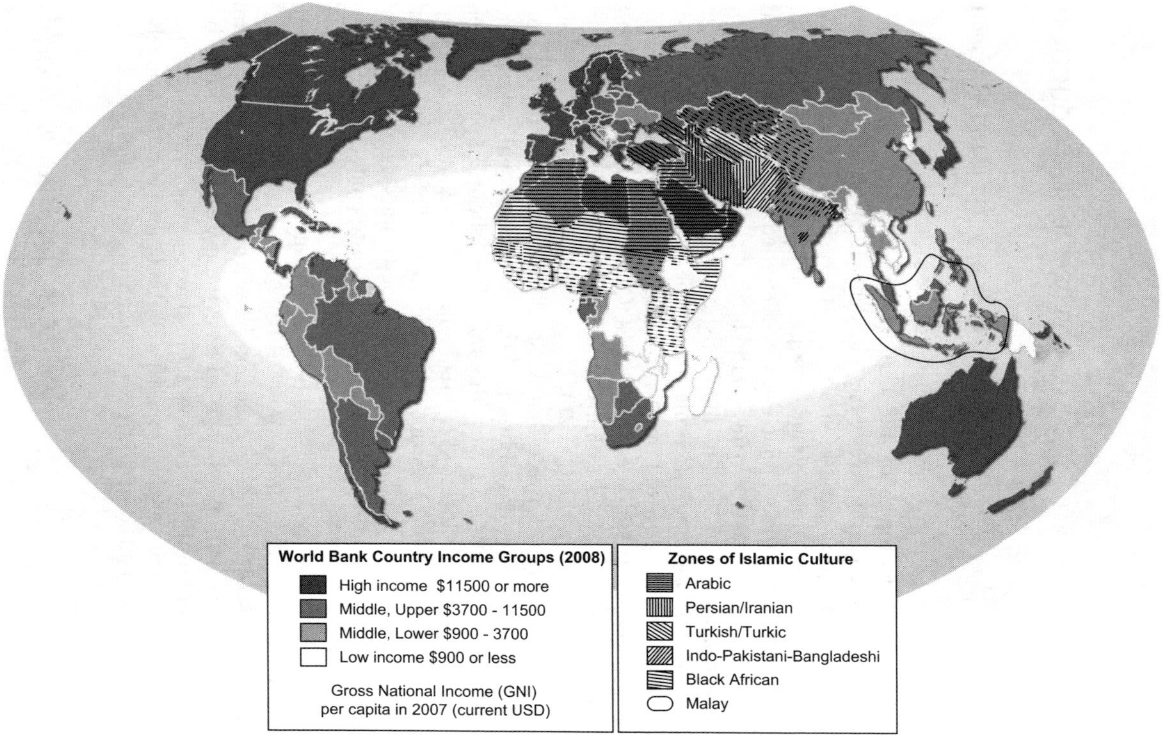

Figure 1.1 2008 World Bank Country Income Groups and Islamic Zones Map. Mixed cultural areas are indicated by dotted lines and are present in Africa (Guinea, Sierra Leone, Liberia, Cote d'Ivoire, Ghana, Nigeria, Camaroon, Central African Republic, Uganda, Kenya, and Tanzania), and in Asia (Kazakhstan, China, and India).

Sources: Seyyed Hossein Nasr, *The Heart of Islam: Enduring Values for Humanity* (San Francisco: Harper San Francisco, 2002); World Bank.

culture represents many ethnicities involving approximately 250 million people, who are united linguistically rather than ethnically. Although Arabic is the sacred language of Islam (not a liturgical language like Latin in the medieval West), 80% of Muslims do not use Arabic as a language of daily discourse.

The second zone of Islamic culture is the Persian zone consisting of present-day Iran, Afghanistan, and Tajikistan. It represents the second major ethnic group, a branch of the Aryan or Indo-Iranian-European peoples, who embraced Islam and who participated in building classical Islamic civilization without becoming Arabized. The dominant language in this zone is Persian, although it contains different dialects such as you might find in England or Texas. Although today it is common to identify the Persian zone with Shīʿism and the Arab zone with Sunnism, this is only partly correct at present and is completely incorrect if projected into the past, since much of the Arab east was Shīʿite in the tenth century and most of Persia was Sunnī until the sixteenth century. Both denominations are orthodox interpretations of the Islamic revelation that for the most part only differ regarding the function of the political leader of the community rather than the essential tenets of faith or religious practice.[3] Today this zone comprises over 110 million people.

The third zone of Islamic culture is that of Black Africa, where Islam started to spread in the seventh century, establishing powerful kingdoms in Ghana by the eleventh century and Mali in the fourteenth century. Although Swahili is perhaps the most important Islamic language of this zone, there are many subzones with distinct languages, in contrast to the Arab and Persian worlds where one language dominates. This sub-Saharan zone of Islamic culture represents approximately 200 million people.

The fourth zone is the Turkic, embracing those people who speak one of the Altaic languages, with Turkish being the most important. This zone includes present-day Turkey and much of Central Asia, but stretches from the Balkans to Siberia, making it the most geographically widespread zone of the Islamic world. Although it is ethnically different from the Persian zone, it is culturally very similar and comprises approximately 170 million people.

The fifth zone is that of the Indian subcontinent, the most populous zone of the Islamic world with nearly half a billion people. It includes Pakistan and Bangladesh, as well as the Muslims of India, Nepal, and Sri Lanka. Ethnically this zone is mostly homogenous, but culturally and linguistically quite diverse, with several local languages such as Sindhi, Gujrati, Punjabi, and Bengali gaining some prominence, and Urdu as the official language of Pakistan, although Persian was the intellectual and literary language of Indian Muslims for nearly a thousand years.

The sixth zone embraces the Malay world in Southeast Asia, which includes Malaysia, Indonesia (the most populous muslim majority country in the world), Brunei, and minority communities in Thailand, the Philippines, Cambodia, and Vietnam. Malay Islam has been deeply influenced by Sufism, the esoteric dimension of Islam, reflecting a mild and gentle aspect consistent with the principal ethnic characteristics of the people. In fact, Sufism played a major role in the spread of Islam into the Malay world in the fifteenth century, coloring the intellectual and spiritual life of approximately 240 million people, much as it did in the African and Indian zones.

Besides these six major zones, there are smaller ones that deserve mention, such as the up to one hundred million Chinese Muslims, as well as new Islamic communities in Europe and the United States that play an important role as bridge between Islam and the West. In fact, several chapters in this volume present the voice of a new generation of Western Muslim scholars who have studied in the best Western institutions of higher learning and who know Western thought in depth. They are also practicing Muslims deeply rooted in the Islamic intellectual tradition. So the Islamic world consists of far more than the Arab zone, or even the troubled Middle East, while, unfortunately, Westerner's knowledge of Islam and Muslims is not what it should be. Accordingly, this book hopes to provide enough knowledge to promote preliminary engagement.

The map also illustrates the diversity of income levels within the Islamic world following the World Bank's standard country income level groupings. The broader picture suggests a need for collaboration on global challenges of economic development and the environment, which "A Common Word" provides a framework to address. Although in the Middle East there are a small number of very rich nations due to oil and natural resources, there are also Muslim nations in the poorest parts of the world, such as Sub-Saharan Africa, with other countries in between. On the whole, it is fair to say that most of the Islamic world consists of low- to middle-income countries in World Bank terminology.

"A Common Word" in Theory and Practice

This book is the first to expand the "Common Word" inquiry addressing religious commonalities (starting with love of God) from a comparative exploration of theology, mysticism, and metaphysics, or "vertical" issues, while addressing "horizontal" issues of governance and legal development (emphasizing love of neighbor) in the practical context of international challenges such as development, the environment, and human rights. We refer to these two areas of focus as the theory and application of "A Common Word," given an intention to look beyond conventional approaches to interfaith dialogue and ethics per se to better engage the practical level of shared international challenges.

Theory

Our book commences with introductory statements and exhortations of distinguished Muslim and Christian religious leaders. His Excellency Shaykh Ali Goma'a speaks as Grand Mufti of Egypt and one of the leading Sunnī religious figures in the Islamic world. He addresses the motivation behind "A Common Word" in the context of globalization, outlining practical initiatives that Muslims and Christians should address together. This does not involve compromising religious principles, as some erroneously fear, which underscores the importance of the theory section of the book. He also emphasizes the role of religious leaders in confronting shared challenges, underscoring the importance of its applications elements.

Seyyed Hossein Nasr speaks as arguably the leading Islamic scholar living in the West, hailing from a Shī'ite and Persian background. He addresses the theory of "A Common Word" in the original sense of *theoria*, or vision, and not theory as ordinarily understood. Thereafter, he discusses practical steps to realize this vision on the level of and through *praxis*. He emphasizes that both are necessary to confront the shared challenges of a desacralized worldview and its applications. This brings out the interconnections between the theory and applications sections at the most profound level.

The Right Reverend William O. Gregg speaks as a Bishop of the Episcopal Church and former chair of its Standing Commission on Ecumenical Relations. He begins with three images—one from a Muslim source, one from a Christian source, and one from the natural world—to illustrate the opportunities and possibilities offered by "A Common Word." Accordingly, he outlines some of the major scriptural, theological, and practical questions that occupy much of the book.

The book's heart, on the side of theory, addresses vertical issues of comparative theology, mysticism, and metaphysics. Ibrahim Kalin speaks in his individual capacity as scholar of Islamic philosophical thought, but also as official spokesperson of "A Common Word." He argues that Christian-Muslim theological dialogue remains understudied and undertheorized, resulting in a lack of communicative rationality as a basis for theological interaction, which "A Common Word" seeks to fill. Although a full-fledged theology of comparative religion may not have been a compelling necessity before the modern era, it is clearly desirable in our tense times. He accordingly examines how obstacles in the flourishing of such dialogue might be overcome.

One of the key issues he focuses on is the different ways that Islam and Christianity have encountered and reacted to the European Enlightenment and secular modernity, leading to important differences in the way Christian and Muslim communities have interacted with one another and conversed, or failed to converse, on such issues as reason, freedom, human rights, and religious freedom. He maintains that the "Common Word" initiative has broken new ground in Muslim-Christian relations to address such vested historical, theological, and political issues, and that the growing debate over the issue should be read as a sign that a serious theological dialogue between Christians and Muslims is just beginning.

Daniel Madigan speaks as a Jesuit priest who has served as consultor of the Vatican's Commission for Religious Relations with Muslims of the Pontifical Council for Interreligious Dialogue. He notes that properly theological questions are often not even on the table in official interfaith discourse. Meanwhile, he rejects the claim that such dialogue is impossible, and argues that it is in fact essential. He employs the superb image of how out-of-town guests often provide a chance for people to explore their hometown in ways they're not normally accustomed. Invoking this image of mutual hospitality, he illuminates new possibilities for mutual learning and understanding in the context of "A Common Word." However, he warns that a confusion of categories in the typical discourse on prophets and scriptures comparing Jesus—whom Muslims also revere as a Messiah destined to return before the final judgment—with Muḥammad, the prophet of Islam, or the Bible with the Qur'ān, leads to a theological dead end.

Madigan therefore calls for a common language in which meanings, not just utterances, are shared even if it turns out to be a common language in which to disagree. This suggests that the trade-off sometimes offered implicitly by Christian partners in theological dialogue with Muslims that involves exchanging a lowest common denominator understanding of the nature of Jesus Christ for a lowest common denominator understanding of the nature of the Qur'ān is unnecessary. In fact, the opposite tact in commencing theological discussion from an elevated understanding of Christ's Divinity is, contrary to expectation, a much more promising point of departure. Later chapters on comparative metaphysics build upon this move toward a theology of comparative religion complementing Kalin's analysis. These views may reflect the Islamic insight that the three Abrahamic faiths (Islam, Christianity, and Judaism) all focus on the same God, hence would profit from listening more closely to one another talking about God.

Caner Dagli speaks in his academic capacity as a scholar of Islamic philosophy and Sufism, but also with the perspective of a former interfaith affairs consultant in the Royal Hashemite Court of Jordan, where he participated in "An Open Letter to the Pope" (in response to the Regensburg lecture) and "A Common Word." He examines the need for and role of (Islamic) mysticism in interfaith dialogue, maintaining that those who are attached to the inner dimension of their traditions are better able to have a deeper dialogue with their counterparts. This is particularly true in light of the great potential of mystical teachings open to believers looking for the discernment of truth in other religions.

From Dagli's point of view, Muslim and Christian saints and sages share not only the supreme commandments to love God and love their neighbor, but also the realization of these commandments. This merges *theoria* and *praxis* in the deepest sense of those terms. Those who are attached to this inner dimension therefore tend to be at the core of much good work, such as "A Common Word," but tend not to lay their public emphasis there. Meanwhile, Islam is commonly perceived as a formalistic, rule-based religion (in fact reflecting different dimensions within Islam, and the idea that some schools within Islam, such as Salafīʿism, adhere to more narrow views). The role of the inner dimension of Islam is not explicit in broad-based documents such as "A Common Word" despite its significance on multiple levels. The problem at hand is that Christians often regard esoteric approaches to Islam as not being truly "Islamic" on the basis of an assumption that only formalistic, rule-based Islam is the real Islam. Denying the legitimacy of this dimension in interfaith dialogue on any level would represent an irretrievable loss.

John Chryssavgis speaks as a Greek Orthodox priest, but also with the perspective of theological advisor to the Ecumenical Patriarch. He explores the fundamental mystical principles underlying Orthodox efforts to promote understanding, tolerance, and compassion through interfaith dialog, taking as example Ecumenical Patriarch Bartholomew who has made building bridges between religions, races, and cultures a foremost priority in his theology and ministry. Chryssavgis points out the global implications of the fact that even the most complete and comprehensive definition of God can never approach the fullness of divine nature, highlighting the implications for Orthodox spiritual thought and practice in approaching theological differences. He evokes the powerful image of Abraham's hospitality to an unexpected visit from three strangers as an icon of interfaith dialogue, an interesting parallel to Madigan's appeal for mutual hospitality, showing that dialogue is itself a gift from above.

Chryssavgis' open appeal to the mystical tradition of the Eastern Orthodox Church in the name of interfaith dialogue provides an interesting contrast to the role of mysticism in the Islamic context as outlined by Dagli. The distinction between the exoteric and the esoteric, or the public versus private faces of belief, is not as sharp in the Christian East as it is in the Islamic world, which implies much for the role of mysticism in building bridges between traditions. But both Chryssavgis and Dagli approach the role of mysticism in reconciling theological differences within a shared view of pre-modern intellectual space alluded to in Kalin's paper, rejecting rationalist secularism and its relativistic elements.

Joseph Lumbard speaks in his capacity as a scholar of Islamic philosophical thought, as well as former adviser on interfaith affairs to the Royal Hashemite Court of Jordan. He addresses the metaphysics of religion, understood as seeking the true nature of things beyond theological doctrine as such. Lumbard examines the understanding of "God's word" in Islamic theology and the manner in which the Islamic understanding of God's uncreated word provides an opening within Islamic theology to a fuller understanding of the Christian concept of Jesus as Divine Word. He then proposes ways in which Qur'ānic passages regarding the nature of Jesus can be understood by Muslims when read in relation to Christian theology rather than in opposition to it. The objective is not to provide conclusive arguments, but to examine ways in which Islamic theology can understand Christian teachings within the structure of Christianity itself. We see how much can be gained by engaging in comparative theology from a higher metaphysical point of view, and conversely how much may be lost by categorically ruling out such discussion, paralleling Madigan's concerns.

James Cutsinger speaks as an authority on the theology and spirituality of the Christian East with a special interest in comparative metaphysics. He responds to "A Common Word" by arguing that the profoundest form of unity between Christians and Muslims can be achieved if, and only if, one first acknowledges the radical disparity that exists between their traditions on a doctrinal or theological level, paradoxically reversing the popular notion of politely agreeing to disagree. He argues toward a resolution of opposing Muslim and Christian viewpoints of the nature of Christ (and Adam) and issues with Christian theology's Trinitarian doctrine in metaphysical rather than purely theological terms. Accordingly, he attempts to bring together central Christian and Muslim convictions in such a way as to show how their apparently contradictory claims can help both come to a deeper understanding of their own beliefs.

Maria Dakake rounds out the section on comparative metaphysics in her capacity as a scholar of Islamic philosophy and mysticism. She points out that the figure of Christ and the concept of the Word of God are intricately connected in both Christianity and Islam, but that the two apparently parallel concepts are defined theologically in radically different ways in the two religions. Agreeing with Lumbard and Cutsinger on the potential for using these concepts to advance interreligious dialogue between Christians and Muslims, she argues for a further analysis of these theological concepts through the lens of shared Christian and Muslim views of human creation and the figure of Adam. In a sense, she brings together several insights found in previous chapters, arguing that where the door of theology shuts on certain questions of interfaith dialogue, those of metaphysics and mysticism might yet open.

Practice

The chapters in the initial section of the book thus collectively demonstrate on the one hand how Muslims and Christians can engage in interfaith dialogue without either compromising their religious integrity, or on the other simply reducing dialogue to the level of polite diplomacy. In fact, academic approaches to interfaith dialogue are frequently reductionist in character, while dialogue between religious authorities is often theologically defensive. This book is probably the first to balance both elements in the context of "A Common Word," taking advantage of the openness of the academic environment (in which those who do not represent large constituencies risk less when venturing new approaches to theological differences), while simultaneously reinforcing the integrity of the traditions. But do we engage simply to understand each other's religion better, or also with a view to cooperation on our common problems, commencing with the environment and climate change? An underlying thrust of "A Common Word" is that there are global problems requiring undivided attention, so that the world of politics and action would profit through coordinated efforts of Muslims and Christians working together.

Waleed El-Ansary speaks as an Islamic economist with special interest in the environment. His chapter represents a bridge from the theological focus of the book's first half addressing the theory of "A Common Word" to the book's second half covering our application topics, namely the environment, human rights, and development. He begins with the observation that, in certain areas of the Islamic world, it is an observed fact that religion in the form of God's law seems a more effective protector of the environment than secular regulation. Why is this so?

The key is the idea lost to secular regulation that the environment represents God's creation, with the result that it cannot be subjected to cost-benefit analysis in a customary regulatory mode (meanwhile, those who might be unconcerned about violating secular laws may follow the dictates of God's law). Further, the theological view that man may subjugate the environment is wrong, at least in Islamic eyes, because man is the steward of God's creation, rather than its owner. As a practical matter, Islamic law establishes a hierarchy of use in economic terms, articulating principles analogous not only to international environmental law's precautionary principle, but also establishing social justice-based rules that prioritize prevention of harm to the poor above gains to the wealthy. Religion ultimately calls into question any purely technological approach to addressing issues like climate change, suggesting the need for a new environmental economic understanding based on the intellectual and esoteric dimensions of religion in addition to the legal or ethical dimension in order to develop a common word on the environment as neighbor.

Cinnamon Carlarne speaks as an environmental scholar working principally on evolving systems of domestic and international environmental law and policy, especially in the area of climate change. She sees religion as an inescapable part of the climate change debate. In chicken-and-egg fashion, if you seek change you need to alter beliefs before behavior will shift. The reason is that religion is an integral part of culture, and culture drives beliefs. Addressing climate change involves altering behavior, so beliefs rather than simple commands must drive change to enable effective enforcement.

Part of the problem in involving religion in a climate change discussion is the longtime separation of religion and the environment in North American environmentalists' eyes. Environmentalism has approached the status of secular religion, and traditional religion was correspondingly rejected, in the alternative, because of twisted scriptural interpretations attributing to man unlimited dominion over the environment, or because of beliefs that technological rationalism was superior as an approach to a supposedly more emotive religious sensibility. However, organized Christianity in the form of Catholic and mainline Protestant denominations have begun to push religious involvement in the environment. Evangelicals in particular are developing an affinity for the environment as God's creation.

Nicholas Adams speaks as an Anglican theologian addressing a perceived reluctance among Protestant theologians to embrace secular ideas of human rights along the lines of the United Nations' 1947 "Universal Declaration of Human Rights." Why is this, and what does it tell us about the understanding of human rights in modern Christianity and Islam? Adams sees "A Common Word" itself as seeking a partnership of differences, not just unity on commonalities, arguing that its method of scriptural juxtaposition (as opposed to strong interpretation) offers a model for how members of different traditions might reason together about human rights.

Adams' underlying issue is whether human rights are best realized in practice under a single, universal maximalist approach—understood in philosophical terms as the Kantian view—or whether human rights should be rooted rather in the indigenous views of different communities, here based in religion and history, subject to certain minimum standards, understood in philosophical terms as the Hegelian view. The underlying difference is whether, in the longer term, views of human rights across countries and religious communities are advanced more by striving toward an artificial common maximalist standard, versus seeking shared roots in local cultures and beliefs. Adams' picture of the proper approach to human rights across religions and cultures is to hearken back to the early modern political settlements between Catholics and Protestants in the wake of the Reformation, employing as examples the Peaces of Augsburg (1555 CE) and Westphalia (1648 CE), designed to allow European Catholics and Protestants to live together and contribute peacefully to the life of the same, diverse community.

Harkristuti Harkrisnowo speaks in her personal capacity as Indonesian legal scholar and longtime human rights proponent, but with her parallel perspective as serving director general for human rights in the Indonesian Ministry of Justice (in which capacity she bears official responsibility for human rights in the world's most populous Islamic country). Her perspective on human rights involves a lawyer's sensibility in pursuing specific legal solutions rather than a theologian seeking general moral outcomes. She sees in Adams' discussion of Kantian versus Hegelian views a parallel to discussions a decade ago opposing Asian values to Western values, and challenges the idea that human rights are solely Western concepts.

The hidden issue in practice involves assumptions that beliefs within, much less between, religions are homogeneous, when in fact views on Islamic law's content can sometimes vary widely across Islamic zones and within individual Islamic communities. Thus, looking at Indonesian experiments like Islamic law's recent introduction in Aceh, the problem in practice for Muslim jurists is how properly to apply Islamic law in specific local contexts, particularly when political statements are often made about the requirements that may perversely violate true Islamic principles as articulated by respected Islamic scholars.

Indonesia's extremely diverse ethnic groups and society are the multicultural core of shared Indonesian historical experience, notwithstanding incidents involving religious and ethnic tensions in certain geographic areas. The difficulty is that friction may arise by reason of competition for land and resources between groups at a social level, which may be translated into religious friction if the ethnic groups follow different religions for purely historical reasons. Problems have multiplied recently due to the activities of religious militias from outside local communities who may seize upon a conflict-laden situation for their own purposes. The government often becomes involved to preserve the peace, but meanwhile must challenge party propaganda that it is taking sides in a religious dispute. However, the vast majority of ordinary Indonesians live peacefully with their neighbors of all religious persuasions. Further, ordinary Muslim Indonesians are horrified at claims that Islam justifies murder (as in the Bali bombings). Indonesia works proactively against religious extremism via religious leaders, most recently via youth programs. Here, "A Common Word" might play a role.

Joseph Isanga speaks as African Catholic priest and scholar of human rights. His chapter represents a bridge between human rights and development as two different applications for "A Common Word." Isanga recognizes Africa as the most conflict-ridden area of the world, but also as an environment of strong religious traditions. Social disputes triggering religion tension may under some circumstances divide Africans, but religion has a place in human rights and development.

Religious conflicts may arise in part because there are strong majorities, minorities, pluralities of Christianity and Islam across Africa. Conflict is more possible where there are strongly contending groups, as opposed to an essentially homogenous population, or a largely fragmented population. But the African problem goes beyond competing religions, as witnessed by the recent misuse of religion in the horrific human rights record of the nominally Christian Lord's Resistance Army. Catholic social doctrine provides for the development of the individual, for which purpose education is a pressing need, meanwhile remaining critical toward both liberal capitalism and Marxist collectivism. "A Common Word" could have a special place in Africa, as part of a program to involve religious institutions more in dealing with both shortcomings of African states and international financial institutions (IFIs, meaning chiefly the World Bank, International Monetary Fund, and various regional development banks).

Zamir Iqbal and Abbas Mirakhor speak as economists with extensive experience within the IFIs, now trying to articulate a distinctively Islamic view of development. Islam contains a blueprint for society and its members' proper behavior, but one only fully applied briefly at Islam's inception. Islamic ideas of development would share the focus on institutions under the new institutional economics current in IFIs as a leading explanation for economic growth. However, Islam would distinguish between individual self-development, physical development of the earth, and development of the human collectivity. Such insights should apply beyond Muslim majority countries as such. But Islam's concepts of social justice and development infer that physical resources were created for all mankind, so holders of those same resources may be in a trust-like relationship (and redistribution remains possible). "A Common Word" thus may be a catalyst for a shared theology of development able to address distributive justice concerns.

David Linnan speaks from the perspective of a legal scholar engaged in legal and economic reform work at the Southeast Asian end of the developing Islamic world since long before 9/11. He reviews the ideas and history behind secular development reaching back to the 1950s, as well as specifically Catholic and Protestant ideas touching on development. One lasting problem is a general lack of consensus on what precisely constitutes development, linked with disputes on a technical level about how to accomplish that ambiguous goal. Should development be measured purely in material terms, versus also employing social indicators like public health and education, versus newer concepts like sustainability in the face of challenges like climate change? How can you know when you have succeeded when there is substantial dispute concerning what constitutes the proper yardstick?

The bottom line is that all of the developing world started from a similar position in the 1940s through the 1960s. Some developing countries have become resounding successes, at least in achieving material development comparable to the West, while others have not made substantial progress. Typically Asian countries have been among the most successful, African countries have been among the least successful, and Latin American countries lie somewhere in between. Those who did succeed typically adopted market-based liberal economic policies by the 1980s, linked with strategies like export-oriented development premised upon industrialization, which often had as collateral effect increasing inequality within countries even as GDP grew.

These approaches keying on industrialization as development strategy also brought environmental and related problems, which now may be more difficult to sustain in the face of general complications like climate change. If industrialization is the traditional first step on an economic growth ladder, and increasing economic resources is key to achieving development under almost any definition, how can a developing country substantially increase income levels in the face of complications like climate change? Speaking of the Islamic world, it shares economic development concerns with much of non-Muslim Africa, Asia, and Latin America. For such countries, economic development is typically the first priority, but what are the social dimensions to sustainability? There are scientific arguments revolving around what levels of atmospheric carbon dioxide versus degrees of warming would occur, however, the effects are typically treated on a macro level rather than on an individual country basis. What is the proper answer if we cannot all fit through the eye of the needle at the same time, and to what extent can "A Common Word" help to address this next step in a practical sense?

Quo Vadis?

This returns us to the issue first raised by Seyyed Hossein Nasr concerning the shared challenges of a desacralized worldview. Applying the full resources of the Islamic and Christian traditions to the exigencies of our time, including the need for a new economic understanding to deal with concerns about sustainability and climate change, requires *theoria* in the deepest sense of the term. But in the Islamic world, the traditional Islamic sciences and educational system have been weakened by the imposition of secular modes of thought and institutions.[4] The advent of this era is often dated to Napoleon's 1798–1801 Egyptian campaign, representing the beginning of European domination of the heartland of the Islamic world.[5] Indeed, this led to an internal perception of crisis, particularly among the youth who associate power with truth, and for whom nothing is more humiliating than colonization.

Today, many Westerners have a queasy feeling about adoption of Sharīʿah law in Muslim majority countries as a looming threat perceived in terms of a battle between modernists and fundamentalists, (although parallel claims of Sharīʿah law's adoption in the West seem overwrought). This book suggests that the actual situation in the Islamic world is quite complex with many different reactions and competing strains of thought following in the wake of colonialism. At one end of the spectrum are secular fundamentalists who completely reject religion as a normative force for guiding society, and for whom Islamic civilization is something to be left behind in favor of modern Western civilization as part of the modernization exercise itself.[6] The aggressive secularism of Kemal Atatürk in modernizing Turkey is one example of this approach. At the other extreme are *takfīris*, militants who claim that anyone who stands in the way of their very narrowly defined vision of Islam are legitimate targets of violence, much like the group that assassinated President Anwar Sadat of Egypt. Less extreme versions of each end of the spectrum are those who hold that Islamic teachings should change with the times on one hand, and those who claim that anything after the first century following the Prophet of Islam is an undesirable innovation on the other. In the center are the silent majority of Muslims who view religion as the source of meaning and guidance for the inward and outward life, and for whom Islamic civilization offers a precious source of nourishment.

This traditional middle represents the overwhelming majority of Muslims, with less than one hundredth of one percent (i.e., less than 0.01 percent, or less than one in every 10 thousand Muslims) in the militant category, and perhaps less than 10 percent in all other categories combined.[7] Accordingly, the 90 percent of Muslims in the traditional middle are essential for addressing global challenges with their Christian counterparts in the applications context of "A Common Word" going forward. Since Islam asserts the universality of revelation, the traditional middle is in fact anxious to partner with fellow people of scripture on shared challenges of the environment, drug abuse, poverty, and other issues that the Grand Mufti of Egypt, Shaykh Ali Goma'a, outlines in his introductory remarks. Conversely, "A Common Word" is crucial for greater Western understanding of this traditional Islamic middle, sometimes erroneously conflated with aggressive fundamentalism by the West, to avoid marginalizing the very group that could provide the antidote to extremism in all its forms.

Notes

1. For the text of the Pope's Regensberg address, see http://www.zenit.org/article-16955-?l=english. For commentary on the Pope's address, see http://www.newsweek.com/id/45693. On the theological motives and expectations of "A Common Word," see Prince Ghazi bin Muhammad, "*A Common Word Between Us and You*: Theological Motivations and Expectations," http://www.acommonword.com/en/Ghazi-Biser-Speech.pdf.
2. For a fuller examination of the history of "A Common Word," the responses to it, and its influence, see Joseph Lumbard, "The Uncommonality of 'A Common Word,'" *Crown Paper*, http://www.brandeis.edu/crown/publications/cp/CP3.pdf. For a live discussion of many of these issues, see the streaming video of the conference underlying this book in concept, *Theory and Application of A Common Word,* March 26–27, 2009, http://www.lfip.org/barnes/2009/videopage.htm.
3. See Seyyed Hossein Nasr, *The Heart of Islam: Enduring Values for Humanity,* 65–76.
4. See for instance Seyyed Hossein Nasr, *Traditional Islam in the Modern World* and Joseph Lumbard, ed., *Islam, Fundamentalism, and the Betrayal of Tradition: Essays by Western Muslim Scholars.*
5. See Ghazi bin Muhammad, *The Crisis of the Islamic World.*
6. For a brief, but excellent summary of the following spectrum, see Caner Dagli, *Jihad and the Islamic Law of War,* 57–67. http://www.haqqani.org.es/Contenidos/jihad.pdf.
7. Ibid, pp. 60–61. See also John Esposito and Dalia Mogahed, *Who Speaks for Islam: What Over a Billion Muslims Really Think.*

Religious Leaders' Introductions

2

"A Common Word Between Us and You": Motives and Applications

HE Shaykh Ali Goma'a

Previously, the call to dialogue between religions could not find its place between nations. Such a call—if one were ever delivered—was received with disdain and dismissed due to the then prevalent isolation of communities in the world that caused a deterrent to communication, and man's inability to recognize the importance of this dialogue despite the presence of a clear religious perspective promoting it. But now such dialogue appears to be a necessity in the wake of extremists from both the East and the West who have succeeded in swaying the future course of humanity toward the theory of a clash of civilizations while dividing the world into warring factions. Dialogue has become an intellectual and pragmatic necessity in order to put an end to humanity's slip into barbarism, especially now that we live as neighbors in a world where barriers have been lifted through communication, transportation, and new technologies. Everyone has become interconnected, and ideas are flowing from everywhere. We live in a world that is referred to as a "small village" or a "global village" in which any action in any place now has a global impact, whether positive or negative. For this reason, there remains no possibility for self-isolation or segregation from others. There is no choice but to live together in the world. So what is to be done? We must engage in dialogue, establishing its foundations as God Most High intended.

Dialogue is one of several types of exploration in a quest for clarification, which is one of the essential bases of dialogue. When I sit with the other, I want to discover who that person is. I want to seek that which is common between us. I want to correct some of my misconceptions, which come from either the result of history and its unfolding events, or the reading of books that are written by those who criticize or disagree with the other thereby causing great potential for misunderstanding or ill intent. I want to know the truth. When we make language and its terminology one, many of our differences fade away. Ibn Ḥazm (994–1064 CE), an Andalusian jurist and theologian, said that if terms in any domain are reassigned and agreed upon, three quarters of the differences between all of humanity would dissipate. We would realize that the area that is shared between the other and ourselves is much greater than the area on which we differ. That is the focus of "A Common Word" initiative. And the greatest thing we share that brings us together is love of God and love of neighbor.

I do not think I exaggerate if I say that "A Common Word" initiative has become the most prominent exchange between Muslims and Christians in the world today. This initiative was launched on October 13, 2007, as an open letter signed by 138 Muslim scholars and intellectuals addressed to church leaders and Christian communities throughout the world, starting with Pope Benedict XVI. The essence of this letter, as affirmed in verses of the Qur'ān and the Bible, was that Muslims and Christians share values of the utmost importance, namely love of God and love of neighbor. Building on this common ground, the letter called for peace and love between Christians and Muslims throughout the world.

Since its release in 2007, prominent Christian figures, including the Pope, Dr. Rowan Williams, the Archbishop of Canterbury, and Mark Hanson, the Presiding Bishop of the Evangelical Lutheran Church in America, have reacted positively.

In November of 2007, over 300 American evangelical leaders responded in an open letter published in *The New York Times*. During 2008, the number of Muslim scholars who signed on to the initiative reached 300, in addition to 460 Islamic institutions and organizations. The exchange resulted in other social initiatives being enacted in countries such as India, Bangladesh, the United States, Canada, and Great Britain. And we have heard unofficial reports of other efforts undertaken in many different places that have taken this initiative as their launching point. Conferences have been held at Yale University, Cambridge University, and Lambeth Palace, and it was discussed at global gatherings such as the World Economic Forum in the spring of 2008. It was also the topic of discussion at the annual Catholic-Muslim Forum at the Vatican in November 2008.

There were a number of activities in 2009, including the release of a documentary film, several publications such as A Common Word and the Future of Christian-Muslim Relations,[1] an important political conference at Georgetown University in Washington D.C., and a large religious conference in Malaysia. There were also high-level meetings between Muslims and the Orthodox Churches, and between Muslims and the World Council of Churches. There is now a multilingual Web site that includes a list of recommended books on Islam and Christianity, a Muslim Theological Press Conference in Spain, a Muslim-Christian Institute for Peace based in Europe that will affirm the Common Word in its charter, and much more. I think that "A Common Word" initiative has, praise be to God, achieved an unprecedented success. And we hope, by the will of God, that it will enjoy unprecedented acceptance and dissemination in the next year as well.

The cause that inspired us to act was, in all honesty, peace. We aim to spread peace and harmony between Christians and Muslims throughout the world. Not by way of governments or treaties, but on the most widely accepted level, utilizing popular leaders with the most influence and impact. By this I mean religious figures.

We were fully aware that efforts to achieve peace were in need of another component: knowledge. Based on this we have sought to disseminate essential and precise knowledge of our religion in order to correct the notion the Western world has of Islam thereby removing the darkness and clamor that surrounds it.

I consider some of the things leading to the theory of a clash of civilizations between Muslims and Christians since the collapse of the Soviet Union in 1990. These include the Jerusalem and the Palestinian issue, anger over American foreign policy (particularly in connection with the war in Iraq and the situation in Afghanistan), terrorism, fundamentalism and propaganda spread by fundamentalists (on both sides), missionary work, and the role of the media in forming stereotypes of the other. According to the findings of the largest world poll of religious populations in history (also published in summary form in a book by John Esposito and Dalia Mogahed of the Gallup organization),[2] 60% of Christians are prejudiced against Muslims, while up to 30% of Muslims are prejudiced against Christians.

After speaking about what inspired us, permit me to mention the things that did not serve as motives for us in light of the suspicions that we have seen cast on the Internet. The aim of "A Common Word" initiative is not to trick Christians, impose the Islamic faith upon them, or to convince them to enter our religion, as some have erroneously thought. "A Common Word" was not intended to reduce our religions to an artificial unity on the basis of the two principles (love of God and love of neighbor), rather it was only an attempt to create an essential common ground deeply rooted in the shared Abrahamic tradition in order to put an end to the misgivings between us that act as stumbling blocks in the way of our respecting one another.

The goal was to affirm that religion is a part of the solution, not the problem. The truth is that the two principles (love of God and love of neighbor) serve as the shared standard of behavior concerning what we expect from others and how we behave ourselves. The point of "A Common Word" was not to deny what Christians believe and reiterate that God created us out of His love. The issue of God's love for the servant preceding the servant's love for God is clear in Islam. We do not feel that it is something that we need to advertise because it is so clear that God exists before human beings and creation. It is also clear in the phrase, "In the name of God the Most Merciful, the Most Compassionate," which begins the chapters of the Qur'ān and with which Muslims begin all of their actions. And God says in a Divine tradition, "I am the All Merciful [*al-Raḥmān*], I created the womb [*al-raḥm*] and gave it a part of my name," which indicates that God created the whole of the cosmos through the effulgence of His love.

This matter is apparent in the Qur'ān in the beginning of the chapter titled "The All-Merciful" where God says, "The All-Merciful, He taught the Qur'ān, He created humanity, He taught humanity speech." In other words, the name the All-Merciful must be understood in light of its containing these meanings, that is, God creates through His love. And the name the All-Compassionate (*al-Raḥīm*) means "the One who saves out of His mercy."

"A Common Word" initiative did not aim to exclude Judaism or diminish its importance. We began with Christianity alone for a very simple reason, namely that Islam and Christianity are the two major religions of the world and of history. Christians now comprise two billion people, while there are one-and-a-half billion Muslims, but there are no more than 25 million Jews in the world. This does not mean that we, as Muslims, are aloof from other religions, or even those who do not follow any religion at all. Muslims do not object to the idea of Christian-Jewish dialogue, and do not object to not having been invited. Based on this, there is no cause for Jews to feel excluded from Muslim-Christian dialogue, and Christians should likewise not feel excluded from Muslim-Jewish dialogue. These conversations are where we may overcome many oft-repeated issues.

I would like to reaffirm that "A Common Word" does not mean that Muslims are prepared to depart one iota from their beliefs in order to build relationships with Christians, and I do not think that the opposite is true either. Let us make it explicit: "A Common Word" is an initiative about peace, not about surrendering principles.

Some have alleged that extending our hands through the language of love is a kind of compromise of principle. I reaffirm to you that this is not true at all. It is a personal joy to be able to focus our exchange on the aspect that is most often ignored between us: the principle of a supreme love. The truth is that we have over fifty synonyms for love in the Qur'ān; English does not have this wealth of synonyms. If Muslims do not use the same language of love as Christians do in English, this may be because the word *love* carries many different meanings for Muslims.

Today, we aspire to move beyond conversation to cooperation. There are many doorways to dialogue that can open up to new and attainable horizons, adding to intellectual, faith-based, theoretical discussions new applications that bring individuals and institutions together on one level in order to work for the betterment of humanity.

I have previously suggested that both sides undertake translating some of their most cherished religious literature. I am very pleased indeed that Cambridge University has started taking practical steps in turning this dream into reality.

In this blessed gathering I call for an opening of new doors to interfaith and cross-cultural dialogue, in particular collaboration on development, taking as its starting point the religious vision inherent in every aspect of authentic advancement. I also ask that we research the role of religious leaders by positively engaging these objectives and utilizing their tremendous moral authority to improve the quality of human life. In this regard, I would like to mention the following major issues, which are by way of example and not intended to be exhaustive:

- Religious leaders cooperating on protecting the environment. This is a matter that has become a global concern and to which Islam has always given great care and importance. It requires the formulation of a comprehensive Islamic vision in order to provide Muslim scholars and preachers an opportunity to play their role in expanding religious awareness of the importance of this issue through a variety of means such as: sermons, lessons, seminars, workshops, and conferences, as well as publications and the media. In light of the concern of the Western and Eastern churches on this issue, and the publication of many studies and recommendations by the church supporting protection of the environment and forbidding its harm, the door is open for Muslim-Christian cooperation as well. In this regard, it is my pleasure to share with you that Egypt's Dār al-Iftā', over which I preside, has initiated a sequence of measures to reduce harmful carbon emissions, and I hope to announce that Dār al-Iftā' will be carbon neutral by the end of 2010.
- Religious leaders cooperating in the fight against drug abuse that contributes to the loss of our young people. We know that Islam forbids and opposes this affliction, and we find the same conviction among Christian religious institutions. There is no doubt that formulating a common discourse will provide greater protection for our youth, and that this should be one of our top priorities.
- Religious leaders cooperating on media ethics and protecting our kids from campaigns of corruption and immorality. These are shared problems from which our communities suffer, opposition to which may be taken from Islam and Christianity that call for respect of moral and social boundaries. By way of hundreds of religious institutions that have influence in the media and in society, we may arrive at a Muslim-Christian code of ethics for media and advertising. This will directly reduce the level of moral decline found in many media outlets.

- Religious leaders cooperating in the realm of religious tourism and cultural exchange in an effective and appropriate manner based on a framework of mutual understanding of all different backgrounds. This can offer an important economic element as well by promoting tourism among Muslim countries, and between Muslim and Western countries, after considering moral boundaries consistent with religious and practical goals.
- Religious leaders cooperating in raising health awareness and fighting against widespread afflictions, benefiting from religious principles and guidelines, both Islamic and Christian, which forbid fornication and adultery and all forms of moral indecency.
- Breaking the cycle of poverty and unemployment and eradicating illiteracy and social injustice.
- Training people concerning the new situation in which we are all living as neighbors. This must be based on getting to know one another, and then searching for that which is commonly held between us. Then we can chart a course for cooperation and work continuously to achieve peace and lasting justice.

There is a long road ahead of us, and the area for intellectual and practical cooperation is immense. We ask God to bless our efforts and to grant us the strength and courage to enjoy the peace for which we all strive.

Notes

1. John Borelli, ed., "A Common Word and the Future of Christian-Muslim Relations," Prince Alwaleed Bin Talal Center for Muslim-Christian Understanding Occasional Paper, Georgetown University.
2. John Esposito and Dalia Mogahed, *Who Speaks for Islam: What Over a Billion Muslims Really Think*.

3

"A Common Word" Initiative: *Theoria* and *Praxis*

Seyyed Hossein Nasr

Although in its early stages, "A Common Word" initiative already has a significant history. The initiative was begun four years ago through the efforts of Prince Ghazi bin Muhammad bin Talāl in cooperation with a number of eminent Muslim scholars, to create a new atmosphere based on mutual understanding between Islam and Christianity and the "Common Word" (*al-kalimat al-siwā'*) to which the noble Qur'ān refers. The initiative led to the now famous letter signed by a large number of eminent Muslim scholars from all over the globe, who belong to different juridical and theological schools. The letter called for our meeting within a spiritual framework defined by the hallowed principles of the love of God and of neighbor, which both Christians and Muslims consider to be sacrosanct. It was addressed first of all to Pope Benedict XVI, and then to leaders of other major Christian churches, the Orthodox, the Protestant and the Eastern. This act was itself historic, both because never before had such an appeal been formally supported by such a wide array of authoritative Muslim voices from so many diverse schools and perspectives, but also because of the enthusiastic responses from leaders of so many different Christian churches.

The first step in this effort led to very significant conferences and gatherings organized around the theme of "A Common Word" initiative at Yale and Cambridge Universities, then at the all-important meeting at the Vatican last November. These gatherings were followed by a smaller academic exploration at the University of South Carolina in Columbia leading to a significant gathering at Georgetown University in Washington D.C., a venerable Catholic institution located in the capital of the nation, where decisions are made that often in one way or another affect the lives of numerous Christians and Muslims, and their relationships worldwide.

This is a short history, yet laden with much significance because it deals with one of the central issues of today. It is now time to take stock of what we have so far learned, and one might say also unlearned, from this initiative. It is time to review what the *theoria*, in the Latin sense of this term meaning vision and not theory as ordinarily understood in English, of this initiative is, and what practical steps can be taken from here on to realize this *theoria* on the level of and through *praxis*.

Our *theoria* was from the beginning not the creation, but rather the discovery of a common ground between us. I say discovery and not creation, because this common ground has always been there in the inner and quintessential realities of our faiths, created according to those who are people of faith by God, and not based simply on human creation for the sake of expediency. Moreover, this *theoria* has been based not on repudiating some of the tenets of our religions in order to create common human understanding, not on casting aside what is sacred to us for some worldly goal and a convenient least common denominator. Instead, it is based on penetrating beyond the formal order to that "Abode of Peace" that transcends formal differences, and in light of that reality to gain a more sympathetic understanding of why there are irreducible differences between us on the formal plane.

The "Common Word" initiative has made many who have participated in it realize that we *do* have irreducible differences on the level of theological dogmas, external ritual forms, etc. First of all, we have been reminded, in case we had forgotten or not been aware, that there are exclusivists in both religions who are opposed in principle to this initiative. Some among them are happy in their religious exclusivism. They worship God according to the tenets of their own religion without wanting or being able to bother with the question of religious pluralism, but also without bearing enmity toward the religious other. We have to respect their attitude, their faith and their piety. It is not for us to castigate them. But there are other exclusivists whose exclusivism leads to the demonization of the other, to aggression and even violence. In its extreme form, this exclusivism can result in the bombing of innocent people, whether these lethal weapons come at the innocent horizontally or vertically.

We have been reminded that there are people in both religions who identify their religion less with the unadulterated content of God's message, and more with nationalism, cultural imperialism, ethnic and tribal identity, and also political expediency. We are faced with a situation in which many followers of one religion find it very easy to criticize the actions of the other, but difficult to criticize those of their own co-religionists. They choose to disregard the universalist message of accord with the other and love of the neighbor. They sow instead the seeds of hatred while claiming to love and obey God as if the supreme commandments mentioned by Christ did not include both the love of God and of the neighbor, and also as if the noble Qur'ān did not teach the same truths in another language.

Such is the reality of our present-day predicament. And then there are the irreducible theological, legal, and culturally and historically determined differences. We have learned through our many discussions that Muslims will not be able to convince Christians to put aside the doctrine of the Trinity, nor Christians persuade Muslims not to insist that God "does not beget nor is He begotten." During our gatherings, Muslims have heard Christian presentations based completely on Christocentrism, while Muslims insist on a theocentric perspective. This difference in the understanding of revelation has also made clear that a chasm separates the Islamic meaning of revelation as a universal reality stretching from Adam to the Prophet of Islam from the particularism that Christians associate with the advent of the coming of Christ, which remains for most of them a unique event in human history.

We came to realize more fully the different understandings of the meaning of the Word of God in our traditions. To the question who or what is the Word of God, the Christians would answer without hesitation Christ, and for the most part reject the Qur'ān as His Word. For Muslims, the answer would be the inner reality of God's prophets and His revealed books, particularly the Qur'ān. A title of Moses in Islam is the Word of God, and he is referred to as *kalīm Allāh* (the Word of God), hence the term *kalīmī,* which is sometimes used by Muslims for

Jews. But this title of Word of God could certainly be extended also to Christ, one of whose names in Islam is *rūḥ Allāh* (the Spirit of God). But for Muslims, the central and concrete embodiment in their lives of the Word of God, and in fact that Word itself, is the Qur'ān, which we often refer to simply as *kalām Allāh* or Word of God. Of course Christians also refer to the Bible as the Word of God, but technically, at least, the Gospels are the account of the words of the Word of God, and are the Word of God only if the Word of God is considered as God.

On many occasions during our discussions it became clear that the Islamic perception of Divine Law or *al-Sharīʿah* differs from the Catholic perception of canonical law. It is also not identical with the Christian perception of Divine Law pertaining only to the spiritual realm and the domain of ethics, and not positive law. Concerning this subject, it also became clear that there is a greater proximity of the Islamic view to the Jewish idea of *halakhah* than to the Christian concept. Many differences between our views of religion in public life, and the whole question of the opposition between the sacred and the profane and the relation between religion and the secular, issue from our diverse understanding of the meaning of Divine Law and its domains of application.

We even came to find important differences stemming from the similarities that each religion claimed, namely that their message was addressed not to a single group or nation, but to the whole of humanity. Rivalry for the souls of men and women could not be ignored in our dialogues. The whole question of missionary activity by the Western Christian churches that is abetted by superior economic means and greater political support in comparison to what is available to Muslims, along with various Muslim responses to Christian's missionary zeal, remains a powerful source of discord between us. It is a problem that will not disappear through mere diplomatic niceties. It presents all of us who seek to create deeper harmony and understanding with a great challenge. In this case and in contrast to some of the theological issues, our very initiative can play a role to provide from both sides, Christian and Muslim alike, suitable responses to this challenge. It can help to bring about a change in the dynamic of the present situation, which has caused, and continues to cause, so much bitterness, enmity, and occasionally out-and-out strife in lands as far apart as Nigeria and the Philippines. Surely we could at least try to understand the motivations of the actions and reactions in this domain that continue to make the creation of harmony between us difficult in so many instances.

One could go on and cite other differences that seem to pose insurmountable obstacles to coming together within the framework of the "Common Word" initiative. But this is not the whole reality of the matter. There are all these, and other unmentioned, differences that form a portion of the present day interaction of our religions and, in fact, religions in general. There is, however, also the immense reality of our accord on what is most essential in our worldviews, which begins with faith in the one God beyond all the different cataphatic theological formulations of the nature of the Divine Reality. Both Muslims and Christians believe in the transcendent God who is above and beyond all change and becoming, who creates, loves, and has Mercy for His creatures, whose Will dominates over everything, who is the All-Good, the Infinitely Merciful, and who hates evil that nevertheless exists in His creation for metaphysical and theological reasons that our sages—our Saint Thomases and Meister Eckharts, our Ghazālīs and Ibn 'Arabīs—have explained in the most profound and also diverse ways over the centuries. For both of us, although God is ultimately the Godhead, the ground of

Being, the *Urgrund*, *al-Ḥaqq*, or *Huwa*, He is also the Person who addresses us and whom we can address as Thou. If for both of our religions, God is the greatest reality, and, ultimately, the only Reality, how can our common faith in Him not be the greatest source of accord, which no discord on any plane could ever match or annul?

We both believe in the gift of faith whose object is not only God, but also His revelations and the spiritual and angelic worlds. We live with awareness of the reality of the soul and its immortality, and with knowledge of the responsibility we have for our actions before God, and therefore the consequences of our actions for our souls even beyond the grave. And despite some differences, how similar are our eschatologies? They are so similar that the greatest work of Western literature on the Christian view of hell, purgatory, and paradise, *The Divine Comedy,* by that supreme Christian poet, Dante could draw its structure from a Muslim work on the nocturnal ascent (*al-mi'rāj*) of the Prophet of Islam.

As Christians and Muslims, we both believe in the ethical character of human life here on earth. We hold firm to the reality of divine justice and seek justice as well in the social order. While realizing the centrality of God's love, mercy, and goodness that are abiding realities in our lives and, in fact, in the life of all beings, we also believe in the supreme importance of the virtue of justice and our responsibility to be just in both our individual and social lives. Furthermore, over the centuries our religions have taught us that life is sacred, given by God, and is not simply the result of some cosmic accident. In the societies molded by the teachings of our religions, laws pertaining to human life have been based on this shared belief in the sanctity of life, which includes the sanctity of the family, upon which we both insist.

On the level of religious practice, we both pray and perform sacred rites and divinely ordained rituals. The formal aspects of these rites are different, but inwardly they point to the same religious realities. Yes, we both pray, and pray to the same God, no matter what some in our communities may say. In fact, we realize this sameness when as sincere Muslims and Christians we pray together. In such cases, we feel existentially that the grace that flows during our prayers through both of us *is* divine grace, however its perfume might differ in Christian and Islamic forms. Can we in our heart of hearts claim that God hears only our prayers and not the prayers of the other?

It becomes clear how vast and profound is the common ground on which we can meet when we delve in depth into all these similarities and many others, including metaphysical knowledge, the reality of the spiritual life, the virtues we are called upon by our religions to cultivate within our souls, and the vices we are commanded to shun. How close are Muslims and Christians to each other when compared with those who deny the reality of the sacred altogether, and all that such a denial entails? Christians and Muslims are, in fact, closer to each other than we are to those members of our own nation, culture, community, or ethnic stock who deny the basic truths we hold so dear. The *theoria* of the "Common Word" initiative is none other than the vision of this common ground without any recourse to reductionism, and with full respect for the sacred traditions of each other.

Theoria, however, is one thing, and its realization, which becomes related to *praxis*, is another. Having journeyed so far to this point, we must now ask ourselves what it is that we can do in addition to that primary action of praying to God for succor? As a first step, we can begin to cooperate together in those fields where cooperation is the easiest, and in many instances of vital importance to the well-being of each of our religions. Let us recall some of these domains. There is before everything else a common challenge presented by a desacralized worldview that manifests itself in numerous ways, including a virulent campaign of aggressive atheism that has appeared in recent years in Europe, especially in Great Britain but also in America, that concerns not only Christianity but religion as such. Then there are the numerous issues related to the encounter between religion and science, and especially the ideology of scientism with its totalitarian claims. There are problems resulting from the applications of modern science in the form of modern technology. These include difficulties arising from bioengineering,new questions involving medical ethics, and the environmental crisis that now threatens whole ecosystems and even human life itself . There are issues of social and economic justice that concern both religions. The recent encyclical of the Pope on unbridled capitalism could not but be joined by authentic Muslim thinkers. Why can we not sit together and devise a new economic philosophy based on our mutual understanding of human nature in its full reality and our sense of justice that is a reflection of a divine quality in human life? Why simply be passive observers to the attempt now being made to infuse new life by artificial means into the cadaver of greedy and selfish capitalism that has already done all of us, or should we say almost all of us, so much harm?

As followers of the teachings of Christianity and Islam, we both believe in human rights, but ones that are combined with human responsibility toward God, human society, and the natural environment. Rather than criticizing each other's understanding of this issue, we can come together in the realization of the consequences for human beings "made in the image of God," of the substitution of the "Kingdom of Man" for the "Kingdom of God," and the absolutization of the rights of man reduced to a merely terrestrial being with total indifference to the rights of God and other creatures. We could render the greatest service not only to our own communities, but also to the whole of humanity, by bringing the full weight of our traditions together to bear upon this crucial issue.

On the political plane there are numerous crises where both our religions are involved in one way or another. Examples include the prevailing conditions in Nigeria, the Sudan, Lebanon, Israel, Palestine, Indonesia, and the Philippines, along with the situation of Christian minorities in some Muslim countries and Muslim minorities in Europe. Rather than simply taking sides automatically or remaining silent, could we not try to stand together on the side of truth, justice, and compassion? One might say we should take God's side, without claiming blindly that God is always on our side, no matter what our side does. We can criticize in unison senseless violence, extremism and terror carried out both by those wearing uniforms and those without them, no matter to which "side" they may belong.

And now some practical suggestions that, rather than discord, can implement this vision of harmony. There have been many international organizations created during the last century in fields dealing with politics, economics, and health that have met with various degrees of success and failure. Such attempts have also been made in the realm of religions. The former types of organizations have, until recently when NGO organizations appeared upon the scene, often been supported by individual nations and in many cases by their governments, but a similar situation has rarely been the case *mutatis mutandis* for those concerned with religion. Religious institutions that hold authority in their societies have hardly ever come together to create international organizations of a religious nature, or give full support to those founded by various individuals and groups. Attempts in this domain have in fact usually been confined to marginal religious groups, lacking orthodoxy and in most cases of an antitraditional nature.

Perhaps we could now establish a forum or council consisting of Christians and Muslims, and supported formally by established traditional authorities from both religions. Later members of other religions including not only Judaism but also the primal religions, Hinduism, Buddhism, etc. could also be invited to join in the discussion of various issues. But at the beginning, the forum would devote itself to the implementation of the ideals of "A Common Word" initiative carried out between Christians and Muslims. During its formation, members could be appointed by the established religious authorities of Christianity and Islam, and henceforth be self-perpetuating. In order for this organization to be effective, however, its members would have to be recognized as persons of great knowledge and theological and/or scholarly expertise in their religions, and be respected in their communities as such. But they would also have to possess complete moral integrity and devotion to the truth above all else, rather than being pawns of political forces. It would not be too much to hope that they would also have a spiritual perspective and possess spiritual virtues that would provide them with innate attraction and gravitas. These qualities would enable them to have a vision of the inner unity of our religions beyond the world of forms. If they were to be chosen simply on the basis of political opportunism, the whole effort would become more or less worthless. There is now an effort underway elsewhere to create an international council of elders to face the common problems of humanity. Even if this ideal is realized, however, it will not impinge upon the functions of the forum being proposed here. Our forum would concentrate on the issues mentioned above along with similar subjects, seeking to provide solutions that draw from the resources of both traditions, and supervising research where it is needed that would be carried out by Muslim and Christian scholars, often working together. The forum would also have the major duty of giving its formal view, much like a *fatwā* or religious edict, on current problems and issues where both religions are involved. Our hope is that the forum would carry so much weight that its edicts would be accepted by a large number, if not all, of Muslims and Christians whom the subjects of the edicts concern.

Today there are a very small number of Christians in Islamic educational institutions and vice versa. Of course, there are universities and colleges in the Islamic world, and especially the West, where both Christianity and Islam are taught, and students from both religions study. But in most such schools, especially those in Europe and America, a secularist and historicist view of the study of religion as *Religionswissenschaft* is taught with little interest in theology and the life of faith, or in fact in religious truth. In many cases the teaching of religion results paradoxically in the destruction of religion as a living reality for those who are undergoing training in academic religious studies. I must add, however, that such is not the situation everywhere. There are some exceptions, but as far as having both Christianity and Islam taught as living realities with existential concern for the life of faith and spiritual experience, with a perspective that is more spiritual and theological than just historical, sociological, or philological, the exceptions are few indeed. One such exception is the Selly Oaks Colleges in Birmingham, England, affiliated with the University of Birmingham. I have the honor of being a patron of Selly Oaks, which seeks to bring Muslim and Christian students to study together and to learn the religion of the other. I can bear witness to the fact that this school has done much good. But still, as far as I know, many of its students, especially those from Sub-Saharan Africa where Christianity and Islam vie with each other for the souls of men and women, have the attitude of confrontation vis-à-vis the other rather than the sharing of a "Common Word" that we seek. The same can be said of some of the teachers.

Why then not create an institute of advanced studies or academy for the purpose of training a whole new generation of scholars, both Muslim and Christian, who would know well the religion of the other? Let them have knowledge that is combined with empathy and love of the other, rather than enmity, and is based on both the study of scholarly sources and personal encounters with the other. Steps could be taken to create an institute that one might say would be at once a *madrasah* and a divinity school or seminary, teaching both Islam and Christianity as living sister religions, while also training the students to be able to deal with theological differences and historically troubling experiences on the plane of the truth, but also in the spirit of reconciliation. The institute should have two campuses, one in the Islamic world and the other in a European country in which the Christian tradition has been strong in recent centuries and is still a living presence.

The institute could also be a research center where joint efforts would be used to address so many issues of common concern to Christians as well as Muslims. In addition, it would further the cause of authentic ecumenism, while the difficult task of self-criticism could unfold alongside critical thinking, so prevalent today only when it comes to the negative criticism of religion, and could be investigated in a new light. The research would be of the highest intellectual order and be always carried out in light of the truth that both of our religions hold to be central to human life. There is no reason why love of God and the neighbor should weaken our intellects, no matter what opponents of religion claim.

The forum and the institute or academy as both a propaedeutic and a research institution and other efforts, including perhaps the establishment of a publishing house devoted to the realization of the *theoria* of "A Common Word" initiative, could over time create a new living space, a *Lebensraum*. Here Christians as devout Christians, and Muslims as devout Muslims, could meet, to live in harmony together and to face together so many threatening challenges that we confront in common. Many of our co-religionists would not want to enter into such a space. That is understandable, but what is important is to realize that the very creation of such a space or common ground would change the present dynamic between our religions. It would augment the already existing number of Muslims and Christians who see in each other friends rather than enemies in a world that poses many dangers for what we both hold dear, and marginalize the exclusivists and extremists bent on demonizing the other.

Hope is a theological virtue, as St. Augustine reminded us so eloquently, and it is a virtue that the Qur'ān commands us not to lose. So let me conclude with a note of hope amidst this darkness that continually threatens to dim our vision. Many a skeptic will say, "Of what use is the voice of a few Muslims and Christians amidst the deafening din of a world in strife and burning in so many places with the fire of hatred?" Let us remind ourselves of two cases drawn from Western history that reveal how the voices of the few can in fact become those of the many in a relatively short time. In the early seventeenth century, a handful of scientists in Italy, France, Germany, Holland, and England embarked upon the creation of a new purely quantitative science and the creation of a mechanistic picture of the cosmos. These men associated with such institutions as the Royal Academy and the Accademia dei Lincei often corresponded with each other, and in a sense formed a new and distinct body of thinkers that continued to grow (but they were at first very small in number). The vast majority of their contemporaries, and even some of their own scientific colleagues, rejected the mechanistic view of the cosmos that they were proposing. Yet, within less than a century, a new paradigm came to dominate the whole of the modern West, a paradigm based on the mechanistic worldview.

Let me also turn to a personal experience. Over 40 years ago in the Rockefeller Series lectures that I gave at the University of Chicago, whose text appeared later as *Man and Nature—The Spiritual Crisis of Modern Man*, I was one of the first to speak of the impending environmental crisis in terms of the religious and spiritual, not simply economic and engineering, causes of the tragedy we were about to face. Both the lecture and the subsequent book met with great opposition from many quarters, including from a number of Christian theologians. Few showed any interest in these matters, and I felt like a lone voice crying in the wilderness. Even in my own country, Iran, where I lived at that time, this book received less attention than any of my other works. How many Jewish, Christian and Muslim theologians, religious thinkers, and philosophers were concerned with "the theology of nature" in the 1960s when my book appeared, and how many are concerned with such issues today? It is an eye-opener to ponder upon the response to this question in light of what we hope to be the effect of our "Common Word" initiative.

And so although our voice is still weak, let us not lose hope. There is much that can be done to implement that *theoria* upon which our initiative is based, despite the enormous problems and obstacles that exist, ranging from the political to the personal, not to speak of the long history between our two religions of confrontation and mistrust, whose effects are still with us and that we have yet to overcome. As members of the family of Abraham, as followers of the message of Christ and the Prophet, we should be the first to remember and the last to forget that the Mercy of God is infinite, and that with God all things are possible.

4

The Power of Finding Common Ground: "A Common Word" and the Invitation to Understanding

The Right Reverend William O. Gregg

I begin with three images. One is from nature, one is from a Christian source, and one is taken from a Muslim source. They seem to me to be iconic of the opportunities and possibilities offered by "A Common Word Between Us and You."[1]

Each year, there is a migration of Humpback alpha whales in the Pacific Ocean that results in their coming together for a time. During this time together, they sing the songs of their particular herd to each other. Oceanographers have discovered that during this time together, the various particular songs are modified by what each hear from other whales. There is an exchange of sounds and adaptation of songs that takes place. When the whales go back to their herd, they teach the new song to the rest of the herd. They sing that song for the year until the next migration and they receive their new song.[2]

The whales teach us that singing and sharing our song is natural. They teach us that when we sing our songs to one another, and each listens, our songs touch and modify each other and, in turn, transform us. The whales teach us that this process is perpetual.

The second image is from a Christian source, the African-American Howard Thurman. It is a poem entitled, "I Will Sing a New Song"[3]:

I will sing a new song…
I must learn the new song for the new needs.
I must fashion new words born of all the new growth
[O]f my life, of my mind and of my spirit.
I must prepare for new melodies
[T]hat have never been mine before,
[T]hat all that is within me may lift my voice unto God.
How I love the old familiarity of the wearied melody[,]
[H]ow I shrink from the harsh discords of the new untried harmonies.
Teach me, my Father, that I might learn with the abandonment and enthusiasm of Jesus,
[T]he fresh new accent, the untried melody,
[T]o meet the need of the untried morrow.

Thurman captures the image of singing a new song and situates it in the theological realm. He makes the essential connections between the necessity of a new song, the challenges of change, the needs of the day, and living and singing the new song in the context of relationship with God. Thurman's poem is also one of compelling commitment. It is a poem of refusing the seduction of the known and comfortable and embracing the unknown and the uncomfortable. Theologically, he knows that the new song cannot be learned and sung without God's help. In his Christian context, he prays that, "...I might learn with the abandonment and enthusiasm of Jesus / The fresh new accent, the untried melody / To meet the need of the untried morrow."[4]

At the heart of the new song and our capacity to sing it faithfully is God who is with us and for us. God gives us the capacity, strength, and courage to live faithfully, moving forward in new ways into uncharted waters, into unknown and untried morrows. The ways we live and move forward are the ways we sing the new song, the ways we manifest our love of God and one another and our praise and devotion to God.

Like the whales and Howard Thurman, God has called us into a new opportunity and opens for us new possibilities through our Islamic brothers who have given us "A Common Word." The challenge is to see anew, listen anew, hear anew the ancient song within both our faiths, and to learn to sing the songs God is now giving us in theory and application. In so singing, God's love for us and our love for God and each other will grow and deepen as we work together in our distinctness and our commonalities so that the world may be one of justice, peace, mercy, and compassion.

The third image is from a young Muslim scholar, author, and founder of Interfaith Youth Core here in the United States, Eboo Patel. In a recent interview, when asked about the principles of the Interfaith Youth Core, he replied that there were four basic steps in their work: "[First,] We try to put the idea of interfaith cooperation into the culture. Step two: [We] teach a different song. So we sing the song of interfaith cooperation, the song of religious pluralism, the song of [Martin Luther] King [Jr.] learning from Gandhi, the song of King marching with [Abraham] Heschel, the song of the South African liberation movement being a multifaith movement. Step three: Teach that song to the choir and make sure they sing it. Now you've added your voice to the noise [of the world], and hopefully you're singing a different song in the world. Instead of just the voices of religious extremists, religious bigots, and aggressive atheists, there's now the voice and song of religious pluralists. The fourth piece: Teach your choir members to start their own choirs. ... [W]e don't seek to grow exponentially as an organization; we seek to tell the story, inspire young people to tell it themselves, and then act on it."[5]

I am also put in mind of the story of Abraham and Sarah (Gen. 17–25). What strikes me is that "A Common Word" invites us to take much the same kind of journey with God. We do not know exactly where we are going, how we are going to get there, or when we shall arrive. The good news is that, like Abraham and Sarah, an increasing number of us are hearing the call and saying, "Yes. Yes, we will take the journey. Yes, we will learn the new song. Yes, we will teach it to our neighbors. Yes, with God's help, we will go forward in love together into the 'untried morrow.'"

"A Common Word" is a singularly important document for our time, not only in the religious world, but for the world at large. Its publication marks a substantive shift in the sea of interreligious relationship between Muslims and Christians, and by extension with Judaism.[6] It is a demonstration that if we choose to frame the question or issue well in a realistic but positive mode, it can be a powerful instrument of transformation, creativity, and new possibilities. The unexpected outcome of Pope Benedict XVI's speech of October 13, 2006, in Regensburg, Germany, has become, because of the thoughtful, creative response of a broadly representative group of Muslim scholars, a moment of grace and invitation, opening profound and major possibilities and opportunities. As a Christian and Bishop of The Episcopal Church, I join with Dr. Rowan Williams, the Archbishop of Canterbury, in being immensely grateful to God and the initial group of Muslim scholars who graciously and wonderfully crafted their initial letter to the Bishop of Rome and a year later, "A Common Word," and for those who have since joined as signatories.

The significance and power of "A Common Word" lies as much in its methodology as in its content. Without ignoring or minimizing the real differences of experiences, understandings, and theology, the methodological choice of common ground as the starting point, and specifically our common word, love, is in itself an act of love and faithfulness that possesses immense power to connect.

The constructive methodology of "A Common Word" opens possibilities that draw us together in ways that enhance our capacities to work and live together in the world. This approach also develops and strengthens our self-understandings as Christians and Muslims through ongoing participation in conversations that seek mutual understanding, develop mutual respect, and bring us to appreciate each other in the broadest and deepest sense. Our common experience of and belief in God who unites us in love, is an essential message of the Holy Qur'ān, the Hebrew Scriptures, and the Christian Scriptures.

From the scriptural and theological traditions of both Islam and Christianity, it is clear that who we understand ourselves to be and how we are to live in this world are grounded in our experiences and understandings of God, which have developed out of God's revelation of God's self to us, especially through Jesus for Christians and through the Holy Qur'ān for Muslims. The concurrence among responses to "A Common Word" demonstrates that our understandings and applications of the fundamental revelations of God bring us to a common place. That is, we arrive at a common commitment to live in the world by embracing its diversity, respecting the dignity of every human being, and striving for peace and justice as we live and work with compassion and mercy for and with one another, grounded in God's love of us and our love for God.

Indeed, love identifies the fact that we are, by our very nature, connected to God and to one another, created in God's image and likeness, as we read in the creation story of Genesis 1. At the heart of that image and likeness—and so at the heart of our humanness—is love. This word, "love," is a common gateway into rich, fertile, and holy ground that is God's gift to both Christians and Muslims. Yet, the possibility of our love of God and neighbor cannot happen without the prior primordial love of God for us. Just as God makes known God's love for us, we too must make our love of God and others known concretely in daily life. Our experience and understanding of who God is provides the foundational dynamic and shape of authentic human life.

This love, however, is not a matter of sameness, nor is it about becoming or convincing the other to become one or the other, Christian or Muslim. Rather, precisely in our diversity of persons, religions (including our internal diversity), cultures, heritages, and current realities, this common love identifies fundamental common ground that makes possible, with God's help, the realization of our natural, essential connectedness in ways that empower us to live and work together for justice and peace, to be deeply and richly people of compassion and mercy, people of great mutual respect, honoring both our differences and our commonalities, people who respond to God's love both through our prayers of praise and thanksgiving and in our love of our neighbors. Again, different as we may be, our common word brings us to the same place.

As "A Common Word" reminds us, "the unity of God, the necessity of love of Him, and the necessity to love our neighbor is thus the common ground upon which Islam and Christianity (and Judaism) are founded."[7] An essential part of what that means is, I think, this: no matter how difficult it is at times to live and work together, no matter how hard it may be to engage each other, no matter what our differences are or may be, no matter how well we do or do not understand each other, always, everywhere, for all eternity, we are held in the infinite steadfast love of God. This love is the condition of possibility for us to realize the potential and possibilities of "A Common Word."

Among the responses, I would commend especially the response of the Archbishop of Canterbury, *A Common Word for the Common Good* (July 2008),[8] the statement of the Yale Conferences (July 2008),[9] the Communiqué of the Cambridge Conference (October 2008),[10] the speech of H.R.H. Prince Ghazi at the Biser Award Ceremony (November 2008),[11] and the Final Declaration of the Rome Conference (November 2008).[12]

Clearly, to engage in the depth and breadth of conversation and working together that "A Common Word" presents, requires much of both Christians and Muslims. We need to know who we are and to articulate with clarity, coherence, and conviction what being a Christian or a Muslim means to us. We need to know how to live our faith in daily life with integrity. And then we need to live that way. "A Common Word" invites us to respect and support one another in this faithful work. "A Common Word" also gives us the opportunity to name and acknowledge the real differences between us in constructive, critical, and life-giving ways.

In this context, I would offer these as basic areas of exploration and conversation for our ongoing meeting and working together:

I. Questions regarding the Holy Qur'ān and the Bible: These questions would include, but not be limited to, hermeneutics and the interpretation of texts, critical exegesis of our texts, translations of our texts, the history of our sacred texts and study of commentaries, the roles or functions of sacred texts in our traditions, and how we apply these sacred texts in daily life.

II. Questions of theology: We need to be excellent thinkers in at least two ways: as theologians within the context of our faith, and as ones committed to the discipline of religious studies as we engage the faith of the other.[13] Both leaders and followers of Christianity and Islam need to be educated and formed in our faiths so that we know how to think well about who God is, who we are in relation to God, and what that means for how we live with one another in this world.

From the perspective of religious studies, we have the opportunity to study together each other's faith in an orderly, intentional way so as to come to understand one another better, to deepen our theological and spiritual conversations and to ground our common work in the world. We might engage in such basic questions as: doctrine of God, theological anthropology, revelation, Christology, our theology of creation, and moral theology, and our theology of social action (e.g., relative to justice, peace, law, mercy, compassion).

III. Questions of spirituality and mysticism: Muslims and Christians also need to be well disciplined in the spiritual care and nurture of our hearts and souls, as well as in our theological thinking and *praxis* in daily life. This area might well include theological and practical reflecting on and teaching about the life of prayer, our life of common worship, the connection between our spiritualities and liturgies on the one hand and the living of daily life on the other. This is an area where we can learn much from one another. We both hold rich and diverse traditions and experiences of spirituality and mysticism, prayer, and engagement in liturgical worship.

IV. Questions of application: As fascinating as theology and theory are, ultimately we must ask and answer the question: "So what? Why and in what ways can or does taking up the opportunities afforded by "A Common Word" to live into its possibilities really matter in daily life? Among its great strengths, practically speaking, "A Common Word" provides a framework within which we can work together for the common good based on common interests, and provides an intellectually and theologically cogent framework that makes it possible to choose creative and generative ways of engagement.[14]

We can create the space in which we learn to honor each other and our faiths in such a way that we draw out the very best in ourselves and each other. We come, with God's help, to love one another as God loves us.

The "Common Word" process offers us, therefore, the possibility and opportunity:

1. To choose to be intentional about engaging one another to learn to hear one another accurately. This choice involves us in learning to know each other, removing the chimera of abstraction; and giving us faces, names, and voices of real people, good people, faithful people who live real lives in real places and who matter deeply to us. We can learn to speak the truth in love (Eph. 4:15) and to speak truthfully and accurately about one another.
2. To choose to be intentional about collaborating with one another in practical applications of our faith, especially our love for God and our neighbor in joint work. For example, to work together on projects in areas of mutual concern and value, such as education, public health, the safety and welfare of women and children, shelter and hunger, energy and environmental stewardship and development, scientific explorations, or advocacy for justice and peace.
3. To choose to be intentional about meeting for substantive conversations to build broad understanding and respect. We might do this by:
   a. Continuing and even more vigorously encouraging and promoting mutual exchanges in the academy (faculty and students) and through other exchange partnerships and agencies (e.g., culture, fine arts, music, science, and government); and,
   b. Seeking out additional resources, such as the United Religious Initiative and other worldwide religious organizations and bodies to build and strengthen worldwide networks of conversation and work that promote and sustain healthy relationships between Muslims and Christians in a larger interfaith context.
4. Choosing to be intentional about committing ourselves to structures and processes of mutual accountability and responsibility that foster respect that transform us, our institutional manifestations, and our world.

I close now with an image from a nineteenth century Christian hymn that speaks to me of the common core values of the invitation in "A Common Word" and the possibilities it offers. For indeed, I would say to us all, if we faithfully live what we faithfully claim in belief, then Christians and Muslims will know and can bring to reality what we know that:

> There's a wideness in God's mercy
> like the wideness of the sea;
> There's kindness in God's justice,
> which is more than liberty...
> For the love of God is broader
> than the measure of the mind;
> and the heart of the Eternal
> is most wonderfully kind.
> If our love were but more faithful,
> we would take him at his word;
> and our life would be thanksgiving
> for the goodness of the Lord.[15]

Notes

1. Hereafter, "A Common Word".
2. See generally, Salvatore Cerchio et al., "Temporal and Geographical Variation in Songs of Humpback Whales, *Megaptera Novaeangliae*: Synchronous Change in Hawaiian and Mexican Breeding Assemblages," *Animal Behavior* 62 and http://www.whaletrust.org/whales/whale_song.shtml.
3. Howard Thurman, *Meditations From the Heart*, 206–07.
4. Ibid., 207.
5. Rose Marie Berger, "Radical Possibility," *Sojourners*.
6. H.R.H. Prince Ghazi bin Muhammad, "A Common Word Between Us and You: Theological Motives and Expectations."
7. "A Common Word Between Us and You," 2.
8. Williams.
9. Loving God and Neighbour in Word and Deed: Implications for Muslims and Christians (New Haven, Connecticut, July 24–31, 2008).
10. A Common Word and Future Muslim-Christian Engagement (Cambridge, October 12–15 2008).
11. Ghazi bin Muhammad.
12. "Final Declaration of the Catholic-Muslim Forum." (Presented at The Catholic-Muslim Forum, Rome, Italy, November 4–6, 2008).
13. This is more than a technical distinction. In this context, it is a matter of both respect and intellectual integrity. Theology, properly understood, can only be done from within a faith tradition, as clearly articulated in the Anglican theologian John Macquarrie's definition of theology: "Theology may be defined as the study which, through participation in and reflection upon a religious faith, seeks to express the content of this faith in the clearest and most coherent language available." *Principles of Christian Theology*, 1. Religious studies, by contrast, is the serious, disciplined study of the content and practices of a religion from the outside, by one not of that religious faith. Thus, a Christian can do Christian theology, but can only do religious studies when he or she engages in the study of the content and practices of Islam. The same applies to the Muslim, who does theology of Islam, but religious studies of Christianity.

14. John Macquarrie, "Christ and the Saviour Figures," in *Jesus Christ in Modern Thought*. In this chapter, Macquarrie writes a profound and challenging theological essay focusing on Jesus' words in the Fourth Gospel, "No one comes to the Father but by me." At the heart of his argument is a crucial distinction between "exclusive" and "definitive" theological claims and beliefs within the Christian faith in the context of the world religions. In the context of "A Common Word Between Us and You," Macquarrie compellingly sets aside the conundrum of exclusivity that so often precludes creative, transforming conversation among different faiths, especially from a Christian context. With a proper understanding of his distinction, one is able to sustain one's faith with integrity and simultaneously engage persons of another religious faith with openness, receptivity, and respect, such that the possibility of living together, grounded in our common word, love, can actually happen.
15. "There's a Wideness in God's Mercy," *The Hymnal 1982*.

Part I

Theory

A. Theology

5

Islam, Christianity, the Enlightenment: "A Common Word" and Muslim-Christian Relations

Ibrahim Kalin

Muslim-Christian relations have been shaped by the different Christian and Muslim experiences of history, theology, and politics. In the classical and modern periods, Muslims and Christians have interacted with one another in diverse fields such as theology, exegesis, philosophy, science, art, and politics. Their historical experiences, theological prerogatives, and political development, however, have varied considerably and led to parallel and divergent histories. Premodern Jewish, Christian, and Muslim thought shared a common intellectual space in which the central doctrines of Abrahamic monotheism were expressed and elaborated in the philosophical vocabulary of Greek thought, though non-Greek forms of philosophical and theological discourse had a history of their own before the eventual demise of Greek philosophy. As I shall discuss below, this shared space of cosmology, science, philosophy, and even spirituality was replaced by the new adventures in the seventeenth century of European modernity and the Enlightenment, leading to a further distancing of the two traditions from one another. Despite the rich literature of Christian and Muslim polemics in the first three centuries of Islam, the field of Muslim-Christian relations remained underdeveloped and fell short of developing a sustained discourse on comparative theology.

The religious and theological distance that grew between Muslims and Christians in later centuries was due to a combination of religious, communal, and political reasons. While Christian communities in the lands of Islam enjoyed a relative degree of religious freedom and social integration, occasionally they also faced hostile circumstances. A typical example is the 'Abbāsid Caliph al-Mutawakkil (d. 861 CE) who, in contrast to his predecessors, ended the Miḥnah debacle, which started out as a debate among the theologians as to whether the Qur'ān was created or not, but quickly turned into a political dispute and persecution of those who opposed the createdness of Islam's sacred book. While al-Mutawakkil ended this internal strife and returned the focus to a more tolerant view of theology, he followed stringent policies against Christians (and Shī'ites) and put unprecedented restrictions on his Christian subjects, including barring them from government offices and ordering them to wear special dresses. Another example is the Fāṭimid ruler Ḥākim bi-Amri'Llāh, who ordered the destruction of the Church of the Holy Sepulcher in 1009, an incident that Pope Urban II was later to use to launch the Crusades in 1095. The destruction of this oldest and one of the most sacred Churches came as a shock to both Christians and Muslims.

A few years later, to the surprise of many, Ḥākim bi-Amri'Llāh changed his view and used money from his own budget to rebuild some of the churches.

These periods of religious intolerance and communal tension were counterbalanced by the largely successful experience of social cohesion and communal harmony in cities and provinces such as Baghdad, Andalusia, Istanbul, Cairo, and Isfahan. Some strands in Muslim thought, the Sufis in particular, advocated a form of spiritual universalism and expanded the horizon of religious boundaries, even though a full-fledged comparative theology was not a compelling necessity before the modern period. Today, the situation is radically different and the recognition of the plurality of religious forms is a compelling reality. Yet Muslims and Christians fail to obtain a reasonable degree of communicative rationality as a basis for theological interaction. In most cases, they end up having a very narrow definition of theology and use it as a tool for creating oppositional identities. Differences at the human level are taken up all the way to the level of the understanding of the Divine.

"A Common Word Between Us and You" seeks to fill this vacuum. In this regard, it is one of the most important attempts to develop a dialogical discourse and a leadership engagement between Islam and Christianity in recent years. Identifying the love of God and love of the neighbor as the basis of a meaningful and serious dialogue, the "Common Word" asserts, against the claims to the contrary, that there *is* a ground for theological conversation between Muslims and Christians.[1] It also argues that the differences over theological issues, including the way Muslims and Christians formulate their notions of God, do not obviate serious engagement and interaction.[2] While the command to love God connects the believer to the Divine, love of the neighbor extends to the domain of human relations and seeks to fuse it with love and compassion. Equally important is the fact that the "Common Word" anchors its claims in the Qur'ān and the Bible and thus expresses a "desire to meet each other not 'at the margins' of our historic identities but speaking from what is central and authoritative for us."[3]

In one respect, this is a call for the acknowledgement of a Judeo-Christian-Islamic tradition. The claim to such a tradition, however, is as novel and understudied as the Judeo-Christian tradition when this phrase began to be widely used after the Vatican Council II. Until then, the phrase was an anomaly and, given the troubled history of Jewish-Christian relations, an oxymoron.[4] The "Common Word" does not make a specific case for an Islamic-Christian tradition or argue for a united tradition of the three Abrahamic faiths, even though the Islamic sources have numerous references to Abraham as the unifying figure of the three religious traditions.[5] Rather, it calls for an engaged conversation between Islam and Christianity, while fully acknowledging the theological and historical differences between the two traditions.[6] The impressive list of Muslim signatories on the one hand, and the large number of Christian responses to the "Common Word" on the other hand, attest to the emerging potential for a new course of Muslim-Christian relations in the twenty-first century.[7]

"A Common Word Between Us and You" promises to chart a new course in Muslim-Christian relations in a way that respects the claim of orthodoxy and authenticity by both traditions and maintains an open horizon. By going back to the two commandments of the love of God and love of the neighbor, it invites Christians, Muslims and other people of conscience to the Qur'ānic injunction of "vying for the common good (*al-khayrāt*)" (al-Mā'idah 5:48). It is this universal outlook and spiritual ecumenism rather than the embattled legacy of modernity that should decide the future of Muslim-Christian relations.

This chapter has a twofold argument. On the one hand, I argue that Christians and Muslims talk to one another within a theological and historical context that their respective traditions have provided for them. At this level, the traditional differences between Islamic and Christian scriptures present a contested history but also an understudied field, shaping the main contours of the religious conversation. Instead of repeating it, both traditions need to build on this history in order to respond to the spiritual and political challenges facing their followers and the world at large today. On the other hand, I argue that the conceptual ground of the current Muslim-Christian dialogue, like all other interreligious discourse, is effectively determined by the modern notions of truth, epistemic pluralism, and human agency. The different ways in which Islam and Christianity have reacted to modernity and the Enlightenment project reflect, in their myriad modalities, the philosophical and theological differences that define the Islamic and Christian intellectual traditions in the modern period. While the two have their theological and historical differences in the traditional-medieval context, the divergences have become particularly accentuated in the post-Enlightenment period. I maintain that a critical reading of the legacy of the Enlightenment is crucial for charting a new discourse of dialogue between Islam and Christianity in the twenty-first century. While the traditional differences between Islamic and Christian theologies on the Trinity, the crucifixion, the prophethood of Muḥammad and other theological and scriptural issues remain intact, the questions posed by the Enlightenment on truth, reason, the self, belief, and science present a new set of challenges. The positions which the two traditions will develop on the key philosophical and spiritual issues of late-modernity will also shape the future of their dialogue.

I shall analyze these two aspects of Muslim-Christian thinking with references to history and contemporary philosophy. But there is also a third element and it pertains to what we might call the political-economy of Muslim-Christian relations in the twenty-first century. The "Common Word" addresses this issue when it says that "Muslims and Christians together make up well over half of the world's population. Without peace and justice between these two religious communities, there can be no meaningful peace in the world."[8] It should be pointed out that the issues of political engagement, war, poverty, economic inequality, migration, minority rights, and missionary activities generate and sustain many of the intractable problems and communal tensions between Christians and Muslims in the West and in the Muslim-majority countries. They shape religious attitudes and create spaces of suspicion and mistrust.

The group of over three hundred leading Protestant-Evangelical Christians who responded to the "Common Word" took note of this fact when they said that "though tensions, conflicts, and even wars in which Christians and Muslims stand against each other are not primarily religious in character, they possess an undeniable religious dimension. If we can achieve religious peace between these two religious communities, peace in the world will clearly be easier to attain."[9] Dr. Rowan Williams, the Archbishop of Canterbury, has underlined the importance of this point in his response when he said:

> [P]eace throughout the world is deeply entwined with the ability of all people of faith everywhere to live in peace, justice, mutual respect and love. Our belief is that only through a commitment to that transcendent perspective to which your letter points, and to which we also look, shall we find the resources for radical, transforming, nonviolent engagement with the deepest needs of our world and our common humanity.[10]

As the two responses above indicate, any genuine Muslim-Christian dialogue of necessity goes beyond theology and extends to social and political domains. Just as in the past, the political-economy of Muslim-Christian relations today is as important as theology for all dialogue and engagement initiatives to succeed. This, however, requires a number of other measures. A Muslim-Christian dialogue will not take root until and unless trust and confidence has been built between the two communities around the world. Given the size and complex problems of the followers of the various denominations of Islam and Christianity in the twenty-first century, it takes more than theology and scriptural reasoning to deal with the pressing issues of our world today.

Establishing religious and cultural accord is admittedly a difficult enterprise anywhere in the world. This is especially true given the long and checkered relationship between Islam and Christianity. Islam's meteoric rise to the stage of world history in the seventh century, when Christianity was struggling both in the East and in Europe, created a sense of rivalry and urgency among European Christians.[11] Islam's claim of restoring Abrahamic monotheism and rejection of the Christian Trinity was received as a theological challenge.[12] There were also other elements of theology that drew the attention and ire of Eastern Christians and Byzantine theologians to Islam and caused consternation among them. The first Christians who encountered Islam did not fail to see that the Qur'ān devoted a large amount of space to Judaism and Christianity as well as their theological and historical claims.[13] The Prophet Muḥammad spoke of the previous prophets claimed by Jews and Christians as his brothers, and presented himself as completing their mission. Besides theology, Islam introduced a new legal status for Jews and Christians calling them the People of the Book (*ahl al-kitāb*), who thus shared one more basic element with Muslims. In all of these cases, the new Muslim faith was inviting Jews and Christians to a serious dialogue on key religious and historical issues shared by those who considered themselves to be the children of Abraham.[14]

Common ground does not mean uniformity, and there are obviously important theological differences between Islam and Christianity that need to be addressed for a genuine dialogue and engagement. The Christian view of Christ as the Son of God and suffering Savior is different from Islamic notions of salvation and eschatology. In contrast to Islam's concept of salvation, Pope Benedict XVI, for instance, affirms that "faith in Jesus Christ as the only Savior and the indivisibility of Christ and the Church is the foundation."[15] The Muslim Jesus remains within the confines of Islamic prophetology, and Muslims accept him as one of the preeminent prophets. While the Qur'ān calls Jesus a Word and a Spirit from God (Q 4:71), Islam rejects assigning any divine attributes to him. As for the Virgin Mary, she is mentioned more in the Qur'ān than in the Bible and her name decorates the *miḥrāb*s of countless mosques around the world. The Qur'ān presents Mary as the most blessed of all women (Q 3:43) and as a model of modesty, chastity, and devotion to God. By contrast, Christianity rejects the Qur'ān as God's revelation, and the Prophet Muḥammad is vilified by both secular and religious groups in the West.[16] These theological and scriptural differences have originated from the canonical sources of Islam, and both Christian and Muslim polemical works have discussed them extensively during the Middle Ages.[17] A quick look at the earliest interactions between Muslims and (Eastern) Christians confirms the decisive role these issues and their interpretations by posterity have played in the later history of Muslim-Christian relations.

The Legacy of the First Muslim-Christian Encounters

Muslim interaction with Christians goes back to the beginning of Islam and, in one well-known instance, to the life of the Prophet before the advent of the first Islamic revelation. Five major encounters seem to have shaped the positive image of Christians among the first Muslims. The first is the Christian monk Baḥīrā who had recognized the "seal of prophethood" in the 12-year old Muḥammad who was at the time traveling with his uncle Abū Ṭālib to Syria.[18] Struck by the young boy's appearance, Baḥīrā asked Abū Ṭālib a number of questions about Muḥammad and his "qualities" and then talked to him directly. Baḥīrā's questions establish an interesting link between the Christian tradition and the future mission of the young Muḥammad. Ibn Hishām describes Baḥīrā as possessing the "knowledge of the Christian people."[19] Later Muslim historiography interprets this incident as a foretelling of Muḥammad's future as a prophet on the basis of Christian sources.[20]

The second is the famous incident when Muḥammad, then 40 years old,[21] received the first revelation through the Archangel Gabriel. Bewildered by the extraordinary experience of receiving the first revelation, he rushed to his wife Khadījah and asked her to cover him, not sure how to interpret the incident that would change the course of history. He was reassured by a "wise and knowledgeable" Christian with the name of Waraqah ibn Nawfal, who was also a cousin of the Prophet's wife.[22] The reason Waraqah was consulted was because "he was a Christian and read the scriptures and learnt from the people of the Gospel and the Torah."[23] After listening to the Prophet Muḥammad, Waraqah confirms that he was visited by the "same *Nāmūs* (*nomos*, Archangel Gabriel) who descended upon Moses, the son of 'Imrān."[24] Thus the beginning of the prophetic mission of Muḥammad is certified by a Christian tradition of "books, angels, and prophets."

The third incident is of a different nature but confirms the previous experiences. After the Prophet Muḥammad began openly to preach the new religion, he sent a small group of Muslims to the Christian kingdom of Axum or Abyssinia to escape religious persecution in Mecca, a fact that early Muslims believed they shared with Christ and his disciples. The Christian king of the time had the title of Negus, known in Arabic as Najāshī. He welcomed the Muslim delegation and refused to turn them in to the Meccans. This was taken as a further sign of Christian compassion and friendship towards Muslims.[25] The Mu'tazilite theologian al-Jāḥiẓ (d. 868 CE), the author of *al-Radd 'ala'l-Naṣārā* ("The Refutation of Christians"), mentions Najāshī among the reasons as to why Muslims regard Christians closer to themselves than others.[26] In his *al-Jawāb al-Ṣaḥīḥ* ("The Correct Answer"), one of the most extensive responses to Christianity in medieval Islam, Ibn Taymiyyah goes so far as to call Najāshī a Muslim and narrates that the Prophet Muḥammad prayed for his soul when he died—an act which Muslims typically perform for fellow Muslims.[27]

The fourth incident takes place in Medina, where the new Muslim community had taken refuge. In a striking episode that we might call the first Muslim-Christian interfaith dialogue, Prophet Muḥammad permits a group of Christians from the town of Najrān to say their mass in the mosque where Muslims prayed. After the prayers, the Prophet invites the Christian delegation to embrace Islam. They refuse but agree to live in peace with Muslims. This was more than an incident of religious tolerance; it was also the expression of a special bond that was forming between the first Muslims and (Eastern) Christians.[28] This is corroborated by the fact that the Qur'ānic verse that stipulates against forced conversion ("there is no compulsion in religion," al-Baqarah 2:256) was sent, according to

Ibn Kathīr, as a response to a specific incident when Banī Sālim b. 'Afw, one of the companions of the Prophet from Medina, had forced his Christian sons to accept Islam.[29] An interesting application of this verse is attributed to 'Umar ibn al-Khaṭṭāb, the second caliph of Islam (d. 586–590 CE), who asks an old Christian woman to embrace Islam. The old lady responds by saying, "I am an old lady and death is nearing me." Upon hearing this, 'Umar reads the verse al-Baqarah 2:256 and leaves her.[30] Finally, we should mention the Byzantine Emperor Heraclius, who was a contemporary of the Prophet Muḥammad and is said to have interacted with the first caliph Abū Bakr.[31] He was held in high esteem as a wise and just ruler because of his political wisdom as well as religious devotion.

Muslims thus had a clearly more favorable view of the Byzantine Empire than they did of the Sassanids for no other reason than the fact that the former was Christian.[32] But this was true also theologically due to the Qur'ānic verse al-Mā'idah 5:82–84, where Christians are praised as being closer to Muslims in affection than others. While the Muslim tradition has treated the Christian Trinity as compromising God's absolute oneness (*tawḥīd*), enshrined in Islam's robust monotheism, the Christian devotion to God has been largely acknowledged. In his commentary on Mullā Ṣadrā's *Kitāb al-Mashā'ir*, Mullā Muḥammad Ja'far Langarūdī Lāhījī, one of the important nineteenth century expositors of the school of Mullā Ṣadrā (1571–1641 CE), develops a striking concept of the ontological servitude of all created beings and applies it to religious pluralism. Following the Qur'ānic tradition, Lāhījī states that all creatures depend on God for their existence and thus worship Him because "everything worships that which effaces its poverty [i.e., brings it out from nothingness into existence]. So nothing and nobody escapes His praise and worship." The Qur'ān (17: 44) describes all things in the "heavens and the earth" as praising God and prostrating before Him. Those who worship Him in a "general and absolute way" profess His oneness (*muwaḥḥidūn*); whereas, those who worship Him in a "limited and conditioned way" take partners unto Him (*mushrikūn*). In this sense, the disbelievers (*al-kuffār*), the Magians, the materialists (*dahriyyah*), and the naturalists (*ṭabī'iyyah*) are all within the plane of ontological dependence and servitude. Despite their differences with Muslims, Jews and Christians also worship God but in an incomplete way because they mistake some of His Names and Qualities for His absoluteness.

After these remarks, Lāhījī adds that "among all the past nations, Christians are closest to God the Exalted and they are below the *Muḥammadiyyīn*." The reason is that Christians worship God in the person of Jesus, Mary, and the Holy Spirit. This does not befit God's absolute oneness and moves Christians away from the "state of those who affirm the oneness of God (*al-muwaḥḥidūn*)." Yet they remain closer to the truth of the Divine because "whoever has witnessed God in man (*al-insān*) has a witnessing more perfect than all those who have witnessed God in anything other than man."[33] This is a reference to the Islamic belief that while God has revealed His Names and Qualities in all of His creation, they are manifested most perfectly in the human state. All other attempts to see God's glory in His creation while forgetting His absolute oneness and transcendence have ended up in paganism or polytheism. For Lāhījī, the Christian concept of God comes closer to His oneness, which is what Islam affirms, because it sees God through the human state, which is closer to God than anything else He has created.

Such theological formulations, however, do not change the fact that the nascent Muslim community and the Byzantines were also engaged in a political and military battle for dominance in the upper Mesopotamia and Asia Minor. The rapid expansion of Muslim societies into areas that were once under Byzantine rule fueled the Byzantine polemical works against Islam with a heightened sense of contention and threat. The Muslim attitude toward other religions also displayed considerable changes in different periods from tolerance and engagement to exclusion and assimilation. The overall experience was a mixed one: political rivalry and military hostility on the one hand and religious, cultural, and artistic interaction on the other. Both were part of the early Muslim-Byzantine relations in the seventh and eighth centuries.

Finally, the spread and ascendancy of Islamic culture and civilization in the eastern Mediterranean, North Africa, and Southern Spain after the tenth and eleventh centuries were a cause of alarm to Christians in Europe. The sense of insecurity and threat was felt in every field of cultural and religious life. The rising popularity of Muslim culture among European Christians caused many to see Islam as an enemy.[34] Periods of peaceful coexistence in places like Baghdad, Istanbul, and Andalusia, where the experience of *convivencia* flourished among Jews, Christians, and Muslims, did not change this threat perception.[35] The cultural and religious attitudes of premodern Christendom towards Islam remained mostly hostile and exclusivist, and some of these attitudes continue to shape the views and perceptions current in Western societies today, even if they are called post-Christian.[36]

Talking about Truth in the Modern Context

These religious, political, and cultural experiences have shaped Muslim-Christian relations from the classical to the modern period. The sense of suspicion, rivalry, and hostility continues to emerge in the very diverse facets of encountering one another in the religious and secular contexts of late modernity. Both religious traditions are faced with other challenges that go beyond the comfort zone of religious uniformism and cultural isolationism. The key components of European Enlightenment, including secularism, relativism, pluralism, and political liberalism have changed the intellectual and social landscape of the West as well as much of the rest of the world. The shared theological and philosophical ground between Islam and Christianity has now been replaced by a new framework that posits the rejection of all absolute truth claims as key to a humane worldview and civilized social order. Habermas, for instance, argues that "the self-understanding of modernity... has been shaped by an egalitarian universalism that requires a decentering of one's own perspective. It demands that one relativize one's own views to the interpretive perspectives of equally situated and equally entitled others."[37] It is, however, questionable to what extent this definition properly describes the main thrust of modernity because modernity has its own claims of absolute truth and epistemic monopoly. One of the reasons for modernity's clash with religion is precisely its attempt to supplant religious truth with its own equally absolute, secular truths. Nevertheless, the challenge which Habermas' concept of modernity poses for religious truth is clear.

The new truth-claims of modernity are vastly different from the traditional ontologies that engendered and maintained Christian and Islamic views of reality. The God-centric metaphysics of the three Abrahamic traditions, regardless of the differences of their specific religious languages, refused to grant the world a self-regulating status and insisted on placing everything within a larger context of meaning. The world was meaningful to the extent to which it was not only "itself" but something that always pointed to something more, something higher. The notion of the world as a self-authenticating and independent reality was anathema to all premodern traditions. The self-regulating world of modern Western philosophy is coupled with a self that assumes an ontology of its own and is based on a radical form of subjectivism. By subjectivism, I do not mean arbitrariness, subjective judgment, or lack of objective standards. Subjectivism is the closure of the subject upon itself with a claim to enclose the nonsubjective and the supra-individual within it. It is an attempt to construct a context of justification by a subject that sees itself above and beyond points of references and context of relations. This meaning of subjectivism is evident in what Charles Taylor has called the "disengaged agent" of modernity, an agent that is in a position to thrust itself over the world to give it meaning, order, content, and structure.[38] The modern concept of the self is conceived to be an agent disengaged from any context of relations, whether these relations are attributed to the world, human language, existence, or the Divine.

In its subjectivist claims, the modern self is a "world-less subject" set against a "subject-less world."[39] It is a world-less subject because it is thought to be cut off from all contexts of relation, having a god-like position over the world. It is set against a subject-less world because the world is conceived to be an aggregate of entities that obtain meaning only when penetrated by a knowing subject. The modern self does not investigate reality. It defines it.[40] To use Berger's characterization of the modern individual, "The concept of the naked self, beyond institutions and roles, as the *ens realissimum* of human being, is the very heart of modernity."[41] The rational procedures of the mind are read thus into the ontological structure of the world. The knowing subject assumes the privileged position of the "view from nowhere" with an attempt "to view the world not from a place within it, or from the vantage point of a special kind of life or awareness, but from nowhere in particular and no form of life in particular at all."[42] Such a self knows itself and the world through a self-professed mastery over the world.

The ontological closure of the knowing subject unto itself was a critical step toward the secularization of knowledge. A knowledge that is closed upon itself has to work from within itself without a supra-individual and transcendent principle. Here we have the emergence of modern reason as disengaged, objective, free, and secular all at once. Modern reason cut off from all external references, however, can pretend to be autonomous only as an abstraction. In reality, reason, just like any other human attribute, is firmly embedded in frameworks of relations that go beyond the individual. As Huston Smith points out, "[T]he deepest reason for the current crisis in philosophy is its realization that autonomous reason—reason without infusions that both power and vector it—is helpless."[43]

The autonomous subject powered by an autonomous reason is projected to be free and emancipated from all contexts of relations. But reason cannot be a solipsistic entity, otherwise, it can never have access to objective reality, (i.e., what the Muslim philosophers have called the nonsubjective and extra-mental, *fi'l-khārij*) reality of our world.[44] Furthermore, the claim of the autonomous reason to be the sole source of meaning and reference goes against the basic insight of medieval Jewish, Christian, and Islamic metaphysics that existence precedes cognition. In contrast to Descartes, one *is* before one knows. The self-intelligibility of existence preempts the possibility of a knowing subject constructing a world of meaning on its own. Such a subject can only function within the context of existence and its modalities. As I have argued elsewhere[45] that the self can be itself to the extent to which it ceases to be itself and reaches out to the non-self. We can conceive a self only by seeing it embedded within the larger context of existence.

A self-authenticating world coupled with the ontology of the modern self invites a radical secularization of the world-picture to which religions cannot remain indifferent. The challenge that this problem poses for interfaith discourse is that while religious traditions try to talk to one another, they operate in a context that undercuts religious talk in a manner that may not always be apparent. The truth-claims of religions are subjected to the same rules of scrutiny and verification as any truth-claim in science, philosophy, or politics. Religions run the risk of losing all truth-value in the face of the nonrealist ontology of late modernity. Reduced to social utility, religions cater to the needs of their followers but without the moral authority that underwrote their tradition. In a world of competing truths, religions cannot talk to one another in isolation from the numerous ways in which the autonomous reason fashions, maintains, and falsifies the modern truths. They do so at the expense of either religious fundamentalism, which rejects everything outside its own religious universe, or religious antirealism, which gives up all claims of authenticity. Thus, we return to the age-old problem of relativism, which Pope Benedict XVI considers to be "the most profound difficulty of our age."[46]

If the new foundations of truth pose problems for the justification of religious belief, believing in an absolute truth poses another set of problems in an age of lessening commitments. The religious claim to truth is seen not only as incoherent because it refers to something transcendent (i.e., beyond my understanding of reality) but also as something deadly because it introduces a categorical distinction between true and false, pure and impure, godly and satanic, and so on. Such distinctions invite violence of various kinds, for the moral commitment that accompanies them is susceptible to radicalism and intolerance. In his book *Moses the Egyptian: The Memory of Egypt in Western Monotheism*, Jan Assmann discusses what he calls the "Mosaic distinction" and claims that Moses' deadliest mistake was to introduce "a distinction between true and false in the realm of religion. Hitherto, religion had been based on the distinction between pure and impure or between sacred and profane, and had no place at all for the idea of 'false gods'...whom one should not worship." In the pre-Mosaic Egypt "no one disputed the reality of foreign gods or the legitimacy of foreign ways of worshipping them. The concept of a religion being untrue was wholly alien to the ancient polytheistic religions."[47] It was the Mosaic redefinition of religion in terms of truth and falsity that created the alleged arrogance and violence of monotheistic religions. Assmann's conclusion is clear: If we are to create a humane, pluralistic world free of religious violence and intolerance, we must go back to the premonotheistic and pagan world of "international" and "interchangeable" deities.[48]

Assmann's view that rejecting all claims to truth and authenticity guarantees religious tolerance and pluralism is unwarranted. One can be violent with or without committing oneself to a religious truth. After all, "pagan societies," to the extent there was such a thing in the modern sense of the term, were as violent as any other society. The same holds true for modern secular societies, which have in fact been no less violent and in some cases more so than traditional societies. Furthermore, violence committed in the name of religion is too complicated a phenomenon to be reduced to a single factor such as blind faith, social conservatism, or communal politics.[49] The problem is how one formulates the concept of truth and lives by it. All claims to truth involve some notion of boundaries and require commitment. Integrity entails a certain degree of exclusion (i.e., the exclusion of that which one does not associate with). In the final analysis, this is a relative measure because no identity can be absolutely exclusive or inclusive. This, however, does not in itself lead to violence. There must be some other elements to produce violence. Religious faith can produce violence but also nurture love and compassion. Regardless of Assmann's faulty logic, the symbolic and actual violence presumed to issue from the truth-claims of the major religions of the world present challenges to religious thinking in the twenty-first century. Muslims and Christians can claim no immunity.[50]

Muslim and Christian Responses to the Enlightenment

How do these challenges affect Christians and Muslims in their interfaith thinking? At the beginning of the twenty-first century, the two traditions do not have a shared language because they work from different sets of theological priorities. In the modern period, they have hardly made an effort to encounter the challenges of secular modernity in a spirit of critical engagement and mutual reflection. While Christians received modernity as an essentially anticlerical and anti-Christian movement, the Muslim world came into contact with it through European colonialism, occupation, cultural imperialism, and missionary activities supported by European governments in the nineteenth and even twentieth centuries. Especially in its French version, the Enlightenment developed as a philosophical movement to overcome the Catholic Church as a source of moral and political authority. This has made the Catholic-Christian encounter with modernity substantially different from that of other traditions, including that of Eastern Orthodox Christianity. Christianity had to choose either fideism or secularism to survive the relentless attacks of eighteenth century rationalism and anticlericalism. With the expansion of European colonialism and modernity, the post-Christian Europe envisioned by the Enlightenment *philosophes* went beyond Europe and came to have a deep impact on the non-Western world.

The postreligious and postmetaphysical world in which modern man lives today is related to the process of creating a specifically post-Christian world. The nineteenth century bourgeois revolution was anticlerical and had to be so to protect its new interests. The original meaning of the secular was related to the political-economy of secularization and it meant the transfer of property owned by the clergy to laypersons and the " 'freeing' of property from church hands into the hands of private owners, and thence into market circulation."[51] In the Muslim world, this meaning of secularization was well captured in Badger's *English-Arabic Lexicon* published in 1881, where the entry on secularization (*'almāniyyah*), the first definition in any Islamic languages, read as the "transfer to worldly purposes of endowments and properties pertaining to worship and religion (*tahwīl al-awqāf wa'l-amlāk al-mukhtaṣṣa bi'l-'ibādah wa'l-diyāna ila'l-aghrād al-'ālamiyyah*)."[52] In essence, secularization meant the process of the weakening of the sociopolitical and religious authority of the Catholic Church.

The Enlightenment project took aim at the excesses of what came to be known as "institutional religion" in Europe (i.e., the Catholic Church). Some in the Muslim world have taken this point further and argued that it was the "dogmatic" and "irrational" aspects of Christian theology and political history that invited the Enlightenment attacks on religion. In their eyes, one should not generalize the Enlightenment critique of Christianity to other religions. The experience of European Christianity, the argument goes, remains specific to European history and cannot be fully extended to other traditions such as Judaism, Hinduism, and Islam.

Christian theologians attempted to defend Christianity by using the arguments of post-Christian philosophy in an increasingly aggressive secular and skeptical age.

The so-called "Christian reconciliation" with the Enlightenment produced many mixed results. For both theological and historical reasons, Catholic and Protestant thinkers developed different, and at times, opposite positions. The conceptual framework of such notions as reason, personalism, human rights, and the dignity of the human person, all of which received their modern connotation from the Enlightenment, has been largely embraced as an attempt to find a modus vivendi between traditional Christian doctrines and modern secular ideas. The Second Vatican Council's concept of the dignity of the person and the inalienable rights of the human, for instance, fits the broad outlines of Kant's post-Christian and post-metaphysical theology. It is defended by Christians and some Muslims alike as a confirmation of the privileged position God has granted to humans in His creation.

There is, however, a world of difference between a human state anchored in the Divine and a self-authenticating man who carves out his own ontology and theology in a Promethean fashion. Such a notion of the person ends up either in a subjectivist theology or anthropocentric humanism. In both cases, the autonomous individual and his or her choices in the Weberian sense of the term have the final say over what counts as normative theology. Weber's concept of freedom as the ability to choose without accounting for what one chooses becomes the hallmark of modern agency: Modernity enables the modern subject to choose what she wants without asking questions about the content of her choices. While tradition is thought to provide meaning for its followers, modernity promises freedom, leading to a "dilemma of rootless freedom and oppressive tradition."[53]

It is clear that both Islam and Christianity need to develop a religious discourse that would accommodate meaning and tradition on the one hand and freedom and an open horizon on the other. An equally critical question is how thinking on these issues affects Muslim-Christian relations. The religious defense of reason and freedom does not always lead to a greater understanding across religious boundaries. A case in point is Pope Benedict's defense of a "reason-based Christianity" against the allegedly irrational and violent nature of Islam, which he claimed in his Regensburg speech to have shaped the Muslim experience. It is this experience, Pope Benedict further argues, that urges Christians to treat Islam as a culture rather than a religion.

In an interesting essay dealing with the "other of Europe," Pope Benedict posits Islam as "Europe's real opponent." He contrasts the merging of Hellenization and Christianity in Europe with Islam's rejection of both. His analysis is worth quoting in full:

> Already in its emergence Islam is to a certain extent a reversion to a monotheism which does not accept the Christian transition to God made man and which likewise shuts itself off from Greek rationality and its civilization which became a component of part of Christian monotheism via the idea of God becoming man. It can of course be objected to this that in the course of history there were continually approaches in Islam to the intellectual world of Greece; but they never lasted. What this is saying above all is that the separation of faith and law, of religion and tribal law was not completed in Islam and cannot be completed without affecting its very core. To put it another way, faith presents itself in the form of a more or less archaic system of forms of life governed by civil and penal law. It may not be defined nationally, but it is defined by in a legal system which fixes it ethnically and culturally and at the same time sets limits to rationality at the point where the Christian synthesis sees the existence of the sphere of reason.[54]

Pope Benedict's tacit claim that Islam has failed to develop a system of reason of its own because it rejected the Christian trinity on the one hand and remained "ethnically and culturally bound" on the other is unsubstantiated both historically and philosophically. What is interesting is the way in which Islam is contrasted to Christianity in its painful experience of Hellenization and modern Enlightenment. Curiously, the fact that Islam has not gone through the same stages of historical encounter and transformation is presented as an obstacle to dialogue and engagement. It is this sort of perspective that undercuts serious engagement between Muslims and Christians and adds mistrust to an already troubled relationship in the modern period.[55]

A (re)interpretation of Enlightenment humanism from a religious point of view has been tried in order to dovetail the secular spirit of the modern age with the Christian faith. After all, not all Enlightenment thinkers rejected religion in toto. Instead, they invented a new religion for themselves and called it deism.[56] They hoped to maintain a sound belief in God while rejecting supernatural revelation and Christianity as an institutional religion.[57] Edmund Burke, for instance, was unambiguous when he wrote in 1790 that "man is by constitution a religious animal."[58] One can also mention John Wesley and Methodism as one of the new religious movements of the modern era—a popular religious current that differed from mainstream Christianity but that also went against the antireligious spirit of the French *philosophes*.[59]

In his famous work *The Secular City*, first published in 1965, Harvey Cox embraced secularization as the fulfillment of the Biblical concept of religiosity—a concept of God and a form of religion free from the metaphysical burdens of Greek philosophy and arrogant claims of religious institutions. Cox's joyous celebration of secularization as humanity's maturation, something God wants of His children, may be seen as making virtue out of necessity in the sense that secularization has already happened and all we need to do is to learn to live with it. One can also argue that God wanted his religion to manifest itself in the first century in the form of a rural faith culture; whereas, today His will is manifested in the creation of the secular city. However one imagines religions to be in the postmedieval world, there is room for the multiple interpretations of religious commitment even in a purely secular context.

Since the publication of *The Secular City*, Cox has revised his view in a number of important ways and no longer sees secularization as the only emancipatory power in the modern world. But Cox makes an important point about the state of religion in the modern world. Secularization does not oppose religion but simply bypasses it and moves on to other things. It does not promise a traditional, religious heaven on earth but presents to us a mere world, a world that is nothing more than what it appears to be. It sets a different set of priorities and convinces its modern believers that their view of the world as a mere world with no metaphysical rings attached to it is no less cogent or significant than that of traditional religions. The world can be lived in with no expectation of a hereafter. According to Hegel, one should celebrate the "recognition of the Secular as capable of being an embodiment of Truth: whereas it had been formerly regarded as evil only, as incapable of Good—the latter being essentially ultramundane."[60] So much can be done through science, technology, development, innovation, trade, art, and literature, and none of these calls for a religious presence. Religions end up in a serious problem of relevance.

Just like Christian responses, the Muslim reactions to the Enlightenment have produced varied results. The vast majority of Muslims have abstained from humanizing the Divine and divinizing the human in the name of bringing theology down to earth or raising man up to the heavens, respectively. Instead, they have continued to consider God in anthropomorphic terms and see man as a theomorphic being.[61] They still see the world as the work of God who created it for a purpose, a purpose that is in harmony with the *telos* of man's earthly existence. The ideas of progress, individualism, rationalism, and secularism have been imposed by top-down state policies as part of the sociopolitical modernization of Muslim societies. However, they have not found a home in the hearts and minds of ordinary Muslims who still live in a "sacred" and "enchanted" world. The Muslim notions of human reason, the individual, family, the universe, the transcendent, and religion are imbued with a sense of the sacred that defies the subjectivist epistemologies and secular ontologies of our days. Even the Muslim modernists who lament the "backwardness" of Muslim societies and propose religious reforms to overcome it have for the most part rejected the excesses of modern secularism.

It should, however, be underlined that Muslim modernists attempted to embrace modernity on the basis of the naïve assumption that the project of modernity would have worked better in Islam than it did in the Christian West for theological and political reasons. While this is an anachronistic assumption and betrays a Eurocentric sentiment, it does point to an interesting fault line between Islam and Christianity in the modern period. The argument goes something like this: theologically speaking, the Islamic faith has never had an apocalyptic fallout with reason and has rarely resorted to fideism as a basis of faith. True, Islam is not a rationalistic religion in the modern ideological sense of the term and such movements as Ḥanbalism have advocated a robustly pietistic and anti-intellectualist position on issues of faith. Nevertheless, the Islamic intellectual tradition developed its own system of rationality whereby sound reason and free will were the preconditions of acceptable faith. That is why, for instance, Islamic law does not hold the insane (*majnūn*), those who have lost their mind and free will, legally responsible. Numerous Qur'ānic verses enjoin people to use their reason and senses in order to understand reality. One Western scholar of Islam goes so far as to say that, "Christianity speaks of the 'mysteries' of faith; Islam has nothing like that. For Saint Paul, reason belongs to the realm of the 'flesh,' for Muslims, reason, *'aql*, has always been the chief faculty granted human beings by God."[62]

Politically, Islam did not produce institutions like the Church or the Papacy. Separation of the religious from the secular and the political is conceptually difficult to imagine in Islam because the canonical sources treat them as one. There has always been a struggle between those who were pious and upheld the principle of justice and those who committed oppression and injustice. But no Muslim clergy developed to claim a strict monopoly on religious truth or political power. Orthodoxy in Islam was shaped and maintained by a set of very different elements and processes. When the *'ulamā'* and the populace who followed their lead rejected the modern reforms introduced by the state to Westernize traditional Muslim societies, they reacted not only because they were against the core values of secular modernity. They also saw a great danger of tyranny and authoritarianism at the hands of Westernized political elites who considered the traditional elites as an obstacle to their political agendas. To the vast majority of ordinary Muslims in the nineteenth century, modernization was a program of Westernization underlined by secularism on the one hand and European colonialism and missionary Christianity on the other. It involved the new ideas of freedom, equality, science, and constitutionalism, and so on but also Western dominance and imperialism.

The antimodernist movement led by the *'ulamā'*, the Sufis, local leaders, and others was directed at foreign dominance as well as local tyranny. Their resistance cannot, therefore, be brushed off as simply "obscurantist and obstructive."[63]

Claiming modernity in the name of religion has produced different versions of the same religious modernism in the Islamic and Christian worlds. But they have not brought the two traditions closer to one another in the intellectual or political senses of the term. They only confirm that attitudes toward modernity, shaped by the history of the Enlightenment since the eighteenth century, constitute an essential part of the mutual perceptions of Christians and Muslims toward one another in the modern period. A critical comparative theology entails orthodoxy, tradition, and authenticity on the one hand and an open horizon on the other. But in the case of Muslim-Christian relations, it also involves a critical examination of the legacy of the Enlightenment in the twenty-first century.

Notes

I would like to thank Seyyed Hossein Nasr, H.R.H. Prince Ghazi bin Talal bin Muhammad, John Borelli, Waleed El-Ansary, and David Linnan for their helpful comments on an earlier draft of this paper.

1. See *A Common Word Between Us and You.* http://www.acommonword.com.
2. Ibid.
3. Rowan Williams, the Archbishop of Canterbury, "A Common Word for the Common Good," *A Common Word Between Us and You*, 128.
4. See Wolfgang Huber, "The Judeo-Christian Tradition," *The Cultural Values of Europe*, 43–58.
5. 'Alī ibn Sahl Rabbān al-Ṭabarī (d. circa 870 CE) says that "The Prophet, peace be with him, called to the unity of God and to the same subject as that included in the faith of Abraham and all the Prophets, peace be with them". See N. A. Newman trans., *The Early Christian-Muslim Dialogue: A Collection of Documents from the First Three Islamic Centuries*, 568–657.
6. See *A Common Word Between Us and You.*
7. For the Catholic, Protestant, Orthodox and other responses to the *Common Word*, see ibid.
8. Ibid., http://www.acommonword.com/lib/downloads/fullpageadbold18.pdf.
9. Ibid., 84–5.
10. Ibid., 124.
11. Ibrahim Kalin, "Sources of Tolerance and Intolerance in Islam: The Case of the People of the Book," *Religious Tolerance in World Religions*), 240–43.
12. Ibid., 243–49.
13. Ibid., 240.
14. Granting legal protection to Jews and Christians, however, does not mean theological laxity. For the People of the Book in the Qur'ān and early exegetical sources, see ibid. For the Qur'ān's engagement of Christians, see also Jane Dammen McAuliffe, *Qur'anic Christians: An Analysis of Classical and Modern Exegesis.*
15. Joseph Cardinal Ratzinger, trans. Henry Taylor, *Truth and Tolerance: Christian Belief and World Religions*, 53.
16. In his address to Pope Benedict XVI and the Muslim-Catholic Forum on November 6, 2008, Seyyed Hossein Nasr has given an excellent summary of the main points of convergence and divergence between the Islamic and Christian traditions. See "We and You: Let Us Meet in God's Love" (address given at 1st Catholic-Muslim Forum Conference, Vatican City, November 6, 2008), http://acommonword.com/en/

attachments/107_Nasr-speech-to-Pope.pdf. See also Seyyed Hossein Nasr, "Comments on a Few Theological Issues in Islamic-Christian Dialogue," in *Christian-Muslim Encounters*, 457–67; "Islamic-Christian Dialogues: Problems and Obstacles to be Pondered and Overcome," *Muslim World* (1998), 218–37.

17. Jacques Waardenburg, *Muslims and Others: Relations in Context*, 181–91.
18. Ibn Isḥāq, "Sīrat Rasūl Allāh," *The Life of Muhammad*, 79–81.
19. Ibn Hishām, *al-Sīrat al-Nabawiyyah*, 144.
20. See 'Alī ibn Sahl Rabbān al-Ṭabarī, *Tārīkh al-Umam wa'l-Mulūk*, 303–4.
21. Ibn Hishām, *al-Sīrat al-Nabawiyyah*, 179.
22. Ibn Isḥāq, "Sīrat Rasūl Allāh," in *The Life of Muhammad*, 83.
23. Ibn Hishām, *al-Sīrat al-Nabawiyyah*, 182.
24. 'Alī ibn Sahl Rabbān al-Ṭabarī, *Tārīkh al-Umam wa'l-Mulūk*, 309.
25. The numerous references to Najāshī in the exegetical sources confirm his positive image among Muslims. Ibn 'Abbās, one of the earliest authorities of Qur'ānic commentary, believes that al-Mā'idah 5, 82–84 is a reference to Najāshī. The verse says "...thou wilt surely find that, of all people, they who say 'Behold, we are Christians' come closest to feeling affection for those who believe [in this divine writ]: this is so because there are priests and monks among them, and because these are not given to arrogance..." See Ibn Kathīr, *Tafsīr* (Beirut: Dār al-Ma'rifah, 2006), 521. See also Ibn Qayyim al-Jawziyyah, *Zād al-Masīr fī 'Ilm al-Tafsīr*, 401.
26. Al-Jāḥiẓ, *al-Radd 'alā'l-Naṣārā* in *Rasā'il al-Jāḥiẓ al-Rasā'il al-Kalāmiyyah*, ed. 'Alī Bu-Malham, 260. Al-Jāḥiẓ mentions other reasons: Christianity was common among Arabs, trade helped their relations, and Christians had a more advanced culture. For a partial English translation of al-Jāḥiẓ's treatise, see Al-Jāḥiẓ, *al-Radd 'alā' Naṣārā*, in *The Early Christian-Muslim Dialogue*, trans. N.A. Newman, 699–709.
27. Ibn Taymiyyah, *al-Jawāb al-Ṣaḥīḥ li-man Baddala Dīn al-Masīḥ*, ed. 'Alī b. Hasan b. Nāṣir al-Alma'ī, Vol. I, 162. Cf. Ibn Hishām, *al-Sīrat al-Nabawiyyah*, 250.
28. See Hugh Goddard, *A History of Christian-Muslim Relations*, 22.
29. Ibn Kathīr, *Tafsīr*, 239–40.
30. Abū 'Abdullah Muḥammad ibn Aḥmad al-Anṣārī al-Qurṭubī, *al-Jāmi' li-Aḥkām al-Qur'ān* 2, 280.
31. Nadia Maria El Cheikh, *Byzantium Viewed by the Arabs*, 39–54.
32. For the favorable Muslim view of the Byzantines against the Persians, see El Cheikh, *Byzantium Viewed by the Arabs*, 24–33. See also Ahmad M. H. Shboul, "Byzantium and the Arabs: The Image of the Byzantines as Mirrored in Arabic Literature" in *Arab-Byzantine Relations in Early Islamic Times*, ed. Michael Bonner, 235–60.
33. *Sharḥ Risālat al-Mashā'ir*, ed. Sayyid Jalāl al-Dīn Āshtīyānī, 207.
34. As early as the ninth century, a Spaniard named Alvaros was lamenting the increasing popularity of Islamic culture: "My fellow Christians delight in the poems and romances of the Arabs; they study the works of Mohammedan theologians and philosophers, not in order to refute them, but to acquire a correct and elegant Arabic style. Where today can one find a layman who reads the Latin commentaries on Holy Scriptures? Who is there that studies the Gospels, the Prophets, the Apostles? Alas! The young Christians who are most conspicuous for their talents have no knowledge of any literature or language save the Arabic; they read and study with avidity Arabic books; they amass whole libraries of them at a vast cost, and they everywhere sing the praises of Arab lore." Alvaro, "Indiculus luminosus," in *Medieval Islam* by Gustva von Grunebaum, 57.
35. For an accessible account of the experience of *convivencia* in Andalusia, see Maria Rosa Menocal, *The Ornament of the World: How Muslims, Jews, and Christians Created a Culture of Tolerance in Medieval Islam*.
36. See Ibrahim Kalin, "Roots of Misconception: Euro-American Perceptions of Islam Before and After September 11th" in *Islam, Fundamentalism, and the Betrayal of Tradition*, ed. Joseph Lumbard, 149–85.

37. Jurgen Habermas, *The Divided West*, ed. and trans. Ciaran Cronin, 35.
38. Charles Taylor, "What is Human Agency?" in *Human Agency and Language: Philosophical Papers 1,* 15–44. See also Charles Taylor, "Lichtung or Lebensform: Parallels Between Heidegger and Wittgenstein" in *Philosophical Arguments*, 61–78.
39. Ibid.
40. Cf. Louis Dupré, *The Enlightenment and the Intellectual Foundations of Modern Culture,* 46.
41. Peter Berger, Bridget Berger, and Hansfried Kellner, *The Homeless Mind*, 213.
42. Thomas Nagel, *Mortal Questions,* 208. See also Thomas Nagel, *The View From Nowhere.*
43. Huston Smith, *Beyond the Post-Modern Mind,* 137.
44. I have dealt with this issue in the context of Mullā Ṣadrā's *wujūd*-centered ontology and non-subjectivist epistemology. See Ibrahim Kalin, *Knowledge in Later Islamic Philosophy: Mullā Ṣadrā On Existence, Intellect and Intuition.*
45. See Ibrahim Kalin, "Knowing the Self and the Non-Self: Towards a Philosophy of Non-Subjectivism," *Journal of Muhyiddin Ibn 'Arabi Society* 43 (2008), 93–106.
46. Cardinal Ratzinger. *Truth and Tolerance: Christian Belief and World Religions*, trans. Henry Taylor, 72.
47. Ibid., 211.
48. Jan Assmann, "The Mosaic Distinction: Israel, Egypt, and the Invention of Paganism," *Representations* 56 (1996), 48.
49. In this regard, Pope Benedict's following claim is highly questionable: "Yet even Islam, with all the greatness it represents, is always in danger of losing balance, letting violence have a place and letting religion slide away into mere outward observance and ritualism." Cardinal Ratzinger. *Truth and Tolerance: Christian Belief and World Religions*, trans. Henry Taylor, 204.
50. See Ibrahim Kalin, "Islam and Peace: A Survey of the Sources of Peace in the Islamic Tradition," *Islamic Studies* 44, 327–62.
51. Talal Asad, *Formations of the Secular,* 192.
52. Quoted in ibid., 207.
53. David Kolb, *The Critique of Pure Modernity: Hegel, Heidegger and After*, 17.
54. Cardinal Joseph Ratzinger, *Church, Ecumenism and Politics: New Essays in Ecclesiology* 223.
55. Ibrahim Kalin, "Seeking Common Ground Between Muslims and Christians," 7–22.
56. Cf. Jonathan Israel, *Enlightenment Contested: Philosophy, Modernity and the Emancipation of Man 1670-1752*, 663–96.
57. In one of the earliest instances of the use of the word deism, we find John Dryden defining it as "the opinion of those that acknowledge one God, without the reception of any revealed religion" in John Dryden, Preface *Religio Laici*, by John Dryden (1682), in "Deism," in *Encyclopedia of Religion*, 2nd ed. 4, 2251.
58. Edmund Burke, *Reflections on the Revolution in France*, 104.
59. For a discussion of Methodism in the context of the Enlightenment, see Gertrude Himmelfarb, *The Roads to Modernity: The British, French and American Enlightenments*, 116–30.
60. G. W. F. Hegel, *The Philosophy of History*, trans. J. Sibree, 422.
61. William Chittick, *Science of the Cosmos, Science of the Soul: The Pertinence of Islamic Cosmology in the Modern World,* 87.
62. Josef Van Ess, *The Flowering of Muslim Theology*, 153–54.
63. Cf. Richard W. Bulliet, *The Case for Islamo-Christian Civilization*, 71.

6

Mutual Theological Hospitality: Doing Theology in the Presence of the "Other"

Daniel A. Madigan

The publication of "A Common Word Between Us and You" has raised anew the issue of whether it is even possible to have a theological dialogue between Muslims and Christians. Voices claiming some authority have been raised on both sides of the argument and in both communities. Most recently, we have the example of Pope Benedict XVI's letter to the right-wing Italian politician Marcello Pera—ironically a declared atheist whose book is entitled *Why We Must Call Ourselves Christians*! In endorsing this rather curious book, the Pope writes that a dialogue that is interreligious in the strict sense or, perhaps better, in the *narrow* sense, of that word, is impossible.[1]

Like Pope Benedict XVI, many Muslim groups engaging in and initiating dialogue have preferred the notion of intercultural or intercivilizational dialogue. One can think of the Iranian initiative on the Dialogue of Civilizations[2] or of Al-Azhar's policy on the annual dialogue with the Vatican.[3] There, properly theological questions are not on the table, and discussions have focused rather on peace, mutual respect, and human rights. Perhaps there is a suspicion on the part of all these authorities that theological dialogue is a form of negotiation in which the parties gradually renounce certain of their claims in order to arrive at an agreed position. The model they have in mind may be, on the Christian side, ecumenical agreements such as the agreed statements between Lutherans and Roman Catholics on the question of justification; or on the Muslim side, consensus statements like the Amman Message of 2004,[4] or the Makkah Appeal of 2008.[5]

In a certain sense, Pope Benedict XVI is right to be sceptical about a dialogue that is inter-religious only "in the narrow sense of the word." There is no real interreligious space, in the sense of a no-man's-land between religions where faith commitments are bracketed or ignored. In dialogue we speak from within our communities and commitments and with respect for the commitments of others. More importantly, as Pope Paul VI wrote in 1964, "Before speaking, we must take great care to listen not only to what [people] say, but more especially to what they have it in their hearts to say."[6] Thus dialogue is not, as some fear, the negotiation of a new hybrid religion. Rather it means taking other people seriously as believers. My paper begins, then, with a conviction, born of experience, that theological dialogue between Muslims and Christians is not only possible, but also, in spite of its undoubted difficulties, essential. There can be no other sound basis for the urgent political and cultural dialogues that also confront us, than to take each other seriously as believers.

Indeed, it is far too late for the Catholic Church to say that theological dialogue is not possible. At the Second Vatican Council (1962–1965), both in the document *Nostra Aetate*[7] on the Church's attitude to believers of other traditions and in *Lumen Gentium*,[8] the Council's solemn statement on the nature of Church, we have made positive theological declarations about Muslims' faith and piety—not, it should be noted, about Islam as such.[9] We have affirmed, both at the Council and since, that God's "plan of salvation also includes those who acknowledge the Creator. In the first place amongst these, there are the [Muslims], who, professing to hold the faith of Abraham, along with us adore the one and merciful God, who on the last day will judge mankind."[10] One cannot, it seems to me, say that we adore together the one God and then say that we cannot or may not talk together about that God, or about that sense of adoration that God evokes in us. This is, after all, precisely what theological dialogue means.

I certainly acknowledge that a theological dialogue, even if it were to yield some increased measure of understanding of our differences, will not resolve all the issues that lead to tension and conflict between Muslims and Christians. Indeed, it is extremely rare for theological issues to be the real cause of strife between us. Nonetheless, to speak of dialogue without including theology seems to me impossible. This is particularly important in a Western situation, where there is a tendency, or perhaps it should be called a temptation, to think of Muslims principally in social and political categories without recognizing the centrality of their religious commitments.

Another Religion?

In the Middle East—though not always in other Muslim-majority environments like, for example, Pakistan—Christians are strongly aware that Islam is not an exotic "other religion." Instead, it is a post-Christian and quite novel reading of the Judeo-Christian tradition. The dialogue is, therefore, qualitatively different from what it tends to be in more pluralist situations, or at least in situations where Islam and Christianity have not had a long history of living together. It is essential to understand that our theological dialogue with Muslims is not simply the polite study of the exotic beliefs and customs, some of them strangely familiar, of a foreign people—as it might be, for example, with Hindus, Buddhists, or Jains. Rather our dialogue is a sometimes quite lively disagreement about how to read and understand the history of God's engagement with humanity from the creation of Adam and Eve, through Noah, Abraham, Isaac, Ishmael, Moses, David, Solomon, right up to Jesus, and beyond—a history we both, along with the Jews, see as our own.

The fact that we are appealing to the same history raises the question of whether and to what extent it is appropriate for Christians to approach Islam as another—an "other"—religion. Islam did not, indeed does not, present itself as a new religion. It rather sees itself as the reestablishment of the original religion that has existed from the beginning, and of which Judaism and Christianity are examples—even if the Qur'ān holds that they have needed to be purified of certain extraneous elements. Indeed, Islam could be seen as a reform movement within the Judeo-Christian world of its time, a movement that proposes a substantial rereading of the Abrahamic, Mosaic, Christian tradition that had developed in biblical and postbiblical literature and practice. For believing Muslims, it is not simply a human reform movement, but God's reform—first as a restoration of what Meccan religion had disfigured of the original Abrahamic worship and second as a warning to Christians and Jews that their grasp of and adherence to the revelation God had given them was seriously lacking. (Q 5:66, 4:171, 9:30–31)

Precisely because of this, the faith of Muslims has a very particular claim on the theological attention of both Christians and Jews. Most Jews have come to accept gracefully the idea that Christianity, with its radically alternative reading of the biblical tradition and of the figure of Jesus of Nazareth, is not going to fade away. So too, we Christians may have to accommodate ourselves to the idea not only that Islam as a religion is not going to fade away, but also that it will remain a lively challenger of our reading of the Jesus event, and will call us to an ever-clearer expression of our faith.

Historically speaking, what theological dialogue that has existed among these three traditions has been what we might call a boundary discourse—defining, disputing, and policing the borders that separate us.[11] More recently, however, we have witnessed between Jews and Christians a different kind of discourse emerging—one that cautiously, and perhaps over-politely, recognizes that we both inhabit a common theological space. That is to say, our respective God-talks are not foreign languages to each another. It has been my privilege to witness something similar beginning to happen in various forums between Muslims and Christians, particularly with my Muslim students and colleagues at the Gregorian University in Rome and at Ankara University in Turkey, but also in the annual Building Bridges seminars convened by Dr. Rowan Williams, the Archbishop of Canterbury, as well as in the ongoing friendships and conversations that have grown out of them.

"A Common Word" begins with an implicit recognition of our common faith, since it is based upon the conviction that it is conceivable for us to seek a word in common about God and about how things are between God and humanity. We could satisfy ourselves with a minimal word in common—a few agreed statements of ethical principle—yet the divine command in Qur'ān 3:64 would have us come to a word in common about the most important thing of all, the worship of nothing other than God:

> Say: "O People of the Scripture! Come to a common word between us and you, that we worship none but God, and that we do not associate anything with Him, and do not take each other for lords, beside God."

It is at this point that I want to introduce the image of mutual hospitality. The border-negotiation discourse gives way to an acceptance, perhaps at first it is just toleration, of the presence of the other in that space of reflection on our faith that we call theology. We would like our new guests to behave themselves; we want them to sit quietly in the corner, as it were, and not interrupt us by raising objections or posing questions. Yet if we are at all hospitable, we gradually start to take more notice of our guests and we learn to speak their theological language so that we might communicate our positions more clearly. Little by little our guests learn to understand how to converse in our language and they begin to take a hand in shaping the conversation themselves. When this kind of hospitality is mutual, something new emerges, and what starts out as doing theology *in the presence of* the other becomes doing theology *together with* the other.

Yet there is a further step. The risk of all theology—let's define it as systematic discourse about God—is that discourse and system become more important than *Theos*, God. The risk of theological dialogue is that it becomes a defense of our systems of discourse rather than an opening to the divine. The space of theology belongs primarily to God, not to our systems. When we acknowledge that neither of us is the proprietor, but that we are both guests in God's space, something new in theology can emerge. This is the point that the more nervous observers of this process usually begin to speak of as relativism. Yet I think there is a significant difference between a theology that is relational and one that is relativistic. Relativism would suggest that we have different truths and that is fine. A relational theology recognizes that being in search of the one truth means also being in relation to those other seekers of the truth who do not—one might even be tempted to say do not yet—believe as I do.

But perhaps we are getting ahead of ourselves here. Let us first examine briefly the categories of our theological dialogue and some of the points of contention that have defined our relationship.

The Categories of Our Discourse

In the pluralist situation of many Western countries, it is quite common to make the various religions fit into a kind of standard schema with predetermined categories: founder, scripture, leadership, symbols, feasts, dress, laws and practices, food and fasting, ceremonies, and ideals. In terms of Islam and Christianity, this leads to a categorizing mistake that places Qur'ān and Gospel, Jesus and Muḥammad on the same plane. It is important to understand the correct parallels in order to recognize the specificity of each tradition. I propose the notion of the Word (not in the first place "scripture") as the common term around which we can build an understanding of our specificities.

It is essential in order to understand the relationships among the Abrahamic traditions that we get our categories right. The most important common belief our traditions share is that the Word of God has been spoken in our world—the eternal divine word that is of the very essence of God, God's self-expression, we might say. One way of looking at it is that the thing that distinguishes our three traditions from each other is where we believe we can hear most definitively that Word of God. Unfortunately this has led all too often to a competition over the relative value of each other's founders, prophets, and scriptures. However, this is a category mistake and leads to a theological dead end.

For Jews, the Word of God has been spoken in a privileged way at Sinai, and thus in the Torah, understood not only as the Five Books of Moses, but as the whole edifice of rabbinic reflection and study right up until our own day. For a Muslim, God has spoken His Word in Arabic in the Qur'ān—and indeed in other languages in earlier scriptures. For Christians, on the other hand, God's Word is spoken not primarily in words but, as John says in the prologue to his Gospel, in the flesh—in "body language" as it were.[12] The words of scripture, then, are not simply the words of God but also words written by the believing community inspired by the Spirit in order to put us in touch with the capital-w Word that they had experienced in the flesh. As John puts it at the beginning of his first letter, what he is writing is "about the Word of life," and that Word was able not just to be heard but also to be touched and seen (1 John 1:1). For Christians, therefore, Scripture is not simply revelation itself, as it is for a Muslim. It is in the first place the witness to the event of revelation in the Word-made-flesh, and so it is revelation in a derivative sense.

Although most Muslims may see Jesus and the Gospel as being parallel to Muḥammad and the Qur'ān, the Christian tradition does not see things this way. We need to avoid being drawn into a discourse of prophets and scriptures that ultimately leads us into a theological dead end. As Seyyed Hossein Nasr observed more than 40 years ago, what Jesus is for the Christian (God's Word expressed in history), the Qur'ān (*not* Muḥammad) is for Muslims.[13] What Muḥammad is for Muslims (the human channel through which the Word of God entered the world), Mary could be said to be for Christians.[14] Of course, that Mary role—being the bearer of the Word—does not exhaust the reality of who Muḥammad is for Muslims. He is also a Moses figure, as the leader of the community and its lawgiver. He is like Constantine in having united religious and political authority in his own person.

Confusing these categories leads to endless misunderstanding. Muslims find Christians' estimation of Jesus exaggerated, and Christians in their turn find Muslims' assessment of the Qur'ān far too exalted. Each seems to the other to be raising something holy but ultimately only human to the level of the divine. Muslims claim that what might seem to many people to be only a seventh-century Arabic text is the eternal Word of God. Christians are claiming that, although he might seem to many simply a first-century Palestinian with a prophetic bent, Jesus is the very self-expression of God. These are extraordinary claims and anything but self-evident. They are statements of faith, not simply descriptions of observable fact.

I do not wish to propose here that clarifying this language and these categories (along with others, some of which I will mention) will lead to an agreement among us. It may very well sharpen our disagreements. Yet at the moment some of our disagreements arise from the fact that we think we are speaking the same theological language—we are surely using similar vocabulary, but those vocables do not function in the same way. They do not mean the same thing. We need a common language, certainly, but perhaps it will turn out to be a common language in which to disagree.

Muslims as Theological Interlocutors

Western and Asian theologies, for all the pluralism of their contexts, have not, by and large, taken Islam as a significant interlocutor in the way Eastern churches have, though even there, not a great deal of progress has been made since the first few centuries of Arabic theological writing.[15] In the West, although there has been recent growth in comparative theology and theology of religions, our discourse is still substantially carried on with an eye to those who do not believe, rather than those who believe differently. Thus, there is a need to recognize the increasing presence of Muslims in the theological (and catechetical) contexts in which Christians function, and to take seriously the long-standing Islamic critique of Christianity.

I say this not in order to suggest that Christians are about to let go of the key elements of the Christian proclamation in order to develop a lowest-common-denominator theology to which any monotheist believer could subscribe. No, rather Christians have to recognize that we have yet to find a way to express these central elements of faith in a way that is convincing or even understandable to a fifth of the world's population. We are not doing our theology in isolation. We are doing it in the presence of people who believe differently. My own experience of teaching Christian theology to Muslims over the last decade, for the most part in the West, has convinced me that taking seriously their questions and perplexities can lead Christians deeper into the particularity of our faith. It has convinced me, furthermore, that it is possible to make some progress in finding new expressions of Christian faith that are accessible to Muslims while still being faithful to the Christian tradition. It is only arrogance to presume that the last theological word has been said in response to honest questioning.

The Two Big Issues

Although some Christians, theologians, and non-theologians, are ready to jettison the doctrines of Incarnation and Trinity as archaic embarrassments,[16] most Christians in dialogue will still want to maintain their centrality. At the same time we recognize that these elements of our faith have, from the beginning, been points of contention; therefore, if we wish to maintain them, we need to find more fruitful ways of expressing them for a Muslim audience.

In their discourse about the identity and nature of Jesus, or Christology, Christians use two general approaches: from below and from above, low-ascending and high-descending Christologies. To caricature the approaches slightly, we could say that the former begins on earth with the humanity, whereas the latter begins in heaven by considering the divinity. Low-ascending Christologies have become much more popular of late. Even if among the New Testament's many Christologies it is not difficult to find such approaches,[17] the Christian tradition overall has privileged a high-descending approach, as witnessed by the prominence of John's prologue[18] and its notion of Incarnation in Christian faith. Experience shows that Muslim interlocutors prefer and appreciate a low-ascending Christology, as long as it doesn't ascend too high.

If we were to apply these terms to Muslim discourse about the Qur'ān, we would say that it is traditionally high-descending: The Qur'ān is God's eternal Word that comes down to us. A low-ascending approach that would see the Qur'ān simply as an inspired composition by the Prophet is hardly acceptable. Even the idea that the Qur'ān might be a created rather than eternal word has not been favored in the tradition, yet Muslims are constantly challenged by their critics to adopt this kind of low-ascending approach to the Qur'ān.

In a well-motivated attempt to promote theological dialogue, a trade-off is implicitly offered by many a Christian partner: "I would be prepared to lower my claims about Jesus to something nearer your claims for Muḥammad, if you would just lower your claims about the Qur'ān and treat it the way we treat the gospels." This trade-off might be thought of as a "lowered" Christology in exchange for a "lowered" Qur'ān-ology, or what we could call a Jesus-seminar approach to Christ in return for a trenchantly historical-critical approach to the Qur'ān. This is what Hans Küng , a Swiss Catholic priest and one of the best-known and most influential voices of theological modernism, sometimes seems to be hoping for, or even demanding, when he deals with Muslims—something to restore some balance to the schema of prophets and scriptures that tends to dominate our approach to theological interaction.[19]

Given what has already been pointed out about the parallel between Jesus and the Qur'ān, it would seem that this trade-off is unnecessary. It seems to me that a robustly Johannine, high-descending, Word-Christology is, perhaps contrary to expectation, a more promising point of departure for a theological dialogue with Muslims, than are the low-ascending Christologies often adopted as being most appropriate to interfaith engagement.

Low-ascending Christologies have a tendency to confirm Muslims in their belief that what Christians are up to is the elevation of a merely human messenger to the divine plane where he has no place. Interestingly, the Islamic theological tradition in its reflection on the Qur'ān as the Word of God had to grapple with a number of issues that quite parallel those that emerged in the Christological controversies of the early centuries of the Christian tradition.[20] These became issues precisely because the Muslim community professed that what on the Qur'ān's own testimony many thought of as merely a human text—poetry (Q 36:69), stories of the ancients,[21] or a soothsayer's mantic utterance was actually a divine revelation; and furthermore that this revelation had—to use a Qur'ānic as well as Johannine turn of phrase—come down from heaven, had been sent by God. Questions about the relationship of God's Word to God's self, about the relationship between the obviously human and historically conditioned elements of the word and its divinity, about the eternity or otherwise of this word, all these exercised the theologians of both our traditions.

In this conversation, Christians recognize once again that many of our core professions of faith emerged from a long history of disagreements—that may be putting it too mildly—and only after repeated unsuccessful attempts to express in words the mystery of God and God's action in the world. Muslim participants, too, come to recognize that even though some of their own theological positions may appear settled, this is not because they have reached a point of equilibrium. Rather it is because the exploration of these questions was cut short due to a growing sense of the futility of speculative theology and its methods. If Christians can share with Muslims our own theological perplexities—both those that led us eventually to the authoritative definitions, and those that still keep us probing those definitions centuries later—they sometimes come to see that we are all "in the same boat" theologically. That is, we are both in a position of having to account for the series of questions and apparent contradictions that arise from the shared basic affirmation that the eternal and transcendent God has spoken a word—God's own Word—in and to our world. They come to realize that for both of us the appropriate response to the Word we perceive to have been given us by God is not a sceptical analysis but rather the obedience of faith.

A satisfactory Logos-Christology gives us a first opening into a more accessible theology of the Trinity, because Muslim theology has already settled on an expression about God's Word or Speech (*kalām Allāh* in Arabic) to the effect that it is an essential attribute of God, which although it is not simply identical with God, is nothing other than divine. In the classic Arabic formulation it is *ṣifah dhātiyyah lā 'aynuhu wa-lā ghayruh*. That is a paradox which to my mind is almost identical to the one John leaves us with in the very first verse of his Gospel.[22] He tells us first that "The Word was in relationship to God." This Logos, God's creative and authoritative speech, was *pros ton theon*. We usually translate that phrase as "was with God," but the preposition *pros* has a much more dynamic sense, involving a movement toward, not simply a presence beside. So the Logos is not simply identical with God—if we can place a preposition between two things, then they are surely not the same thing. Yet John goes on immediately to tell us that the Logos is nothing other than divine: *kai theos ên ho logos*, "and the *logos* was God."[23] So the Logos is not simply identical with God, yet is nothing other than divine. God is not reducible to the Word, yet the Word is no less divine than is God.

However, our approach to Trinitarian questions will begin, as it seems to have in the New Testament, from the experience of God's activity in the world as Word and Spirit rather than from speculation about the internal life of God.

Muslim belief in the ongoing and immediate divine creativity in the world provides a basis for reflecting together on the Christian belief in God as Spirit. For both our traditions God is absolutely transcendent and therefore distinct from creation, and yet at the same time, God is recreating and sustaining the world at every moment, since the world is incapable of guaranteeing and maintaining its own existence.

Much has been written in recent decades—though perhaps not yet enough—about the difficulties raised by the term "person" in Christian Trinitarian proclamations, and this deserves much more study.[24] Since, in the West, we have been engaged in a largely internal theological conversation for so many centuries in this area, we have not benefited from a careful listening to the Muslim critique of, or even simply to their puzzlement at, our Trinitarian language. Karl Rahner puts it rather bluntly:

> For the most part, we Christians talk a little too ingenuously of *three* divine persons and then say that each one of these three is God, so that (as we should readily admit to ourselves) we are exposed to the danger of being regarded as tritheists.[25]

Rahner maintains that, even without having recourse to the term *person* at all, it is quite possible to express what Christians mean when they affirm the Trinity.[26] The need to reexpress our faith in dialogue with Muslims will necessarily involve finding different expressions and what Rahner calls "more restrained formulations" than we are accustomed to use when we are on our own.[27] The purpose of these new and more careful formulations is not to conceal the truth about what we believe but rather to make that belief accessible to those who have for centuries found it at best incomprehensible, and at worst scandalous. This should not be seen as an imposition on us, but rather an opportunity for exploring our beliefs anew. People often comment on how having guests from out of town gives them the chance to explore their hometown in ways they are not accustomed to do normally. The same, I venture to suggest, is true theologically.

I have found in teaching mixed groups, that the questions the Muslim students are prepared to voice are the same ones that perplex the Christian students, though the latter are sometimes hesitant to express them. It seems to me, therefore, that in the first place, the effort required to develop a theology appropriate to our dialogue and truly responsive to Muslims will have a benefit for the Christian community itself. But more than that, this is a sign that there is something natural about welcoming Muslims into our theological space. Their questions may seem surprising at first to those who are used to particular ways of thought and expression. However, we gradually discover that those questions are not extraneous and barren, but can be natural and fruitful. Not everything natural is easy, of course. Ask any woman in childbirth. Yet in our dialogue, when the questioners and their questions are welcome, something new is aborning.

Notes

1. Marcello Pera, *Perché Dobbiamo Dirci Cristiani.* The Pope's letter-preface is available at http://www.marcellopera.it/index_en.php?page=english_zoom.php&sct=4&cnt=138.
2. See generally, Michael Rubin, "'Dialog of Civilizations'—A First-Hand Account," *Middle Eastern Quarterly* 7:1.
3. See generally, Final Declaration of Annual Meeting of the Joint Committee for Dialogue of the Permanent Committee of Al-Azhar for Dialogue Among the Monotheistic Religions and the Pontifical Council for Interreligious Dialogue (Vatican) (Cairo, February 25–26, 2008), http://www.ilvelino.it/archivio/documenti/allegato_documento_355.pdf.
4. The Amman Message, http://www.ammanmessage.com/.
5. The Makkah Appeal, http://www.saudiembassy.net/announcement/announcement09260806.aspx.
6. Pope Paul VI, *Ecclesiam Suam* 87.
7. Pope Paul VI, *Nostra Aetate.*
8. Vatican Council II, *Lumen Gentium.*
9. It is important to note the hesitation the Council shows in speaking about Islam as a whole or the essential elements of it, like Muḥammad and the Qur'ān. Both are passed over in silence. For a discussion of this point, see Daniel A. Madigan, "*Nostra Aetate* and the Questions it Chose to Leave Open."
10. Vatican Council II, *Lumen Gentium.*
11. Daniel Boyarin, *Border Lines: The Partition of Judaeo-Christianity.*
12. See, e.g., Daniel A. Madigan, "People of the Word: Reading John's Prologue with a Muslim," *Review and Expositor.*
13. Seyyed Hossein Nasr, *Ideals and Realities of Islam*, 43–4.
14. See Daniel A. Madigan, "Mary and Muhammad: Bearers of the Word." *Australasian Catholic Record* 80, 417–27. See also Seyyed Hossein Nasr, *Ideals and Realities of Islam.*
15. See Sidney Griffith, *The Church in the Shadow of the Mosque* and Samir K. Samir and Jorgen S. Nielson, ed. *Christian Arabic Apologetics During the Abbasid Period, 750–1258.* See David Thomas, *Early Muslim Polemic Against Christianity: Abū `Īsā al-Warrāq's "Against the Incarnation,"* 37–59. See also David Thomas, *Anti-Christian Polemic in Early Islam: Abū `Īsā al-Warrāq's "Against the Trinity,"* 1–66.
16. See, e.g., John Hick, "Islam and Christian Monotheism," in Dan Cohn-Sherbok, ed., *Islam in a World of Diverse Faiths*, 1–17.
17. Consider, for example, Peter's speech in Acts 2:14–36.
18. John 1:1–3.
19. See, for example, Hans Küng, *Christianity and the World Religions.*
20. See generally Walter Bauer, *Orthodoxy and Heresy in Earliest Christianity.*
21. Qur'ān 6:25; 8:31; 16:24; 23:83; 25:5; 27:68; 46:17; 68:15; 83:13.
22. See Daniel A. Madigan "People of the Word." *Review and Expositor* 104.1, 81–95. See also Daniel A. Madigan, "Gottes Botschaft an die Welt: Christen und Muslime, Jesus und der Koran," *Communio* 32.1, 100–12. A slightly enlarged English version will appear as "God's Word to the World: Jesus and the Qur'ān, Incarnation and Recitation," in *Godhead Here in Hiding: Incarnation and the History of Human Suffering*, Terence Merrigan and Frederik Glorieux, ed. (Leuven: Peeters, forthcoming).
23. Our standard translations do not always capture the actual mirror image structure of John's sentence (*logos–theos* / *theos–logos*), because it becomes ambiguous in English. The Revised English Bible translation captures the complexity and keeps the word

order of the second part of John's sentence by rendering it, "What God was, the Word was."

24. See, for example, Karl Rahner, "The Oneness and Threefoldness of God in Discussion with Islam," in *Theological Investigations, Volume XVIII: God and Revelation*, 105–21. See also Nicholas Lash, *Believing Three Ways in One God: A Reading of the Apostle's Creed*, 30–33.
25. Rahner, "Oneness and Threefoldness of God in Discussion with Islam," 119.
26. Ibid., 120.
27. Ibid.

B. Mysticism

7

Spirituality and Other Religions: Meditations upon Some Deeper Dimensions of "A Common Word Between Us and You"

Caner Dagli

The relationship between mysticism and "A Common Word" is not readily apparent. Nothing particularly mystical is to be found in this historic interfaith document, and the goals and means set out in it are not mysterious or esoteric at all. Indeed, if we look at the actual text of "A Common Word," we notice that very little recourse is had to the Islamic intellectual tradition. No theologian, philosopher, or mystic is quoted as an authority in the text. Of course the mainstream interpretations of the Qur'ān and the *ḥadīth* given rely upon the scholarly tradition, but the reasoning in the document is taken directly from the so-called transmitted sources (mainly the Qur'ān and the Bible), as opposed to the intellectual tradition which grows from those sources.

This structure was not accidental. The signatories to "A Common Word Between Us and You" include preachers, intellectuals, and leaders from the length and breadth of the Islamic world. It is a practical impossibility to craft a consensus document as sensitive as "A Common Word" by relying upon the intellectual position of any scholar or saint, no matter how great. One need only examine the questions of authority or governance within the Christian world, and reason by analogy that achieving a unified position on any matter within the world of Islam is only possible when the basis is the Qur'ān and the agreed upon Sunnah or Tradition of the Prophet Muḥammad. Palamas, Aquinas, or Luther are all taken as authoritative or inspired by discrete sectors of Christian civilization. But it would do little good to quote any one of them to prove a point in a consensus document meant to represent the entire Christian world, or even most of it. After the Prophet, the only figure who even approaches some kind of universality and religious authority is 'Alī ibn Abī Ṭālib, the fourth Caliph of the Sunnis and the First Imam of the Shī'ah. But even here the disputes over the status and teachings of this great figure make it difficult to use his teachings as font of consensus, when it comes to questions such as those addressed in a "A Common Word."

For some time, the origins of "A Common Word Between Us and You" remained obscure. Practically no one knew who drafted it, although recently it was made known that the principal author was Prince Ghazi bin Muhammad of Jordan.[1] Most people who are interested in the issue know that Prince Ghazi of Jordan was and continues to be a public pivot around which the "Common Word" initiative moves, and that there have been many important clerics in the Islamic world (such as Ḥabīb ʻAlī al-Jifrī) who have been instrumental in making it more than a nicely worded letter. But the public spokespeople for the initiative, including Prince Ghazi himself, have always been firm that "A Common Word Between Us and You" was a group document. The drafting of it was of little moment; only its signing was consequential. And this, it must be said, is quite true. Many who are involved in interfaith activity know how often something beautiful is written, or some political position is articulated well, and it goes nowhere. It is published somewhere and soon falls into obscurity. What makes "A Common Word" a new event in the history of religions is the caliber of the men and women who have chosen to stand behind it. But it is significant that the main force behind "A Common Word" were Muslims of a mystical and deeply spiritual bent, and that is the dimension of the document that I would like to discuss here.

Sufism, or Mysticism in the Muslim Tradition

Scholarship in Islamic Studies, whether it is carried out by Muslims or otherwise, has long debated the orthodoxy of the mystical and spiritual dimension of Islam often called *taṣawwuf*, or Sufism. Within Islam, Sufism is sometimes chided or condemned for being a heretical innovation, an improvisation of ritual and doctrine alien to the spirit and letter of the Qur'ānic revelation and the Prophetic sunnah. From outside, Sufism is sometimes seen as a foreign import from Christianity or the mysticisms of Asia, or as a homegrown movement that nevertheless is somehow intrinsically foreign or at odds with mainstream Islam. In the past, some Western scholars have referred to an orthodox or even a "high" Islam as opposed to more heterodox or popular expressions of religion. For the purposes of this essay it must be stated clearly that, in the view of this author, Sufism, or *'irfān* ("gnosis"), or *sulūk* ("traveling [the spiritual path]"), or the *ṭarīqah* ("the [spiritual] path"), is Islam. It is not an accretion or improvisation. What follows will not make much sense if we take as our starting point the stale and overused assumption that Islam is more or less the juridical and theological establishment's version of it. To be more specific, Islamic orthodoxy is not restricted to or exhaustively defined by the *fuqahā'* (jurists) of the *madhāhib* (such as the Ḥanafī or Shāfiʻī schools), or by *mutakallimūn* (scholastic theologians such as those of the Ashʻarite and Māturīdī schools).

One way in which we can understand this desire to exclude is by reminding ourselves of the even more stale and overused assumption which non-Muslims, and even some Muslims, have had about the Qur'ān itself. According to this assumption, the Qur'ān must be taken, above all, as an utterly unoriginal text. This imputed thoroughgoing unoriginality is the closest thing to a consistent approach to have been offered by much critical scholarship on the Qur'ān. Thus, stories which have material in common with the Bible are borrowings, and usually badly executed borrowings at that. Important terms are not to be understood by their usage in the Qur'ān, but rather by their supposed etymology. For example, one learns something more important about the word *ṣirāṭ* (meaning "path" as in *Set us upon the straight path* of the Qur'ān's first chapter) by studying its history as a word, than by trying to understand how it is used in the Qur'ān. These assumptions strangely echo some of the same accusations made in the Qur'ān, namely, that the Prophet was not actually a recipient of a Divine message, and, also, that he could not have possibly come up with the Qur'ān on his own. The modern theories of foreign borrowing are often sophisticated and etymologically based versions of the accusations leveled against the Prophet that he had a kind preceptor who taught him many of the things about which the Qur'ān speaks.

It is moreover curious that those who reject either the provenance, originality, or unity of the Qur'ān are quite ready to accept that there is such a thing as the so-called real Islam or Islamic orthodoxy, and they typically define it as, in the case of Sunnī Islam, the Shāfi'ite Ash'arite consensus (the Ḥanafī-Māturīdī consensus is not significantly different), which I referred to above as the juridico-theological consensus. Insofar as Muslims are legalistic, unoriginal, misogynist, warlike, and authoritarian, they are part of Islamic orthodoxy. Insofar as they are spiritual, compassionate, creative, peaceful, and libertarian, we must search for causes outside of the Islamic tradition for it.

And so it often happens that at meetings where Muslims give voice to the spiritual dimensions of their tradition, an objection of the following sort will be made: "That is all good and well, but you are giving a very Sufi interpretation of things. Who really pays attention to that? Is that really at all representative?" Imagine a Catholic who, in describing his own spirituality and morality to members of another faith, bases himself heavily upon the life and writings of St. Francis of Assisi. Should the Catholic be anything but baffled if a Muslim interlocutor challenges him, "That is all good and well, but Francis was a mystic and spiritual man. But who does he *really* represent? What about real Catholicism?"

Indeed, there is no real dichotomy between the orthodox *'ulamā'* (clerics) on the one hand and the Sufis or the mystically minded on the other. Abū Ḥāmid al-Ghazālī (1058–1111 CE) was a Sufi, while being a major authority in the fields of Islamic law and theology. Jalāl al-Dīn Rūmī (1207–1273 CE) was a conventional *shaykh* before he was a famous poet and saint. Ṣadr al-Dīn al-Qunawī (d. 1274 CE), the famous disciple of Ibn al-'Arabī (1165–1240 CE), was a *ḥadīth* specialist. Today and in recent times many of the greatest figures in the Islamic world have been Sufis, or drew heavily and proudly from the tradition of Sufism. In Turkey, one thinks of the Naqshbandī shaykh Mehmet Zahid Kotku. Kotku was not merely a spiritual figure, but exerted an immense influence over politics.[2] He did not do this directly, but in his function as spiritual teacher and mentor to some of the most important political actors in the last several decades of Turkish history. Among those who were his disciples or who were closely associated with the Iskender Paşa group are Turgut Özal, Korkut Özal, Necmettin Erbakan, Abdullah Gül, and Recep Tayyip Erdoğan, that is, presidents and prime ministers.[3] Futhullah Gülen, leader of one of the largest Islamic movements in the world, is heavily influenced by Sufism and makes use of it in his writings, even though he is careful not to describe himself as Sufi, for complex reasons.[4]

In recent history the Grand Mufti of Syria, Ahmad Kuftaro, whose son now holds that position, was also a Sufi Shaykh. Both the grand mufti of Egypt and the president of al-Azhar University are steeped in the tradition of *taṣawwuf*. One of the most famous of the recent rectors of al-Azhar, 'Abd al-Ḥalīm Maḥmūd, was also in the tradition of Sufism. (Historically, the vast majority of Azharī *'ulamā'* have been members of the Sufi orders.) Major *'ulamā'* today such as 'Abdullah bin Bayyah of Algeria, Ramaḍān Būṭī of Syria, and Ḥabīb 'Alī al-Jifrī of Yemen are also part of this tradition. They are not known primarily as Sufis; rather they are scholars and preachers with mainstream authority and appeal, whose spiritual life is nourished in *taṣawwuf*. Despite the recent influx of foreign influence, the spirituality of the Caucasus has always been deeply ingrained by Sufism, not only in the time of Imam Shāmil (1797–1871 CE) but through the Soviet period and until today. The religious life of the subcontinent, despite the admittedly important role of fundamentalism there, is still permeated through and through by the Sufi tradition.

It should not be thought that *taṣawwuf* is a separate set of doctrines and teachings. It is primarily a spiritual psychology, consisting of a method based upon a doctrine. For Sufis throughout the centuries, the primary source of doctrine has been and continues to be the Qur'ān. This is both obvious, and completely surprising. Obvious, because even the most famous documents in the history of Sufism–such as Ibn al-'Arabī's *al-Futūḥāt al-Makkiyyah* and the poetry of Jalāl al-Dīn Rūmī–are mainly extended meditations upon the Qur'ān. With the difficult conceptual language of Ibn al-'Arabī and the beautiful poetics of Rūmī it is easy to be distracted from the presence of the Qur'ān in their writings. But for anyone who is very familiar with the Qur'ān, it becomes obvious that it is the main source of inspiration. Beyond literature, the content of Sufism is utterly Qur'ānic. The prayers and formulas that Sufis use in their *dhikr* (methods of remembrance) are thoroughly taken from the Qur'ān and from the Sunnah.

Still, it is commonplace to assume that Islamic law and scholastic theology are most closely in line with the Qur'ān, whereas the spiritual heights and depths of Sufism are rather alien to the Qur'ānic message. This is often the opposite of the truth. Recall that scarcely one-tenth of the Qur'ān is devoted to matters of law. *Kalām*, or scholastic theology, for its part, does not set itself the goal of interpreting the Qur'ān as a whole and providing the basis of a spiritual life. It seeks only to protect certain important points of creed and to safeguard God's authority in all matters. Despite the bias in favor of giving kalām pride of place in Islamic intellectual life, very few people in the Islamic world live their spiritual life with reference to the teachings of the theologians.

Sufism and "A Common Word"

Returning to "A Common Word," it is important to note that there is a significant sector of active Muslim intellectuals whose sensibilities are very noteworthy when it comes to interfaith relations, the Wahhābī-Salafis or simply Salafis. (I do not mean to use these labels pejoratively, but they do represent a distinct set of interpretations in the spectrum of Islamic thought.) An attitude common to the Wahhābī-Salafī sector is a rejection of the spiritual tradition of *taṣawwuf*, not to mention most philosophy and theology as well, with the exception of certain figures like Ibn Taymiyyah (1263–1328 CE). Their general aversion to the intellectual tradition also extends to the legal schools (the madhāhib) of the Hānafis, the Mālikis, the Shāfi'is, and the Ḥanbalis. Rather than seeing the intellectual tradition of classical Islamic civilization as a treasure to be explored, they view most of it as the blind following the blind, or to be more precise, the ignorant imitating the ignorant. Rather than seeing the legal schools as interpretative traditions which each seek to best understand the Qur'ān and Sunnah, the Salafis view them as intellectually corrupt institutions that prefer their own authority to that of the Qur'ān and the Sunnah. For example, once a Salafī friend proudly told me the story of a new Muslim who was confused by the legal wrangling in a book he was reading, where Abū Ḥanīfah said one thing, Imam Mālik said another, and Imam Aḥmad yet another. Frustrated, he said, "But what did the *Prophet* say?" as if this were not the precise thing which Abū Ḥanīfah and Mālik were trying to understand themselves. The Salafī attitude is "Islam without madhāhib (schools of thought)" which means precisely, "Only our *madhhab*." This applies equally, or even more so, to Sufism.

Dealing with the Salafis, who are a numerical minority of no more than 10 percent, is one of the great challenges in crafting a consensus document of the nature of the "Common Word," because many of the most profound meditations on the relationship between religions, on the spiritual core of faith, is to be found within *taṣawwuf* and within the general philosophical tradition.

In the fifteenth century, when the *shaykh al-islām* or chief muftī of the Ottoman empire (Molla Fenārī) was himself an author and an authority in the theoretical mystical school of Ibn al-'Arabī, in a country where Jalāl al-Dīn Rūmī was the patron saint, one could imagine a political and cultural environment where the mentioning of, and even reliance upon, mystical ideas would not have been altogether difficult. If there were still a similar situation today, perhaps the "Common Word" document and other possible consensus documents could be even more clear and powerful, taking advantage of the elaborations and articulations of religious ideas of the Sufis, which appeal both to intellectuals and to laymen.

But such a thing can never be expected from a consensus document today. From the Sufi point of view, this should present no great problem, since Sufi doctrine's first source is the Qur'ān. The Qur'ān itself is rather clear on the question of spirituality, mysticism, and the status of other religions—they would say—and really all the great *shuyūkh* can ever offer are clarifications and teachings about the Qur'ānic doctrine. But as twenty-first century believers grappling with the meanings of the Qur'ān, we are denying ourselves a great resource of teaching and clarity when we exclude the meditations of the Sufis from the outset. Must we do so?

Moses and the Shepherd, or Perspectives and Problems

Rūmī tells of an encounter of Moses and a shepherd.[5] The shepherd is praying to God in terms that appear to Moses as grotesquely anthropomorphic, telling God he would wash His robe and clean His lice, and Moses upbraids him for his ignorance and insolence. Moses is then chastised by God for interrupting the glorification of a man who was glorifying God as he knew him. Let us keep that parable in mind.

In *A Guide for the Perplexed*, the economist E.F. Schumacher elaborates upon a useful distinction between two kinds of problems and solutions, what he calls divergent problems and convergent problems.[6] In a convergent problem, one's efforts towards a resolution zero in on a single, once-and-for-all solution. For example, what is the best shape for a stone bridge? There is precisely one curve that represents the maximum strength, and it can be defined independently of a human being's consciousness. A computer could calculate it. Given the proper inputs it would give a correct output. One could show the solution to someone on a piece of paper without reference to virtue, beauty, goodness, or their opposites. A convergent problem has a certain external verifiability about it. Such problems are in a sense reducible.

A divergent problem is one whose solution comes in transcending an opposition, or in maintaining the proper balance between externally irreconcilable forces. An example given by Schumacher is justice and mercy in matters of law, or freedom and discipline in matters of education. Just how much justice and mercy shall we have? Just how much freedom should be balanced with just how much discipline when we educate children? Problems of this sort are irreducible by their very nature. They require the conscious, living holding of a tension.

We run into problems when we attempt to solve divergent problems as we would convergent ones, leading to all sorts of terrible solutions. Many of the utopian movements of the twentieth century can be seen in part as the application of convergent thinking to divergent problems. In answer to the question, "What kind of society is the best one?," the communists, fascists, and neoliberals all have in common a tendency to reduce the solution to one fundamental insight which, if only applied widely and universally enough, would solve all of our problems. In these solutions, the living breathing consciousness of human beings and their capacity to hold competing forces in balance is de-emphasized. The underlying assumption of these utopian ideologies is that we can indeed engineer a structure so perfect that the quality and content of the individuals will be a secondary matter.

Strange as it may seem at first, this useful distinction between convergent and divergent problems is relevant because there is a kind of tension, a holding of opposition, which the spiritual person or the mystically minded person must hold in these questions of interfaith relations. Indeed, if all there were in the world were Zen masters, Sufi shaykhs, Christian monks, and Native American medicine men, there would hardly be any need for documents such as "A Common Word" at all. Everyone would be able to discern the spiritual content and truth in the other religion, since it is much easier for a master of the school of Ibn al-'Arabī to understand Advaita Vedānta than it is for an Ash'arite to understand, say, Nyāya Vaisheshika or Samkhya.

But spiritual people who are open to the common elements in our religions cannot demand or expect that most, or even many, people will come around to their way of thinking. Interfaith relations need not, in this sense, be predicated on an explicitly Sufi or mystical interpretation of texts, or on a vision of reality derived from the metaphysics of Ibn al-'Arabī or the Vedānta or something else. Even a Sufi who engages in interfaith dialogue and relations need not predicate his own activity on a specifically Sufi way. He need not quote Ghazālī or Rūmī. It may be that Sufism, and the teachings of the Sufi masters completely and thoroughly informs an individual's desire to reach out and engage with other religions in a positive way. A Sufi may even believe that he has received inspirations from Heaven to do so. But even then it does not follow that this activity exhibit a narrowly Sufi or mystical character.

This is actually how things tend to work out, at least in my experience with the open letter to the Pope and "A Common Word" initiative, and other similar good work that is done in interfaith relations. Those who are attached to the inner dimension of Islam tend to be at the core of this activity, although by no means exclusively so. In fact, the signatories did their level best *not* to make any great conceptual leaps and deal with matters that were least controversial. It is, at root, a call to recognize that what is most central to Islam and Christianity is also what is common to them. It was not, as many feared, a subtle attempt to undermine Christianity or dilute Islam. Indeed, a Sufi perspective made it easier to be open to this common element and to speak about it with some eloquence, but the desired effect was not a transformation of doctrine, but a desire for peace and an avoidance of bloodshed, predicated on theological understanding, not theological competition. Competition, as it were, can happen elsewhere. It simply was not the purpose of "A Common Word."

It is not false or hypocritical for a Sufi or his mystically oriented counterpart in another religion to do this. The Sufi does not diverge from other believers in a way that requires him to believe that they are believing falsely, even if he does disagree with them. Most Sufis are comfortable with the notion that God looks favorably upon doctrines and beliefs which the Sufi might see as limiting or superficial. A Sufi can appreciate that an Ash'arite theologian has a role in society and has a positive effect in the overall economy of the Muslim community. This is neither patronizing nor hypocritical, unless it is patronizing to believe that people's understanding of a religious text or phenomenon can be limited without it rendering that understanding false or wicked. That is the point, I believe, of the story of Moses and the shepherd.

So, if a mystically minded Muslim sought a convergent solution for how to deal with his disagreements with other Muslims on interfaith relations, he would feel frustrated because there is no once-and-for-all external solution for reconciling such apparently competing views. But if he approaches it as a divergent problem, he can allow the Ash'arite or Salafī to have his belief, affirming its virtues without affirming its absolute truth. He can consciously maintain himself between the unqualified truth and that portion of truth sufficient for what God expects of all human beings. (By the way, it is not true that the labels of Sufi, Salafī, and Ash'arite necessarily refer to distinct groups of people. There are Sufi Ash'arites, for example, and even Salafī-Wahhābis who accept the authority of Ibn Taymiyyah and must accept some form of Sufism, as Ibn Taymiyyah clearly did. Ibn Taymiyyah spoke well of Ibn al-'Arabī's *al-Futūḥāt al-Makkiyyah*, for example, but condemned Arabi's other work, the *Fuṣūṣ al-Ḥikam*.)

It is probably true that mystical or spiritual ideas will never be the main engine driving healthy interfaith relations, but it is likely that mystical and spiritual people will be. Speaking from the Muslim side, Sufis have in the past balanced their mystical inner life with an outer pastoral function. Ghazālī was perhaps the greatest example of this. His writings on scholastic theology are apparently at odds with his Sufi metaphysical writings. And they are, if one treated spiritual writings like mathematics. But his theological writings were written more for a general audience and for the preservation of the religious community, while his mystical writings for a smaller and select few. So the apparent contradiction can be resolved, as long as we do not insist on a convergent solution to the question: what was Ghazālī all about? For so complex a man and author, no single answer will likely suffice.

More recently, when Seyyed Hossein Nasr delivered a talk on behalf of the Muslim delegation at the Vatican, he did not present a Sufi or philosophical interpretation of Islam.[7] He was true to Islam and to the truth without expressing those truths in such a way so as to exclude other Muslims who may not have agreed with his own more full and profound positions.

It is certainly not a new idea that a mystic should keep his inner life private, not exposing subtle spiritual truths and states to a hostile and perverse environment where such realities can only be misunderstood and deformed. I am only here suggesting that this extends also to matters such as interfaith relations. The spiritual person, guided and nourished by the inner dimensions of faith, cannot abdicate his responsibility to be pragmatic and worldly (in the positive sense). For Muslims this lesson is most clearly demonstrated in the Treaty of Ḥudaybiyyah, when the Prophet Muḥammad was willing to have the title "Messenger of God" struck from the treaty—much to the consternation of prominent companions such as ‘Alī and ‘Umar. This was done for the simple reason that the other side would not assent to its conclusion.

I might also note that much of the consternation from certain evangelical quarters, such as the influential reaction of John Piper[8] to the Yale response to "A Common Word," stems, as I see it, from an inability or refusal to maintain an inner dimension that is not exhausted by or synonymous with outward activity. The utter centrality of "spreading the good news" as a religious duty of the first order renders evangelicals somewhat unable to take a pragmatic approach to interfaith relations. Piper, to use an important example, seems unable to imagine any worthwhile religious encounter between Muslims and Christians that is not a kind of evangelizing joust. It is as though this type of evangelical feels himself a phony or a hypocrite if he engages in a dialogue whose subject matter is religious without "bearing witness" or "testifying," to use their language. I believe part of the reason for this is that evangelical doctrine does not provide the conceptual tools, as it were, to differentiate between the inward and the outward in a strong enough way.

If we follow the useful schema of British historian David Bebbington in outlining the defining traits of evangelicalism, we encounter a structure that is fundamentally different than that found in traditional Islamic civilization, and indeed in the minds of most Muslims today regardless of sect or interpretation. He describes the four central features of evangelical religion as:

1. *Conversionism*, the belief that lives need to be changed
2. *Activism*, the expression of the gospel in effort
3. *Biblicism*, a particular regard for the Bible
4. *Crucicentrism*, a stress on the sacrifice of Christ on the cross.[9]

Evangelicals believe that to "testify" and to "share their faith" is a core principle that applies in one way or another to all Christians, not only some. Thus they believe that to "testify" and share their faith with others is as integral to their religious practice as the *ṣalāh* (canonical five daily prayers) are to a Muslim. Indeed the very name *evangelical* means "of the good news." They place the preaching of their message on the same level as other fundamental questions.

When some evangelicals are asked what they hope to accomplish through their testifying and their sharing, they will often say (and I have often heard them say), "Of course we want you to become Christians, just as you desire for us to become Muslims." But it simply is not true that Muslims view the conversion of Christians in the same way that evangelicals view the conversion of Muslims. In fact, the evangelical focus on conversion, what Bebbington called "conversionism,"[10] is rather unique among the world religions.

What most religions share is a basic structure, where a spiritual, liturgical, and ritual core of truths and practices unfolds into way of life and a social community. For Muslims, inviting others to Islam is not one of the pillars of faith, nor is it one of the main articles of faith (belief in God, the angels, the prophets, the revealed books, the Day of Judgment). In Hinduism the question of missionary work does not arise, and even those who take upon themselves the teaching and spiritual edification of others do not view this activity as an essential, indispensable part of their spiritual life. Besides, the object of their teaching is usually other Hindus. The same is true for Judaism, where missionary activity has no role (at least today). Missionary work is a significant aspect of Buddhist civilization, and indeed Buddhism spread through the work of missionaries, but Buddhist teaching and practice do not hinge on the sharing of what it means to be a Buddhist in the form of converting others. Indeed, very often being a monk or an enlightened person is hindered by too much contact with other people.

Putting aside small sects and religious movements which can be found anywhere, the evangelical strain in Christianity is unique in elevating the 'sharing of the good news' to the level of what the canonical prayer (*ṣalāh*) is to a Muslim, or what the Mass is for a Catholic, or *puja* is for a Hindu, or meditation is for a Buddhist, just to name a few examples. That is to say, if we can view religious obligations and worship as a set of concentric circles, for Muslims the very center would be the testimony of faith (not to others first and foremost, but to God) that, "There is no god but God, and Muḥammad is the Messenger of God." In that first circle would also be the aforementioned articles of faith, as well as the other four pillars of prayer, fasting, pilgrimage, and alms (the *zakāh*, which is not a spiritual charity but a straightforward economic assistance for the poor and needy). The performance of *da'wah*, or bringing others to Islam, would not be found in this first circle, nor would *jihād*, but in the second or third, if one can extend the metaphor.

For evangelical Christians, the spreading of the good news does not come second, after the establishment of some ritual and liturgical core. It *is* that very core, or at least, it is a crucial dimension or aspect of it. It is not a branch, but a root. One cannot really be a Christian without it, according to them. In this sense one could say that evangelicals such as Piper treat the divergent problem of interfaith relations in a convergent way. "How shall we deal with other faiths?" Answer: share the good news; that is, must always be, the answer.

The mystic or spiritually minded person, for his part, must also not fall prey to this kind of convergent thinking. The evangelical, and his counterparts in other faiths, must allow for the independence of the spiritual, while the mystic, and those like him, must allow for the independence of the material. Each must avoid a totalizing tendency to solving complex problems with a single solution.

One can see the mirror image of the evangelical tendency in what one might call New Age thinking, though this is a very general term encompassing many ideas and ideologies. One of the more sinister dimensions of New Age thinking, which often masquerades under the label of mysticism but is usually a thin brew of various traditional doctrines shorn of their more distasteful demands, is to impose sentimentalist programs which could only appeal to a small segment of humanity (relatively affluent, socially isolated, and unrooted). New Age thinking is the mirror image of evangelicalism, in that it tends to erase the distinction between the world and the spirit in favor of the spirit, not by transcending the dichotomy, but by interpreting the realities of the world such that they can be subsumed into a sentimentalist framework. The New Age often asks little more than the follower is already willing to give, resulting in a flabby mysticism obedient to the demands of modern life.

This New Age treatment is often perpetrated upon great figures such as Jalāl al-Dīn Rūmī, whose poetry, if read as a whole, is both beautiful and terrible, both welcoming and demanding, loyal to the tradition without pandering to its baser aspects, affirming traditional morality while reaching to spiritual heights of love. In the hands of newer translations he is rendered into some rambunctious wisecracker, or a mawkish aesthete such as one might see during a public television fundraising drive.

Interfaith Dialogue and Relations in Practice

Interfaith dialogue is difficult if one adopts an uncompromising conversionistic mind-set, and it is rendered ineffectual and ephemeral by a pseudo-mystical drive to "just get along." All of us must be prepared to hold ourselves between apparently contradictory demands of the spiritual and the material, the *ākhirah* and the *dunyā*, without insisting upon one or the other in an absolute, unbending way. Life cannot address only one or the other, and neither should interfaith activity. In moving forward, it is perhaps fitting to describe some steps Muslims and Christians in particular can take to improve the environment for interfaith relations, and to enhance those relationships themselves.

Christians must accept that Islam is not a monolithic juridico-theological block, but rather a religion and civilization where matters of the spirit and matters of the world interact in complex and unpredictable ways. They must acknowledge that Islam possesses authentically Islamic expressions of mysticism, psychological sophistication, and spiritual depth, often existing side-by-side with more vulgar manifestations of fundamentalism and puritanical zeal. Evangelical Christians, for their part, must understand that Muslims are not similarly constrained in their worldly activity vis-à-vis other faiths, and can have a dialogue with Christians not predicated upon missionary activity or religious competition. Each and every evangelical must desire the conversion of Muslims, but all Muslims need not carry this desire for Christians in order to fulfill the requirements of their faith.

Muslims, for their part, must understand the difference between evangelicalism and the teachings of the ancient churches with which they are more historically familiar. They should also make an effort to understand the more profound and intellectually sophisticated interpretations of such difficult doctrines as the Trinity and atonement. If Muslims can rightly expect Christians to go beyond the surface appearance of Islamic law to understand the spirit and love within the tradition, Muslims should make a similar effort to examine the claim made by Christians that belief in the Trinity is not a violation of monotheism, and that atonement is not a sidestepping of moral responsibility. It might be that Islam is readily misunderstood as being legalistic, but Christianity is often misunderstood as being polytheistic.

These basic changes in attitude can help foster a more respectful and welcoming environment on both sides. However, those souls on both sides with sensitivity to the truth within the other religion must also show restraint. It has happened that representatives from one religion have fallen victim to their own mystical exuberance, and unwisely (though innocently) have risked the ire of their co-religionists by seeming to erase the unique claims of their own religion.[11] Beautiful intentions notwithstanding, it is unreasonable to expect that, in some great flourish of love, all our conflicts will melt away. But small, well-placed and well-phrased flourishes, balanced with level-headed awareness of the world and its caprices, can go a long way toward improving interfaith relations and the state of the world in general.

Notes

1. See the official Web site of "A Common Word," http://www.acommonword.com/index.php?lang=en&page=faq#link7.

2. See Martin van Bruinessen and Julia Day Howell, *Sufism and the "Modern" in Islam*, 54–55.
3. Ibid.
4. See *M. Fethullah Gülen: Essays, Perspectives, Opinions*, 111–13.
5. Jalāl al-Dīn Rūmī, *The Mathnāwī of Jalālu'ddīn Rūmī*, 2, 1720–1749. A version is available at http://www.dar-al-masnavi.org/n.a-II-1720.html.
6. E. F. Schumacher, *A Guide for the Perplexed*, 121–24.
7. For the text of the speech, see http://acommonword.com/en/attachments/107_Nasr-speech-to-Pope.pdf.
8. See his video response at http://www.desiringgod.org/Blog/1032_a_common_word_between_us/.
9. David W. Bebbington, *Evangelicalism in Modern Britain: A History from the 1730s to the 1980s*, 2–3.
10. Ibid., 3.
11. For example, I was present when the Dalai Lama visited with Muslims in San Francisco in April 2006, a Muslim cleric exclaimed something to the effect of "You are the ocean of love [or knowledge]" leading one prominent Muslim cleric present to privately shake his head in disappointment, even though he shared a high opinion of the Dalai Lama's spiritual station and his work. In his eyes, such a statement added little, and risked the dignity and integrity of Islam in the eyes of Muslims who had little understanding or interest in the Dalai Lama.

8

Ecumenical Patriarch Bartholomew and Interfaith Dialogue: Mystical Principles, Practical Initiatives

John Chryssavgis

In his response to the open letter accompanying *"A Common Word Between Us and You,"*[1] Ecumenical Patriarch Bartholomew cited various consultations organized jointly (1986–1998) between the Royal Aal al-Bayt Institute for Islamic Thought in Jordan and the Orthodox Center of the Ecumenical Patriarchate in Switzerland, affirming seven basic values of dialogue between Christians and Muslims:

First, (as he observes) our religions are not willing to disturb *world peace* to serve the deplorable military hysteria of political leaders.
Second, our religions are not willing to overlook their teaching about the *unity of the human race* to serve recent ideologies of fragmentation.
Third, our religions are not willing to replace the call put forward in their teachings for *peace* and *justice in the world* with the demand for war.
Fourth, our religions are willing, through interfaith dialogue, to heal the wounds of the past in order to jointly *serve the weak and suffering.*
Fifth, our religions are willing to jointly publicize the *principles of mutual respect and understanding* in educational curricula, so that blind fanaticism and religious intolerance may gradually be eliminated.
Sixth, our religions are willing to cooperate through ecumenical dialogue to defend peace, social justice, and *human rights among people*, irrespective of religious, national, racial, social, or other differences.
Seventh, our religions support governments and international organisations to achieve *fuller awareness* of these fundamental principles.

My chapter is an attempt to explore the fuller dimensions of some of these principles.

The Orthodox Church and Interfaith Dialogue

Ecumenical Patriarch Bartholomew

Not every Orthodox Christian leader responded warmly to the open letter; indeed, some bishops were quite critical of the document. In light, then, of Dr. Caner Dagli's concluding remark that "mystical or spiritual *ideas* [may] never be the main engine driving healthy interfaith relations, but it is likely that mystical and spiritual *people* will be,"[2] permit me, with very broad strokes, to paint a portrait of one such spiritual leader. Ecumenical Patriarch Bartholomew is the 270th Archbishop to the 2,000-year-old Church of Constantinople (Istanbul), "first among equals" of Orthodox bishops worldwide, and spiritual leader to 300 million faithful. Patriarch Bartholomew was born in 1940 on a small island off the coast of Turkey.[3] From his enthronement in 1991, the Ecumenical Patriarch outlined the parameters of his vision: continuation of ecumenical engagements with other Christians, initiation of awareness and action against ecological degradation, and intensification of inter-religious dialogue for peaceful coexistence. For this reason, he has been dubbed the "Green Patriarch" by such environmental visionaries as Al Gore.[4]

Patriarch Bartholomew is as comfortable preaching about the spiritual legacy of the Orthodox Church as he is promoting sociopolitical issues or advocating for respect toward Islam and global peace. He has traveled more widely than any Orthodox Patriarch in history; he has received sympathetic, albeit at times controversial, attention in the media and even offered public lectures on Christian-Muslim relations. His role as the spiritual leader of the Orthodox Christian world and transnational figure of global significance is becoming more vital by the day. He has cosponsored international peace conferences—as well as meetings on racism and fundamentalism—gathering Christians, Muslims, and Jews to generate greater cooperation. In this regard, he has addressed the European Parliament, UNESCO, the World Economic Forum, and numerous national parliaments. He can do this precisely on account of his unique perspective and prophetic position in the world.[5]

The Patriarch's efforts to promote religious freedom and human rights, his initiatives to advance religious tolerance and mutual respect among the world's faith communities, and his work for international peace and environmental protection earned him the US Congressional Gold Medal (1997).[6] "To build a bridge between the East and West has long been a major concern for His All-Holiness," noted the Chancellor of Leuven University, adding: "Such bridge-builders are desperately needed."[7] In 1994, Patriarch Bartholomew joined with the Appeal to Conscience Foundation to organize the International Conference on Peace and Tolerance held in Istanbul.[8] In 2001, weeks after the tragedy of September 11th, Patriarch Bartholomew initiated a major interfaith conference in Brussels, cosponsored by the President of the European Commission.[9] The Patriarch played a key role there in forging the Brussels Declaration that affirmed, echoing the Berne Declaration of 1992: "War in the name of religion is war against religion."[10]

The Ecumenical Patriarch knows what it is like to be under siege. His See, established in the fourth century and once possessing holdings as vast as the Vatican, has been reduced to a small enclave, the Phanar, in a decaying corner of Istanbul. Most of its property was seized by successive Turkish governments; its schools have been closed and its prelates taunted by extremists who demonstrate almost daily outside the patriarchate calling for its ouster from Turkey. The Patriarch's effigy is periodically burned by Muslim fanatics. Petty bureaucrats harass him. The Turkish government as a whole follows a policy that deliberately belittles him, refusing to recognize his ecumenical status as the spiritual leader of a major religious faith.

Yet none of this abuse has diminished Bartholomew's compassion for the Turkish people or his determination to serve as a bridge between Turkey and

Europe. Indeed, he has supported international efforts to strengthen Turkey's economy and democracy often inviting severe criticism from Greek conservatives. He has been a fervent advocate of Turkey's efforts to join the European Union by traveling widely throughout Europe to speak out in favor of its admission. "The incorporation of Turkey into the European Union," he has declared in several capitals, "may well provide a powerful symbol of mutually beneficial cooperation between the Western and Islamic worlds and put an end to the talk of a clash of civilizations."[11] The unqualified support of an eminent Christian leader has blunted opposition by skeptics who doubt the wisdom of admitting a predominantly Muslim country of 70 million. "It is our strong belief that Orthodox Christians have a special responsibility to assist East-West rapprochement," Bartholomew affirms. "For, like the Turkish Republic, we have a foot in both worlds."[12]

Finally, pointing out that Orthodox Christians have a 550-year history of coexistence with Muslims in the Middle East, he has initiated a series of meetings with Muslim leaders throughout the region. To that purpose, he has traveled to Libya, Syria, Egypt, Iran, Jordan, Azerbaijan, Qatar, Kazakhstan, and Bahrain, meeting with political and religious figures, whom no other Christian hierarch has ever visited, and earning greater credibility than any other prominent Christian leader.[13]

The Ecumenical Patriarchate and Interfaith Dialogue

The Ecumenical Patriarchate has always been convinced of its wider role and ecumenical responsibility. "Standing as it does at the crossroads of continents, civilizations, and faith communities, the Ecumenical Patriarchate has always embraced the idea and responsibility of serving as a bridge between Christians, Muslims, and Jews."[14]

Two symbolical images adorn the foyer of the central offices at the Ecumenical Patriarchate, silently representing decisive moments in the rich and complex story of a city, where Orthodox Christians, Muslims, and other believers have coexisted over centuries. One image portrays St. Andrew, patron saint of the Patriarchate; beside him is Stachys, first bishop of Byzantium (38—54 CE) variously called Constantinople and Istanbul through the centuries. A second mosaic depicts Gennadios Scholarios (1405—1472 CE), first Ecumenical Patriarch of the Ottoman period. The Patriarch stands with hand outstretched, receiving from the Sultan Mehmet II (1432—1481 CE) the "firman" or legal document guaranteeing the continuation of the Orthodox Church and the protection of its traditions through Ottoman rule. It is an icon of the beginnings of a long, even if nervous, coexistence and uneasy interfaith commitment.

Throughout his tenure, Bartholomew has addressed issues of racial discrimination and religious tolerance before diverse audiences in Western and Eastern Europe, the Middle East, Africa, Australasia, and the Americas. He has also hosted or sponsored such international initiatives as:

- The Peace and Tolerance Conference, which met for the first time in Istanbul in 1994 and published The Bosporus Declaration, affirming (based on the Berne conference on peace in 1992) that "a crime committed in the name of religion is a crime against religion";
- The Conference on Peaceful Coexistence between Judaism, Christianity, and Islam held in Brussels in 2001, in the aftermath of September 11th;

- A special session held in Bahrain in 2002 on the occasion of the 10th anniversary of the commencement of [the] Christian-Muslim Dialogue;
- The Conference on Religion, Peace, and the Olympic Ideal held in Athens in 2004, on the occasion of the imminent Olympic Games;
- The Peace and Tolerance Conference, held again in Istanbul in 2005, stating: "As spiritual leaders of the children of Abraham, it is incumbent upon us to diminish ethnic and religious tensions" while "deploring those who preach violence toward other faiths and ethnic communities" and "rejecting violence and totally and unconditionally condemning the use of force, ethnic cleansing and brutalities."[15]

Such gatherings proved pioneering in purpose and historical in substance, opening participants' eyes to the cultural and religious diversity of our fragmented world as well as to the complexity of the global reality.

Fundamental Mystical Principles

Human Rights and Religious Tolerance

The Orthodox Church has long searched for appropriate language to address racial and religious intolerance amid the strife that this new ideology created in the countries of Eastern Europe for much of the 19th century. In 1872 a Pan-Orthodox synod held in the Patriarchal Church of Constantinople issued an unqualified condemnation of the sin of racism:

> We renounce, censure, and condemn racism, that is racial discrimination, ethnic feuds, hatred, and dissensions....[16]

However, the Patriarch recognizes that the problem still plagues our world.[17] Thus, for the Patriarch, the exploitation of religious symbols to further the cause of aggressive nationalism is a betrayal of the universality of faith. Freedom of religious conscience is imperative for all; it is the greatest of divine gifts, representing most clearly the divine reflection in the human soul. In proclaiming that God created humanity in "[His] image and after [His] likeness" (Gen. 1:26, RSV), Orthodox theology claims that humanity is endowed with spiritual qualities, such as free will, that correspond to God.[18] While certainly the concept of freedom is understood differently in Churches of the Reformation and Enlightenment than in religions of the East and the Orthodox Church, it remains nonetheless a crucial notion for global coexistence in the twenty-first century. In many ways, the real debate—the real "clash"—is not between East and West, but with the concept of freedom as variously perceived in contemporary religious and political circles.

Whenever freedom is subjected to necessity, particularly in the form of restriction or repression of worship, this offends the original blessing bestowed indiscriminately by God on all human beings. Emphasizing this notion of freedom, the second-century *Epistle to Diognetus* affirms: "God persuades; God does not compel. Violence is foreign to God."[19]

> Communities of faith are able to provide a counterbalance to secular humanism and exclusive nationalism by proposing a more spiritual form of humanism. That applies to Christians, Jews, and Muslims alike; while we cannot deny our

differences, neither can we deny the need for solidarity and fellowship in order to deter and dispel the forces of intolerance and racism. If we believe in a "God who is love" (1 John 4:16), then we must proclaim that "perfect love casts out fear" (1 John 4:18), and "pursue what makes for peace" (Rom. 14.19). And peace is more than the mere absence of war. Peace is the invocation of a divine name; it is the very presence of God (cf. John 14.27).[20]

The Bane of Fundamentalism and Fanaticism

Nevertheless, our world appears to be witnessing a rapid rise in religious fundamentalism. Of course, while the notion of the "free individual" is more germane to eighteenth-century Western thought and the notion of "free will" is perceived more communally in non-Western circles, the Patriarch emphasizes "personal respect and freedom of choice with regard to one's religious convictions."[21] As Orthodox Christians, we would vehemently disapprove of any form of proselytism, in the sense of placing pressure on others to change their religious affiliation. We most certainly do not participate in dialogues between Christians and Muslims or Jews in order to convince them to accept our faith;[22] that would imply a sense of arrogance and prejudice, undermining the very purpose of encounter and dialogue.

Indeed, if there is one fundamental principle drawing Christians to the discussion table with Muslims and Jews alike in a world torn by division and turmoil, it is the passionate desire to recognize and declare that it is not religious differences that create conflict. In our times of tension, many single out religion as the forum or scapegoat for problems plaguing our world. Indeed, as global conflicts intensify, they argue more passionately against religion and for a secular approach to international relations. And to some degree, these critics may be right. Nevertheless, religion is not the primary issue at stake; religion is not the source of the problem at hand. While there are many misconceptions about religious fundamentalism,[23] it is also true that religion has undoubtedly been manipulated and sacred texts deliberately misinterpreted[24] as a means toward political ends or personal interests.[25]

Religion and Absolutism: Apophatic Theology in Political Practice

The most delicate and simultaneously difficult issue in relation to religious fundamentalism is absolutism. Every religion asserts that it contains the absolute truth concerning God and the world. Every faith preaches that God is the absolute being, the One from whom all pure attributes uniquely derive and in whom all evil attributes are entirely absent. This conviction is common ground among all three Abrahamic religions.

At the same time, our perceptions as thinkers and believers are not determined by the divine Object of our observation and worship but rather primarily by our subjective condition. The confession of this radical truth incites within us the Socratic admission with regard to ignorance: one thing we do know, that we do not know anything! In other words, we humbly accept the fact that when we speak of absolute values we are dealing with truths beyond our capability and experience; we are dealing with truths beyond debate and discussion. As a direct consequence of this humble recognition, we are at the very least obligated to be open to and tolerant of the views of others. For insofar as we stand in mystical ignorance before God, ultimately we can only be united in utter silence before God's transcendent being. Even the most complete and comprehensive definition of God can never appropriate or approach the fullness of divine nature which always remains incomprehensible, indeterminable, and unqualified.

In Orthodox spiritual thought and practice, this is called *apophaticism* (or *via negativa*), and it surely has political and global implications.[26] The fact that we do not know God's inner being or nature—the fact that we can never know God's essence, which forever eludes us—means that any certainty with regard to God is dangerous inasmuch as it tends to polarize cultural discourse and deepen cultural division. The truth is that one cannot debate with fundamentalist Muslims any more than one can debate with fundamentalist Jews or fundamentalist Christians. Their certainty about God renders global discourse or religious discussion almost impossible. The alternative is humble engagement and moderate conversation. It is an expression not only of dignified respect toward other human beings but of due response to God who lies beyond all certainty and comprehension.

God is by definition and by nature beyond all human understanding and perception; otherwise, God would not be God. This is the teaching of the great theologians and mystics, like Saint Gregory of Nyssa in the fourth century and Saint Gregory Palamas in the fourteenth century, both of whom underlined the radical transcendence as well as the relative immanence of God: God as unknowable and yet as profoundly known; God as invisible and yet as personally accessible; God as distant and yet as intensely present. The infinite God thus becomes truly intimate in relating to the world.[27] Could Gregory Palamas' contact with Muslim leaders have led him to emphasize the incomprehensibility and inaccessibility of God?

There is always something in divine nature that we can never fully grasp, and there is always something in human nature that always includes uncertainty and imperfection. This conviction allows us the freedom and space to sit with our Muslim brothers and sisters, as well as with our Jewish colleagues, in order to determine how best to worship God and dwell with one another in peace and harmony. Love transcends law; mystery transcends doctrine; and practice transcends theory. So a genuine and humble faith will be tolerant of other faiths; it will not be threatened by other religions but instead freely and fearlessly embrace other faiths.

> [The] Book of Exodus, revered by all three monotheistic religions, itself reveals the same apophatic truth, namely that "no one shall see the face [of God] and live" (Exod. 33:20). The language of Scripture is metaphorical and symbolic. Its goal is to preserve—and not dispel—the mystery of God; the purpose is to pray to—and not dismiss—the transcendent God. God "is who God is" (Exod. 3:14); the face of God is veiled in mystery.[28]

The ancient Greeks long ago warned against any temptation toward rational projection. The early Fathers warned against worship of rational idols. What, however, is even more unacceptable is the imposition on others of our image of God which may be refracted—even deformed—through the prism of our passions and prejudices; what always remains intolerable is presenting this image as the only valid and absolute truth about God. Such a "God" could surely be manipulated to bless someone's fundamentalism and fanaticism, pitting the cross against the crescent.

The many names of God in Islam offer a crucial point of encounter with Muslim believers. Indeed, while the correspondence may not be precise, the diverse and wonderful names of God in Islam[29] resemble the names attributed to God in Christian mysticism and preserved in the Orthodox liturgy.[30] Both religions describe God as merciful, compassionate, and holy. Both religions call God creator, king, peacemaker, and repairer. Both religions pray to God as forgiver, provider, and judge. Both religions refer to God as first and last but also as light and hidden. Nevertheless, above and beyond such similarities—some will be quick to add, above and beyond numerous contrasts and dissimilarities—the various names in both religions underline an important truth: divine names reflect the power both of encounter and of mystery. They reveal a personal relationship between God and a world initiated and sustained by God through love and forgiveness. They also conceal the ultimate incomprehensibility of God preserved by the peoples of the Book. The names then are metaphors and symbols, albeit powerful and personal, of a nameless God. It is the same truth known by mystics and celebrated in prayerful song through the centuries.

Thus, the great monotheistic religions agree not only on the name (or many names) of God, but they agree on the namelessness of God. For while they may disagree on the content of the divine names—on the precise details of the faith that they confess—yet they agree on the mystery of God who transcends all names and knowledge. Put simply, while Jews, Christians, and Muslims may disagree on the partial truth that "we see in a mirror dimly" (1 Cor. 13:12), they agree with one another in their humble recognition that the absolute truth can never be conceived, contained, or exhausted.

Abraham's Hospitality: An Icon of Interfaith Dialogue

Personal encounter then, among the adherents of these religions—and honest conversation between those, who, like Moses, seek the true face of God—is the only way worthy of the God of Abraham, Isaac, and Jacob. This God chooses to establish dialogue with the world in many and diverse ways. I am in agreement with Dr. Dagli's introductory remark: "Practically no one [knows] who drafted ["A Common Word Between Us and You"]. . . .But the public spokespeople for the initiative. . . have always been firm that. . . the drafting of it was of little moment; only its signing was consequential."[31] In truth, the broad spectrum of signatories indicates the desire for authentic dialogue. Indeed, dialogue is a gift from above. According to St. John Chrysostom (347–407 CE), fourth-century Archbishop of Constantinople, God is forever speaking to us: through Prophets and Apostles, through saints and mystics, even through natural creation that "[declares] the glory of God." (Psalm 19:1)[32]. In *Encountering the Mystery,* His All Holiness Ecumenical Patriarch Bartholomew states:

> As religious leaders responsible before God to preserve the teachings and traditions of our faith, to whatever degree we are of course cognitive of this faith, we are obligated consciously to reject any projection of personal whim that seeks to replace the will of God. At the same time, however, we are obligated humbly to demonstrate a profound mutual respect, which allows our fellow human beings to journey on their own personal path to God, as they understand the will of God, without interfering with the journey of anyone else. This kind of profound mutual respect on the part of one person toward the religious journey

> and conviction of another is the foundational responsibility of each of us. It is also the fundamental presupposition for peaceful coexistence and goodwill among people.
>
> Even in the sacred texts of the monotheistic religions, there is no evidence whatsoever that God is in any way pleased with conversion by means of force, obligation, or deceit. Indeed, there is no evidence that God forcefully draws people to the divine will or way. On the contrary, at least from the Judeo-Christian Scriptures, as we have already observed, the idea that emerges is of the human being created in the image and likeness of God, adorned with the divine characteristic of personal freedom. Surely it would be paradoxical, if contradictory, for God to endow humanity with free will on the one hand while forcefully curtailing that freedom on the other hand. Therefore, what modern and even secular Western society promotes as cultural achievement, namely the expression and protection of free will in relation to the inviolability of religious conscience, is also essentially espoused by and directly derived from the teaching of the three monotheistic religions of Christianity, Judaism, and Islam. This is what forms the basis of interfaith encounter and dialogue.[33]

The world's monotheistic religions owe it to their common heritage to imitate their patriarchal forefather. Sitting under the shade of oak trees at Mamre, Abraham received an unexpected visit from three strangers (recorded in Genesis 18; see also Hebrews 13:2) whom he did not consider as a danger or threat; instead, he spontaneously shared with them his friendship and food, extending such generous fellowship and hospitality that, in Orthodox Christian spirituality tradition, the scene is interpreted as a symbol of divine communion. In fact, the only authentic image of God as Trinity in the Orthodox Church is the depiction of this encounter scene from rural Palestine. As a result, Abraham was promised the impossible, namely multiplication of his barren seed for generations. Is it too much to hope that our willingness to converse and cooperate as people of different and diverse religious convictions might also result in the seemingly impossible coexistence of all humanity in a peaceful world?

In the Orthodox icon of "Abraham's Hospitality," iconographers traditionally depict the three guests on three sides, allowing an open space on the fourth side of the table, namely on the side closest to the eye of the beholder. The icon thus serves as an open invitation to each of us. Will we sit at table with these strangers? Will we surrender prejudice and arrogance to assume our place for the survival of our world and the future of our children? Will we welcome others without inhibition or suspicion? This icon is a profound image of encounter and communion.

Religious leaders and intellectual thinkers bear a special responsibility not to mislead or provoke. Their discretion is a key factor in people's interpretation of God's will. Their integrity is vital in the process of dialogue.

> In the mid-fourteenth century, Saint Gregory Palamas [1296–1359 CE], Archbishop of Thessaloniki, conducted theological discussions with distinguished representatives of Islam. One of the Muslim leaders expressed a wish that the time would come when mutual understanding would characterize the followers of both religions. Saint Gregory agreed, noting his hope that this time would come sooner than later. It is my humble prayer that now will be that time. Now, more than ever, is the time for [deep encounter and open] dialogue.[34]

Notes

1. In a letter addressed to HRH Prince Ghazi bin Muhammad bin Talal of Jordan (April 11, 2008). From the Archives of the Ecumenical Patriarchate. This chapter is essentially based on and directly cites from passages found in Ecumenical Patriarch Bartholomew's *Encountering the Mystery: Understanding Orthodox Christianity Today, New York: Doubleday, 2008.*
2. See Caner Dagli, chapter 7, this volume, 75 (emphasis mine).
3. In the discussion following his paper, Dr. Kalin mentioned the papal visit to Turkey in 2006. What few people recognize is that the Pope's visit to Istanbul was in response to a formal invitation by the Ecumenical Patriarch; indeed, the timing in late November was scheduled to coincide with the Patronal Feast of the Church of Constantinople on November 30, namely the feast of St. Andrew the Apostle.
4. Cain Burdeau, "Orthodox Patriarch Pleads for Environmental Action," *USA Today*, October 21, 2009, http://content.usatoday.net/dist/custom/gci/InsidePage.aspx?cId=thenewsstar&sParam=31867547.story.
5. Bartholomew, *supra* note 1, 195–96.
6. "Congress Bestows Medal on Orthodox Christian Leader," *LA Times*, October 22, 1997, http://articles.latimes.com/1997/oct/22/news/mn-45441.
7. John Silber, "Patriarch Bartholomew—A Passion for Peace," The Ecumenical Patriarch of Constantinople, http://www.patriarchate.org/patriarch/passion-for-peace.
8. "The Bosporus Declaration: Joint Declaration of the Conference on Peace and Tolerance," The Ecumenical Patriarch of Constantinople, http://www.patriarchate.org/documents/joint-declaration.
9. Silber, *supra* note 7.
10. Bartholomew, *Encountering the Mystery*, xxxviii.
11. Silber, *supra* note 7. The Ecumenical Patriarch vehemently resists (even resents) any generalization about a "clash of civilizations," if only because such a thesis grossly oversimplifies both East and West, which comprise far more complicated, and not monolithic, realities (even deeply divided within themselves). By the same token, Christianity and Islam, too, are not monolithic realities. With regard to Christianity, it should be remembered that there is an entire body of the Christian Church (the Orthodox East) that never suffered the effects of the Reformation and the Enlightenment.
12. Silber, *supra* note 7.
13. Ibid., xxxvii.
14. Ibid., 175.
15. Ibid., 176–77.
16. In Communion: Web site of the Orthodox Peace Fellowship, "The Heresy of Racism," http://incommunion.org/?p=263.
17. Bartholomew, *supra* note 1, 136.
18. Ibid., 137.
19. Roberts-Donaldson, trans., "The Epistle of Machetes to Diognetus," 7.4, http://www.earlychristianwritings.com/text/diognetus-roberts.html.
20. Bartholomew, *supra* note 1, 137–38.
21. Ibid., 182.
22. This is clearly the policy of the Ecumenical Patriarchate and it defines the openness of its ecumenical dialogues and interfaith relations.
23. See R. Scott Appleby and Martin Marty, "Fundamentalism," *Foreign Policy* 128 (January-February, 2002) on several misconceptions about the problem of fundamentalism.
24. In fact, if critics blame religion (whether Islam or Christianity) for being "inherently flawed," it is not so theologically but more so historically and socially. The Qur'ān is

no better or worse than other sacred texts which depend on interpretation to determine their tolerance or intolerance.

25. Bartholomew, *supra* note 1, 183–84.
26. As Dr. Michael Allen remarked while chairing the session on "Mysticism and A Common Word": "In the Eastern Orthodox Church, the contrast between exoteric and esoteric is not as sharp [as in Islam]: mysticism is in a sense incumbent on every Orthodox Christian, if not in practice then at least in principle, insofar as dogmatic theology and mystical theology are intimately related. A Muslim can still be a Muslim and yet not be a follower of Ibn al-'Arabī or Rūmī; but no Christian can be an Eastern Orthodox Christian without accepting the teachings of Maximos the Confessor or Gregory Palamas."
27. Bartholomew, *supra* note 1, 186.
28. Ibid., 187.
29. See M.R. Bawa Muhaiyaddeen, *Asmā'ul-Ḥusnā: The 99 Beautiful Names of Allah.*
30. See the Liturgies of St. John Chrysostom and St. Basil the Great. In particular, the latter refers to God as: "without beginning, invisible, incomprehensible, indescribable, and without change."
31. See Caner Dagli, chapter 7, this volume, 69–70.
32. See John Chrysostom, *Homily VIII on 2 Corinthians*, http://www.newadvent.org/fathers/220208.htm.
33. Bartholomew, *supra* note 1, 189–90.
34. Ibid., 221.

C. Metaphysics

9

What of the Word Is Common?

Joseph Lumbard

During its short life, the "Common Word" initiative has proven to be one of the most promising interfaith movements for the whole of the historical relationship between Christianity and Islam. It initiated a series of conferences in leading religious and academic institutions including the Vatican, Lambeth Palace, Yale and Cambridge Universities. The open letter[1] has received hundreds of thoughtful responses from theologians, politicians, and academics and spawned hundreds of articles in leading publications the world over.[2] The open letter, "A Common Word Between Us and You" was also the central impetus for the Wamp-Ellison Resolution, adopted in the US House of Representatives on September 23, 2008,[3] and has recently given rise to proposals for a United Nations Resolution to declare a worldwide interfaith acceptance week. Furthermore, the initiative is at the heart of The C-1 World Dialogue,[4] which aims to continue the work of the C-100 of the World Economic Forum, and to be the foremost organization for the orchestration of dialogue between Islam and the West to advance peaceful and harmonious relations between the two.

All of these accomplishments should be applauded, and one hopes that they will bear further fruit. Nonetheless, as many participants in the "Common Word" initiative have noted, several of the more nuanced theological implications of Christian-Muslim dialogue have yet to be addressed in the course of the this initiative. As indicated by the World Council of Churches' response to "A Common Word," there are central theological questions to which this new initiative gives rise or (one might say) to which it reopens.[5] Among these is the question of our relationship to God through revelation. As expressed in the World Council of Churches' response:

> ...while both Muslims and Christians claim to receive revelation from God, what is meant when Muslims claim to perceive the will of God revealed in the Qur'ān–what has been called the word of God become book—and what is meant when Christians claim to perceive God's self revealed in Jesus Christ—who is called the Word of God become flesh?[6]

Statements like this indicate that "A Common Word Between Us and You," although it may not be theological in nature, nonetheless gives rise to fundamental theological questions about the relationship between Christianity and Islam. These questions have received various treatments throughout their complicated history. However, if the "Common Word" initiative is to proceed, such questions can only remain unexamined for so long. At some point, we must confront the deeper theological, philosophical, and metaphysical issues. This is not to say that we must come to radical new theologies wherein we embrace the tenets of one another's creeds. Rather, we can take advantage of the opportunities provided by this newfound spirit of dialogue and cooperation to see what new theological potential it may augur. We all too often encounter the theology of the other in a spirit of polemic, seeking division, rather than in the spirit of faith, seeking understanding. These attitudes prevent us from understanding the central teachings that exist at the core of each other's traditions. Reading these traditions in a spirit of polemic and opposition has given rise to some theological insights,[7] but it also prevents Muslims and Christians from learning what the other truly believes and teaches. This in turn prevents us from taking the initiative to accept the invitation "to think afresh about the foundations of our own convictions," as the Archbishop of Canterbury, Rowan Williams, has stated.[8]

There are many theological issues which could be reexamined in the spirit of coming "to a word common between us and you" (Q 3:64): the nature of God, the nature of prophecy, the nature of revelation, the question of the Trinity, and the Incarnation, among others, as indicated by the thoughtful responses to "A Common Word" issued by the Yale Divinity School, the World Council of Churches, the Archbishop of Canterbury, and the National Council of Churches, among many others.[9] But there is a question that is deeper still. One that lies at the heart of all of them and upon which the whole of this initiative rests: what is the Word of God? Though not addressed by "A Common Word," this question is brought to immediate attention by the title of the document that spurred this entire initiative.

Indeed, it is our response to the "Word" that defines who we are as Muslims, as Christians, or as Jews. As the Prophet Muḥammad has said, "The superiority of the Word of God over all other words is as the superiority of God over His creation."[10] And as the Book of Proverbs says, "Every word of God proves true; he is a shield to those who take refuge in him" (Prov. 30:5). Our effort to respond with faith to God's Word is truly what we hold in common. From one perspective, to declare oneself a Jew, a Christian, or a Muslim is to join with the psalmist in singing to God, "The sum of thy word is truth; and every one of thy righteous ordinances endures forever" (Ps. 119:160). It is our response to God's Word, be it through the Qur'ān, the Torah, or in the person of Christ, from which we derive our identity, through which our life achieves meaning, and through which we attain to salvation (John 6:68; 1 Pet. 1:23). This belief could apply to other religions as well (though it would be phrased differently for each). For the purposes of this paper, I will focus upon the understanding of God's Word in Islam and Christianity.

Theology and Metaphysics

To endeavor to understand the Word of God is the true meaning of theology in Islam. The phrase that is usually translated as theology is *'ilm al-kalām*, quite literally, "Knowledge of the Word." Although theology is related to the study of the Word of God in both the Christian and Islamic traditions, the function of theology in investigating the nature of the Word is limited when contrasted to metaphysics. The function of theology as a discipline is to provide dogmatic representations of the truth that answer doubts and objections in order to allow for faith to be more fully manifest in a particular religious universe. In this respect, theology is a historical phenomenon shaped by the challenges and questions posed to a particular faith at different times. The response to these questions and challenges has led to particular formulations, which then take on the form of dogma when some consensus has been reached.

Whereas the Divine Word itself is beyond the world of form and matter, theology pertains to the world of forms and is by its very nature polemical and apologetic (in the classical meaning). It seeks not only to defend the truth as such, but in doing so cannot but defend a particular manifestation or iteration of the truth that has been transmitted through revelation. Thus, while it takes the revelation of God's Word as its starting point, theology then translates a particular revelation into dogmatic language, which is by definition limited. This process often leads to the confusion of the form that conveys truth (theological dogma) with absolute truth itself. This process in turn leads theologies to reaffirm outward oppositions between religions and even different theologies within the same religion rather than seek their inward connections.

By contrast, metaphysics seeks to transcend antagonisms between forms and dogmatic formulations when understood as the science of the real and not simply as a branch of philosophy. When looking at these forms, metaphysics seeks to emphasize the absolute truth that they are meant to convey rather than the expressions of it, which cannot but be relative. Most theologians, who are by definition dogmatists of one degree or another, focus upon reaffirming the truth of their relative expressions or of the relative expressions they have inherited. Meanwhile, the metaphysician seeks the naked, supraformal and absolute truth, which lies beyond all expressions of it. When all is said and done, truth is absolute or it is nothing. Thus, when the theologies (i.e., formal defenses) of religion are viewed from a metaphysical perspective, many believe that they are being unduly relativized, hence compromised. Yet the metaphysician seeks to reaffirm and thus revivify the form by illustrating how it derives from and conveys, albeit within its own relative framework, the supraformal absolute itself.

When viewed from the standpoint of theology, external religious perspectives and doctrines cannot but be contested in the light of another religious perspective and doctrine—that is to say in light of another external orthodoxy. But when viewed metaphysically, there is not a question of extrinsic orthodoxy, but of intrinsic orthodoxy such that we attempt to understand the internal logic of each doctrinal system and evaluate its capacity to serve as a means of expressing the total truth. Such an approach will certainly not resolve all of the disputes between Christians and Muslims. It can, however, help many come to a deeper understanding of the treasures that lie buried within each tradition and thus to a deeper appreciation of Divine Mercy and Infinitude. Though dogmatic theologies often claim scripture for themselves, many aspects of scripture call us to look beyond these formal antagonisms. "All the paths of the Lord are steadfast love and faithfulness, for those who keep his covenant and his testimonies" (Ps. 25:10). As the Gospel says, "The wind blows where it wills, and you hear the sound of it, but you do not know whence it comes or wither it goes ..." (John 3:8). This call in turn may help Christians and Muslims move from discourse and tolerance toward understanding and acceptance, seeing that in God's house there are many mansions (John 14:2).

While the Bible provides openings whereby the supraformal transcendence of metaphysical contemplation can influence the form of theological articulations, the Qur'ān is more emphatic, providing the building blocks for a Qur'ānic hermeneutics by which pre-Qur'ānic scriptures and the theologies that derive there from can be read with a view to finding the truths expressed or conveyed therein, truths to which the Qur'ān bears witness. In this vein the Qur'ān says in a verse addressed to Prophet Muḥammad, "And We have revealed to you the Book with the truth confirming the Book that was before it and watching over it" (Q5:48). Several other verses reiterate that the Qur'ān confirms previous revelations and even religions (e.g., Q 2:97; 3:3; 10:37; 35:31; 46:30).[11] The notion that previous scriptures have been abrogated, as some Muslims maintain,[12] would seem to be contradicted by verses such as Qur'ān 5:43: "But how is it that they make you (Muḥammad) their judge when they have the Torah, wherein is God's judgment?" And Qur'ān 5:68: "Say: 'O People of the Scripture you have no basis until you observe the Torah and the Gospel and what was revealed to you from your Lord.'" In this same vein, Qur'ān 5:47 says of Christians: "So let the people of the Gospel judge according to what God has revealed therein."

It would make no sense for the Qur'ān to speak of the efficacy of judging by the Torah and the Gospel while also maintaining that the scriptures are abrogated or excessively distorted. It would also make no sense to say that the religions in which these scriptures are applicable are defunct, or were defunct at the time the Qur'ān was revealed, for it is the methodologies developed within the religions that would provide them with the ability to judge in accord with them. Were previous religions abrogated, they would also have no soteriological efficacy, which would stand in direct contrast to Qur'ān 3:113–14: "Some the People of the Scripture are a community upright, who recite God's verses in the watches of the night, prostrating themselves. They believe in God and in the Last Day, enjoining decency and forbidding indecency, vying with one another in good works; those are of the righteous."

Based upon these and many other verses,[13] one could go so far as to say that the challenge posed to a Muslim by the Qur'ān is not simply to bear witness to the oneness of God and the veracity of the Qur'ānic revelation and to live in accord with it, but to be able to bear witness to the truth within other religious traditions while living in accord with one's own tradition—to be able to uphold the letter of one's own tradition while understanding its relativity in the face of the Absolute. This principle could even be seen as what is called for in the oft-cited Qur'ānic verse: "We have…made you nations and tribes that you may come to know one another" (Q 49:13). As the Prophet Muḥammad has said, "The prophets are half-brothers; their mothers differ, but their religion [*dīn*] is one."[14]

The Uncreated Word

True "Knowledge of the Word" (*'ilm al-kalām*) is a weighty thing indeed. The most widely accepted understanding of *kalām* (word) in the Sunnī Islamic tradition is that it indicates a beginning-less attribute of God abiding with His being or essence. Understanding how Muslims have grappled with the questions raised by God's beginning-less, uncreated eternal Word that is nonetheless present in the created world is one aspect of Islamic theology that can help Muslims better understand the Christian doctrine of Jesus.[15]

Some Muslims who oppose this notion of the uncreated Word of God have even observed that admitting to an uncreated Word of God lends more credence to the understanding of Jesus as the Word who is coeternal with the Father. This is especially true if one emphasizes the expression of "Word" found in the Gospel of John rather than the emphasis upon "Son" found in the synoptic Gospels (though as will be seen, even this aspect of the Qur'ānic treatment of Jesus merits a closer reading). While most Muslim theologians maintain that the Qur'ān is itself eternal and uncreated (the Word "inlibrate" as some have expressed it[16]) critics may question whether one can formulate arguments against the dual nature of Christ—fully Divine and fully human—that might not in some way rebound upon certain aspects of the traditional Islamic understanding of the Qur'ān as an uncreated supratemporal Book.[17] This criticism was foreseen by the ʿAbbāsid Caliph al-Ma'mūn (786–833 CE), an opponent of the belief that the Qur'ān is uncreated, who wrote that those who believe in the uncreatedness of the Qur'ān are "like Christians when they claim that Jesus the son of Mary was not created because he was the word of God."[18]

For proponents of the view that the Qur'ān is created, it was thought that the Qur'ān was God's speech but that were it eternal and uncreated this would undermine the absolute unity and uniqueness of God.[19] Others, twelver Shīʿites in particular, would not say that the Qur'ān was created (*makhlūq*) because such a pronouncement could lead some to think the Qur'ān was constructed or composed of other parts, but maintained that it was produced in time (*muḥdath*).[20] The issue so deeply involved Muslim thinkers that many of the Christian arguments regarding the dual nature of Christ as fully divine and fully human (or not) are replayed, albeit in a different manner, in many of the Islamic debates regarding the nature of the Qur'ān as the Word of God that is at once eternal and uncreated yet temporal and created (or not). For example, the Muʿtazilite position mentioned above came to assume a position (vis-à-vis Ashʿarism) similar to that of the Arianism heresy (vis-à-vis Christian orthodoxy) in so far as the Arians held that Jesus, though unlike other created beings, was nonetheless created.[21]

Three Qur'ānic verses serve as the central textual referents for the Islamic belief in the uncreatedness of the Qur'ān: "This is indeed a noble Qur'ān, in a Book guarded" (Q 56:77–78); "Nay, but it is a glorious Qur'ān in a tablet, preserved" (Q85:21–22); and "Lo! We have made it an Arabic Qur'ān that perhaps you may understand. And it is indeed in the Mother Book, [which is] with Us [and it is] indeed exalted." (Q 43:3–4). The "Book Guarded," the "Tablet Preserved," and the "Mother Book" are understood by many to refer to a single uncreated, supratemporal Book that is the eternal source of all Scripture of which the Qur'ān is one particular manifestation.[22] Others say that it is the Qur'ān itself. In either interpretation, Ashʿarī theologians maintain that it is the Word of God that is an attribute abiding with the Divine Essence.

This is the Divine Logos that, according to some Muslim theologians, partakes of divinity. To illustrate this point, many scholars cite a famous saying of the Prophet Muḥammad, "Whoever dismounts at any place and says, 'I seek refuge in the perfect words of God from the evil that is created,' nothing will harm him until he moves from his stop."[23] Given that in Islam invoking protection from anything other than God in this fashion is tantamount to *shirk* (attributing partners to God—the only unforgivable sin in Islam), scholars such as Imam Bukhārī (810–870 CE) take this statement as proof that the Prophet himself considered the Word of God to be eternal and uncreated.[24]

While those theologians who maintain that the Qur'ān is uncreated have debated its exact meaning, the consensus of the majority of Sunnī Ashʿarī theologians is presented in the words of Abū Ḥāmid al-Ghazālī (1058–1111 CE):

> He speaks, commanding, forbidding, promising, and threatening, with a speech from eternity, ancient, and self-existing. Unlike the speech of the creation, it is

> not a sound which is caused through the passage of air or the friction of bodies; nor is it a letter which is enunciated through the opening and closing of lips and the movement of the tongue. And the Qur'ān, the original Torah, the original Gospel of Jesus, and the original Psalms are His Books sent down upon His Messengers. The Qur'ān is read by tongues, written in books, and remembered in the heart, yet it is, nevertheless ancient, abiding in the Essence of God, not subject to division and or separation through its transmission to the heart and paper. Moses heard the Speech of God without sound and without letter, just as the righteous see the Essence of God in the Hereafter, without substance or its quality.[25]

This statement seems straightforward enough, but each and every phrase expresses a position that was achieved after centuries of debate and is still debated today. The majority of Sunnī scholars maintain, and have maintained as does al-Ghazālī, that the Qur'ān is in itself the uncreated word of God but that the utterance of the Qur'ān that one hears, the physically written Qur'ān that one reads, and the Qur'ān that one has memorized, are all created. As Abū Ḥanīfah (699–765 CE) writes, "The Qur'ān is the Word of God Most High, written in texts (*maṣāḥif*), preserved in hearts, recited on tongues, and sent down to the Prophet, upon him be blessings and peace. Our uttering of the Qur'ān is created, and our recitation of it is created, but the Qur'ān is uncreated."[26] The actual recitation and writing are believed to be created because they result from acts originated by human beings and as such are subject to the vicissitudes of time and space and thus could not be eternal. But as all prophets are said to attest that God has the attribute of speech, but that a created thing could not subsist within God's essence, the speech is considered to be eternal.

Abū Ḥanīfah, al-Ghazālī, and many others felt the need to emphasize the relativity of the expressions that convey the Divine uncreated speech because others maintained that the spoken, written, and memorized words are still the uncreated Word of God itself, not mere allusions to it. Proponents of this view call upon Qur'ān 9:6 to support this claim: "And if any one of the idolaters (*al-mushrikūn*) seeks your protection, then grant him protection so *that he might hear the words of God*" (emphasis added). The majority of Asha'arite theologians would maintain that this last phrase indicates that what one hears of the Qur'ān, although conveyed by created sound waves, is indeed the actual uncreated Word of God. Yet the Ḥashwiyyah, an early group that sought to preserve a literal reading of the Qur'ān and *ḥadīth* that verged on anthropomorphism, are said to have insisted that every aspect of the Qur'ān was uncreated.[27] In this way they can be likened to the Christian monophysite heresy, which maintained that Jesus was only divine because his divinity had overwhelmed his humanity.

While we cannot address the details of all of the debates regarding the complex relationship between the uncreated word and its created expressions, we can identify at least four different positions that Muslim scholars have maintained:

1. That God's speech and revelations are created (mu'tazilite);
2. That God's speech is produced in time (*muḥdath*) but not necessarily created (Twelver Shī'ī);
3. That God's speech is beginning-less and uncreated, abiding with the essence of God. But that God's speech is not letters and sounds, so that what is found among us is an expression of it (*lafẓ*) not it itself (Ash'arite and Maturidite);

4. That God's speech is letters and sounds that are beginning-less in essence, and that God's speech is actually these written letters and sounds that are heard (Ḥashwiyyah, among others).

As most Islamic scholars maintain that the uncreatedness of the Qur'ān derives from the very nature of God's speech as an attribute of God's Divine Essence, many Muslims also maintain the uncreatedness of previous revelations as seen in al-Ghazālī's reference to Moses above. As the ninth century *ḥadīth* scholar ʿUthmān b. Saʿīd al-Dārimī (d. 895 CE) states:

> God knows all languages and speaks in which ever language He wishes. If He wishes He speaks in Arabic and if He wishes He speaks in Hebrew, and if He wishes in Syriac. So He has made the Qur'ān His word in Arabic, and the Torah and the Gospel His word in Hebrew, since He has sent the prophets with the language of their peoples.[28]

To support this claim, some cite Qur'ān 2:75, which says of the Jews, "seeing there is a party of them that *heard God's Word ...*" (emphasis added). It could thus be argued that the notion of the dual nature of God's Word, the Divine Logos, as both an uncreated eternal Word that is an attribute of God's very Essence and a created book that conveys that Word to humankind, is something that Muslim theologians attribute in some way, shape, or form to all revelations because that dual nature is understood as being inherent to the phenomena of revelation itself. Muslim theologians then maintain that this applies to the Torah, the Gospel, and the Qur'ān. But such thinking implies a misunderstanding of the structure of Christianity, wherein the Word is incarnated rather than made into book or "inlibrated," as some have put it. This is a reasonable approach for Muslims, as Christians do have a book in the form of the Gospels, and the Gospels are referred to in the Qur'ān. But this belief ignores the very structure of traditional Christianity, and thus seeks to interpret its central teachings based upon the internal logic of Islamic theology rather than the internal logic of Christian theology. But when viewed in accord with its own internal logic, the Christian understanding of Jesus as the Word of God as both Divine and human could be understood from within an Islamic context as something that derives from the nature of revelation itself. This does not mean that Muslims must accept the Christian understanding of the Incarnation, only that they have keys within their own tradition that would help them to better comprehend it. Important Qur'ānic verses bear witness to Jesus as the Word of God. Though Jesus is referred to as a messenger of God in the Qur'ān (Q 4:157; 4:171; 61:6), he is unlike all other messengers in that he is "His [God's] Word which He cast to Mary" (Q 4:171), and thus directly embodies the message with which he was sent or is the very message itself. In verse Q 3:45, Jesus is also referred to as "a Word from Him...son of Mary." In this vein, one can also read Q 19:34 as follows: "That is Jesus, son of Mary, a statement of truth [(i.e., God)] concerning which they are in doubt."

Most Muslims would argue that the Qur'ānic references to Jesus as "His (God's) Word," "a Word," and "a statement of truth" merely indicate that he is a word like every other element of creation, of which the Qur'ān says: "When He decrees a thing, He says to it only: 'Be!' and it is" (Q 2:118; 3:47; 19:35; 40:68), and "His command when He wills a thing, is just to say to it 'Be!' and it is" (Q 36:82). But all other existent things are here referred to as things created through the Word of God. Jesus, however, is referred to as "His Word which He cast to Mary." So unlike all created things that come about through God's command "Be!" the Qur'ān indicates that Jesus, by virtue of being God's very Word, in some way participates directly in this Divine Command.

Furthermore, Muslim theologians from the time of Abū'l-Ḥasan al-Ashʿarī (874–936 CE), the eponymous founder of the most widespread school of Islamic theology, have employed similar verses, such as 16:40, "All that We say to a thing, when We will it, is to say to it, 'Be!' and it is," to emphasize that God's speech is an attribute of His Essence and that the Qur'ān is therefore uncreated. As al-Ashʿarī writes,

> If the Qur'ān had been created God would have said to it "Be!" But the Qur'ān is His speech, and it is impossible that His speech should be spoken to. For this would necessitate a second speech and we should have to say of this second speech and its relation to a third what we say of the first speech and its relation to a second. But this would necessitate speeches without end—which is false. And if this be false, it is false that the Qur'ān is created.[29]

To argue that verses, which refer to God's creative speech, prove that the Qur'ān is uncreated, while also arguing that they mitigate against the reference to Jesus as "His word" being interpreted as a reference to the uncreated word of revelation, would seem to be disingenuous at best. Furthermore, the very notion that God's word is a thing, though superior to other things, is part of the argument that the Muʿtazilite and others have employed to argue that the Qur'ān itself is created or that it is a thing originated in time *(muḥdath)*. This is not to say that individual theologians are necessarily contradicting themselves, but that when we read the tradition as a whole, some contradictions can arise.

In addition to testifying that Jesus is God's Word, other Qur'ānic passages bear witness to a creative, healing, life-giving power in Jesus that was not granted to any other prophet—a life-giving power akin to God's Word through which He says to things "Be!" and they are. For example, verse Q 3:49 says of Jesus: "I have come to you with a sign from your Lord, I will create for you out of clay like the shape of a bird then I will breathe into it, and it will be a bird by leave of God. I will also heal the blind and the leper; and I bring to life the dead, by the leave of God." And in verse Q 5:110:

> When God said, "O Jesus, son of Mary, remember My favour to you and to your mother, when I strengthened you with the Holy Spirit to speak to people in the cradle and in maturity, and when I taught you the Scripture, and wisdom, and the Torah, and the Gospel; and how you create out of clay the likeness of a bird by My permission, and you breathe into it and it becomes a bird by My permission, and you heal the blind and the leper by My permission, and you raise the dead by My permission.

Many Muslim theologians will argue that the phrases "*by the leave of God*" and "*by My permission*" employed in Q 3:49 and Q 5:110 respectively confirm that this power ultimately lies with God alone, and thus distinguish the Qur'ānic account from the Biblical account, or the Islamic account from the Christian account. But the Qur'ānic account is not so far from the Biblical understanding. For the distinction between Jesus and God the Father is made clear throughout the Gospels, as in John 20:17, "I am ascending to my Father and your Father, to my God and your God" In several passages, Jesus states that he is subordinate to the Father: "I can do nothing on my own authority; as I hear, I judge; and my judgment is just, because I seek not my own will but the will of him who sent me" (John 5:30); "For I have not spoken of my own authority; the Father who sent me has himself given me commandment what to say and what to speak" (John 12:49); and "I go to the Father; for the Father is greater than I" (John 14:28). Yet despite this duality between Jesus and the Father expressed in these and other verses, Jesus also says, "I and the Father are one" (John 10:30).

Christian theologians thus insist that the Word or Son can never be separate from God but that there is nonetheless a sovereignty of the Father in relation to the Son—such that nothing can be done by the will of the Son but that it also be done by the will of the Father. Thus Qur'ān 3:49 and 5:110 do not contravene the Christian understanding of the relation between the Father and the Son but in fact reaffirm it. While the manner in which Christian theologians understand the Word differs from that of Muslim theologians, that the Word partakes of divinity in some way is nonetheless a principle that, as we have seen above, is intrinsic to the Sunnī Muslim understanding of the Divine Word, of the Qur'ān, and of revelation as such.

One may argue that if God's Word gives rise to several different revelations, it is somehow multiple and fragmented and would therefore introduce multiplicity into the Divine Essence if it were part of the Divine Essence. But according to Muslim belief, God's Word is on a "Preserved Tablet" as an attribute of the Divine Essence that is one with His knowledge with which He "encompasses all things" (Q 6:80; 7:89; 20:98) and is therefore infinite. In this sense, the multiplicity of revelation does not contradict the immutability of God's Eternal Word but actually manifests another of its intrinsic qualities—infinitude. The following verses are interpreted by some exegetes as an allusion to the inexhaustible infinitude by which words of revelation emanate from the single Word of God: "If the sea were ink for the Words of my Lord, the sea would be spent before the words of my Lord were spent even though We brought the like it as replenishment" (Q18:109); "And if all the trees on earth were pens, and the sea replenished with seven more seas, the words of God would not be spent" (Q 31:27). Based upon such verses, each word of God in the revelation of the Torah, the Psalms, and the Qur'ān is understood as an extension of the eternal, uncreated Word of God.

Though the words of each revelation are multiple in order to convey the fullness of God's Word to human beings, each word nonetheless partakes of the uncreated essence of the Word. Hence the Qur'ān states: "There is no changing the Words of God" (Q 10:64); "There is none to change the words of God" (Q 6:34); "none can change His words" (Q 6:115); "And recite that which has been revealed to you of the Book of your Lord. There is none who can change His words. And you will not find, besides Him, any refuge" (Q 18:27). All the individual words, letters, and even sounds are thus understood to partake, as regards their inmost substance, of the inimitable immutability that is ultimately due to God alone (though as mentioned above this is understood in different ways).

For Muslims, it is difficult to understand the Christian belief that Jesus is "seated at the right hand of the Father." But when this is seen as a reference to the uncreated Word, it can be understood from within a Qur'ānic context. For, like the second person of the Trinity, the Word of God is co-eternal with God, partaking of divinity, though God is its cause and principle. In its own way, the

Qur'ān could be read as testifying to such an understanding of the Christian position when it confirms the ascension of Jesus into heaven in two passages: "When God said, 'O Jesus, I am gathering you, and raising you to Me, and I am cleansing you of those who disbelieved, and I am setting those who follow you above those who disbelieved until the Day of Resurrection' " (Q 3:55); "and they did not slay him for certain. Nay, God raised him up to Him. God is ever Mighty, Wise" (Q 4:157–158).

Seeing Jesus as the eternal, uncreated Word of God, or one of the faces of that Word, also helps explain certain dimensions of Islamic eschatology. For like Christians, Muslims believe that Jesus will return at the end of time to make justice reign on earth. As the Prophet Muḥammad says: "By Him in whose hand is my soul, the son of Mary will soon descend among you as a just judge."[30] If Jesus has indeed been preserved from death, has dwelled in heaven for over two thousand years, and will be sent again, then Islamic theology must admit that he has a nature that is different not only from other human beings but from other prophets as well.

This interpretation need not lead to full acceptance of traditional Christian Logos theology, but can lead to a better understanding of what is meant by Incarnation, Trinity, and sonship, and thus to better dialogue between Muslims and Christians. There should be no illusions. Muslims will never accept that Jesus is "the divine cause of the continuing effects of *theosis* among other men," to quote from Cutsinger's parallel chapter in this book written from the Christian viewpoint.[31] Nonetheless, they can acknowledge that the question of the relationship between the Divine and the human through the Divine Word is one over which they too have grappled and, in fact, never reached an overall consensus.

Some of the similarities between the Christian doctrine of the two natures and the Islamic doctrine of the uncreated/created Qur'ān can also help to mollify the offense some Christians may take when hearing that the Qur'ān says of Jesus, "The Messiah would never disdain to be a servant of God" (Q 4:172), and "The Messiah, the son of Mary, was only a messenger; messengers passed away before him; his mother was a truthful woman; they both used to eat food" (Q 5:75). When read in the spirit of coming "to a word common between us and you" (Q 3:64), these can be seen as an extension of the many verses in the Gospel of John in which Jesus states that he was sent by the Father (John 5:23; 5:30; 5:36–37; 6:39; 6:44; 6:57; 8:16; 8:18; 8:29; 8:42; 10:36; 12:49; 14:24; 17:21; 17:25; 20:21; *et passim*); for what is a messenger but one who is sent?

In a more subtle reading, such Qur'ānic verses can be seen as a reference to Jesus' human nature and as an affirmation that the Word, divine by nature from all eternity, became fully human. In Christian theology, it is an essential aspect of the supreme sacrifice that Christ in his earthly manifestation fully submits to the mortality of the human condition.[32] As Philippians 2:6–8 states:

> [Jesus], though he was in the form of God, did not count equality with God a thing to be grasped, but emptied himself, taking the form of a servant, being born in the likeness of men. And being found in human form he humbled himself and became obedient unto death, even death on a cross.

Likewise, the similarities in these doctrines can help Muslims to better understand (though not necessarily accept) such verses as "I and the Father are one" (John 10:30), when viewed as an expression of the Divine Word itself.

Son of God

The question of the nature of the Word is also important as regards the Qur'ānic critique of "those who say that God has a son." Three Qur'ānic verses explicitly deny that God has a son:

"They say, 'God has taken to Himself a son;' Glory be to Him! Nay, to Him belongs all that is in the heavens and the earth; all obey His will" (Q 2:116). "The Jews say: Ezra is the son of God; and the Christians say: The Messiah is the son of God. That is the utterance of their mouths, imitating the utterances of those who disbelieved before [them]. God assail them! How they are deviated!" (Q 9:30). "It is not [befitting] for God to take to Himself a son. Glory be to Him. When He decrees a thing, He only says to it, 'Be!' and it is" (Q 19:35).

These verses appear to flatly contradict the traditional Christian position that Jesus is the Son of God. However, the meaning of "son" in the phrase "Son of God" employed by the Christian Creed is very different from the meaning of "son" as it would be understood by most readers of the Qur'ān, especially at the time it was revealed. For Christianity, the term "Son of God" refers to Jesus as the pre-temporal, uncreated Word of God that is begotten of the Father before time;[33] this interpretation is based in large part upon the beginning of the Gospel of John:[34] "In the beginning was the Word, and the Word was with God, and the Word was God.[35] He was in the beginning with God; all things were made through him, and without him was not anything made that was made" (John 1:1–3).

Here, "the Word" is taken as a direct reference to Jesus, who exists as the "Son" and "Word of God" before all creation. As Paul writes of Jesus, "He is before all things, and in him all things hold together" (Colossians 1:17). The Nicene Creed, the most widespread and authoritative declaration of Christian belief, confirms this, stating that he was "begotten of the Father *before all worlds*" (emphasis added).[36] This statement indicates that Jesus is the "Son of God" in a pretemporal fashion, not through the physical process of human birth through the Virgin Mary. The virgin birth brought the Word of God into the world, but it is not through the virgin birth that Jesus becomes God's "only begotten son." The process of begetting can thus be seen as a reference to the generation or emanation of the Divine Logos, or Divine Word, from the Divine Principle, God, conceived of as "the Father."

Against this background one can discern the deeper significance of the Islamic denial of the sonship of Christ. When not read in the background of and with the need for dogmatic reaffirmations, the Qur'ānic position is more subtle than what is usually presented. As seen above, verse Q 19:35—"It is not [befitting] for God to take to Himself a son. Glory be to Him. When He decrees a thing, He only says to it 'Be!' and it is."—denies that God can take a son. But it also alludes to the Divine command "Be!" which constitutes, precisely, the very Word of God. The verse can thus be taken to deny direct biological procreation by God, as sonship would have been understood in the pre-Islamic pagan environment, but to subtly confirm that the Word flows directly from God. And as seen above, Jesus is "His [God's] Word that He cast to Mary" (Q 4:171).

The view that what the Qur'ān seeks to repudiate are crude pagan notions of sonship is supported by verse Q 6:101, which denies the possibility of God having any physical offspring: "He is the Originator of the heavens and the earth; how should He have a son, when He has no consort?" Only a few minor sects within the early Christian heresies of Adoptionism and Arianism have ever claimed that

Jesus was the result of a physical relationship, and this has been repudiated by all existing denominations of Christianity.[37] When read in light of these and other heresies, the Qur'ān can actually be taken to support the traditional Christian position, which rigorously distinguishes between the human nature of Jesus and his divine nature as uncreated Word. It is this uncreated nature which, alone, can legitimately be referred to as the "Son," the third Person of the Trinity, precisely on account of the Son's transcendence of the temporal and material conditions presupposed by physical procreation. This is not to say that this is how the Qur'ān should be read; it is only to demonstrate that the Qur'ānic verses regarding this most crucial of issues can be read in different ways when we come to the text with a different set of questions.

The Qur'ānic Chapter of Sincerity (*Sūrat al-Ikhlāṣ*) is considered by many to be the most concise summation of Islam's position regarding the inimitable unity of the Divine: "Say, 'He is God, One. God, the Self-Sufficient, Besought of all. He neither begot, nor was begotten. Nor is there anyone equal to Him.' " (Q 112:1–4). The chapter is also interpreted by many as a direct denial of the Christian understanding of Jesus. But the words translated as "beget" (*yalid*) and "begotten" (*yūlad*) have a specific physical connotation. The verse (v. 3) that would appear to deny that Jesus is the "Son of God" could thus be translated, "He does not procreate, nor is He procreated."

When read this way and viewed in light of other verses (such as Q 5:75, 6:101, and 19:35) that can be read as denying the views advanced by heretical Christian sects rather than traditional Christian theology itself, verse three would appear to refer to the notion of a created "Son of God." Indeed, that is how most Muslims interpret the verse. They have repudiated the Christian position because they have misinterpreted the Christian creed to be supporting the notion of physical sonship that both Christians and the Qur'ān repudiate. Seen in this way, the Qur'ān is not necessarily denying this central tenet of Christianity but may even be joining with the Church Fathers in denying egregious misunderstandings of the virgin birth. This is exactly why the Nicene Creed says of Jesus that he is "begotten, not made." Translated into Islamic philosophical terms, this attestation of the Nicene Creed could be rendered, "emanated not procreated."

Conclusion

Such potential openings within the Qur'ānic treatment of Jesus augur great theological potential. Nonetheless, there will always be lines of division, and irreconcilable antagonisms cannot but persist on the plane of theology. Muslims can only accept the efficacy of the Christian understanding of Father, Son, and Holy Spirit so long as the Father remains God as such, the one transpersonal and ineffable source of divinity, as in the opening apposition of the Nicene Creed: "I believe in one God, the Father Almighty, Maker of heaven and earth, and of all things visible and invisible."[38] But Muslims cannot accept that the Father, Son, and Holy Spirit are all of the same essence (*homoousios*) and thus equally divine, such that what can be predicated of one can be predicated of the other. Even when phrased in a manner that seeks to preserve the sovereignty of the Father as "the 'cause' (*aitia*) and the 'principle' (*archê*) of the divine nature, which is in the Son and in the Spirit,"[39] the fact that anything is seen as sharing in any way with the Ultimate Divine Principle will appear as the ultimate sin of *shirk*—associating others with God.

In other words, when the Trinity is presented in terms of "the Father is greater than I" (John 14:28) such that the Father is maintained as the source of all divinity, it could be understood in Islamic terms. But when presented in terms of "I and the Father are one" (John 10:30), such that "each [is] God because [they are] consubstantial,"[40] it is more difficult to find common ground.

The fundamental difference between the Qur'ānic and Biblical presentations of Jesus is that the Qur'ān always seeks to reaffirm the transcendence of the Divine by focusing upon Jesus' humanity, while only hinting at the divinity of the Word, while the Bible focuses more upon his divinity while also confirming his humanity. This may be due in part to the different historical and sociological circumstances under which God sent Jesus and the Prophet Muḥammad. Jesus was sent to a mostly Jewish community that was already well versed in the teachings of Abrahamic monotheism and alert to the dangers of idolatry. The Prophet Muḥammad was sent to a community still in the throes of polytheism and idol worship. The community to which Jesus was sent was accused of having forgotten the true meaning and purpose of scripture—focusing upon the minutiae of the law instead of the spirit. The community to which the Prophet Muḥammad was sent was accused of having completely forgotten that there was even such a thing as revelation. Each message thus emphasized different aspects of the Divine Word while implicitly comprising the whole.

The message that Jesus embodied focuses upon Jesus as the Divine Word "begotten of the Father before all worlds."[41] The message that the Prophet Muḥammad delivered focused upon the perennial truth of the Divine Word in the Qur'ān and in all previous revelations. It thus relegated all prophets to a secondary function in relation to the Divine Logos through which all scriptures are revealed; this does not mean that each revelation is historically and sociologically conditioned. Rather this seeming difference is what is alluded to in Qur'ān 14:4: "We have not sent any Messenger except with the tongue of his people, that he might make [the Message] clear to them." Each revelation necessarily contains the whole of God's wisdom because the revelation is the Divine Word as such. But each revelation also emphasizes different aspects of that Word in accordance with the needs of the human collectivity to which it is sent.

Seen in this light, many other aspects of the Qur'ānic account of Jesus and Christianity merit further investigation. For example, does the Qur'ān criticize traditional Christian Trinitarian theology? Or could it actually be read as opposing the tritheistic misunderstandings of Christian theology that Christians themselves have opposed?[42] Does the Qur'ān deny the Crucifixion of Jesus, or is there a more subtle understanding of the text?[43] It may be that when subjected to close reading not shaped by centuries of polemic, the Qur'ānic verses regarding Jesus can lead to more common ground than is often assumed. But we must first recognize that our interpretations will always reflect the premises we bring to the text and the spirit in which we choose to read them. Only when our texts are read in relation to one another in a spirit of faith seeking understanding, rather than a spirit of polemic seeking division that so often plagues us, can we establish a dialogue that is based upon the central teachings that lie at the core of our religious traditions. In all likelihood, we will not come to agreement, but at least we will better understand what it is we disagree about.

From one perspective, seeking such understanding between those who disagree is a central calling of both the Qur'ān and the Bible. As one famous Qur'ānic verse states: "O mankind! We have indeed created you from a male and a female, and made you nations and tribes that you may come to know one another" (Q 49:13). And as another declares:

> To every one of you, We have appointed a law and a way. If God had willed, He would have made you one community, but that He may try you in what He has given to you. So vie with one another in good works; to God you shall all return, and He will then inform you of that which you differed. (Q 5:48)

Similarly, Paul writes: "Now there are varieties of gifts, but the same Spirit; and there are varieties of service, but the same Lord; and there are varieties of working, but it is the same God who inspires them all in every one" (1 Cor. 12:4–6). In light of such verses, perhaps we can find elements of our traditions that will help us to view the Divine Word in a manner that transcends the bounds of one particular tradition, understanding that it is infinite and therefore cannot be limited to a single revelation, or that Divine Mercy will not be confined to one religious tradition. For one thing that Christians and Muslims can agree upon is that the Divine Word is, by definition, beyond the ken of the human word. Knowledge of the word, ʿilm al-kalām, in the ultimate sense is thus something to which we can only attain by transcending our words and being absorbed within God's Word.

Notes

1. "A Common Word Between Us and You," *Sophia: The Journal of Traditional Studies* 14, no. 2 16–38. See also "A Common Word Between Us and You," The Official Web site of A Common Word, http://www.acommonword.com/index.php?lang=en&page=option1.
2. For an examination of the history of *A Common Word,* the responses to it, and its influence, see Joseph Lumbard, "The Uncommonality of 'A Common Word,'" *Crown Paper.* Also available at Joseph Lumbard, "The Uncommonality of 'A Common Word,'" Crown Center for Middle East Studies, http://www.brandeis.edu/crown/publications/cp/CP3.pdf.
3. *Concurrent Resolution Supporting Christian, Jewish, and Muslim Interfaith Dialogue that Promotes Peace, Understanding, Unity, and Religious Freedom*, HR Res. 374, 110th Cong., 2nd sess., *Congressional Record* 154, no. 151, daily ed. (September 23, 2008): H 8655–57. Also available online at "Latest Major Action: 9/23/2008," The Official Web site of A Common Word, http://www.acommonword.com/index.php?page=newcontent&item=3.
4. Alistair Macdonald-Radcliff and Roland Schatz, ed., *C1 Annual Dialogue Report on Religion and Values: 2009*, http://www.yale.edu/faith/downloads/070809%20C-1%20World%20Dialogue%202009%20Report.pdf, 4–6.
5. World Council of Churches, "Learning to Explore Love Together," Oikoumene, http://www.oikoumene.org/fileadmin/files/wcc-main/documents/p6/Learning_to_Explore_Love_Together.pdf .
6. Ibid., 3.
7. See Sidney Griffith, *The Church in the Shadow of the Mosque.* The author offers examples of the cross-fertilization that has occurred between Muslim and Christian theologians (even when they opposed one another). A study that is "put forward with the hope that today Jews, Christians, and Muslims might be inspired to undertake the unlikely task of turning the historical clash of theologies between Islam, Christianity, and Judaism into an exercise in comparative theology, which will hopefully be more successful in promoting a mutually tolerant interreligious dialogue than has proved possible heretofore." Ibid., 22.

8. Rowan Williams, "A Common Word for the Common Good," *Sophia: The Journal of Traditional Studies* 14, no. 2: 41.
9. See "Responses from Christian Leaders," The Official Web site of A Common Word, http://www.acommonword.com/index.php?lang=en&page=responses. The nature of these responses merits a study in and of itself. There are over 60 different responses.
10. al-Tirmidhī, *al-Jāmi'*, *Kitāb Faḍā'il al-Qur'ān*, 25. Unless otherwise noted, all *aḥadīth* in this essay are cited from the most recent collections edited by The Thesaurus Islamicus Foundation.
11. Several verses also speak of Jesus as confirming that which came before him (Q 3:50; 5:46; 61:6), and Moses is said to confirm that which was with his people (Q 2:41; 2:89; 2:91; 4:47).
12. For a discussion of Muslims who maintained that the previous scriptures had been abrogated see Camilla Adang, *Muslim Writers on Judaism and the Hebrew Bible from Ibn Rabban to Ibn Hazm* chap. 6.
13. For an examination of these verses see Joseph Lumbard, "Koranic Inclusivism in an Age of Globalization," *Iqbal Review* 46, no. 2, 95–104. Also available at http://www.allamaiqbal.com/publications/journals/review/oct05/index.htm.
14. *Ṣaḥīḥ Bukhārī*, *Kitāb al-Anbiyā'*, 48.
15. See Wilfred Madelung, "The Origins of the Controversy Regarding the Creation of the Qur'ān," in *Religious Schools and Sects in Medieval Islam*, 504–25 (demonstrating that although the vast majority of Sunnī Muslims maintain that the Qur'ān is uncreated, there are slight variations in how this belief is understood); and Harry Austryn Wolfson, *The Philosophy of the Kalam*. See also Abdullah bin Hamid Ali, "The Speech and Word of Allah (Kalām): In Light of Traditional Discussions," Masud, http://www.masud.co.uk/ISLAM/ust_abd/speech_word.htm (containing a brief examination of the perspectives among those who maintain that the Qur'ān is uncreated).
16. Wolfson, *The Philosophy of the Kalam,* 244–64. The term "inlibrate" in the context of the Qur'ān as God's word appears to have been introduced by Harry A. Wolfson.
17. Some have even observed that the technical theological treatment of the divine attributes in Islam, especially as it relates to envisioning the relationship between God and the created order, may have initially been fashioned through debates with Christians. See Wolfson, *The Philosophy of the Kalam*, 58–64, 112–32; Seppo Rissanen, *Theological Encounter of Oriental Christians with Islam During Early Abbasid Rule*, 11–17.
18. Walter Melville Patton, *Aḥmed ibn Ḥanbal and the Miḥna*, 67.
19. See J.R.T.M. Peters, *God's Created Speech* (for an analysis of the Mu'tazilite position regarding the Qur'ān).
20. For example, the Shī'ite theologian al-Shaykh al-Mufīd writes, "I say the Qur'ān is God's speech and inspiration, and it is produced in time, as God Himself has described it. And I refuse to say unreservedly that it is created." Martin J. McDermott, *The Theology of al-Shaikh al-Mufīd (413–1022)*, 90. The difference between Ash'arī Sunnī theologians and Twelver Shī'ī theologians regarding the nature of the Qur'ān is rooted in different understandings of the Divine attribute of speech which the Ash'aris see as an attribute of the Divine Essence but which the Twelver Shī'is see as an act of God that cannot but be conditioned by some contingencies to which an act is subject. Thus for the Shī'is speech takes place in time and exhibits temporal conditions. While Ash'arī theologians take the uncreatedness of the Qur'ān as a fundamental creed or part of the principles of religion (*uṣūl al-dīn*), Twelver Shī'is do not maintain that one's position on this issue is central to the creed. Their discussion of this matter is thus taken up as a response to a fundamental tenant of Ash'arī theology but does not constitute a fundamental tenant of Shī'ī theology. For a discussion of the Shī'ī perspective regarding this issue, see Al-Sayyid Abū al-Qāsim al-Mūsawī al-Khū'ī, *The Prolegomena to the Qur'ān*, trans. Abdulaziz A. Sachedina, chap. 13.

21. Given the very different theological and historical contexts in which these different groups arise, such similarities can only be approximations. In this particular instance, for example, the Arians maintained that Jesus was still divine, though created, and that he was to be worshipped. Something Muʿtazilites would never claim.
22. See, for example, Abū ʿAbdallāh M. b. Aḥmad al-Qurṭubī, *al-Jāmiʿ li Aḥkām al-Qurʾān* 10, 246.
23. Ṣaḥīḥ Muslim, *Kitāb al-Dhikr waʾ l-Duʿāʾ*, 15.
24. ʿAbd Allāh Yūsuf al-Judayʿ, *al-ʿAqīdah al-Salafiyyah fī Kalām Rabb al-Bariyyah*, 131.
25. Abū Ḥāmid al-Ghazālī, *Qawāʾid al-ʿAqāʾid fī l-Tawḥīd* in *Rasāʾil al-Ghazālī* 162.
26. My translation from Arabic text in Abū ʿl-Muntahā al-Maghnīsāwī, *Imām Abū Ḥanīfaʾs Al-Fiqh al-Akbar Explained*, trans. Abdur-Rahman ibn Yusuf, 89. While the attribution of *al-Fiqh al-Akbar* has been questioned by both Muslim and non-Muslim scholars, the majority of scholars have maintained that it was composed by him; see al-Maghnīsāwī, *Imām Abū Ḥanīfa's Al-Fiqh al-Akbar Explained*, 24–25.
27. See A. S. Halkin, "The Ḥashwiyya," *Journal of the American Oriental Society* 54, no. 1 (1934), 1–28 (discussing the relation of the Ḥashwiyyah to what was to become orthodox Islam).
28. ʿUthmān b. Saʿīd al-Dārimī, *al-Radd ʿalā al-Jahmiyyah*, 123.
29. Quoted in A. J. McCarthy, *The Theology of al-Ashʿari*, 20–21.
30. *Ṣaḥīḥ Bukhārī, Kitāb Aḥādīth al-Anbiyāʾ*, 50.
31. James S. Cutsinger, chapter 10, this volume, 119.
32. Vladimir Lossky, *Orthodox Theology: An Introduction*, 101.
33. Muslims may bristle at the reference to God as "the Father" or "our Father" in Christianity. But as the Qurʾān reaffirms previous scriptures, and the New Testament continually refers to God in this manner, it cannot be completely rejected. When "God, the Father" is understood as a reference to God as the Creator of all and the Lord of all, it can be accepted within an Islamic context. This is alluded to in a saying of the Prophet Muḥammad: "Human beings—all of them—are the dependents of God, the most beloved of them to God are those who are of the greatest benefit to His dependents." (Sulaymān b. Aḥmad al-Tabarānī, *al-Muʿjam al-Kabīr* 10, 86; Abū Yaʿlā al-Tamīmī, *Musnad Abī Yaʿlā*, Ed. Ḥusayn Salīm Asad , 65, 106, 194).
34. For some Muslim reactions to the Gospel of John, see Mark Beaumont, "Muslim Readings of John's Gospel in the ʿAbbasid Period," *Islam and Christian–Muslim Relations* 19, no. 2: 179–97.
35. Cutsinger rightly points out that the end of this sentence literally reads in Greek, "the Word was a god," rather than "God". See James S. Cutsinger, "That Man Might Become God: Lectures on Christian Theology," University of South Carolina, http://www.cutsinger.net/pdf/that_man_might_become_god.pdf, 129–30. But we refer here to the standard translation as "the Word was God" in the context of traditional Christian theology.
36. "The Nicene Creed," Center for Reformed Theology and Apologetics, http://www.reformed.org/documents/index.html?mainframe=http://www.reformed.org/documents/nicene.html.
37. Without any dramatic archaeological discoveries, it would prove very difficult to demonstrate that the Qurʾān critiques any specific Christian heresy or heresies. Various scholars postulated that the Qurʾān addresses particular Christian sects such as the Ebionites, the Nazarenes, the Elchasiates, or the Collyridians, among others. There is, however, little linguistic or historical evidence to support these speculations. As Tor Andrae observes, the available historical evidence indicates that the Arabic-speaking Christians that would have been known to Muḥammad and his community were associated with the Melkites, Jacobites, and Nestorians at the peripheries of Arabia whose

scriptural heritage was largely Aramaean. Tor Andrae, *Les origins de l'Islam et le christianisme*, trans. Jules Roche, 201–11.

38. "The Nicene Creed," Center for Reformed Theology and Apologetics, http://www.reformed.org/documents/index.html?mainframe=http://www.reformed.org/documents/nicene.html.
39. J. Meyendorff, *Byzantine Theology: Historical Trends and Doctrinal Themes*, 183.
40. Ibid., quoting Gregory of Nazianus, *Oratio* 40, 41; PG 36:417b.
41. "The Nicene Creed," Center for Reformed Theology and Apologetics.
42. For further discussion of the Trinity in the Qur'ān see Sidney Griffith, "Syriacisms in the Arabic Qur'ān: Who were "those who said 'Allāh is third of three'" according to *al-Mā'idah* 73" in *A Word Fitly Spoken: Studies in Mediaevel Exegesis of the Hebrew Bible and the Qur'ān Presented to Haggai Ben-Shamma,* ed. Simon Hopkins, Sarah Stroumsa, and Bruno Chiesa, 83–110. For a discussion of the Trinity in Islamic thought see David Thomas, "The Doctrine of the Trinity in the Early Abbasid Era" in *Islamic Interpretations of Christianity,* ed. Lloyd Ridgeon, 78–98; David Thomas, *Anti-Christian Polemic in Early Islam: Abū 'Īsā al-Warrāq's "Against the Trinity."*
43. For a discussion of the many ways in which the crucifixion has been treated in classical Islamic sources see Todd Lawson, *The Crucifixion and the Qur'ān* and Neil Robinson, *Christ in Islam and Christianity*, 78–141.

10

Disagreeing to Agree: A Christian Response to "A Common Word"

James S. Cutsinger

Conform to holy separation to realize holy union.

Frithjof Schuon

Ibn Isḥāq, an early biographer of the Prophet Muḥammad, offers a fascinating account of what may well have been the very first interfaith dialogue between Christians and Muslims.[1] It is an important tradition, for it helps to clarify the context of the opening verses of the third Qur'ānic *sūrah*, "The Family of 'Imran"—a context in which Christians were invited by Muslims to "a common word between us and you" (Q 3:64).

Interfaith Dialogue in the Time of the Prophet

Jesus said unto them, "Who do men say that I am?" And they answered, "One of the prophets."

Mark 8:27–28

Imagine the scene: It is the year of our Lord 632—the tenth of the *hijrah*.[2] A deputation of some 60 Christians, including a bishop by the name of Abū Ḥārithah bin 'Alqamah, has just arrived in Medina from the Yemeni city of Najrān, a dusty seven days' ride to the south. Like many other tribal groups from throughout the Arabian peninsula, they have come seeking to establish a pact and terms of peace with the Prophet of Islam. Muḥammad shows them great hospitality, generously allowing his guests—despite the objections of some of his companions—to say their prayers in his mosque. Discussions afterward naturally turn to the subject of religion and to the theological differences between Christianity and Islam, notably their differing understandings of Jesus.

The Christians say they are puzzled. You Muslims agree—do you not?—that the son of Mary was no ordinary man. On the contrary, you too believe in his miracles, including his healing of the man born blind and his raising of the dead (Q 3:49), and you describe him as "the Messiah," as "illustrious both in this world and the next," as "one of those brought near to God," and indeed as God's very "word" (Q 3:45–46). If—as you also claim to agree—his mother was a virgin (Q 3:47), and if he therefore had no human father, does it not follow that he must have been the Son of God? No, the Prophet responds, this does not in fact follow, and he recites as his reason a Qur'ānic revelation that has just been given him: "Lo! the likeness of Jesus with God is as the likeness of Adam. He created him of dust, then He said unto him: Be! and he is. This is the truth from thy Lord" (Q 3:59–60). The prophetic logic is clear. Adam had neither father nor mother, and yet neither Christians nor Muslims believe that he was anything more than a creature of God. So why would anyone suppose that the absence of only one human parent somehow constitutes a proof of divinity?

Yes, the logic seems clear enough. But realizing that his Christian visitors might require something more than this single sign to convince them, the Prophet is told that he should propose a test to determine which of their divergent Christologies is the true one. He invites them to engage in a *mubāhalah*, an ancient rite in which the parties to a dispute attest to their confidence in their respective positions by "invoking the curse of God upon those who lie" (Q 3:61). We are told that the Christians at first accept this challenge, but when the time arrives for the contest itself, they are daunted to find that the Prophet has returned with his daughter Fāṭimah, her husband, 'Alī, and their children, Ḥasan and Ḥusayn, all of whom he enfolds in his cloak, as if to say: Look! I am prepared for my whole family to be killed if we are the ones whose understanding of Jesus is wrong. According to the Islamic sources, this powerful demonstration of certitude causes the Christians to lose heart, and they decline to proceed with the imprecation.

The Prophet's response to their demurral is especially intriguing. Once again a heavenly sign is given him, and it is precisely this additional *āyah*, bestowed in precisely this interfaith context, that has provided the name for *A Common Word Between Us and You*:[3] "Say: 'O People of the Scripture! Come to a common word between us and you: that we shall worship none but God, and that we shall ascribe no partner unto Him, and that none of us shall take others for lords beside God'" (Q 3:64). According to the traditional sources, the Prophet then tells the Christians that they are free to continue practicing their religion, and in exchange for their payment of the *jizyah*, or poll tax, he pledges to protect their churches and possessions. A treaty is signed, and the deputation returns to Najrān.

I find this account fascinating on many levels, not least because it raises a number of provocative questions. Who exactly were these Christians? Were they members of one of the heretical sects of the era, or were they fully Orthodox adherents of Chalcedon? If they *were* Orthodox, as some of the sources suggest in calling them "Melkites" and in describing them as followers of the "Byzantine rite," then why, unlike the many early martyrs of their faith, do they appear to have been so reluctant to stand up for their convictions regarding Christ's divinity? Or was it reluctance? Did they change their minds and withdraw from the *mubāhalah* because they had lost their self-confidence, as the Islamic report appears to imply? Or did they draw back, though still firmly believing themselves to be right, because they were unwilling to put the Prophet and his family at risk? Who, in other words, was the more confident party, and whose the more generous and effective interfaith diplomacy?

The most important question for me as an Orthodox Christian, however, is whether, and if so how and to what extent, the historical background I have been sketching is germane to contemporary Christian-Muslim dialogue. Are we to read the prophetic overture of Qur'ān 3:64 on its own and in isolation from its Qur'ānic and commentarial context? Or should this verse be interpreted in light of the Christological controversy hinted at in the preceding *āyāt* and detailed in Islamic tradition? In issuing their own invitation to Christians today, the Muslim signatories to "A Common Word Between Us and You" have chosen the first approach, and they have done so in order to underscore precisely the "common ground"[4] shared by our traditions, especially our respective teachings concerning the love of God and neighbor. Moreover, in a spirit of friendship and dialogue, they have provided a conciliatory gloss for three crucial phrases in the verse in question that might have otherwise seemed divisive. To "worship none but God" (Q 3:64), they tell us, is to be "totally devoted to God";[5] to "ascribe no partner unto Him" (Q 3:64) means acknowledging "the Unity of God";[6] and to say that "none of us shall take others for lords beside God" (Q 3:64) implies that "none of us should obey the other in disobedience to God,"[7] which is to say that "Muslims, Christians, and Jews should be free to each follow what God commanded them,"[8] because "there is no compulsion in religion" (Q 2:256).

This is doubtless the most appropriate way of reading the Prophet's concluding words to his Najrāni guests if one's primary aims are peaceful coexistence and the promotion of religious tolerance. It goes without saying, of course, that these are highly laudable goals, and like other Christians who have contributed a response to the online "Common Word" statement,[9] I am very happy to support any effort that may help to reduce tension and violence between the adherents of our historic faiths. Nevertheless, as I study the opening verses of *Sūrah* 3 and the traditional Islamic account of their historical background, I confess that it is the *differences* between our traditions, and especially our Christologies, that appear by far the more prominent feature, and it seems to me we shall miss a valuable opportunity for deepened insight if we focus only on obvious and rather anodyne commonalities.[10] Indeed, speaking as a metaphysician, I would dare to go further. I would say that it is only by first accentuating our theological differences that we can hope to attain a truly transformative unity. For it is not on their surfaces or along their circumferences but at their centers—where outwardly they are furthest apart—that the real "common ground" between genuine religions may be realized.

What I have in mind is something of a paradox, and a visual image may be helpful.[11] Suppose we envision the Christian and Muslim religions as geometrical figures. Several configurations are possible. Exclusivists within each tradition will no doubt prefer to think of these figures as lying in parallel, and therefore never-intersecting, planes and as having different sizes and shapes representing what are perceived to be their respective degrees of perfection and comprehensiveness. One's own tradition will in this case be given the larger shape, no doubt circular in form—whereas a rather cramped and irregular polygon will be employed to symbolize the competing religion! Other Christians and Muslims, more sanguine about the prospects for interfaith concord, will imagine the figures as existing instead on the same plane, where contact is possible. Certain of these hopeful ecumenists may picture the shapes as moving ever closer to each other, while even greater optimists may see them as already touching or perhaps overlapping.

The problem with all these representations, however, is that they end up depicting the relationship between our religions, even at its best, in merely superficial and peripheral ways, as if the possibility of mutual comprehension and respect depended solely on external proximity or juxtaposition, whether between two parallel planes or between two discrete figures in the same plane. But this is to understand ecumenism in merely planimetric, dogmatic, and exoteric categories. I propose we envision a rather different, three-dimensional model, where divergence and convergence are each given their due by means of an intersection of planes. Of course, Christianity and Islam must still be represented by two distinct figures, for doctrinally they are quite dissimilar. But they should both be pictured as circular, for each expresses a unique mode of perfection. Furthermore, I suggest that we inscribe these circles inside a single sphere where, to highlight their exoteric differences, they are deployed at right angles to each other, but where, in order that attention might be directed toward their inward or esoteric commonalities, they are pictured as sharing the same diameter. For the perennialists in my audience, I could add that the sphere is the *religio perennis* while the common diameter, stretching from the north to the south pole of the sphere, is the *axis mundi* and thus the seeming distance between God and man.

I shall return to this diameter and to a discussion of these "inward commonalities" later on in my talk. But first I must concentrate on the divergence of planes so as to underscore for my audience the difference, indeed the radical disparity, between our traditions' respective understandings of Jesus, and by extension our understandings of the relationship between the Divine and the human. Metaphysics comes later. For now I speak as an Orthodox Christian theologian.

Christology, Theosis, and "A Common Word"

> *"Thou, being a man, makest thyself God!" Jesus answered them, "Is it not written in your law, 'I said, Ye are gods?'"*
>
> *John 10:33–34*

The Prophet Muḥammad asked the deputation from Najrān, and contemporary Muslim scholars and leaders are asking my fellow Christians and me, to come to a "common word" or "agreement" with them.[12] Central to what my coreligionists and I are being asked to accept, as the Qur'ānic text of the invitation specifies, is the premise that God has no partners or associates and that it is therefore wrong to regard anyone other than God as divine or to take anyone other than God as one's lord. Fundamental to these claims, of course, are two key points of Islamic doctrine: on the one hand the defining *shahādah*, or testimony, *Lā ilāha illā 'Llāh*,

"There is no god but God"; and on the other hand the resulting conviction that *shirk*—that is, the "association" of others than God with God, the worshipping of others as if they were God, the attribution of God's characteristics to others than God—is the gravest of sins.[13] In deciding whether to accede to a theology thus defined, the first question a Christian must ask himself is whether Jesus Christ, whom Christians certainly do worship and to whom they certainly do attribute divine characteristics, is Himself actually God. According to the Islamic revelation, He clearly is not. Indeed, even if we had never heard of the Najrāni deputation or their meeting with the Prophet Muḥammad or the proposed but then averted test of their respective claims about Jesus, the Qur'ānic text itself is unambiguous: however wondrous His deeds may have been and however exceptional—even prophetic—His stature, Jesus Christ is human and not divine.

Needless to say, the Christian perspective on Christ—whether Orthodox, Catholic, or Protestant—is radically different. In their open letter, the authors of "A Common Word Between Us and You" have asserted that "Christians themselves... have never all agreed with each other on Jesus Christ's nature,"[14] but with due respect I must say that this seems to me a most misleading claim. Disagreements can certainly be found if one includes the opinions of heretics, whether the Arians, Apollinarians, or Nestorians of the first Christian centuries, who had not yet come to terms with the full mystery of the Gospel,[15] or else the demythologizers and other historicist critics of recent times, who, though they may still call themselves "Christian," have capitulated to the reductionist pressures of modernity in their search for a purely "historical Jesus."

Be that as it may, the vast majority of Christians, at least since the Fourth Ecumenical Council in A.D. 451, have been of one mind in believing that Jesus Christ is the divine Son of God, and each time they express this consensus by repeating the words of the Nicene Creed, traditional Christianity's most important statement of faith, they categorically reject the teaching of Qur'ān 3:59 that "the likeness of Jesus with God is as the likeness of Adam." For the Creed makes a point of stating—quite emphatically—that Jesus is "begotten" (*gennēthenta*) but *not* "created" (*poiēthenta*), being "of one essence [*homoousion*] with the Father," and indeed that it is Jesus Himself, the eternal Word of God, "by whom all things were made."[16] Of course Christians also believe that Jesus became fully human, for "though he was in the form of God... He emptied himself, taking the form of a servant, being born in the likeness of men" (Phil. 2:6–7). According to the Formula or Definition promulgated by the Fourth Council, this divine *kenosis* or self-emptying means that the Son of God is now "like us in all things with the exception of sin." But He who thus entered the human condition, the uncreated Word, is not a human being. On the contrary, Christ's *persona* or *hypostasis*—to use the technical theological language—remains strictly divine, though within this Person, the second of the Holy Trinity, there exist two distinct natures, one fully divine and one fully human, each with its own set of distinguishing *idiomata* or attributes.[17]

This traditional Christology developed in part as a way of grasping synoptically what the Bible teaches concerning Christ's divinity. To mention only a few representative passages, Jesus is proclaimed to be "the Light of the world," which "enlightens every man coming into the world" (John 9:5, 1:9); and it is said that "all things... in heaven and on earth, both visible and invisible" were created "in" Him and "through" Him and "for" Him (Col. 1:16), that "He reflects the glory of God and bears the very stamp of his nature, upholding the universe by

His word of power" (Heb. 1:3), and that "He is the Alpha and the Omega"—that is, the beginning and the end of all things—for He is "He who is and who was and who is to come, the Almighty" (Rev. 1:8). Furthermore, contrary to what the "Common Word" initiative would appear to require of those who agree to its terms, Jesus is referred to and worshipped as "Lord" (*Kyrios* in Greek) well over 700 times in the New Testament. In fact, regarding Christ as Lord is said by Saint Paul to be the very key to eternal life: "If you confess with your lips that Jesus is Lord and believe in your heart that God raised Him from the dead, you will be saved" (Rom. 10:9).

Certain Christian respondents to "A Common Word," in an effort to move the conversation forward on this difficult point—and to exonerate their tradition of what might otherwise seem to Muslims the sin of *shirk*—have made a point of insisting that in these and other such Biblical passages, Jesus is *not* in fact being presented as a "partner" of God, or taken as a "Lord" in addition to God, or worshipped as God while nonetheless not being God. He simply *is* God as Christianity conceives of God—not something or someone else or other, but a Christian name for the one and only Divinity. This is the strategy used by Rowan Williams, the Anglican Archbishop of Canterbury, in his June 2008 response to the "Common Word" letter. "It is important to state unequivocally," Dr. Williams writes

> that the association of any other being with God is expressly rejected by the Christian theological tradition... "God" is the name of a kind of life, a "nature" or essence—eternal and self-sufficient life, always active, needing nothing. But that life is lived...eternally and simultaneously as three interrelated agencies are made known to us in the history of God's revelation...In light of what our Scripture says, we speak of "Father, Son, and Holy Spirit," but we do not mean one God with two beings alongside him...There is indeed one God, the Living and Self-subsistent, associated with no other.[18]

There is certainly an important truth in this formulation, for Christians do indeed believe that there is only one God; like Muslims we are monotheists, not polytheists. Nonetheless, as an Eastern Orthodox theologian, I am obliged to point out that this way of expressing Trinitarian doctrine comes rather too close for comfort to the modalist or Sabellian heresy, in which a single God was said to have appeared in three distinct modes or forms, whether successively or simultaneously. No doubt the Archbishop understands this distinction and is fully aware that the early Church rejected modalism. I do not mean to suggest he is consciously opting for heresy. His aim is ecumenical diplomacy, and to this end he is quick to agree with our Muslim interlocutors that nothing and no one should be associated with the only God. The result, however, is a kind of planimetric ecumenism, to refer once again to my geometrical imagery. Like many another enthusiastic proponent of exoteric religious concord, Dr. Williams has pictured Christianity and Islam as if they existed on the same theological plane, and he seems prepared to blur the sharp dogmatic outlines of his own religion so as to make it more compatible, if not congruent, with the Muslim perspective.

But the Trinity is a much greater mystery than this too simplistic equation of theologies suggests. Part of the mystery turns on exactly what, or rather whom, one means by "God." As we Orthodox see it, prayerful fidelity to the witness of Scripture, the decrees of the Ecumenical Councils, and the language of liturgical worship requires that the word *God* be reserved, strictly speaking, not for some generic form of "self-sufficient life," but for God the Father alone, the first Person of the Holy Trinity, who is said to be the Fount (*pēgē*) of all divinity and the uncaused Cause (*aitia*) of the other two Persons, the Son and the Spirit. In defense of this perspective, we cite such Biblical texts as John 17:3, where Jesus prays to His Father, saying, "This is eternal life, that they know thee the only true God, and Jesus Christ whom thou hast sent," or again Christ's response to the rich man, "'Why do you call Me good? No one is good but God alone'" (Luke 18:19). The opening salutations and concluding blessings of several Pauline epistles further support the Orthodox Trinitarian vision, as for example the doxology in the final verse of the Letter to the Romans: "To the only wise God be glory for evermore through Jesus Christ" (Rom. 16:27). What one passes "through" is evidently not the same as what one passes "to," and it follows that Jesus is not to be equated or identified with "the only wise God."

Now admittedly the Biblical language is not systematic, and it would be going too far to claim that Christ is never referred to as "God" in the scriptures. But even when He is thus described, the reader is not allowed to forget that there is Another who is even "more God" than He—if you will permit me this admittedly curious phrase. For, as Jesus Himself insists, speaking as the divine Son and not merely as man, "The Father is greater than I" (John 14:28).[19] The opening chapter of the Letter to the Hebrews offers a memorable illustration of this koanic complexity. Appropriating Old Testament texts from 2 Samuel and the Psalms and applying them prophetically to Christ, the author writes: "To what angel did God ever say, 'Thou art my Son, today I have begotten thee?'...But of the Son He says: 'Thy throne, O God, is forever and ever...Therefore God, thy God, has anointed thee with the oil of gladness beyond Thy comrades'" (Heb. 1:5, 8–9).

Strange as it may sound even to some Christian ears, there is a hierarchy within the divine order itself. Even though Jesus can in one sense be rightly called "God" since He has the same essence as His Father, the "God" that He is *has* a God. This astonishing claim is born out, among other places, in the risen Christ's encounters with Thomas Didymus and Mary Magdalene, as recorded in John 20. Having touched Christ's wounded hands and side, the erstwhile "doubting Thomas" is moved to utter the most exalted profession of faith in the entire New Testament: "'My Lord and my God!'" (John 20:28), a profession Christ in no way rejects or rebukes him for. But when Mary attempts to embrace Him, Jesus stops her, saying, "'Do not hold me...but go to my brethren and say to them, I am ascending to my Father and your Father, to my God and your God'" (John 20:17).

We find this highly paradoxical point reaffirmed in the Nicene Creed, where the grammatical apposition in the opening article shows beyond doubt that the Father alone is unequivocally "God." The Christian recites, "I believe in one God, the Father Almighty, Maker of heaven and earth, and of all things visible and invisible." Once again it is evident that the unity of God is not to be understood as residing in some generic nature shared by three specific Persons. The oneness of God is the specificity of the Father; it is He who *is* the "one God" in whom Christians believe. As Saint Gregory the Theologian puts it, "The union is the Father, from whom and to whom the order of the Persons runs its course."[20] As for Jesus Christ, the second article of the Creed makes it clear that His divinity, while entirely real and efficacious, is in some sense derivative. For He, "the only-begotten Son of God," is confessed to be "Light *of* Light" and "Very God *of* Very God." In Orthodox liturgical texts, this subtle but extremely important distinction is often conveyed by using the word "God" on its own when speaking of the Father while adding the possessive pronoun "our" in phrases referring to the divinity of the Son, as in the frequently recited prayer "Lord Jesus Christ, *our God*, have mercy on us and save us." It is as if the tradition were endeavoring to remind the Christian of the difference between Jesus' words to Mary and Thomas's words to Jesus. Once again it would be misleading to suggest that there is anything systematic or invariable about this usage—devotional piety is not mathematics—but it occurs frequently enough to be worthy of note.

Clearly much more could be said concerning this crucial theological distinction; indeed, to appropriate the final verse of the Fourth Gospel, "The world itself could not contain the books that would be written" (John 21:25) if our hope were in some way to exhaust in prose the mystery of Christ's relation to His Father—let alone to the Holy Spirit. My aim here is merely to raise a question, a question not yet adequately addressed in the responses I have read to "A Common Word." We Christians worship Jesus Christ as God's very Son, and we take this same Christ as our Lord. And yet at least in one sense the Son of God is *not* God, or not at least God as such—not the metaphysical Absolute and sovereign Source of all things, including the Son's own consubstantial divinity. So the question is this: Is it really appropriate for a faithful Christian to accept an invitation to theological dialogue the stipulations of which are that "we shall worship none but God, and that we shall ascribe no partner unto Him, and that none of us shall take others for lords beside God" (Q 3:64)?

But this is by no means the most vexing of the questions we face, for Christology is not the only way in which the Christian and Islamic planes diverge. Nor, I suspect, will it prove the most problematic form of divergence for many Muslim exoterists. Let us assume for the sake of the argument that we all agree to prescind from the historical background in which the faithful of our respective traditions first exchanged views in Medina. Let us assume further that Anglican and other Western theologians are right to prioritize the unity Christ shares with His Father and the Holy Spirit and right to use the word *God* to refer to this unity. And let us assume finally that, since Jesus Christ may thus be regarded as one expression of that unity, worshipping Him is not—or at least *need* not be—an obstacle to interfaith harmony between Christians and Muslims. Even if our discussions were to proceed as swimmingly as these assumptions suggest—and I am none too sure they would, or should—we would still find ourselves facing a tremendous dialogical dilemma. For Jesus is not merely some strange though still acceptable exception to the Islamic rule that God alone is divine. According to Christianity, He is the salvific means whereby this rule is meant to be repeatedly broken.

I said earlier that the traditional Christian understanding of Christ, as expressed by the early Councils of the Church, developed in part as a way of grasping synoptically what the scriptures teach concerning the two natures of the divine Son of God. But it would be wrong to suppose that Christological doctrine came about solely, or even primarily, as a means of collating the titles and descriptions of Christ that one finds in the Bible. On the contrary, Christian understanding of Jesus is above all a way of making soteriological sense of the Christian experience of *theosis* or deification—an experience, promised by scripture and realized in the lives of many saints, in which human beings are enabled to participate in the very powers and properties of God Himself. Granted, it is my Orthodox tradition that has especially stressed this experience as the defining element in salvation and as the ultimate goal of the whole spiritual life. But the essential teaching, firmly based on the Bible and attested to by the entire Patristic tradition, is no more

Eastern than Western. If the conviction that "there is no god but God" is foundational to Islam, the conviction that "God became man that man might become God" is foundational to Christianity.

References to *theosis* can be found throughout the New Testament. One of the most arresting passages comes in Saint Paul's Letter to the Ephesians, where he tells his correspondents that he is praying on their behalf that they "may be filled with all the fullness of God" (Eph. 3:19). What is particularly striking is that the very same phrase is also used by Paul in his Letter to the Colossians in reference to Jesus Himself, in whom "all the fullness of God was pleased to dwell" (Col. 1:19).[21] An equally important formulation is found in the Gospel of John, where we read that those who "receive" Christ are given the "power to become sons of God" (John 1:12). But the most decisive of Biblical supports for this distinctively Christian teaching comes in the Second Letter of Peter:

> May grace and peace be multiplied to you in the knowledge of God and of Jesus our Lord. His divine power has granted to us all things that pertain to life and godliness, through the knowledge of Him who called us to His own glory and excellence, by which He has granted to us his precious and very great promises, that through these you may escape from the corruption that is in the world because of passion, and become partakers of the divine nature. (2 Pet. 1:2–4).

Each of these lines deserves attentive study, but it is enough for our purposes here to focus on the last phrase alone. God has given us the power through Jesus Christ to become "partakers of the divine nature"—*theias koinōnoi physeōs* in the Greek. The word *koinōnoi* is particularly important for our dialogue. Translated here as "partakers," it can also be rendered into English as "participants," "companions," "sharers," "communicants,"[22] and, yes, as "partners." According to Peter, the "precious and very great promise" of God is that man, creature of God though he is, can nonetheless become nothing short of God's "partner." This for Christianity is the divinely willed culmination of human life.

Nor do we Christians regard this *koinōnia*, or "communion," in the divine nature simply as an unrealized human potential or an as yet unfulfilled promise. According to the Fathers of the Church, it is something the greatest saints have already experienced. Saint Athanasius's dictum that "God became man in order to make us God" is one of several Patristic sources often quoted in defense of the doctrine.[23] But it is important to realize that Athanasius was not speaking in a merely speculative or theoretical way; he was talking about the concrete effects of *theosis* as he had personally witnessed them in his spiritual master, Saint Anthony the Great, the first and most famous of the Desert Fathers of Egypt. At the end of his biography of the saint, Athanasius tells his fellow monks that they should read what he has written not only to "the other brothers, so that they may learn what the life of monks ought to be" but to "the pagans as well, so they may understand by this means that our Lord Jesus Christ is God and Son of God."[24] For Athanasius, the quality of Anthony's life—indeed the transfigured nature of his very being—was such that it could not be described except in terms of divinity, but this divinity in turn could not be adequately accounted for without a sufficient reason that was itself divine. To repeat the critical point I made earlier: for Christians, Jesus is not some strange exception that ends up merely proving the rule that God alone is divine. He is the divine cause of the continuing effects of *theosis* among other men, and thus of the ongoing and divinely intended violation of this rule.[25]

I should add that for Orthodox Christians the transformative experience of deification is not merely a thing of the past; on the contrary it is believed to continue right down to our own time. The Greek Orthodox bishop and spiritual writer Hierotheos Vlachos, recalling his encounter in the late 1980s with a *gerondas*, or spiritual elder, on the Holy Mountain of Athos, describes the old man as "participating in the uncreated energies of God" and as having "everything that God has, yet without having His essence."[26] Even supposing that there may be a certain amount of deliberate hyperbole in this formulation, it is clear that the promise of *theosis*, the realization of which such accounts are intended to document, remains very firmly rooted in my tradition, and it points to a hugely important planimetric divergence between Christianity and Islam. As "A Common Word" makes abundantly clear, "partnership" with God is for Muslims the one thing to be avoided at all costs, but for Christians "partnership" with God—indeed partnership *in* God—is the *sine qua non* of salvation. For you it is the greatest sin, while for us it is the distinguishing mark of sanctity. The very thing you proscribe we prescribe.

So is it really possible for us to "come to a common word" with each other?

Toward a Metaphysical Dialogue

I in them, and thou in Me, that they may be perfectly one.

John 17:23

Despite the stress I have been placing on divergence and dissimilarity, I myself certainly believe that it is possible. I agree in other words that it is entirely appropriate, and indeed highly desirable, for traditional Christians and traditional Muslims to seek common ground. But as I have more than once hinted, and shall now endeavor to explain more precisely, I also believe that this search, rather than neglecting or downplaying our differences, should insist they be treated as the very key to our unity. What this means, however, is that any "common word" or agreement between us must be of a metaphysical rather than a theological order.

Simply put, metaphysics is to theology what absoluteness is to relativity. Now of course, the theologian is also concerned with what he rightly regards as absolute and eternal Truth. But his understanding of this Truth is inevitably colored by the revealed forms in which, he believes, it has found its most definitive religious expression.[27] This is obviously the case with Christian theology, where the doctrine of God is ineluctably tied to the saving events of Christ's life, but the general principle applies to each of the Semitic traditions and *mutatis mutandis* to all religions. Compared to Christianity, where the revelational weight is placed on the incarnate presence of God at a particular moment of time, Islam accentuates what God has revealed to all His prophets across the ages. Nonetheless Islamic theology (*kalām*) remains bound in its own way to the conceptual categories with which it articulates the message behind all the messengers. No less an authority than al-Ghazzali goes so far as to say that "spiritual knowledge (*ma'rifah*) cannot be attained by the science of theology," for theology is like a "veil" (*ḥijāb*) and a "barrier" (*māni'*).[28]

By contrast, metaphysics is the science of absoluteness as such, or more precisely of the Absolute as such, and the metaphysician is the person who knows that this Absolute must by its very nature transcend every form, even the relatively absolute forms through which it has revealed itself in his religion. This is obviously not the place for a justification or defense of this science. Fellow scholars of religion who have managed to convince themselves that no one can know anything except relativities will no doubt remain unconvinced by what I say here, and so will fellow religious believers, whether Christian or Muslim, who are intent upon treating their doctrines about God as if they were God Himself. I am not addressing either of these groups at the moment. I am speaking instead to those who have already realized that, without at least some incipient knowledge of a Reality transcending all form, the very concept of form would be meaningless, and I am inviting them to look *through* the forms of their religious traditions, treating them as open windows and not opaque works of art.[29]

Let us remind ourselves of the challenge we face. We have before us two great world religions whose defining doctrines are mutually exclusive, or at least so they appear. Either "God became man that man might become God," or else "there is no god but God"; either Jesus Christ is the uncreated Son of God, or else He is a created human being; either sharing in God's nature is the very pinnacle of holiness, or else it is the abyss of sin. As I noted near the start of this paper, if our traditions are placed within a single plane of theological reference—a plane defined, in other words, by the dogmatic formulations of Christianity alone or, alternatively, those of Islam alone—then confrontation or compromise will be our only options. If the Christian is right, the Muslim is wrong; if the Muslim is right, the Christian is wrong. And in each case he who is wrong must either modify his doctrinal claims or be prepared to face condemnation—whether through a formal rite of *mubāhalah* or by some more terrestrial and less frightening means!

But what if we take a step back from these dogmatically divisive formulations, not to dismiss or abandon them certainly, but to envision them in a new perspective? To revert to my earlier geometrical image, let us picture our religions as circles of equal sizes but placed in different planes. And let us position these planes in such a way that the circles intersect through their diameters and along the axis of a single sphere. Now suppose we ascend above the north pole of this sphere and then descend beneath its south pole, taking turns looking down and then up along the axis. What might we see? What might our apparent oppositions together be pointing us toward? Metaphysics, as I am using the term, is precisely this stepping back, this positioning of planes, and this looking along a shared diameter. There are three basic steps to this process.

First, we must try to understand why "God became man that man might become God" if in fact it is nonetheless true that "there is no god but God." What deep truth within the Christian doctrine of the incarnation is revealed if, but only if, we also profess the *shahādah*?

Second, we must try to understand why "there is no god but God" if in fact it is nonetheless true that "God became man that man might become God." What deep truth within the Islamic prohibition of *shirk* is revealed if, but only if, we also accept *kenosis*, *theosis*, and *koinōnia* as real possibilities?

Third, we must try to understand how these deepened insights into our defining doctrines might together aid us in better knowing the Reality whom Christians and Muslims are both called to love. What deepest truths about God will we glimpse if, but only if, we transcend a merely planimetric ecumenism?

Please understand: there can be no question of somehow solving these three riddles here. What follow are merely a few scattered hints and provocations. The Muslim signatories to "A Common Word Between Us and You" have issued an invitation to Christians. All I am doing is extending in turn an invitation of my own.

Step One

Step one will require that Islamic doctrine be accorded a certain priority. Without giving up their belief that Jesus Christ is the divine Son of God and the saving means whereby others may come to share in God's nature, Christians who take this step must be willing to grant that "there is no god but God"—in other words, metaphysically speaking, that *the Absolute is incomparable to anything else*. In order to do this, however, they must be prepared to rise above the north pole of my imagined sphere in order to look down its axis toward their accustomed immanence by way of transcendence.

Even the most faithful and serious of Christians should be willing to adopt this perspective, whether they are metaphysicians or not. Certainly the Eastern Orthodox, notwithstanding their emphasis on deification, yield to no one in their apophatic insistence that the true God transcends every possible category, even that of divinity itself, and that He therefore remains asymptotically forever beyond His creation. Saint Maximus the Confessor speaks about *theosis* with greater authority and confidence than perhaps any other Father of the Church, and yet he is especially quick to explain that "God is...incomprehensible...altogether excluding notions of when and how, inaccessible to all...He is undetermined, unchanging, and infinite, since He is infinitely beyond all being."[30] This is precisely why the Christian East accentuates the primacy of the Father in relation to the other two Trinitarian Persons, for in spite of the fact that "the only begotten Son, who is in the bosom of the Father, hath declared Him," it remains the case—even "after" the incarnation—that "no one has ever seen God" (John 1:18). This is also why the doctrine of deification is almost always presented with an important disclaimer. Yes, says the Orthodox theologian, we are called to participate in the very life of God, but this participation extends only as far as His uncreated energies, and not to His essence.[31] The description of the Athonite *gerondas* I quoted above may seem overblown to some in my audience, but the writer was actually being very carefully and circumspectly Orthodox when he said that the old man had "everything that God has, *yet without having His essence*."[32]

There need be no opposition, therefore—at least in principle—between the Muslim's conviction concerning God's incomparability and the Christian's conviction concerning the divinity of Christ and the deification of man. But metaphysical dialogue involves a great deal more than a half-grudging, half-apologetic acceptance of minimally compatible truths. In taking Step One, we Christians are not being asked to affirm the transcendence of the divine Absolute in spite of, or even in addition to, our continued belief in the incarnation. On the contrary, we are being invited to plumb the depths of our Christological teachings *by means of* the apparently contradictory doctrine that "there is no god but God." The question, as I have said, comes down to this: What deep truth may be revealed in our claim that "God became man that man might become God" if, but only if, we also profess the *shahādah*?

If nothing else, granting dialogical priority to this Islamic doctrine should help Christians see that whatever the incarnation and deification may involve on the human side, they entail absolutely no change, and certainly no diminution, on the part of God. Christian theologians have always known this, of course; they have known, to quote again the words of Saint Maximus, that God is "unchanging" and beyond all "notions of when and how," and they have therefore known as well—in the classic formulation of the Athanasian Creed—that to "believe rightly in the incarnation of our Lord Jesus Christ" is to understand that it came about "not by the conversion of the Godhead into flesh, but by the taking of the manhood into God." But even theologians can easily forget this fact; even they sometimes talk as if something actually happened in Heaven in the year zero A.D. The impact of the *shahādah* is such as to remind anyone, whether Muslim or Christian, that God simply *is* and that the relativities of the world and the apparent movements of time have no effect whatsoever upon Him. "There is no god but God" means that God is eternal and hence that His acts are all *now*—or rather that He does not truly "act" insofar as action entails change and becoming. But what this means in turn is not only that the world is still being created and that the Second Coming has already occurred;[33] it also means that God has always been man, and man always God.

Can Christians accept the "common word" of such insights? Are we willing to grant that the operative power of the incarnation "for us men and for our salvation" (Nicene Creed) depends on the metaphysical fact that "God begetteth not nor was begotten, and there is none comparable unto Him" (Q 112:3–4)? Can we admit, in other words, that the south would not be fully south without north?

Step Two

In this case the tables are to be turned and Christian doctrine prioritized. Without giving up their belief that "there is no god but God," Muslims who take this step must be willing to grant that "God became man that man might become God"—in other words, metaphysically speaking, that *the Absolute is necessarily Infinite* and that because it is Infinite *there is nothing not it*. In order to do this, however, they must be prepared to descend beneath our sphere in order to gaze upward toward their accustomed transcendence by way of immanence. The first step required Christians to position themselves in such a way as to envision their most important belief from the "northern" perspective of the Islamic *shahādah*. Now I am asking Muslims to return the favor—to position themselves in such a way as to envision their most important point of doctrine from the "southern" perspective afforded by Christian teaching concerning the incarnation and *theosis*.

Unless I am mistaken, this second step will present more of a problem for most Muslims than will Step One for most Christians. While bringing the *shahādah* into direct contact with the doctrine of the incarnation is certainly a strange thing to do, and though it cannot but lead to a de-temporalized—and to this extent unfamiliar—understanding of what is meant when we read that "the Word became flesh and dwelt among us" (John 1:14), there is certainly nothing intrinsically problematic from the Christian perspective in saying "there is no god but God." The situation in this second case is very different, however, and Muslim exoterists will almost certainly be scandalized. For taking Step Two means accepting the idea that the divinity of the one and only true God is in no way threatened or compromised, but is instead most profoundly affirmed, in being *shared*.

Emphasizing the primacy of God the Father in relation to the other two Persons of the Holy Trinity is essential when it comes to Step One. But it would be a mistake for our discussions to stop there, for it is clear in the Gospel that everything the Father has—and is—has been fully given to the Son. Though Jesus Himself testifies to the primacy of the Absolute in saying that "the Father is greater than I" (John 14:28), He at the same time makes a point of insisting that "He who has seen me has seen the Father" (John 14:9) and that "I and the Father are one" (John 10:30). Emphasizing the transcendent incomparability of the divine essence in relation to human beings is likewise essential to the first step of this dialogue. But again it would be a mistake to stop there, for it is also clear in the Gospel that everything the Son has received from the Father He means to give us as well, which is why He can pray—why He who *is* God can nonetheless pray *to* God–that we men be empowered to enter into Their union. John 17 records His potent words:

> Neither pray I for these alone, but for them also which shall believe on Me through their word, that they all may be one, as Thou, Father, art in Me, and I in Thee, that they also may be one in Us...The glory which Thou gavest Me I have given them, that they may be one, even as We are one: I in them, and Thou in Me, that they may be perfectly one (John 17:20–23).

For Christians, the perfect unity *of* God is inseparable from man's own perfect union *in* Him, which is why they believe "God is love" (1 John 4:16) and not just the Loving. But what this means—dare I say it?—is that a God without partners is not really God; interpenetration among the Persons of the Trinity, on the one hand, and the promise and possibility of our own participation in the eternal life of that Trinity, on the other, are essential in Christianity to God's being God.

As noted already, most Muslims will be thoroughly scandalized by the seeming *shirk* of this claim, and theologically they should be scandalized. Unless I am mistaken, the Sufis in our midst will be more amenable, however, drawing as they do on the insights of their esoteric traditions, including an understanding of the divine *tawhīd*, or oneness, that accentuates "union" and not only "unicity."[34] But whether or not there are Sufic approximations to the distinctively Christian doctrines I have stressed in this paper is not the question. The question is whether the parties to our dialogue are willing to adopt, and not just concede, each other's perspectives. In taking Step One, I did not ask my fellow Christians to give a merely provisional nod to the *shahādah*. I asked them to permit this distinctive Islamic doctrine to deepen their understanding of the incarnation. In the same fashion I am now inviting my Muslim interlocutors to accept the incarnation of God and the deification of man not in spite of, or even in addition to, their conviction that "there is no god but God," but *as a means of* plumbing the depths of the divine incomparability. Muslims can—in fact they must—affirm the radiance of the divine Infinite, for "whithersoever ye turn, there is the Face of God" (Q 2:115), and "We are nearer to [man] than his jugular vein" (Q 50:16). No faithful Muslim, whether Sufi or otherwise, can object to the proposition that God is amidst us and in us. But what about the reverse formulation? Is it possible for there to be something amidst and in God—others than God within God who *are* "God" nonetheless, ourselves among them?

I am eager to know what the signatories to "A Common Word Between Us and You" think about this distinctively Christian paradox. Are they willing to grant that "no one hath ascended up to heaven but He that came down from heaven" (John 3:13) and that it is therefore possible to be "born, not of blood, nor of the will of the flesh, nor of the will of man, but of God" (John 1:13)? Can they admit, in other words, that the north can still be north in the south?

Step Three

This third step is going to be the most difficult by far. For here it is no longer a question of simply bringing the central teachings of our religions into contact with each other, however intimate and fructifying that contact might prove, nor of visualizing our defining doctrines from above or beneath the "poles" of each other's perspectives. We cannot simply look toward immanence by way of transcendence or toward transcendence by way of immanence. The challenge at this point is to envision our respective teachings in complete coincidence, as if they had been reduced not just from their divergent planes to a single line but from that line to a point—as if in fact the sphere had collapsed and north and south had met in the center.

Steps One and Two entail rethinking the meaning of our most essential doctrines, and in each case our understanding of those doctrines, under pressure as it were from their theological opposites, must undergo a certain modification. Without denying the southern truth that God became man in Jesus Christ, the Christian remembers, or perhaps realizes for the first time, that God is nonetheless beyond all becoming and that the incarnation is therefore not, or not only, an event in time but an eternal state of being. And without denying the northern truth that there is nothing comparable to God, the Muslim remembers, or perhaps realizes for the first time, that there is nonetheless nothing *not* comparable to God since whatever is—to the measure it is—must be He.

Thus summarized, however, it may sound as if a metaphysical dialogue were no better able than its planimetric counterparts to avoid the dangers of compromise or capitulation. It may seem that each party to our conversation has been obliged to sacrifice at least a part of what makes his religion distinctive: the Muslim at least some of the transcendence implicit in the *shahādah* and the Christian at least some of the immanence implicit in the doctrine of *theosis*. But this is not so, or rather, though it would perhaps be an indirect and unintended result of our dialogue if we stopped short at this point, the aim of Step Three is precisely to reinstate and accentuate our exoteric and theological differences in order to demonstrate how, precisely *as* differences, they point toward an esoteric and metaphysical unity. If we are successful in this quest, Muslims will come to see their transcendence not *through* or even *in* but *as* the deepest immanence; and Christians will come to see their immanence not *through* or even *in* but *as* the highest transcendence.

I shall not presume to try to work this out from the Muslim side. But perhaps I can give you just a hint as to what Step Three might involve for Christians by invoking the authority of one of my tradition's greatest spiritual masters, Saint Gregory Palamas. I have in mind a short passage from his most seminal work, a three-fold collection of treatises written "In Defense of the Holy Hesychasts" of Mount Athos and often simply referred to as *The Triads*. Here is what he says:

> The divine Maximus [the Confessor] taught that [*theosis*] is not only enhypostatic but also unoriginated—and not merely uncreated—as well as indescribable

and supratemporal, and that those who attain it become thereby uncreated, principial, and indescribable, even though in their own nature they come from what is not.[35]

The words *indescribable* (*aperigrapton*) and *supratemporal* (*hyperchronon*) speak for themselves, while the term *enhypostatic* (*enupostaton*) underscores the fact that deification involves an ontological transformation: in the language of Sufism, *theosis* is a permanent station (*maqām*), not just a passing state (*ḥāl*). But the most important words in this passage—and they are nothing short of astonishing—are the adjectives *unoriginated* (*agenēton*) as applied to deification and *principial* (*anarchos*) as applied to deified human beings. They are astonishing because they appear to crack the glass ceiling which my Orthodox tradition is otherwise so careful to maintain—and which I alluded to earlier—between God's uncreated energies on the one hand, in which deified men are permitted to share, and God's essence on the other hand, which is said to remain forever beyond even them. What is perhaps most surprising is that of all the Fathers of the Church Gregory was himself one of the most indispensable in transmitting, and arguably the most assiduous in preserving, this classic distinction.

But now look what he has gone and done! In defending the methods and exalting the attainments of his fellow Athonite monks, he has ended up attributing to the greatest of these brethren a level of realization—to make use of the Anselmian formula—"than which nothing greater can be conceived."[36] First he goes out of his way to insist that deification is more than "merely uncreated" (*aktiston monon*), though transcending the created order would clearly be astounding enough.[37] *Theosis*, however, is something higher: it is "unoriginated" (*agenēton*), which appears to mean that it transcends all becoming.[38] And yet even this word fails to capture the incomparability of those who have arrived at this station, and in "indescribably" describing them Gregory is therefore compelled to stretch for a yet loftier term. Like deification, the deified man can be called "uncreated" (*aktistos*), but he is nonetheless more, and the more in this case takes us beyond even the level of the "unoriginated"—and thus, we may assume, beyond such transcendent realities as the divine *logoi* or ideas, which though eternal, still depend upon God. Wonder of wonders, deified human beings exceed even these, whereas they themselves are exceeded by nothing; for according to Gregory they are now *anarchos*, which means—indeed it could mean nothing else—that they have no principle (*archē*), whether temporal or eternal. But if this is true, it seems we have no choice but to conclude that such men have paradoxically "become" their own Principle, having realized their identity with God as such.[39]

I am not suggesting that the author of *The Triads* would himself have endorsed this startling—and some will say blasphemous—reading. As his well-known disparagement of the Platonists proves, Gregory Palamas was a theologian, not a metaphysician, and as Archbishop of Thessaloniki he would in any case have been obliged *ex officio*, whatever his personal insights, to guard the dogmatic frontiers of the Orthodox tradition. Nonetheless, words mean what they mean, and they are worth taking seriously, especially when they are the words of so important a saint, writing in what is historically so important a treatise. And their meaning in this case, however staggering, appears indisputable. To be deified is to become identified with the very highest Reality, the one and only pure Principle, whom Christians call "Father" and Muslims *Allāh*. It is here precisely—at this supreme level of Being, or rather at a "level" Beyond-even-Being—that the greatest saints find themselves.[40] Were we all Hindus, we could easily cut to the chase and say, *Tat tvam asi*, "Thou art That!"[41] But since ours is a dialogue between Semitic traditions, I must end on a somewhat more allusive note, saying instead that this is how the deepest immanence looks when it is perceived as the highest transcendence; this is what happens, in other words, when south meets north in the center.

I invite my Muslim interlocutors to consider in turn what might happen when north meets south in the center and what the highest transcendence might look like when perceived as the deepest immanence. If they will do this—if they will disagree with me theologically in order to agree metaphysically—we may indeed "come to a common word" not only "between us and you" but *within* us as *I*.

Notes

1. 'Abd al-Malik Ibn Isḥāq, *The Life of Muhammad A Translation of Ishaq's Sirat Rasul Allah*, 270–77. See also Muhammad Saed Abdul-Rahman, *The Meaning and Explanation of the Glorious Qur'an*, 1:602–04; also Martin Lings, *Muhammad: His Life Based on the Earliest Sources*, 326–27.
2. Dates in the sources vary, some indicating that the year was 10 A.H., others 9 A.H.; the meeting may thus have occurred as early as 630 A.D. and as late as 632 A.D. For discussion of this question, see Mahmoud M. Ayoub, *The Qur'an and Its Interpreters,* 2:5.
3. "A Common Word Between Us and You," *Sophia: The Journal of Traditional Studies* 14, no. 2, 16–38.
4. Ibid. at 36.
5. Ibid. at 17.
6. Ibid.
7. Ibid.
8. Ibid. at 35.
9. See "Responses from Christian Leaders," The Official Web site of *A Common Word*, http://www.acommonword.com/index.php?lang=en&page=responses (accessed November 4, 2009).
10. While stressing commonalities, "A Common Word Between Us and You" does acknowledge that "Islam and Christianity are obviously different religions" and that "there is no minimizing some of their formal differences" ("A Common Word," 33).
11. I have adapted this paragraph and the next from the "Introduction" to my *Reclaiming the Great Tradition: Evangelicals, Catholics, and Orthodox in Dialogue*, 10. A similar image was used in that context, though of course for a significantly different purpose.
12. The Arabic phrase *kalimatin sawā'* in Q 3:64 is translated into English as a *word common* by Arberry and as an *agreement* by Pickthall; in Yusuf Ali it is *common terms*, in Hilali-Khan a *word that is just*, in Khalifa a *logical agreement*, in Shakir an *equitable proposition*, and in Sale *a just determination*.
13. "God forgives not that anything should be associated with Him... Whosoever associates anything with God, then he has indeed invented a tremendous sin" (Q 4:48; cf. Q 4:116).
14. "Common Word," 36.
15. A "mystery," according to Saint Paul, "which was kept secret for long ages but is now disclosed" (Rom. 16:25–26). It is possible that the Najrāni Christians were members of the Nestorian sect, and this might account for their apparent lack of resolve. The Nestorians believed that Jesus was a human being joined with the divine Son or Word of God in a unity of "function" or "honor," but that He was not the Son as such.

16. "The Nicene Creed," Orthodox Wiki, http://orthodoxwiki.org/Nicene-Constantinopolitan_Creed. "All things were made by Him, and without Him was not anything made that was made" (John 1:3).
17. Speaking in Orthodox dogmatic terms, Christ has a human *physis*, or "nature," which means that whatever can be truly predicated of us—with the exception of sin—can be truly predicated of Him; but He does not have a human *hypostasis* and is therefore not "a" human person. His humanity is "anhypostatic," though it is "enhypostasized" in the *Logos*, which means that the personal subject of all His thoughts, words, and actions is divine.
18. Rowan Williams, "A Common Word for the Common Good," *Sophia: The Journal of Traditional Studies* 14, no. 2, 44–45.
19. According to Saint Thomas Aquinas, these words are to be predicated of Christ's human nature alone (*Summa Theologica*, Pt. 3, Q. 20, Art. 1). From the Orthodox point of view, however, words can be spoken and deeds performed only by a person, not a nature, and like all of Christ's words this witness to the superiority of God the Father must therefore be attributed to the divine *persona* or *hypostasis* of the Son of God.
20. *Theological Orations*, 42:15, quoted by Kallistos Ware, *The Orthodox Way*, 32. Saint Gregory can be even more direct: "There is but one God, the Father, from whom are all things" (*Theological Orations*, 39:12).
21. Read in context, the phrase follows logically from a description of Christ's creative and salvific power, a power—the Apostle seems to suggest—which would be inexplicable were Jesus not divine: He "is the image of the invisible God, the firstborn of every creature: for by Him were all things created.... All things were created by Him, and for Him: and He is before all things, and by Him all things consist. And He is the head of the body, the church: who is the beginning, the firstborn from the dead; that in all things He might have preeminence. For in Him all the fullness of God was pleased to dwell" (Col. 1:15–19).
22. It is impossible not to hear the Eucharistic overtones of this word. Needless to say, the Mystical Supper, in which Christians assimilate the Real Presence of the Son of God by eating His body and drinking His blood, provides yet another reminder of the divergence between our traditions.
23. *On the Incarnation*, 54. According to Saint Irenaeus, "We were made men at the beginning, but at the end Gods" (*Against Heresies*, 3:19); Saint Clement of Alexandria puts it this way: "God's Word became man so that you might learn how to become God" (*Protrepticus*, 1:9); Saint Gregory the Theologian writes, "I may become God to the extent that God became man" (*Theological Orations*, 3.19); the boldest formulation of all comes from Saint Basil the Great: "Man is a creature under orders to become God" (reported by Saint Gregory the Theologian, *Oration* 43, "In Praise of Basil the Great").
24. *Athanasius: The Life of Anthony and the Letter to Marcellinus*, trans. Robert C. Gregg, 99.
25. According to Saint Maximus the Confessor, full participation in the divine nature comes about when "God suspends in created beings the operation of their natural energy by inexpressibly activating in them His divine energy." "Two Hundred Texts on Theology and the Incarnate Dispensation of the Son of God," in *The Philokalia*, ed. G. E. H. Palmer, Philip Sherrard, and Kallistos Ware, vol. 2, 2:123. Like other Fathers, Maximus understands deification to be a reversal of what happened when Christ became man. In that case an uncreated and eternal being assumed created and temporal attributes, whereas in *theosis* created and temporal beings are granted uncreated and eternal attributes. First articulated at the Council of Ephesus (A.D. 431), the Christological principle of *communicatio idiomatum*, that is, an "exchange of properties" between the divine and the human, also applies to the deified man.

26. Heirotheos Vlachos, *A Night in the Desert of the Holy Mountain*, trans. Effie Mavromichali, 31–32.
27. One recalls the expression of the Sufi Abūal-Qāsim al-Junayd: "The water takes on the color of its cup"; see William C. Chittick, *The Sufi Path of Knowledge: Ibn al-'Arabi's Metaphysics of Imagination*, 341.
28. Abū Ḥāmid al-Ghazālī, *The Revival of Religious Sciences*; see Reza Shah-Kazemi, "God as 'The Loving' in Islam," *Sophia: The Journal of Traditional Studies* 14, no. 2, 81.
29. See James S. Cutsinger, "*Hesychia*: An Orthodox Opening to Esoteric Ecumenism," in *Paths to the Heart: Sufism and the Christian East*, 250. Also available at http://www.cutsinger.net/pdf/hesychia_an_orthodox_opening.pdf, 19.
30. Saint Maximos the Confessor, "Two Hundred Texts on Theology and the Incarnate Dispensation of the Son of God", *The Philokalia* 2:114.
31. "The saints do not become God by essence nor one person with God, but they participate in the energies of God, that is to say, in his life, power, grace, and glory...The energies are truly *God Himself*–yet not God as He exists within Himself, in His inner life." (Ware, *The Orthodox Way*, 125–26).
32. Emphasis mine. The same principle is involved in Saint Gregory of Nyssa's signature teaching concerning *epektasis*, which is a perpetual "stretching forward" or unending progress toward a goal one never reaches. According to Gregory, participation in God entails continual growth in virtue, but man will never understand, let alone attain, God's transcendent perfection. The saint therefore writes, "Whoever pursues true virtue participates in nothing other than God...since this good has no limit, the participant's desire itself necessarily has no stopping place but stretches out with the limitless. It is therefore undoubtedly impossible to attain perfection." (*Gregory of Nyssa: The Life of Moses*, trans. Abraham J. Malherbe and Everett Ferguson, 31 [Sections 7–8]).
33. The Qur'ānic "Be!," (Q 3:47, 19:35), and the Biblical fiats (Gen. 1:3, 6, 14), like all imperatives, do not have tense. In the *Anaphora* of the Divine Liturgy, the trans-temporal reality of the Second Coming is acknowledged when the priest offers thanks to the Father, "who didst bring us from non-existence into being, and when we had fallen away didst raise us up again, and didst not cease to do all things until thou *hadst* brought us back to heaven, and *hadst* endowed us with thy kingdom *which is to come*."
34. I am thinking, for example, of Ibn al-'Arabī's precision with regard to the divine infinitude: "Do not declare [God] nondelimited and thus delimited by being distinguished from delimitation! For if He is distinguished, then He is delimited by His nondelimitation. And if He is delimited by His nondelimitation, then He is not He." (Chittick, *The Sufi Path of Knowledge*, 112). For Saint Gregory the Theologian and other Greek-speaking Fathers, divine unity is a function of *henōsis*, which is the "union" or "unification" among the three Persons of the Trinity, and not merely *hen*, which is the oneness of an arithmetical "unit". The Sufi doctrine of the "unity of being" (*waḥdat al-wujūd*) is clearly pertinent here.
35. James S. Cutsinger, trans., *The Triads*, 3, 1, 31; for the Greek text, see the critical edition: *Grégoire Palamas: Défense des saints hésychastes*, ed. Jean Meyendorff, 2:617.
36. Saint Anselm defines God as "that than which nothing greater can be conceived" (*Proslogion*, 2).
37. One is reminded of the *ḥadīth*: "The Sufi is not created" (*al-Ṣūfī lam yukhlaq*).
38. There is, admittedly, a terminological puzzle here. Beginning with Saint Athanasius, Greek Patristic tradition observed a subtle distinction between *agenēton* (with one *n*) and *agennēton* (with two *n*'s), the former being taken to mean "uncreated" and the latter "unbegotten"; according to this usage, employed by Athanasius in his refutation of the Arians, only God the Father is *agennēton*, while the "only-begotten" (John 1:18)

Son of God is *agenēton*, which is more or less the equivalent of *ou poiēthenta* ("not created") in the Nicene Creed. For Gregory, however, *agenēton* must mean something more, something perhaps closer to *agennēton*, since he sets it in contrast to his own preferred term for "uncreated", *aktiston*.

39. Of course the noun *archē* can also be translated as "rule", and the adjective *anarchos* could therefore be taken to mean only (!) that the deified are "a law to themselves." But given the ontological trajectory suggested by other words in this passage, it seems much more logical to construe this key term in a metaphysical, rather than an ethical or political, sense—though it is difficult to know quite how to put this sense into one English word; "anarchical," to say nothing of "unprincipled," will clearly not do! Since what *has* no principle must in some sense *be* its own principle, possessing the divine property of aseity, "principial" seems the least inadequate solution.
40. John Meyendorff, the editor and translator of the critical French edition of *The Triads*, as well as the editor of an English translation of the work, himself notes—though with surprising reserve—that Saint Gregory has here expressed "a bold thought: The deified saints...are thus to be described by the apophatic adjectives appropriate to the *divine* transcendence" (*Gregory Palamas: The Triad*s 144 [n. 116]). Elsewhere Meyendorff emphasizes, as have I in the second part of this paper, that "the Father is the 'cause' (*aitia*) and the 'principle' (*archē*) of the divine nature that is in the Son and the Spirit" (*Byzantine Theology: Historical Trends and Doctrinal Themes*, 183). Putting two and two together, we are obliged to reason, however strange it may sound, that in "becoming" *anarchos* the deified man "attains" a station that in some mysterious sense is beyond even that of the Second and Third Persons of the Trinity.
41. *Chandogya Upanishad*, 6.8.7.

11

Theological Parallels and Metaphysical Meeting Points: Christ and the Word in Christianity and Islam

Maria M. Dakake

Truly the likeness of Jesus in the sight of God is as the likeness of Adam.

Qur'ān 3:59

Christianity and Islam have many common and substantial elements, from shared prophets and sacred persons to similar ethical concerns. These are embedded, however, in separate theological and ritual schemes, not to mention unique conceptions of sacred history, such that they remain two parallel religious worlds whose beliefs can never be fully reconciled with the other when viewed from within these parameters. At the same time, much understanding and good can come from a faithful yet respectful appreciation of religious systems parallel to one's own; and the rich scriptures and traditions of both Christianity and Islam offer a number of openings onto a metaphysical vision of reality that point beyond their normative theological boundaries. As such, these openings can sometimes provide an intellectual or spiritual place wherein the two traditions can meet in profound and unexpected ways. Joseph Lumbard from the Muslim perspective and James Cutsinger from the Christian perspective attempt to find common ground between Christianity and Islam by examining the conception of Christ in the two religions. However they each seek to do so in different ways by adopting one of the two approaches just mentioned. Lumbard from the Muslim side sees the possibility of enhanced interfaith understanding between Christianity and Islam on the basis of analogous theological principles relating to the nature of Christ as the "Word," Cutsinger from the Christian side argues forcefully that following theological doctrines about Christ to their ultimate conclusions leads Christians and Muslims into inevitable and irreducible conflict. As a result, common ground between the two traditions can only be found on the metaphysical, rather than the narrowly theological, plane.

One of the examples Cutsinger gives from the Christian side of a theological loggerhead that Christians cannot overcome in their dialogue with Muslims concerns the Qur'ānic statement quoted above: "Truly the likeness of Jesus in the sight of God is as the likeness of Adam" (Q 3:59). In this passage, Jesus' extraordinary birth is acknowledged, but the concomitant Christian doctrines of Christ's divinity and "sonship" are apparently denied by noting that, in coming into existence without ordinary human parentage, Christ was no different from Adam—the father of us all, according to both religious traditions. In what follows, I examine both protagonists' approaches to Christian-Muslim dialogue on the nature of Christ, but also seek to reframe the discussion by examining the rich possibilities that open up for interfaith and spiritual understanding when we read the Christian and Muslim stories of Adam and Jesus in light of one another.

Lumbard asserts that Muslims can better understand Christian Christology, with its apparent paradox of Christ as both eternal with the Father and incarnated in time, by seeking to understand it as analogous to Islamic discussions of the eternity or createdness of the Qur'ān.[1] Such an approach is important, especially since Christ and the Qur'ān represent the "Word of God" for Christians and Muslims, respectively. For Christians and Muslims, then, the Word of God, variously understood, has both an eternal reality and a temporal manifestation. Christ is both the eternal second person of the Trinity for Christians, and an historical person born in time; the Qur'ān, as God's Word, is both coeternal with God, and historically revealed in the seventh century CE for Muslims.

The acknowledgement of this paradox in the religion of both the self and the other represents an important watershed in interfaith understanding. It offers each religious tradition a way of seeing the other as both absolute and eternal for its adherents, but also relative insofar as it acquires some of its meaning through its particular historical context, which in turn shapes the conception of history itself for its followers. In other words, it is easier to take seriously the paradox of the eternal and the temporal in someone else's religion, once one is honest about recognizing the same paradox in one's own. From the Muslim viewpoint it is rightly suggested that an awareness of the parallel nature of these paradoxes can help Muslims better understand and appreciate Christian doctrines about Christ.

At the same time, such an awareness might also foster greater understanding among Christians about how Muslims approach their own sacred text. In academic interfaith settings, well-meaning Christian scholars often ask why Muslims are so reluctant to engage in literary and historical criticism of the Qur'ān. What they do not understand is that the essential divinity, and hence infallibility, of the text is a matter of fundamental doctrine for Muslims, despite its inlibration or incarnation in physical sound at a particular moment in history. Seeing this doctrine as parallel to their own belief in the essential divinity and eternity of Christ, despite their belief in his having taken a temporally incarnate form, should help Christians more fully appreciate Muslim views and doctrines about the Qur'ān.

However, the Muslim viewpoint is concerned with more than just the mutual recognition of the presence of theological paradox in both traditions, so Lumbard is interested in finding real theological common ground between them. He argues that a deeper reflection upon the relationship between God and Christ and between God and the "Word" in both the Gospel and the Qur'ān reveals the possibility of a far greater agreement between the two religions on this issue than is usually assumed. He notes that in Islamic theology, the Word of God is an attribute of the Divine Essence, and so coeternal with God and uncreated, but always subordinate to the "Ultimate Divine Principle."[2]

This presents a clear parallel with Cutsinger's discussion on the Christian side of the Christic incarnation as both "of the same Essence" as God the Father, and so coeternal with Him, but also secondary to Him (at least in Eastern Orthodox formulation) in that he is still "begotten of" the Father.[3] Since, in Islam, God creates through the word ("Be!"),[4] and Jesus is identified in the Qur'ān as a "word from Him [God]," "His word," and "the Word of Truth,"[5] Lumbard states, from the Muslim viewpoint, that "the Qur'ān therefore indicates that Jesus . . . in some way participates directly in this Divine Command," that is, in the divine creative process.[6] According to this interpretation, the Qur'ānic conception of Christ would seem to be very much in line with the traditional Christian doctrine that sees the world as brought into existence by God but *through* Christ as "Word."

Here it seems we have a real *theological* parallel that can be influential in increasing mutual understanding of the other's doctrinal positions, or even viewing them as somewhat consistent with one another. However, it should be noted that the interpretation Lumbard offers from the Moslem viewpoint relies on a particular interpretation of the Qur'ānic description of Christ as "Word," one that sees this "Word" as metaphysically identical to the "word" through which God brings creation into existence. This interpretation is not explicit in the Qur'ānic text or even in its more esoteric commentaries.

Traditional Islamic theology does not make anything—especially any human being—a "partner" with God in creation. As a Muslim, Lumbard, of course, does not use this term, or mean his statement to be understood in this way, but this is how a Christian, anxious for interfaith accord, might hear it. It should thus be reiterated that the Qur'ān is quite clear that God creates alone. The connection of the divine creative fiat with the "Word of God" is simply not made in Islam, as it is so clearly and compellingly made in John 1. The Qur'ān, too, is the "Word" of God, but Muslims do not connect this notion of the "Word of God" to the "word" through which He speaks things into creation; Muslims do not speak of things being created *through* the Qur'ān, for example.

A final word of caution one might make with regard to this discussion concerns the fact that if Christ is considered to be God's "word" in the Qur'ān, the Gospel he brings is also considered to be the "word of God," just as both Muḥammad and the Qur'ān are referred to as "reminders" in the Qur'ān and in Islamic piety.[7] There is no doubt that for Christians, there is hierarchy between Christ, as the Word of God, and the Gospel, which is the word of God insofar as it conveys the Word to mankind, just as there is for Muslims a hierarchy between the Qur'ān as the "Reminder to the Worlds,"[8] and Muḥammad as the "reminder" insofar as he brings the Reminder to humanity. Nonetheless, the identification of Jesus as the "word of God" in the Qur'ān may have more to do with the Qur'ānic assimilation of message and messenger than with a connection between Jesus and the divine creative fiat.

All of the above caveats and cautionary notes notwithstanding, however, Lumbard's larger point from the Muslim side about the unique Qur'ānic description of Jesus among the Islamic prophets, and its approximation of certain Christian Christological doctrines, is well taken. It is quite true that if any Qur'ānic figure comes closest to manifesting something of the divine creative power, it is undoubtedly Jesus. This can be seen most strikingly in Qur'ān 3:49 and 5:110 where, in an unmistakable parallel to the process by which God is said to create human beings, Christ makes a bird out of clay and breathes (*nafakha*) into it its spirit, bringing it to life. In the same passage he is said to have raised the dead.[9] No other Prophet is accorded such extraordinary existentiating capabilities in the Qur'ān—capabilities that clearly echo those of God Himself. The Qur'ān makes clear that in performing these extraordinary acts, Jesus is merely acting as the instrument of the divine creative power; but even so, even as a mere instrument of the divine existentiating force, Jesus is absolutely unique among the Islamic prophets in this regard, and this uniqueness does provide an opening to consider how Muslims might understand Christian Christology.

But if Jesus is granted such exceptional capabilities according to the Qur'ān, then what does the Qur'ānic statement that his likeness "is as the likeness of Adam" mean? Is it meant simply to preclude any belief in Jesus' divinity and downplay the spiritual significance of his extraordinary actions and powers by asserting that he is essentially no different from humanity at large, which Adam clearly represents? In context, this would indeed seem to be the most reasonable and straightforward way to interpret the Qur'ānic statement. But what if we read it the other way around: If the likeness of Jesus is as the likeness of Adam, what does it mean to say that the likeness of Adam—who stands for us all—is the likeness of Jesus? If the Qur'ānic comparison "humanizes" Jesus, it also profoundly ennobles Adam, and by extension, all those who share in the human state. Even if we can never participate in the state of prophecy that Jesus shares with Muḥammad and the other prophets, the comparison says much about the spiritual potential and power that lies within all human beings. This notion of the original and essential nobility of human beings is fully manifest in the Qur'ānic story of the creation of Adam. However, such an interpretation might seem initially less salient in the context of Christianity, with its emphasis on the fallen state of humanity and its need for transformative grace. But let us examine Cutsinger's arguments from the Christian side and then revisit the implications of this Qur'ānic comparison for both religions once again.

Cutsinger's provocative piece presents a clear, unapologetic, and creative presentation of important Christian theological differences with Islam. I appreciate the honesty and religious commitment he demonstrates here, even when it presents a strong theological challenge to his Muslim interlocutors. When you hit upon seemingly irreducible obstacles in interfaith dialogue, then you know you are really getting somewhere. Cutsinger notes that the Christian participants in the "Common Word" initiative have answered the Qur'ānic call on which the initiative is based, that is, to try to come to a "common word" or agreement that "there is no god but God."[10] As a representative of the Christian respondents to this call, and having responded in good faith, Cutsinger issues a call of his own: If Christians can try to understand their own religious doctrine in light of "there is no god but God," is it possible for Muslims to understand "there is no god but God" in light of the central Christian belief that "God became man that man might become God."[11] Theologically, of course, any Muslim would have to say "no" to this invitation, and rather categorically at that. At the most basic level, whatever we might say of the relationship between God and man, God does not "become." He is as He was.

So Muslims cannot faithfully respond to Cutsinger's challenge at the level at which he initially poses it. However, mystically, and perhaps even metaphysically, there is the possibility of assimilating this idea to some important Islamic notions concerning the relationship between God and man. Can we accept, first of all, that "God became man"? Perhaps, in a way. A number of Islamic mystical thinkers asserted that all realities preexist their earthly creation—not in themselves, but as realities existing in the knowledge of God.[12] These creations come to exist *in concreto* when God "speaks" these aspects of His knowledge into creation. Insofar as God's knowledge is eternal and unchanging, and insofar as His knowledge is of His Essence, all human beings—indeed all creatures—exist as elements of God's Essence—that is, of His knowledge. When we are created, one can say, some element of God's Essence comes to be *representatively* manifest in us. The important thing here, however, is that this process does not signify any real change or becoming in God Himself—just as I can have an idea in my mind and then write it down, without its representative existentiation in written form in any way diminishing its presence in my mind.

What about man becoming God, or theosis? Again, this is completely unacceptable from the Islamic theological perspective. Nonetheless, Muslim mystics have long approximated this in their discussions of nonduality, arguing that a true understanding of *tawḥīd* (God's oneness) means a recognition that nothing is other than God. "God was and there was nothing with Him," as the Prophet Muḥammad declares in a well-known *ḥadīth*; and the Sufis like to add, "and He is now as He was." So while the mystical goal is not to "become God," the ultimate purpose of all mystical seeking is to come to the metaphysical realization that ultimately nothing exists that is other than God—"all things are perishing, save His Face."[13] The goal is not to become God, but to realize that, to the extent that we "are," we are nothing but an aspect of God's being; all else, all illusion of our independent existence separate from God, is ever-perishing, and thus pure nothingness.

But what if we looked at this idea from the point of view of mysticism and the practice of spiritual virtue by reflecting upon the Gospel account of Christ's suffering and death. Muslims do not accept this account scripturally, of course—but for a moment let us put aside sectarian questions about the factual accuracy of the story, and consider instead what this story means to Christians. In Christian understanding, it is precisely Christ's suffering and death that makes salvation—and indeed theosis—possible for all mankind. How did Christ open this door to theosis and salvation, according to Christian theology? He did so by completely surrendering his will to God's will (as his prayer in the Garden of Gethsemane makes clear), by emptying himself of his own desires and offering up his very life to God. By becoming "nothing," in the earthly sense, he demonstrated that the way to "becoming God" was through completely emptying oneself of oneself, and filling oneself with God. This is the teaching of Islamic mysticism, too, that one only achieves union with God through a complete emptying of the self—by "dying before you die so that you don't die when you die,"[14] as another famous *ḥadīth* of the Prophet says. Dying, in other words, that you might truly live. This brief and simple reflection would seem to prove the accuracy and usefulness of Cutsinger's larger methodological point in this paper: Namely, that where the door of theology shuts on certain questions of interreligious dialogue, those of metaphysics and mysticism might yet open.

Within his larger discussion of the theological issues that divide Muslims and Christians, seemingly irreparably, Cutsinger mentions from the Christian side the Qur'ānic comparison of Jesus and Adam, discussed above, as a Qur'ānic statement and Muslim theological belief that cannot be accepted by Christians. He notes that the implications of such a comparison are expressly rejected by the Nicene Creed's identification of Jesus as the begotten (and therefore, unlike Adam and all other human beings, uncreated) son of God.[15] But I would like to revisit the relationship between Adam and Jesus as articulated in the Qur'ān, for, as I noted above, I think it is an important and compelling one for the larger questions at hand: the relationship between God and man, creation and "word," prophecy and theosis. Adam represents an important focus for all of these issues, in part because he represents for both traditions a kind of "incarnation"—not an incarnation of God (which Muslims reject outright and which Christians would limit to Christ), but an incarnation of His *spirit*, which, according to both traditions was breathed (*nafakha*) into the clay and carnal form of Adam.[16] While neither Muslims nor Christians tend to speak of Adam in this way, for the reasons mentioned above, let us consider, for a moment, what this might mean.

In Islam, God "speaks" all things into creation with the command "Be!" But Adam is different, for although he, like all creatures, is subject to the existentiating command "Be!," he is also said to be formed and fashioned by the "two hands" of God,[17] and animated directly by His spirit. Islamic interpretative tradition further asserts that while this is a distinction that is explicitly attributed to Adam and Jesus in the Qur'ān, all human beings share in the nobility of having been formed by God's "two hands" and blown into of "His Spirit" by virtue of our descent from Adam.[18] Adam represents mankind in general—and so we are all incarnate divine spirit, in a way. This distinction gives human beings, through Adam, a cosmological nobility that places them above all other creatures—so much so, according to the Qur'ān, that God commanded the angels to bow down before Adam,[19] a sign of veneration otherwise offered to God alone.[20] The Qur'ān does not say explicitly that Adam was created in God's likeness (as it does in Genesis), but there is a well-known, if controversial, *ḥadīth* to that effect (*khalaqa'llāhu Ādama 'alā ṣūratihi*: "God created Adam upon His form") and the Qur'ān asserts that God taught Adam the names of all things,[21] thereby granting him knowledge otherwise known only to God. Adam before the fall, then, can be considered a perfect theophany, or as perfect a theophany as can be imagined within the context of Islamic theology. It is true that the Islamic Adam, like the Judeo-Christian one, "falls"; but he immediately and unreservedly repents.[22] Though he is exiled, he receives a divine promise that God will send him guidance, and that guidance will lead him back.[23] As children of Adam we all share in his nobility, in his weakness and exile, but also in the divine promise that we will be given, not the grace to transform our fallen human nature (as one has it in the Christian formulation) but the guidance that can lead us back home. Adam represents both our original nobility and the guidance we are promised so that we may realize it once more. It is not theosis through the existentially transformative power of grace that is Islamic humanity's greatest hope, it is the return to our original theophany through the epistemologically restorative power of prophetic guidance.

If the Qur'ān says that Jesus is like Adam, it is perhaps because Jesus, as one of the greatest of the Islamic prophets, represents a particularly perfect human form—one who, unique among all the other Islamic prophets, is granted the nearly divine power of bringing clay figures to life with his breath and raising the dead. While the theophanic nature of humanity is said to be visible in all the prophets, as representatives of the "perfect man" or "Adam before the fall," it is particularly luminous and stunning in Jesus. If Jesus is not the path to theosis in Islam—as indeed nothing could be—the Qur'ānic Jesus nevertheless presents an exceptionally clear window onto our original, and potential, theophanic character, while also being one of the major bearers of saving, prophetic guidance.

The connection between Adam and Jesus in the Qur'ān is also something that is worth considering for Christians, I think, because some connection (albeit a dialectical one) also exists between the two in Christian theology. Adam does not have prophetic nobility in Christianity; and while Adam's theophanic nature and original distinction is made clear enough in Genesis 1:26, his primary significance in Christianity is as the portal through which sin and death enter the world.[24] Christ, on the other hand, is the means through which this sin and death is overcome.

Jesus would thus seem to be the anti-Adam, in that while Adam caused man to descend from his paradisal state, Jesus offers the way of return thereto. However one interesting New Testament passage does not speak of Jesus as the anti-Adam, but as the "last Adam." This formulation makes Jesus and Adam spiritual opposites, but at the same time suggests that they share a common "Adamic" nature:

> Thus it is written, "The first man, Adam, became a living being"; the last Adam became a life-giving spirit. But it is not the spiritual that is first, but the physical, and then the spiritual. The first man was from the earth, a man of dust; the second man is from heaven. As was the man of dust, so are those who are of dust; and as is the man of heaven, so are those who are of heaven. Just as we have borne the image of the man of dust, we will also bear the image of the man of heaven.[25]

Not only do Adam and Christ share the human state (they are both "Adam"), but it seems that all human beings share in the nature of both Adam and Christ. Adam represents the physical side of man, his dust, his fallen state, his descent from God and his exile; while Christ represents what is heavenly in man, the ability to give life, not just to receive it. The passage thus seems to indicate that men bear within themselves both the cause of their own exile and their path of return, through their metaphysical and mysterious connection to both Adam and Christ. In Christianity, men fall (or are born) into sin and are saved by grace through the existentially transformative, dichotomous realities of Adam and Christ, respectively. But what is most striking in the above passage is the implication that these two dichotomous beings, Adam and Christ, "the man of dust" and "the man of heaven" are also "images" that all human beings, at least potentially, bear within themselves. If Adam represents what all human beings are, Christ represents what all human beings might become through grace.

In Islam the dichotomy is not between a state of sin and a state of grace, but between the confusion generated by spiritual or moral error and the clarity of guidance after repentance; it is not about rebirth, but about remembering; not about transforming, but about coming home. It is a story fully embedded in the nature and account of Adam alone, independent of the other prophets. For Muslims, the promise of guidance and theophanic restoration made to Adam, and so to us all, was historically renewed with the coming of each prophet, but has one of its most brilliant demonstrations in the miraculous power of the prophet Jesus.

There are important and fundamental differences between these Christian and Muslim conceptions of human nature and the process of human salvation, and these differences should not be diminished or overlooked in any way, as they form the core understanding, in each tradition, of meaningful human life. But the relationship between Adam and Christ, as suggested both in the Qur'ān and in the New Testament in very different ways, may provide us a metaphysical, if not a theological, door to a better understanding of theophany and incarnation, prophecy and theosis, as they relate to the human spiritual vocation we all share. We can all agree on the exceptional luminosity that the figure of Jesus brings to the human or Adamic state, and that he provides a model for our own spiritual becoming. For Christians, Jesus is himself divine, and offers through his sacrifice and grace the only path to divinity, or theosis, for humanity. For Muslims, Jesus, like all prophets, is an example of the "perfect man," the Adamic reality in its prefallen state. He along with all the prophets represents our path of return to this original perfection of the Adamic reality in its prefallen state—not through grace, but through the guidance they bring and the example they offer. The differences between these two conceptions lie on the theological plane and cannot be reconciled on that level. But to the extent that they both call us to, and give us hope of attaining, what is "God-like" in ourselves, they point to our common moral vocation, to an analogous, if not identical, metaphysical vision of our theophanic nature, and to a shared human nobility that transcends religious difference.

Notes

1. Joseph Lumbard, chapter 9, this volume, 96–97.
2. Ibid., 102.
3. James Cutsinger, chapter 10, this volume, 115–16.
4. Qur'ān 2:117; 3:47; 6:73; 16:40; 19:36; 36:82; 40:68.
5. Qur'ān 3:45: "O Mary, truly God gives thee glad tidings of a Word from Him, whose name is Christ Jesus son of Mary..."; and Qur'ān 4:171: "Verily the Messiah, Jesus son of Mary, was only a messenger of God, and His Word, that He committed unto Mary..."; and 19:34 "That is Jesus, son of Mary—the Word of Truth, which they doubt." See also 3:39 where John (the Baptist) is said to confirm "a word from God," meaning Jesus.
6. Joseph Lumbard, chapter 9, this volume, 100.
7. The Qur'ān and other divine scriptures are referred to as "reminders" throughout the Qur'ān, and the Prophet Muḥammad himself is referred to as a reminder in 88:21, e.g. In Islamic piety, *dhikr Allāh* is one of the many names of the Prophet Muḥammad.
8. Qur'ān 6:90; 12:104.
9. Qur'ān 3:49; 5:110.
10. Qur'ān 3:64.
11. Cutsinger, chapter 10, this volume, 118–19.
12. There are many examples of this concept in Islamic mystical thought, and the idea is particularly pronounced in the work of Ibn al-'Arabī, a twelfth century Andalusian mystic. For example, see William Chittick, *The Self-Disclosure of God*, pp. 21, 29–30 for citations from Ibn al-'Arabī's writing on this subject and discussion thereof.
13. Qur'ān 28:88.
14. This *ḥadīth* is commonly attributed to the Prophet Muḥammad in Sufi treatises and other works, and is usually cited without a supporting chain of transmission. One of the most influential discussion of this *ḥadīth* can be found in Jalāl al-Dīn Rūmī, *Masnavi-i ma`navi*, Book IV: 2270–75.
15. Cutsinger, chapter 10, this volume, 115.
16. Qur'ān 15:29; 32:9; 38:72; Genesis 2:7.
17. Qur'ān 38:75.
18. See, e.g., the commentary of Fakhr al-Din al-Rāzī in *al-Tafsīr al-kabīr* on 4:1, which speaks of humanity as being created from a single soul.
19. Qur'ān 2:34; 7:11; 15:29; 17:61; 18:50.
20. For example, Qur'ān 41:37 instructs people not to bow down to celestial bodies, but only to "God Who created them."
21. Qur'ān 2:31.
22. Qur'ān 7:23.
23. Qur'ān 2:37–38.
24. Romans 5:14; 1 Corinthians 15:22.
25. 1 Corinthians 15:45–49.

Part II

Applications

A. Environment and Climate Change

12

Islamic Environmental Economics and the Three Dimensions of Islam: "A Common Word" on the Environment as Neighbor

Waleed El-Ansary

The island of Misali, part of the Zanzibar archipelago in the Indian Ocean, is a wonderful example of the remarkable role that religious values can play in confronting the environmental crisis in the Islamic world.[1] The coral reef surrounding this largely uninhabited island is home to a rich variety of fish and turtles, providing direct livelihood to people in neighboring Pemba, which is over 95 percent Muslim. A rising human population and depleting fish stocks, however, led fishermen to adopt desperate and unsustainable fishing methods to maintain their catch, including dynamite fishing and the use of guns. Although these destructive methods were damaging the corals and harming species that lived there, government bans had practically no impact. Local religious leaders were able to restore sustainable fishing and a rich underwater life to the island, however, by highlighting Islamic teachings about conservation. One local fisherman aptly summarized why the religious message succeeded, whereas government decrees had failed. "It is easy to ignore the government," he said, "but no one can break God's law."[2] The Care International project, which started in 2001, was apparently the first time such a religion-based environmental strategy was employed in Tanzania.

Similar lessons apply to Nigeria in annual tree-planting campaigns that are organized mostly by the government in order to check desert encroachment:

> [T]rees planted by the government through these campaigns die off almost immediately after the campaigns. In contrast, environmentalists have carried out tree planting projects using the Islamic notion of tenderness toward the natural environment and the injunction encouraging planting of trees. The communities involved make good their commitments to volunteer to take care of the trees. Realizing the impact of such Islamic environmental success stories, more environmentalists have become interested in exploring Islamic input in solving specific ecological problems of the region.[3]

Given the critical role of religious scholars and preachers in protecting the environment in the Islamic world, Shaykh Ali Goma'a, the Grand Mufti of Egypt, has committed Egypt's Dār al-Iftā' to become carbon-neutral by the end of 2010;[4] this commitment is done in the context of a Muslim Seven Year action plan that includes Medina, the second holiest city in the Islamic world also known as "the City of the Prophet," becoming a model "green" city.[5] Since millions of pilgrims visit the city each year for in conjunction with the *ḥajj* (the annual pilgrimage to Mecca) and *'umrah* (a pilgrimage to Mecca that can be undertaken at any time), this sends an extremely powerful signal to Muslims throughout the world.[6]

Religious ethics is an essential part of any solution to the environmental crisis from this perspective. Indeed, most of the people in the world may only heed religion in this regard. But "religious ethics cannot cohabit with a view of the order of nature that radically denies the very premises of religion and that claims for itself a monopoly of the knowledge of the order of nature, at least any knowledge that is significant and is accepted by society as 'science.'"[7]

To employ the categories of Islamic thought, *al-'ilm* or knowledge must accompany *al-'amal* or action. Therefore, the balance of this paper is structured according to the famous *Ḥadīth* of Gabriel that has been used as a model for discussing the essentials of Islam for over 1,000 years. It divides Islam into three dimensions: submission or "right action" (*islām*), faith or "right understanding" (*īmān*), and virtue or "right intention" (*iḥsān*), corresponding to the legal/ethical, intellectual, and esoteric dimensions of an integral tradition to fully realize love of God and love of neighbor, which includes the natural environment.[8] As we shall see, all three are necessary for socioeconomic and environmental equilibrium from an Islamic perspective.

The Need for a New Approach

Current environmental economic paradigms are generally inconsistent with at least two and sometimes all three of the above dimensions, leading to environmental disequilibrium from an Islamic point of view. For example, conventional or neoclassical economic theory, which dominates much of the discourse in environmental or resource economics, is premised upon certain utilitarian and efficiency-based ideas. These essentially reduce values to tastes and needs to wants, excluding a hierarchy of spiritual and other needs as we shall see. This approach recognizes *ex ante* several of its technical shortcomings when faced with issues like externalities, or costs to the public not captured in standard analysis, which contribute to problems like "mis-pricing" pollution (and so are at the heart of many standard environmental policy instruments, such as carbon taxes or the whole concept of tradable emissions permits).[9]

Nevertheless, neoclassical economic theory *claims* to accommodate any set of instrumentally rational, or internally consistent, values or tastes, including choices that "may themselves involve truth, justice, or beauty, just as easily as the consumption of goods and services."[10] In fact, there is a spectrum of applications of neoclassical theory in environmental economics, ranging from strongly anthropocentric so-called frontier economics, which treats nature as an infinite supply of physical resources and an infinite sink for the by-products of consumption,[11] to environmental protection approaches upon which the American environmental regulatory system of point source permitting or regulating pollution is traditionally based, to resource management based on integrating social and other factors into environmental policy.[12] Although the last represents neoclassical environmental economics at its best, it is still unable to accommodate Islamic environmental values as we shall see. One hidden problem is neoclassical theory's lasting affinity for psychological hedonism, or the "pleasure-pain calculus" of English philosopher Jeremy Bentham as determinative of right and wrong.[13] And deep ecology, which treats man as equal but not superior in importance to other species in the ecosphere and so at the opposite end of the spectrum to frontier economics, is often inconsistent with the intellectual foundation of religious ethical teachings concerning the environment, including the centrality of the human state as bridge between Heaven and earth.[14]

The neoclassical claim to accommodate these and any other internally consistent values and tastes implies that any other approach to environmental economics is a special case of conventional theory at best, making any real alternative logically impossible. Therefore, the first step in demonstrating the need for a new approach from an Islamic perspective is to test the neoclassical claims and assumptions against Islamic legal principles. Abū Ḥāmid al-Ghazālī (1058-1111 CE), the renowned twelfth century Muslim jurist and theologian with tremendous knowledge of all three dimensions of Islam, explicitly articulated the various objectives of Islamic law (*maqāṣid al-Sharī'ah*) in terms of a hierarchy of spiritual and other needs (*maṣāliḥ*).[15] The intent of each Divine ruling according to this approach is the protection of one or more of these interests, and the ultimate purpose of the Divine Law is the universal common good or welfare of all of God's creation (*maṣāliḥ al-khalqī kāffatan*).[16] This prohibits excluding any species or generation from consideration and requires including both "material" and "non-material" dimensions of welfare. The intimate connection between the "right" and the "good" in this view is indicated by the fact that *maṣāliḥ* (sing. *maṣlaḥah*) is derived from the root word *ṣalaḥa*, which means that something has become "pure, correct, and right."[17]

Al-Ghazālī and other jurists classified *maṣāliḥ* for human society into three levels. The first concerns fundamental necessities (*ḍarūriyyāt*), which include the preservation of religion (*dīn*), life (*nafs*), posterity (*nasl*), intelligence (*'aql*), and property (*māl*).[18] Since the disregard of any of these results in disruption and chaos, no valid rule of law can violate any of them. Next are complementary needs (*ḥājiyyāt*), which if unfulfilled, lead to real hardship and distress but not the ruin of the community. Finally, supplementary benefits (*taḥsīniyyāt*) involve the beautification of life and refinement and perfection of ethics.[19] Based on this hierarchy, priority is given to higher level needs if there is a conflict with lower level needs or wants. Jurists have therefore formulated general balancing principles (*qawā'id al-fiqhīya*) to serve as guidelines in solving particular legal problems involving trade-offs between benefits (*maṣāliḥ*) and detriments (*mafāsid*). Such principles inform the science of establishing priorities (*'ilm al-awlawīyāt*) as well as the science of measuring these benefits and detriments (*'ilm al-muwāzanāt*). Important principles that flow from this hierarchy include: "[t]he averting of harm from the poor takes priority over the averting of harm from the wealthy," "[t]here shall be no damage and no infliction of damage," and "[t]he averting of harm takes precedence over the acquisition of benefits."[20] Of course, such general principles need qualification depending on the particular context, but they have major environmental implications and are keys for understanding substantive rulings and legal instruments in Islamic environmental law.

Although this view may appear analogous to the standard cost-benefit analysis, it is very different, for neoclassical theory even denies the distinction between needs and wants. Indeed, it "reduces all wants to one general abstract want called 'utility.' In line with this reduction, one need not say 'these people need more shoes': instead, 'these people need more utility' should suffice."[21] (And although certain other forms of utilitarianism do not necessarily make the same reduction, they still subordinate truth to utility, thereby excluding spiritual needs.[22]) Yet, common sense suggests that, "[h]e who does not have enough to eat cannot satisfy his hunger by wearing more shirts."[23] The conventional economic approach assuming a single use value or mono-utility approach therefore implicitly attributes "to man 'faculties which he actually does not possess,' unless we could drink paper, eat leisure, and wear steam engines."[24] From an Islamic perspective, this misleading notion involves the *post hoc, ergo propter hoc* fallacy.[25] The environmental implications are serious, since this rationalizes the sacrifice of future generations' needs as well as the rest of creation's rights for our generation's wants. Without any qualitative distinction between current wants and future needs, it is easy to overstate current benefits and understate future costs, failing to properly account for negative externalities between generations. The same applies *mutatis mutandis* within generations given the principle that "averting of harm from the poor takes priority over the averting of harm from the wealthy."

But the neoclassical claim to moral neutrality is also incorrect for another reason. Namely, the theory assumes that the amount of money one would be willing to pay to prevent pollution is equal to the amount of money one would be willing to *accept* to allow it. This assumption has been the subject of considerable interest and empirical inquiry (because of practical policy implications in conjunction with measuring nonmonetary or market-determined damages in the environmental setting), with the result that there is a significant body of evidence disproving the assumption.[26] To help illustrate this point, imagine that we have the authority to prevent pollution, and someone is trying to bribe us to permit it. Although we may be unwilling to accept any amount of money to permit what we would consider an evil act for ethical reasons, we may also have a limit, as a result of personal resource constraints, on how much we would be willing to pay to stop the same event that others have the ability to prevent. The two situations are different in the sense that the former is an act in which we participate to accomplish an evil, whereas the latter is an event others perform that perhaps we cannot afford to stop. Neutrality requires that willingness to accept (WTA) may differ from willingness to pay (WTP), along with the fact that WTP can vary.[27] But neoclassical theory equates the two, failing the first criterion.[28] This excludes the ethical values of one who cannot be bought at any price, a characteristic Benthamites would refuse, although it can accommodate the preferences of a miser or (psychological) hedonist. But this is precisely the kind of behavior of which our initial examples from the Islamic world provide evidence. While many ordinary people in Islamic countries may ignore or violate secular environmental law with impunity, once "God's law" is clarified they comply because they consider it an absolute necessity.

Conventional cost-benefit analysis is even more problematic when we take risk and uncertainty into account. The former involves knowledge of the probabilities of different outcomes and states of nature, whereas the latter does not. For example, because the environment is a dynamic, open system, we have no way of knowing the full extent of the damaging effects of pollution, meaning we are in a state of uncertainty as to where we are relative to ecological catastrophe. The prospects of irreversible or serious harm provide a strong justification for adopting what appears as a precautionary principle of Islamic law that the averting of harm "takes precedence over the acquisition of benefits."[29] Common sense similarly suggests that we proceed with caution and err on the side of safety.

But neoclassical theory maintains that we would be willing to accept one dollar for the additional risk of death if we would be willing to pay only one dollar to eliminate such a risk, extending the equation of WTA and WTP to risk as well as uncertainty.[30] Neoclassical theory thus views such *qualitative* differences in strictly *quantitative* terms. Moreover, this approach implies that "there is no difference in principle between buying the right to inflict injury intentionally and buying the right not to take precautions which would eliminate an equivalent number and type of injuries accidentally."[31] Meanwhile, such a position would not be recognized under the common law, since agreements to permit the infliction of injury (or, in the modern context, the sale of human organs *in situ*) are simply unenforceable as against public policy, as are indemnification or insurance contracts covering a party's own criminal acts (and at a certain point reckless endangerment is subject to criminal punishment). All of the objections to the reduction of quality to quantity under situations of certainty, therefore, apply to environmental choices involving risk or uncertainty *a fortiori*.

It is thus a domain mistake to apply conventional cost-benefit analysis to a religious community that makes environmental choices based on the spiritual significance of nature and the divergence between WTA and WTP, meaning this approach only applies to misers and hedonists at the extremes of individualistic preference.[32] Moreover, cost-benefit analysis cannot resolve the differences within a "mixed" community of, for example, saints and hedonists. The only way to resolve the impasse between these two groups is to adopt a substantive philosophical position on the spiritual significance of nature to determine whether WTA *should* equal WTP, thereby excluding the preferences of one of these groups. We cannot avoid the question and suppress debate by claiming that cost-benefit analysis accommodates *both* sets of preferences, as neoclassical economics asserts. It is therefore important for economists to acknowledge that neoclassical theory is limited to a particular domain of preferences and does not simply provide a heuristic analytical tool, allowing critical examination of the substantive philosophical presuppositions that the theory and analysis make.[33] In short, a philosophical doctrine of what is real (a specific ontology) or a view of the world is ultimately necessary to determine how we are to apply cost-benefit analysis, to which we now turn.

The Need for the Intellectual Dimension of *Īmān*

The foregoing analysis suggests questions that the economist cannot answer *qua* economist, and it is here that other sciences come into play. If nature is an aggregate devoid of objective meaning and rights, and the human state is accidental with no given purpose, then people arguably *should* equate WTA and WTP. "To speak of the sacredness of life [would be] little more than sentimental thinking or hypocrisy."[34]

The Islamic position is based on the opposing view that every creature has a face turned toward God, independent of human beings. Accordingly, every creature has its own rights, which Islamic thought refers to as creation's *ḥaqq*, or due. In a sense, all beings in the universe are Muslim in that they are surrendered to the Divine Will, meaning "[a] flower cannot help being a flower; a diamond cannot do other than sparkle. God has made them so; it is theirs to obey."[35] All things hymn the praises of God, as the *Qur'ān*, the Bible, and other sacred texts remind us.[36] Nature speaks to God, and God speaks to things.

Nature is therefore irreducible to its purely quantitative, analytical aspect, just as a book is irreducible to its weight or dimensions. And to deny higher levels of meaning because of the claim that whatever modern science leaves out is unknowable or unreal is to destroy what is in fact most precious in nature, which is to convey to us a message. In this sense, nature is like the *Qur'ān*. Islamic thinkers discussed this correspondence throughout Islam's intellectual history, carefully examining the relation between the composed or written *Qur'ān* (*al-Qur'ān al-tadwīnī*) on the one hand, and the cosmic or ontological *Qur'ān as the whole of creation* (*al-Qur'ān al-takwīnī*) on the other.[37] Accordingly, both the verses of the written *Qur'ān* as well as the signs of God in nature are called *āyāt Allāh* (corresponding to the "vestiges of God," or *vestigia Dei*, in traditional Christian thought). In short, the book of nature is also a revealed scripture, each page of which reveals a truth. But it contains a truth we do not understand unless we accept revelation, in the same way that the truth of revelation is not understood by the person who does not have faith in it.[38]

Environmental values are therefore *not* reducible to tastes, for nature communicates a spiritual truth and presence, and spiritual forces establish and maintain the order of nature. Accordingly, human beings do *not* have the right to equate WTA and WTP, and cost-benefit analysis is wrong as a guide to environmental policy, for the conventional analytical tools in economics do not apply.

Yet, many environmentalists have criticized the Islamic (as well as Christian and Jewish) conception of humanity as the crown of creation—(what Islam calls *ashraf al-makhlūqāt*).[39]Deep ecology, for example, espouses the equality of man and other creatures, or an ecocentric or biocentric approach in place of an anthropocentric one, which allegedly leads to environmental despotism.[40] But such a critique involves a misunderstanding of Islamic (and other Abrahamic) teachings espousing a *theocentric*, rather than purely anthropocentric approach. Indeed, Islam conceives of the human state *both* in terms of God's servant (*'abd Allāh*) and vicegerent (*al-khalīfah*) on earth:

> As *'abd Allāh*, he must be passive towards God and receptive to the grace that flows from the world above. As *khalīfat Allāh*, he must be active in the world, sustaining cosmic harmony and disseminating the grace for which he is the channel as a result of his being the central creature in the terrestrial order.[41]

In this sense, the status of *khalīfah* is not simply a privilege, but a responsibility and a trial, for failure to realize one's spiritual potential leads to disequilibrium.[42] Indeed, the environmental crisis results when *khalīfat Allāh* no longer considers himself or herself *'abd Allāh*, mistakenly identifying oneself as an accidental being not created for a higher purpose. The resulting search for the Infinite in the finite leads to disequilibrium in both man and nature.[43]Anthropomorphism is thus dangerous because it falsely takes the place of theocentrism, not because it is substituted for biocentrism. Denying the central position of the human state would only introduce further disequilibrium from this point of view.

The environmental crisis is thus much more than a question of religious ethics. It is a question of rediscovering the spiritual significance of the world of nature, and this is ultimately a question of challenging modern science's claim to have a monopoly on knowledge itself. Prior to the environmental crisis, interfaith dialogue focused on the Divine Principle, which, of course, is central to all religions, and on the human being, whether in the context of salvation, society, ethics, or other aspects of life.[44] Little attention was paid to the third grand reality of human existence, namely the cosmos or nature. But now it is essential to articulate a harmonious doctrine of the cosmos, the world of nature, and the environment to provide a common religious response to the shared environmental crisis. Clearly stating the Islamic position of the urgent necessity here for interreligious focus:

> A need exists to develop a path across religious frontiers without destroying the significance of religion itself and to carry out a comparative study of the "Earths" of various religions as has been carried out for their "Heavens," if these terms are understood in their traditional metaphysical and cosmological sense.[45]

A "Common Word" on the environment is thus necessary on both the scientific and ethical levels. In short, it is impossible to reconcile the religious view of the order of nature with the scientific understanding of that order when "the first view is based upon certain metaphysical and spiritual principles that the second one denies," with all this implies for the need for a "sacred science."[46]

In fact, there is an increasingly urgent debate over whether the secular paradigm that has created the current environmental crisis can generate new technologies quickly enough to solve it (in addition to the accompanying problems of the depletion of nonrenewable resources and escapism). Whether such a technological "fix" is possible depends on whether the secular paradigm corresponds to the nature of reality. If it does not, attempting to find a fix *within* this paradigm can lead to a vicious cycle of technologies that backfire, ending in a catastrophe. This point can be illustrated with the true story of a man who, having a spot of arthritis in his finger joints, was given tablets by his doctor that resulted in a stomach ulcer.[47] A subsequent operation for the ulcer in conjunction with strong antibiotics interfered with his cardiovascular system to the extent that the doctor felt an obligation to carry out a couple of minor operations. Complications from this then required a heart specialist, and in the patient's weakened condition, he contracted a lung infection. The patient died within two weeks of the heart operation despite the continual care of three doctors and the hospital staff . In short, if science and technology are based on philosophical presuppositions that do not correspond to the nature of reality, then serious unintended consequences follow for both man and nature. The solution is to recognize the erroneous presuppositions in a fragmented view of man and nature and draw the correct conclusions.[48] Technological remediation versus avoidance controversies in climate change discussions surrounding basic choices such as limiting greenhouse gas emissions ex ante, versus pursuing technological fixes such as carbon capture and storage ("clean coal" technologies based on injecting carbon dioxide into geologic structures) or albedo approaches(for example, space-based mirrors) are part of this debate.

In a sense, those who hope for such technological fixes within the current reductionist paradigm are substituting a secular faith for a traditional one (this is quite literally true in light of the history of the notion of progress).[49] What we wish to emphasize here is that all the foregoing issues involve questions that the economist cannot answer *qua* economist: One must kick this debate up to the philosophical level where it belongs. There is no question that the technology must change. The only question is whether the paradigm within which the technology is developed must also change.

Fortunately, good physics is refuting bad philosophy. The discoveries of physics over the course of the last century have proven beyond a shadow of a doubt that a strictly mechanistic conception of the universe is false. The new physics has refuted the naïve realism of billiard ball atomism, the notion that atoms alone really exist and retain their self-identity, prompting a fierce debate on the interpretation of these findings and questions as to what should replace the pre-quantum, scientistic world view. The situation has driven one scholar to speak recently of a reality marketplace.[50] Yet, the different interpretations of the new physics have not succeeded in making the consequences of what is observed and measured intelligible, at least until the seminal work of Wolfgang Smith.[51] A Catholic scientist and theologian, Smith resolves quantum paradox on one hand and integrates the findings of physics into higher orders of knowledge on the other in his seminal book *The Quantum Enigma: Finding the Hidden Key*.[52] Remarkably, Muslim philosopher-scientists such as Ibn Sīnā (980–1037 CE), 'Umar Khayyām (1048–1131 CE), and Naṣīr; al-Dīn Ṭūsī (1201–1274 CE) anticipated this solution centuries earlier based on an Islamic philosophy of nature.[53] As the astronomer Robert Jastrow put it, albeit in a non-Islamic context:

> For the scientist who has lived by his faith in the power of reason, the story ends like a bad dream. He has scaled the mountains of ignorance, he is about to conquer the highest peak; and as he pulls himself over the final rock, he is greeted by a band of theologians who have been sitting there for centuries.[54]

But because these and other of the foregoing arguments may be couched in philosophical terms that many economists are not familiar with, and because different parts of these arguments are found in various writings that do not always explicitly draw their implications for economics, few neoclassically oriented environmental economists may be aware of or understand the implications of such a multidimensional approach. It is therefore necessary to make such arguments explicit (just as it is important to clarify certain details of neoclassical economics for scholars of religion and other thinkers).

It is remarkable that perhaps the most important economist of the twentieth century from this point of view was not a Muslim, but a Christian. I refer to E.F. Schumacher, author of *Small Is Beautiful: Economics as if People Mattered*, remembered as an internationally influential economic thinker who, grounded in religion, pushed the envelope in looking diversely at problems of development economics and environmentalism.[55] His personal library reveals the immense influence of contemporary Muslim philosophers, showing that he took far more extensive notes *within* the books of René Guénon (Shaykh 'Abdul Wāḥid Yaḥyā), Frithjof Schuon (Shaykh 'Īsā Nūr al-Dīn), and Titus Burckhardt (Shaykh Ibrāhīm) than most other authors, including leading Catholic thinkers such as Jacques Maritain. Moreover, this Islamic influence appears in Schumacher's notes for a 24-lecture course he taught at London University in 1959 and 1960 entitled "Crucial Problems for Modern Living."[56] His lecture notes are highly detailed with extensive commentary and references, including notes on the perennial philosophy and Burckhardt's *Alchemy: Science of the Cosmos, Science of the Soul* in German. Tragically, Schumacher died a few weeks before a scheduled meeting on Islamic economics in Tehran with Seyyed Hossein Nasr, prominent participant in "A Common Word" and one of the first scholars to predict the environmental crisis in the 1960s.[57] Despite such profound influences, this foundation of Schumacher's work is not widely known. But it is precisely this type of Muslim-Christian intellectual collaboration in the spirit of "A Common Word" that points the way forward.

The Role of the Esoteric Dimension of *Iḥsān* and the Need for "A Common Word"

Since nature's perfect surrender to God makes it Muslim in the Islamic perspective, the contemplation of nature is intimately related to spiritual realization. Indeed, nature acts as an important, sometimes even indispensable, aid for spiritual recollection.[58] The human counterpart to nature's perfect surrender in Islam is the *walī*, one whose *whole being* is surrendered to God (analogous to a saint in Christianity). But whereas nature surrenders passively, the *walī* surrenders actively, hence the role of the esoteric dimension of *iḥsān*.[59]

Indeed, how many religious believers, Muslim or Christian, can say that they truly love God with all their heart, soul, mind, and strength? Or that they truly love their neighbors as themselves? "Although the *commandments* to love God and to love our neighbors might indeed be an accessible and common ground between all Muslims and Christians without exception, surely the fulfillment of these commandments must remain, for most, a sublime and elusive goal."[60] In this regard, there is a certain innocent equivocation often encountered in dialogue surrounding "A Common Word" between (1) love of God and neighbor and (2) the commandments to love God and neighbor. Only the *walī* or saint can, by God's grace, fulfill these supreme commandments, underscoring the distinction between a commandment and its realization in approaching common ground.

And this distinction implies varying degrees of ability to read nature as a sacred text. As the Qurān states: "We shall show them Our signs in the horizons and in their own souls until it becomes clear to them that it is the truth" (Q 41:53). Traditional Muslims have therefore always "harbored a great love for nature."[61] But only the *walī* or saint is able to fully penetrate its inner meaning and see nature as an earthly reflection of paradisal realities based on fully realizing the supreme commandments. Accordingly, the Islamic love of nature has its most profound and universal expression in the mystical poetry of figures such as Jalāl al-Dīn Rūmī (1207–1273 CE; currently one of the best-selling poets in the United States). Rūmī would therefore join St. Francis of Assisi (1181–1226 CE), who also composed mystical poetry addressing the world of nature as the familiar "thou," in the praise of the Lord through the reflection of His Beauty and Wisdom in His creation. Such figures provide an inspiring example for us who *wish* to fulfill the supreme commandments, including the love of nature as neighbor, but "now we see through a glass, darkly" (1 Cor. 13:12). It is thus highly significant that the Roman Catholic Church selected St. Francis of Assisi as the patron saint of the environment. In short, the esoteric dimensions of Islam and Christianity (as well as other major world religions) are essential for the full realization and implementation of the ethical and intellectual dimensions of the traditions.

Although the mystical dimension of Islam is still strong in various parts of the Islamic world today, it does not control environmental policy. For example, probably as a result of broader modernization paradigms, "[v]irtually all environmental legislation in Muslim countries is borrowed from the industrialized West, in spite of the many principles, policies, and precedents of Islamic law governing the protection and conservation of the environment and the use of natural resources. Much of this legislation remains inadequate and unenforced."[62] For better or worse, secular approaches to environmental policy have dominated much of the Islamic world, at least since the colonial era.

The question then arises as to whether the Islamic world has all the intellectual and practical resources to implement a three-dimensional approach today. In this regard, Shaykh Goma'a points out that Muslim jurists must combine several distinct skills to engage properly the environmental and other contemporary crises: (1) knowledge of both the Islamic legal and intellectual heritage (*turāth*), (2) knowledge of the situation on the ground (*al-wāqi'ah*), and (3) how to link the two.[63] These are somewhat analogous to a doctor's knowledge of the medical literature, ability to make a correct diagnosis, and ability to prescribe the right medicine, three distinct skills at which a doctor may not be equally competent. Indeed, Muslim jurists' skills in the second and third areas have understandably atrophied since the colonial era because of the introduction of secular Dutch, French, and British-based codes and the marginalization of traditional Islamic law in much of the Islamic world. The oddity is that, even while some in the West nervously perceive the media version of *Sharī'ah* law's march across the Islamic world, traditional Islam perceives real Islamic law as currently slumping like canon law in the West.

Another major obstacle to environmental development in the Islamic world is that most governing elites are interested in imitating conventional Western development and related ideas about modernization.[64] Western environmentalists and religious leaders can therefore play an important role in helping to provide political capital for Muslim religious leaders to pursue an authentic Islamic development policy based on the three dimensions.[65] In a sense, the primary problem in the Islamic world regarding the environment has been one of application rather than lack of theory, against which the West may draw as it casts about for the kind of newer sustainable development ideals alluded to in David Linnan's chapter.

The situation in the West is quite different in that there is a need to reformulate a Christian theology of nature. The weakening of religious faith over several centuries coupled with theology's surrender of the realm of nature to science had devastating consequences for serious concern with its sacral dimension. This created an unfortunate breech between mainstream religious organizations still surviving in the West and those who sought a spiritual relation to nature. The thirst for a religious knowledge of nature led many Westerners to "everything from serious Oriental teachings, to cosmologies of religions long dead, such as the Egyptian, to various cults and to the whole spectrum of phenomena now termed new age religions."[66] This often made environmentalism into a religion itself, as explored by Cinnamon Carlarne.

Fortunately, Pope Benedict XVI is making environmental issues a central part of his teachings, and he is now dubbed the "Green Pope," much as Patriarch Bartholomew of the Orthodox Church has been dubbed the "Green Patriarch."[67] In fact, Pope Benedict XVI highlighted the spiritual and intellectual roots of the environmental crisis in his first homily as pontiff:

> The external deserts in the world are growing, because the internal deserts have become so vast. Therefore the earth's treasures no longer serve to build God's garden for all to live in, but they have been made to serve the powers of exploitation and destruction.[68]

He has called on Catholics to be better stewards of God's creation, made Vatican City the world's only sovereign state to become carbon-neutral, and called for global citizens to focus on the needs of sustainable development.[69]

Moreover, the very title of his recent encyclical *Caritas in Veritate* (*Charity in Truth*), which addresses the environmental crisis in the context of development, asserts the need for an intellectual rather than merely sentimental response, for a sound approach must be based on a correct vision of both man and nature:

> When nature, including the human being, is viewed as the result of mere chance or evolutionary determinism, our sense of responsibility wanes. In nature, the believer recognizes the wonderful result of God's creative activity, which we may use responsibly to satisfy our legitimate needs, material or otherwise, while respecting the intrinsic balance of creation. If this vision is lost, we end up either considering nature an untouchable taboo or, on the contrary, abusing it.[70]

He therefore argues that "nature expresses a design of love and truth," indicating an ontological basis for values consistent with nature as *vestigia Dei* or *āyāt Allāh*.[71]

Pope Benedict XVI thus integrates the need for an intellectual as well as moral response to the environmental crisis based on a hierarchy of spiritual and other needs remarkably similar to the multidimensional Islamic approach espoused by Shaykh Goma'a and Seyyed Hossein Nasr.[72] From this point of view, Islamic science can act as a source of philosophical and theological meditation, since it both influenced Western science and was based on another paradigm, as Christian theologians develop a theology of the natural environment and resuscitate a religious understanding of its order.[73] Both the Islamic and Christian worlds need each other for the intellectual and practical resources to develop a three-dimensional approach to confront the environmental crisis. And because a theology of nature is intimately connected to a theology of comparative religion, the recovery of a sacral view of the order of nature is significant for interfaith dialogue as such. "A Common Word" points the way forward in both respects.

Notes

1. See Daniel Dickinson, "Eco-Islam hits Zanzibar Fishermen," *BBC News*.
2. Ibid.
3. Ali Ahmad, "Nigeria," in *Environmentalism in the Muslim World*, 81–82.
4. See Ali Goma'a, chapter 2, this volume.
5. See Louise Gray, "Medina To Go Green," *Telegraph*. For more details on the plan, see Alliance of Religions and Conservation, "Madinah in Saudi Arabia to Become Islamic Eco City: Windsor announcement.".
6. Othman Abd-ar-Rahman Llewellyn, "The Basis for a Discipline of Islamic Environmental Law," in *Islam and Ecology: A Bestowed Trust*, 210.
7. Seyyed Hossein Nasr, *Religion and the Order of Nature*, 273.
8. For an in-depth treatment of each dimension in the *ḥadīth* and corresponding Islamic sciences, see Sachiko Murata and William C. Chittick, *The Vision of Islam*.
9. See for instance Jonathan A. Lesser, Daniel E. Dobbs, and Richard O. Zerbe, Jr., *Environmental Economics and Policy*.
10. Ibid., 42, cited in Mark Sagoff, *Price, Principle, and the Environment*, 4–5. The following statement is also typical of economists:

    > The desires (of *Homo economicus*) can be 'good,' 'bad,' 'selfish,' 'altruistic'–anything you like. The only proviso is that those desires generate a preference

> ordering; that is, the person can always say whether he or she prefers one bundle to another or is indifferent between them, and that the ordering satisfies the following conditions... (of reflexivity, completeness, consistency, and continuity).

Shaun Hargreaves Heap, et al., *The Theory of Choice: A Critical Guide*, 5.

11. Michael E. Colby, "Environmental Management in Development: The Evolution of Paradigms," *Ecological Economics* 3: 195.
12. Ibid., 193–213.
13. See Jeremy Bentham, *Introduction to the Principles of Morals and Legislation.* In a technical sense, this approach implies important restrictions on demand and supply functions without much room for differences in individual preference from an ethical point of view. Another concern is its simple denial of the relevance of substance or truth beyond the individual's perception, regardless of whether or not it corresponds to the nature of reality.
14. For a survey and critique of contemporary approaches to the environment from a traditional religious perspective, see Nasr, *Religion and the Order of Nature*, *supra* n. 7, 191–234.
15. See Imran Ahsan Khan Nyazee, *Theories of Islamic Law*, particularly chapter 12.
16. Llewellyn, "The Basis for a Discipline of Islamic Environmental Law," In *Islam and Ecology: A Bestowed Trust*, *supra* n. 6, 193.
17. For a detailed analysis of *maṣlaḥah* in the context of Islamic economics, see Waleed El-Ansary, "The Spiritual Significance of *Jihād* in the Islamic Approach to Markets and the Environment," chs. 1–3.
18. See Mawil Izzi Dien, *The Environmental Dimensions of Islam*, 134–48.
19. Llewellyn, "The Basis for a Discipline of Islamic Environmental Law," In *Islam and Ecology: A Bestowed Trust, supra* n. 6, 196. Of course, qualitative differences exist *within* each of the three levels as well as between them. The *ḥājiyyāt* and *taḥsīniyyāt* may also simultaneously serve spiritual as well as other needs. See for instance Nyazee, *Theories of Islamic Law*, *supra* n. 15.
20. Llewellyn, "The Basis for a Discipline of Islamic Environmental Law," In *Islam and Ecology: A Bestowed Trust, supra* n. 6, 196–97. Also see Dien, *The Environmental Dimensions of Islam*, *supra* n. 18, ch. 5. The last principle regarding the priority of averting harm over acquiring benefits seems to contradict the central insight of Ronald Coase's landmark paper "The Problem of Social Cost":

> The traditional approach (to factory pollution and other negative externalities)... is commonly thought of as one in which A inflicts harm on B and what has to be decided is: how should we restrain A? But this is wrong. We are dealing with a problem of a reciprocal nature. To avoid the harm to B would inflict harm on A. The real question that has to be decided is: should A be allowed to harm B, or should B be allowed to harm A? The problem is to avoid the most serious harm....

R. H. Coase, "The Problem of Social Cost," *The Journal of Law and Economics* III: 2.

21. Nicholas Georgescu-Roegen, "Utility and Value in Economic Thought," in *Dictionary of the History of Ideas*, 458.
22. For example, John Stuart Mill distinguished between "higher" and "lower" pleasures in his utilitarian ethics, but ultimately negated the distinction in his economics by adding them together in a "composite function" as if they were qualitatively the same. This assumes mathematical continuity, the source of reductionism in neoclassical theory. See John Stuart Mill, *System of Logic*, Part VI. For a critique of utilitarianism from the perspective of virtue ethics, see, for instance, Henry B. Veatch, *For*

an Ontology of Morals: A Critique of Contemporary Ethical Theory. For a critique from an Islamic perspective, see El-Ansary, "The Spiritual Significance of *Jihad* in the Islamic Approach to Markets and the Environment," *supra* n. 17, chs. 1–2.

23. Georgescu-Roegen, "Utility and Value in Economic Thought," in *Dictionary of the History of Ideas*, *supra* n. 21, 457.
24. Mark Lutz and Kenneth Lux, *Humanistic Economics: The New Challenge*, 324.
25. Georgescu-Roegen even points out that it is not possible to construct a "mono-utility," or single use value, function based on the observation of consumer behavior alone, for this requires structuring the data according to *a priori* assumptions. See Nicholas Georgescu-Roegen, *Analytical Economics*, ch. 4.
26. Mark Sagoff, *Price, Principle, and the Environment*; and Thomas C. Brown and Robin Gregory, "Survey: Why the WTA-WTP Disparity Matters," *Ecological Economics*: 323–35.
27. The divergence between WTA and WTP refutes the common neoclassical argument that the psychological discomfort of not doing one's duty can be added to the benefits of compromising it to make a decision on whether to fulfill it. According to this view, a good man's refusal to accept a bribe, as Wicksteed explains:

    only means that to him the total difference between the command of things in the circle of exchange that he already enjoys, and an indefinite, or unlimited command of them, *does not weigh as heavy in his mind* as the dishonour or the discomfort of the specific thing he is required to do. It does not mean that his objection is "infinite." It merely means that it is larger than his estimate of all the satisfaction that he could derive from unlimited command of articles in the circle of exchange, and this is a strictly, perhaps narrowly, limited quantity.

    If this were true, WTA would always equal WTP. The possibility that they can differ proves that such an explanation is false. Philip Wicksteed, *Common Sense of Political Economy*, 405, cited in J. A. Hobson, *Work and Wealth*, 327.
28. In economic jargon, neoclassical theory assumes that preferences are "complete" (one can rank bundles A, B, and C, for example), "consistent" (if one prefers A to B and B to C, then one prefers A to C), and "continuous" (WTA=WTP). Economics textbooks routinely present the latter "continuity" axiom as a technical mathematical condition that has no serious implications. Unlike the other axioms, the continuity axiom is not spiritually neutral, for it reintroduces Jeremy Bentham's hedonistic assumptions into neoclassical theory, excluding spiritual as well as certain other values. For a detailed analysis in the context of Islamic economics, see El-Ansary, "The Spiritual Significance of *Jihad* in the Islamic Approach to Markets and the Environment," *supra* n. 17, chs. 1–2.
29. Llewellyn, "The Basis for a Discipline of Islamic Environmental Law," In *Islam and Ecology: A Bestowed Trust*, *supra* n. 6, 197.
30. See for instance Shaun Hargreaves Heap, et al., *The Theory of Choice: A Critical Guide*, ch. 1. The notion of an "expected utility function," which includes the problematic "continuity axiom," comes into play here. This reductionist approach is one reason why economic theory does not recognize the full danger of various forms of risk-trading, with all this implies for the financial crisis. The inherent problems of this approach reveal themselves in a wide range of paradoxes such as the "Allais Paradox," "Ellsberg Paradox," and the like (in honor of their discoverers). These behavioral results are "paradoxes" because they diverge from the predictions of conventional economic theory, not necessarily common sense. For a summary of these and other paradoxes, see Daniel Kahneman and Amos Tversky, "Prospect Theory: An Analysis of Decision Under Risk," *Econometrica*,, 263–92.

31. John Finnis, "Natural Law and Legal Reasoning," 12.
32. For a classic discussion of negligibility, domain, and heuristic assumptions in economic theory, see Alan Musgrave, "'Unrealistic Assumptions' in Economic Theory: The F-twist Untwisted," *Kyklos*, 377–87.
33. A "heuristic" analytical device makes simplifying assumptions that are neither negligible nor specify a domain of reality, but serves to discover truth (a classic example cited in the philosophy of science literature is Newton's assumption of a single planet in a solar system). See Ibid.
34. Nasr, *Religion and the Order of Nature, supra* n. 7, 6.
35. Seyyed Hossein Nasr, *Science and Civilization in Islam,* 23.
36. See for instance (Qur'ān 17:44).
37. Seyyed Hossein Nasr, *The Need for a Sacred Science*, 130–31.
38. Nasr, "Islam and the Environment."
39. Nasr, *Religion and the Order of Nature, supra* n.7, 218.
40. Colby, "Environmental Management in Development: The Evolution of Paradigms." *Ecological Economics, supra* n. 11, 199.
41. Nasr, *Need for a Sacred Science, supra* n. 37, 134.
42. Llewellyn, "The Basis for a Discipline of Islamic Environmental Law," In *Islam and Ecology: A Bestowed Trust, supra* n. 6, 190.
43. See Nasr, *Religion and the Order of Nature, supra* n. 7, 272.
44. See for instance Yvonne Yazbeck Haddad and Wadi Z. Haddad, eds., *Christian-Muslim Encounters*; and Hugh Goddard, *A History of Christian-Muslim Relations.*
45. Nasr, *Religion and the Order of Nature, supra* n. 7, 3.
46. Ibid., 201.
47. Ezra J. Mishan, *Economic Myths and the Mythology of Economics*, 174–75.
48. Seyyed Hossein Nasr, *Islam and the Plight of Modern Man*, 3–4.
49. For example, the positivist cult of Saint-Simon, who "envisaged an assembly of 'the twenty-one elect of humanity' to be called the Council of Newton," acquired "all the paraphernalia of the Church—hymns, altars, priests in their vestments, and its own calendar, with the months named after Archimedes, Gutenberg, Descartes, and other rationalist saints." John Gray, *Al Qaeda and What It Means to Be Modern*, 30–34.
50. Wolfgang Smith, *The Quantum Enigma: Finding the Hidden Key*, i.
51. Seyyed Hossein Nasr, "Perennial Ontology and Quantum Mechanics: A Review Essay of Wolfgang Smith's *The Quantum Enigma: Finding the Hidden Key*," *Sophia*, 137.
52. Smith, *Quantum Enigma, supra* n. 50. The solution is to drop "Cartesian bifurcation," the tenet that there is an irreducible duality between subject and object in which only what can be measured in mathematical terms such as extension is objective, and what cannot be so measured such as color is subjective.
53. These scholars make a crucial distinction between *al-jism al-tabī'ī* (natural body) in the "corporeal" world of perceptible qualities and *al-jism al-ta'līmī* (mathematical body) in the "physical" world of measured or measurable quantities that concerns physicists central to Wolfgang Smith's solution to quantum paradox. See Seyyed Hossein Nasr, *Islamic Philosophy from its Origin to the Present: Philosophy in the Land of Prophecy*, 169–83.
54. Robert Jastrow, *God and the Astronomers*, 107.
55. For Schumacher's biography, see Barbara Wood, *Alias Papa: A Life of Fritz Schumacher.*
56. See E.F. Schumacher, *Not by Bread Alone: Lectures by E. F. Schumacher.*
57. See his Rockefeller Lecture series at the University of Chicago, originally published as Seyyed Hossein Nasr, *The Encounter of Man and Nature: The Spiritual Crisis of Modern Man*, and most recently published as *Man and Nature: The Spiritual Crisis in Modern Man.*

58. See Seyyed Hossein Nasr, *Islamic Life and Thought*, 196.
59. Nasr, *Science and Civilization in Islam, supra* n. 35, 23.
60. Michael Allen, "Mysticism Panel."
61. Nasr, *Need for a Sacred Science, supra* n. 37, 132.
62. Llewellyn, "The Basis for a Discipline of Islamic Environmental Law," In *Islam and Ecology: A Bestowed Trust, supra* n. 6, 186.
63. Ali Goma'a, *al-Ṭarīq ilā al-Turāth al-Islāmī* .
64. See Seyyed Hossein Nasr, *Traditional Islam in the Modern World.* Concerning the modernization concept generally, see David Linnan, "The New, New Legal Development Model," in *Legitimacy, Legal Development & Change: Law & Modernization Reconsidered* (forthcoming 2011).
65. See El-Ansary, *Spiritual Significance of Jihād, supra* n. 17.
66. Nasr, *Religion and the Order of Nature, supra* n. 7, 6.
67. It is important to note that the Eastern Orthodox Church was far less affected by secular thought and preserved a rich tradition dealing with the spiritual significance of nature for complex historical and theological reasons that are beyond the scope of this chapter. For an account of this difference between the Eastern and Western Church, see Seyyed Hossein Nasr, *Knowledge and the Sacred*, 1–64, 189–220.
68. Pope Benedict XVI (Homily given at the Mass for the Inauguration of the Pontificate of Pope Benedict XVI, Vatican City, April 24, 2005), http://www.vatican.va/holy_father/benedict_xvi/homilies/documents/hf_ben-xvi_hom_20050424_inizio-pontificato_en.html.
69. Daniel Stone, "The Green Pope," *Newsweek.*
70. Pope Benedict XVI, *Caritas in Veritate*, Encyclical Letter, § 48.
71. Ibid., § 49.
72. It is significant that Pope Benedict XVI and Seyyed Hossein Nasr had an opportunity to meet at the First Seminar of the Catholic-Muslim Forum at the Vatican in November 2008, during which Nasr provided an important talk: see Seyyed Hossein Nasr, *We and You: Let Us Meet in God's Love.*
73. See for instance Nasr, *Science and Civilization in Islam, supra* n. 35.

13

Reassessing the Role of Religion in Western Climate Change Decision-Making

Cinnamon P. Carlarne

Environmentalism became a dominant form of secular religion in twentieth-century America.[1] It spawned powerful social movements that derived much of their moral and political authority from a type of "environmental fundamentalism," which has been referred to as "the fourth great religious awakening."[2] This environmental fundamentalism was often a reaction to social optimism grounded in the gospels of economic prosperity and the powers of science.

What we are now witnessing is an increasing number of people worldwide who reject both secular environmentalism and conventional economic gospels. Instead, they call for a more widespread discussion of how values should influence policy choices in the environmental sphere.[3] Here we focus on religious values. For many, the secular religion of environmentalism fails to offer a satisfying response to the social, moral and physical dilemmas underlying the assignment of roles and responsibilities to address global climate change. This is not only true in terms of how religion influences economic policy, and the ways in which it plays a role in the philosophical framing of the debate, but also in terms of how religion influences climate change policy preferences.

Environmental law and policy choices can never be neutral. This is especially true in relation to climate change, which is defined by questions of intra- and intergenerational equity. The inherently value-laden nature of environmental law and policy necessitate a more thorough examination of what role religion plays in influencing the political frameworks that shape environmental decision-making in the climate change context.

Framing the Question

The starting point for this dialogue is a very simple one. Can the religions of the world help the global community come together to find a common way forward in addressing climate change? And, following from this, is this a proper forum for considering religious values in decision-making processes? While it is beyond the scope of this chapter to fully engage with each of these issues, several key questions merit consideration here.

First, is there a real possibility of inter-religion consensus on the role of humans in contributing and responding to climate change and the predicted consequences, considering the often patchy relationship between many religious perspectives and that of mainstream science? Simply put, are we all in it together? Are our diverging approaches prompted by religious views or, to the contrary, by conventional economic and philosophical reasoning divorced from religious perspectives, thus highlighting a need to re-involve religion in the debate?

Second, while many may argue for convergence among religions, convergence must not be confused with incidents of cooperation. Real differences exist concerning humanity's inevitable destiny and the destiny of the organic world (e.g., apocalyptic, cyclical, or transcendent), as well as humanity's place in the universal order of things (e.g., from absolute earthly dominion to a gossamer thread in the web of being). Is it possible or necessary to unify such divergent perspectives to achieve consensus or a shared vision of rights and responsibilities in the climate context?

Third, how much can and does religion influence environmental policy, when we know that economic concerns are often our primary drivers? Should we really be asking how and to what degree religion can influence economic decision-making? This is a question explored in more detail in El-Ansary's chapter on Islamic environmental economics and Linnan's chapter on development, so we leave such matters to them.

Fourth, returning to science, as one commentator notes, "the products of science have proven less unambiguously beneficial than the true believers in economic progress once advertised."[4] Climate change offers a looming example of this reality. Further, questions of uncertainty and of risk dominate climate policy discussions. In this context, we are constantly compelled to make value choices. What role do religious-based values play in this situation? Thus, returning to our previous question: In considering the relationship between religion and economics, must we not also necessarily discuss how religion influences social interpretations and responses to science in climate change decision-making?

Fifth, keeping the preceding questions in mind, let us put this debate in perspective. The current era of human control over nature dates back only 150–200 years.[5] Of course, this time line overlaps precisely with the era within which we can trace the primary root causes of anthropogenic climate change. Can we look back over these past 150 years and trace any critical patterns in how religion and religious values have either influenced, or failed to influence, the decision-making processes that led to our current predicament and, in so doing, begin to think about the role religion can and should play in unravelling this web?

Sixth, the final framing question is arguably the most important from a legal perspective. Does any of this matter in the context of international climate change law and policy making? Ultimately, do political decision-makers at the state level take religious views or priorities into consideration when negotiating international legal agreements?

Bearing these underlying questions in mind, this chapter explores whether and how we can begin to trace the ways that religion and religious values are permeating climate change law and policy debates, focusing primarily on the United States and Europe as the dominant Christian voices in the global climate debate. Ultimately, we argue that the climate change debate has prompted renewed interest in reentwining religious perspectives in environmental lawmaking in the United States and, to a lesser degree, in Europe. The anticipated effect will be to reinvigorate the spiritual and ethical dimensions of the political debate on climate change. Climate change has sparked widespread debate over human roles and responsibilities toward the earth[6] and, in so doing, has generated impetus for reexamining the role of religion in environmental lawmaking. Thus, while religion has been largely absent from the secular world of environmental decision-making over the past half century, climate change has renewed interest in the role of religion.

This chapter briefly reviews the relationship between religion and environmental decision-making, focusing on the United States. It then explores various ways religious leaders have begun to engage in the climate change debate in the United States and Europe. It considers how key differences in religiosity in the United States and Europe impact the role that religion and religious leaders play by influencing the climate change debate. It concludes by suggesting that the far-reaching social and environmental consequences of climate change are prompting both American and European religious leaders to seek ways to influence their congregations' attitudes toward climate change with concomitant influence on climate governance processes. In the United States, this manifests as a new religious-based environmental movement wherein religion plays an increasingly important role in shaping social and political perceptions of climate change. Meanwhile, in Europe, it has a less pronounced effect and serves more often to refine the parameters of the already robust secular political climate change debate. In both contexts, religion is used as a motivating force for mobilizing public support for political change. As a result, while religion continues to play, at best, a supporting role in international climate change lawmaking, it is playing an increasingly relevant role in shaping the contours of domestic climate governance strategies in pivotal countries such as the United States and certain member states of the European Union.

Background of the Religion-Environment Debate

The United States once led the international community in environmental governance. It helped generate the momentum and erect the framework for modern environmental policy. The United States' system of environmental governance arose from the ashes of secular despair over the ongoing devastation of the American wilderness and the pollution of America's growing cities. Inspired by the writings of Henry David Thoreau, Ralph Waldo Emerson,[7] Aldo Leopold, John Muir,[8] and Rachel Carson, the modern environmental movement drew its strength from the perceived failures of religious-based ideologies to foster sustainable human-nature relationships. Thus, while these writers converged in finding spirituality and even religion in nature,[9] the religious roots of, for example, Emerson and Thoreau's writings, did not translate to an intermingling of religious values with modern environmental decision-making.

In fact, the religious underpinnings of many of these writings identify the ways that Judeo-Christian religions encouraged an anthropocentric approach to nature that supported notions of human dominion over nature and views of nature as a human resource lacking in intrinsic value.[10] The perceived failures of religious-based ideologies as translated into notions of manifest destiny and man's dominion over nature[11]—whether textually valid or not[12]—supported a secular approach to environmental protection that shunned religious interference. And, while purist notions of preservation eventually gave way to a largely anthropocentric, conservation-based system of environmental governance in the United States, environmentalism retained its scepticism of religious-based perceptions of nature through most of the twentieth century. Persistent views of secular environmentalism, however, belie underlying similarities between religion and environmentalism. These must be explored both to understand the reasons why many environmentalists defensively reject religious incursions into environmental decision-making, as well as why ignoring the role of religion in this regard is not only disingenuous, but also unwise in that it unduly restricts open debate over underlying values and principles. Exploring these connections, one commentator suggests:

> The environmental movement (at least in its "deep" version)... has great similarities with the religious fundamentalisms sweeping the world.... For though it may appear that the environmental movement is "scientific" and hence "modern," whereas the religious fundamentalists are "non-scientific" and "pre-modern," they both share a fear and contempt of the modernity whose central features are rightly seen to be an instrumental rationality that undermines humankind's traditional relationship with God or Nature.[13]

This analysis is overly narrow in its description of modern environmentalism, choosing to focus on its most fundamentalist branches. Nonetheless, it highlights the value-laden nature of environmental decision-making, and reminds environmentalists and religious leaders alike that existing dichotomies conceal fundamental similarities in purpose and approach. Yet, environmental-religious schisms persist and are a defining feature of modern environmental policy.

Religion and religious institutions have played a marginal role in the development of environmental law and policy in the United States[14] and the member states of the European Union as a result of this enduring dichotomy. Instead, environmental decision-making has been driven by "scientists, politicians, economists, industrialists, preservationists, and developers,"[15] while religious perspectives have been marginalized. This dichotomy is not surprising in states such as the United Kingdom or Germany, where a smaller percentage of citizens define themselves as devout Christians and where religion plays a less overt role in the social fabric of society. It is more surprising in the United States where, despite ingrained notions of the separation of church and state, religion plays a pivotal role in shaping societal policies and preferences (e.g., the abortion debate).

The continuing under-representation of religion in American environmental decision-making can be attributed to the scientific, highly technical nature of environmental management, or equally to fundamental Constitutional notions of the separation of church and state. Yet neither of these explanations is satisfying. Focusing on the scientific foundations of environmental problems ignores larger normative questions concerning the appropriate political response to environmental problems when faced with scientific uncertainty, diverging views of risks, costs and benefits, and questions of distributive justice. Responding to environmental dilemmas requires more than science or technology, it requires a consensus concerning normative principles. Meanwhile, the separation of church and state remains central to the American system of democracy, but it would be disingenuous to argue that religious principles are absent from ongoing political debates on everything from abortion, stem-cell research, genetically modified organisms, the death penalty, torture, to defence and environmental policy.

In a country such as the United States where religion continues as a visible public presence, the marginalization of religion in mainstream environmental dialogue is noteworthy. For many, religion is best kept out of environmental decision-making given its capacity to offer justifications for human exploitation of nature.[16] For others, however, religion and religious values provide "a strong baseline for value judgments from which to launch a pragmatic approach to sustaining our environment."[17] Proponents of infusing environmental decision-making with a headier dose of religion argue that modern environmentalism already mimics organized religion in its adherence to ethics-driven justifications for action. It also maintains a religiously inspired "view of mankind as 'deeply sinful,' a view of the world as corrupted by greed and sin, and a belief that the remedy is to renounce our sinful ways for a more 'pure' lifestyle."[18] Secular environmentalism further reflects underlying associations with religion in its frequent utilization of religious anecdotes, for example, the story of Noah, to support environmental rule-making.[19] Yet, for better or for worse, these shared associations and rationalizations rarely translate into active incorporation of religious values or ideologies in environmental law and policy-making.[20]

The absence of religious values from the repertoire of principles informing environmental lawmaking—as well as environmental economics, as described by the El-Ansary chapter—reflects continuing tensions among religious leaders[21] concerning the proper relationship between humans and nature,[22] as well as enduring opposition amongst many environmentalists to the intertwining of religion with the secularly sacred domain of environmentalism. The lack of continuity within and between the world's religions on the appropriate human-nature relationship, coupled with a historically informed suspicion of religion among environmentalists, creates seemingly impenetrable schisms. However, just as global climate change has inspired renewed dialogue amongst policy-makers working across disciplines such as human rights, law of the sea, biodiversity, development, security, and trade,[23] so has it prompted a rethinking of the role of religion in climate change decision-making.

Religion-Based Climate Change Initiatives

Climate change has spawned a new era in the religion-environment debate. Religious actors ranging from Catholic bishops, Evangelical Christians, the Church of England, the Society of Friends, interfaith alliances consisting of Hindus, Muslims, Christian, Buddhists, and beyond are engaging in concerted efforts to imbue domestic and international climate debates with religious-based moral perspectives. Their efforts focus on both mobilizing religious constituencies and on influencing the contours of political debate.

Religious-based climate initiatives have sprung up in the United States among disparate faith-based traditions. In 2001, for example, the United States Catholic Church bishops approved a document entitled "Global Climate Change: A Plea for Dialogue, Prudence, and the Common Good,"[24] summarizing the bishops' views on the Church's responsibility in responding to climate change. The bishops premise their statement by distancing themselves from scientific debate, declaring: "We make no independent judgment on the plausibility of 'global warming.'"[25] Instead, the bishops review traditional Catholic ideas "such as the goodness of creation, the importance of stewardship, intergenerational responsibility, the virtue of prudence, the special role of humans in creation, and the need to consume with restraint rather than look to population control as the solution to ecological woes,"[26] as grounds for making an appeal to widen the debate and to avoid polarization, partisanship, and interest-based hyperbole that detracts from the real challenge of "search[ing] for the common good." The bishops conclude by making "a plea for genuine dialogue,"[27] before emphasizing the special responsibility that the United States owes the international community as an environmental steward and outlining the importance of incorporating social development programs into any climate change strategy.

The American bishops' Global Climate Change Statement reflects a growing sense of urgency that is impelling religious leaders from disparate traditions to reenter the environmental arena. The bishops' statement begins and ends by criticizing the failings of the secular debate on climate change and pleading for a more inclusive debate that integrates religiously based moral perspectives into an already complex, value laden conversation.[28] It is clear from the bishops' statement that they perceive the secular climate change debate to be inherently flawed and deficient in the absence of religious perspectives.

Similarly, the United States National Association of Evangelicals (NAE)—an umbrella group encompassing 45,000 churches and 40 percent of the Republican Party[29]—has opted into the mainstream climate debate. In 2007, the NAE joined forces with Harvard University's Center for Health and the Global Environment and a group of other public and private actors to advocate immediate action on climate change, along with other environmental issues such as pollution, habitat destruction, and species extinction.[30] The unlikely union was prompted by shared concern over the well-being of life on earth. As its first public statement, the new group issued an "urgent call to action" appealing to American political leaders to adopt fundamental changes in environmental policy. Stressing that "[i]t doesn't matter if we are liberals or conservatives, Darwinists or Creationists, we are all under the same atmosphere and drink the same water and will do everything we can to work together to solve these problems,"[31] the group urged a "creation care agenda" to protect life on earth.

Even prior to the commencement of the Harvard initiative, the evangelical community had begun a very public debate about the proper role of the church in the climate change debate. The evangelical community spawned two competing bodies, the Evangelical Climate Initiative (ECI) and the Interfaith Stewardship Alliance (ISA), in 2005–2006.[32] While the ECI has called for a more vigorous faith-based response to climate change,[33] the ISA has questioned the authenticity of climate change and advised against strong policy measures to address the issue.[34] This internal divide reveals continuing intrafaith dilemmas over the proper role and response of churches to environmental problems.[35] These types of dilemmas overlay the political debate on the proper role for religion in the climate context, creating layers of ethical complexity that add to the already multifaceted nature of the climate debate.

Regardless of continuing intrafaith conflict, large segments of the evangelical community are choosing to engage in the political process. This decision is critically important to the climate debate in the United States, where evangelicals hold a disproportionate amount of political sway. As one commentator notes, "it's the evangelicals, with their close ties to the GOP, who have the power to move the [climate] debate... They could produce policies more palatable to people who have... been [un]moved by secular environmental groups."[36]

The NAE's active involvement with secular organizations on matters of environmental policy suggests far-reaching concern over the implications of environmental degradation. Equally pressing fears over the absence of religion from the debate are prompting religious leaders to risk alienating parts of their congregation in order to reassert the voice of religion into the secular domain of climate change policy. Given the influence that the evangelical community holds in the United States, the NAE's decision to actively push a more progressive climate agenda could help redefine—or, at least, realign—the parameters of climate politics in the United States.

Beyond the United States, in the more secularized societies of Western Europe religion is employed similarly to motivate political action. The less pronounced role of religion in states such as Germany[37] and the United Kingdom[38] moderates the reach and tone of religious-based messages, but does not negate their presence or impact. In the United Kingdom, for example, both the Church of England and the Society of Friends have positioned themselves as advocates for aggressive action on climate change.

The Church of England has published a series of briefing papers on climate change in an effort not only to encourage political action, but also to inject a more nuanced consideration of inter- and intragenerational ethics into the political debate.[39] These papers characterize climate change as "no longer an 'environmental' protection issue, but one intimately connected with a wider world" and suggests that, in order to better address the issue, the Church must:

> [Mainstream] climate change into the wider mission of the Church, not least by recognising more clearly the inter-linkage between the Church's calling "to strive to safeguard the integrity of creation and sustain and renew the life of the earth" and its mission to "to seek to transform unjust structures of society".[40]

Through its briefing papers, the Church of England proceeds to examine multiple dimensions of domestic and international climate change. In "Through the Glass Darkly–Europe and the Politics of Climate Change,"[41] the Church reviews the European Union's response to climate change, focusing on assessing the success of first, its Emissions Trading Scheme, and second, the European Union's ability to integrate climate change into its development policy. The paper extols the European Union on its progressive approach to climate change but cites serious shortcomings in the functioning of the Emissions Trading Scheme and progress yet to be made in supporting the development of local and regional adaptation strategies.[42] The paper then commends the role that churches have played "in lobbying their governments to develop more ambitious climate change programmes" before calling for a "Europe-wide consensus between churches on climate change, that equips the European Union institutions with a moral compass to take the necessary next steps."[43]

Similarly, in its most recent paper, "Towards a Post-Kyoto Climate Treaty for Climate Justice,"[44] the Church of England looked ahead to the December 2009 international climate negotiations. It focused on how the "gaping chasm" between rich and poor countries, the relative responsibilities of developed and developing nations in addressing climate change, and their "diametrically opposed perceptions of climate justice"[45] may impede the development of international consensus. Within this context, the paper suggested that religion has an important role to play in shaping the ongoing political debate. The Church cited the role that faith communities and civil society have played in reforming the international debt regime as a case study in how the Church and its global counterparts can collaborate to help facilitate ongoing climate negotiations, with particular regard to questions of equity.

In October 2009, the Archbishop of Canterbury, Dr. Rowan Williams, reiterated in a public speech many of the themes explored in the Church of England's briefing papers. He described the climate crisis as an "opportunity to become human again, setting aside the addictive and self-destructive behaviour that has damaged their souls" and judged that the failure to address climate change could result in humanity being "choked, drowned or starved by its own stupidity."[46] Reiterating a common theme among religious leaders, the Archbishop made a two-part call to parishioners, asking them both "to keep up pressure on national governments; there are questions only they can answer about the investment of national resources," and "to keep up pressure on ourselves and to learn how to work better as civic agents."[47]

The nuanced and vigorous commentary of the Church of England in its briefing papers, and in the statements made by its senior clergy, demonstrate the extent to which the Church has engaged with the science, politics and economics of climate change in an effort to better inform its congregations and to more effectively contribute to political dialogue. And, while attendance levels for Church of England services may not rival the levels of church attendance in the United States, the Church of England continues to maintain an influential presence in social and political processes that belies the secularization of British society.

Alongside the Church of England, British Quakers have sought to inform and mobilize both the Society of Friends and the larger British community. Through a set of six briefing papers,[48] the Quakers have offered facts and guidance on the causes, consequences, and alternatives for action on climate change. British Quakers have characterized the climate crisis as an opportunity to "remake society as a communion of people living sustainably as part of the natural world."[49] As such, they are leading efforts to promote a low-carbon society and to limit personal ecological impact. British Quakers constitute a small but influential part of the United Kingdom's religious community. The number of Friends attending meetings pales in comparison to most mainstream American congregations, but the activist nature of the Quakers, and their long-standing commitment to peace and social justice, gives them a voice in social and political debate that extends well beyond the confines of their meeting halls.

Religion's role in German climate change policy is more marginal than in the United Kingdom or the United States. This variation is largely attributable to the fact that religion and the churches are noticeably absent from the larger public policy debate, in contrast to Germany's very active secular environmental groups up to and including national political parties (the Greens). This is in part a product of historical and social circumstances that differ significantly from both the United States, with its tradition of religion as a visible component of social life despite the formal legal separation of church and state, and from the United Kingdom where, as previously discussed, religious traditions, including the Church of England (visibly engaged also in the "Common Word" process), have actively engaged in the climate debate.

How should we understand the German view of religion in society and the environment, given that Germany is a driver of climate change politics in the European Union and in global negotiations? Recent ecumenical directions are visible in the outcome of a 2002 Goettingen meeting of leaders of the major religious communities, which stressed their common intent to protect the integrity of nature as life itself.[50] From a Christian viewpoint, one should recognize that Germany is both a cradle of the Protestant Reformation (Martin Luther) and still a bastion of traditional conservative Catholic doctrine. Before he became current Pope Benedict XVI, Cardinal Ratzinger was a well-known theological conservative as professor of theology, Archbishop of Munich and Freising, and later Prefect of the Congregation for the Doctrine of the Faith. Politically speaking, traditional divisions run deep in terms of Southern German Catholicism's association with the (conservative) Christian Democratic (CDU) and Christian Social Union (CSU) Parties, and Northern Germany's more liberal Protestant character arguably sparking intellectual ferment as diverse as Max Weber's *The Protestant Ethic and the Spirit of Capitalism*, social democracy as political movement, and

Marxism understood as economic theory attacking capitalism as rationalized by Weber. Modern German Catholicism's view of the relationship between the environment and religion is arguably *the* Catholic view, to the extent its spokesman is Pope Benedict XVI, whose views are covered in the El-Ansary chapter.

Protestant German views are visible most recently in the 2007 Appeal of the Presiding Bishop of the Evangelische Kirche in Deutschland entitled *It Is Not Too Late to Respond to Climate Change*, stressing that Christians take personal responsibility for climate protection, whether in their private lives or the corporate world, media and public organizations, the sciences, public administration and politics (recognizing that denial of responsibility and shifting it onto others constitute a form of sin).[51] Perhaps this appeal to personal responsibility is best understood as rooted in both general Protestant ethical views, as well as the peculiar circumstance that, in living memory, Germany has experienced organized religion itself being alternatively co-opted and suppressed by the state (in Nazi Germany and the socialist former East Germany). Further, German culture and thus, politics, are manifestly—if indirectly—influenced by a long-standing cultural connection to the land rooted in the morally driven Romantic-Transcendentalist movement of the late eighteenth century. This cultural connection to the land was reawakened first by the Industrial Revolution and later, in the 1980s, by widespread forest loss caused by acid rain.[52] Deeply entrenched notions of the moral imperative of protecting nature inform German policy making. Religion and religious leaders contribute to the continuing presence of spiritual and moral depictions of environmental protection. The overt absence of religion from the political sphere does not equate to the absence of religion from political decision-making in the environmental context.

Despite the generally restrained nature of religion in German politics, religious groups have played critical roles in past and present social movements, including the anti-nuclear and anti-missile campaigns. Further, environmental preservation continues to be a fundamental theme in many of Germany's churches. Religious institutions in Germany, for example, have played an important role in supporting Germany's quest to promote renewable energy and environmental protection, generally. Thus, although the mode of influence is different—being more vocal and centralized in the United States and the United Kingdom and more subtle and decentralized in Germany—environmentalism is a dominant theme in many religious traditions with the effect of promoting healthy religious-based activism in German environmental politics. But, to the extent the emphasis is on conscience and individual action, the outcome may be to channel the active participation of religious persons into secular environmental activism, rather than theologically based institutional involvement on the part of churches. American, British, and German church groups are, thus, more similar than one might expect, although the oftentimes charismatic and pervasive nature of American religious expression and the overtly intellectualized and mainstream nature of British religious expression may create greater opportunities for religion to filter visibly into political debate in those contexts.

Beyond specific intrastate contexts, in late November 2008, approximately 1,000 delegates from Europe and beyond gathered at the Interfaith Climate Summit in Uppsala, Sweden, to debate the proper role of religion in the climate debate.[53] Following Summit discussions, a group of 30 religious leaders hailing from diverse denominational backgrounds released a manifesto calling for "rich countries" to achieve "rapid and large emission cuts" of at least 40 percent by the year 2020.[54] Of particular significance to the discussion at hand, the religious leaders issued a two-part appeal, calling first for greater religious input into the political process and second, for greater leadership on the part of individual followers of religious traditions in acknowledging and responding to the task of caring for the environment. In extolling the value of religious input into the political process, the Archbishop of Sweden stressed that "faith traditions provide a basis for hope and reasons for not giving up" when faced with the threats posed by global climate change. In emphasizing religious-based hope he stressed the shortcomings of the secular debate, stating that: "I am convinced that the issue of climate change is not an issue best left only to politics, natural science, or the market."[55]

In their critique of mainstream climate dialogue, however, the delegates were careful to point-out that religious traditions have fallen short in their response to climate change. The Anglican Bishop of London noted the sluggish response of religious communities and called upon these communities to become active participants in the debate, decreeing that:

> Here is a major human emergency. Have the faiths of humankind got anything to say about this challenge? Many of our constituencies regard this still as a peripheral second-order issue—it's got to be moved up the agenda.[56]

The Archbishop's and the Bishop's comments echo statements by the American Bishops and the NAE that the existing secular climate change debate needs to be interjected with religious ethics and values and that the followers of religious traditions have a moral responsibility to make their voices heard on the issue of climate change.

Why Religion Matters

The question of linkages between religion and the environment has become a source of academic and private interest worldwide. The examples mentioned here are but a few of many efforts initiated by religious, scientific, academic,[57] and political leaders to explore the proper role of religion in the specific arena of climate change politics in the West. Questions about the proper role of religion in climate politics, however, extend well beyond the context of Western, predominantly Christian, countries. The acts and omissions of the United States and the European Union are fundamentally important to global efforts to address climate change, making it important to understand the role of religion in shaping climate politics. The acts and omission of rapidly developing countries in the emerging and developing world, however, are becoming equally if not more important as levels of greenhouse gas emissions rise and countries such as India and China assume greater political and economic authority. Further analysis is needed to explore, for example, what role, if any, the diverse religious traditions present in India and China play in shaping the evolving climate debates in these contexts (and, for that matter, whether religion can play a public policy role in still formally socialist China).

In considering these efforts, it is important to ask not only why religious leaders care about climate change but also why secular environmentalists and politicians should care about religious perspectives on climate change. The first question is relatively easy to answer. Climate change poses dire threats to humans, with the most severe threats being felt by the world's most vulnerable populations. Often pointing to the sacred nature of creation and inherent responsibilities to protect life, religious leaders make varying calls to protect life on earth—sometimes narrowly defined to focus on human life and sometimes more broadly defined to include all living things. The rationale and scope of these calls vary, but often there is a shared focus on the value of life and the role of humans as planetary stewards.

The second question is trickier. Why should environmental decision-makers suddenly care about religion? What, if anything, about climate change shifts the debate? Many political leaders in Europe and the United States welcome the active involvement of religious communities, viewing it as an avenue for broadening the debate and developing grassroot support for national and international climate initiatives. European Commission Vice-President Margot Wallstrom, for example, noted that the interfaith summit would "bring another perspective to the climate change debate, an ethical and moral perspective, and a debate that many politicians might not be willing to engage in."[58] Similarly, many U.S. politicians view religious support for environmental stewardship as a mechanism for overcoming the traditionally partisan nature of environmental politics in the United States. Support from groups such as the NAE offer avenues for engaging constituents who might otherwise instinctively and adamantly oppose governmental regulation of carbon dioxide, for example.

There is also growing awareness among politicians and environmentalists that it is impossible to divorce questions of climate change from their cultural—and, thus, religious—roots. That is, because climate politics are intricately intertwined with deep-seated lifestyle choices and cultural patterns, it is essential to unpack how religious traditions influence cultural patterns and practices, which in turn influence attitudes toward the environment and toward governmental involvement in environmental regulation.[59]

Conclusion

Adopting a pragmatic perspective, even in the secular world of international law, values—including religious values—do matter. Religion may have played a very marginal role in international climate law negotiations to date, but religion plays an increasingly relevant part in shaping the language and contours of domestic climate change debates. These, in turn, influence the parameters of the debate in international forums. Religion does not overtly mould climate agreements, but it increasingly influences cultural perceptions of climate change and helps shape the ethical foundations of this debate at multiple levels. The often obscure and unapproachable terms in high-level theological and philosophical discourse matter little to climate change policy negotiations. However, the conclusions that survive the rigors of these debates and filter out into the public domain do inform cultural perceptions and in turn influence domestic political strategies and international negotiating positions, because they are imbued with moral legitimacy for significant segments of mankind, given their source.

Just as religion and science do not always make easy partners, neither do religion and politics make simple bedfellows. Environmentalists have long spurned religious interference in the domain of environmental decision-making, fearing the inherently anthropocentric, unscientific, and often mechanistic views of the human-nature relationship so closely associated with many world religions, especially Judeo-Christian traditions. Equally, many religious traditions have abstained from active involvement in environmental politics due to internal disagreement over the question of the proper human-nature relationship, the relative low priority of environmental issues on the religious agenda, and disinterest in engaging in secular partisan politics. Climate change, with its heady mix of science and politics, might initially appear to be an unlikely domain for reengagement between religion and environmentalism.

Yet, viewing climate change through a broader lens as a social and cultural crisis that threatens present and future generations of life on earth, it becomes apparent why denying religious traditions a voice in the debate is neither realistic nor desirable. Religious values "are core to many people in this world" and whether one is a religious advocate, agnostic or atheist, it is essential that we engage this sector of society in order to develop comprehensive, culturally informed climate strategies.[60] This is not to suggest that religion offers a panacea to troubled climate change politics; clearly, it does not. Interjecting religion into climate change politics creates ample opportunities for chaos and backtracking, as there is neither religious consensus on the realities of climate change, nor religious consensus on the proper political response to climate change among those religious traditions that accept human-induced climate change as a reality.

Value choices are a defining feature of climate change politics. Religion is a defining feature of cultural value choices. Thus, even given the problems religion brings to the political table, from a secular viewpoint, its presence is required as an integral component of efforts to structure long-term political strategies that are culturally sustainable. Climate law is not immune to religion at any level. Nor is religion immune to climate change. While religion is unlikely to play a central role in the near future of international climate change law negotiations, it is already playing a role in shaping public attitudes toward climate ethics, economics, and law at the domestic level. These influences are subtle but they are real. The challenge for religious and environmental communities is to create a more open and transparent context for engaging with one another on an issue that transcends secular and spiritual divides.

Notes

1. Robert H. Nelson, "Environmental Religion: A Theological Critique," *Case Western Reserve Law Review*, 51. (citing Joseph Sax, Theodore Roszak and John Muir). See also, Joseph L. Sax, *Mountains Without Handrails: Reflections on the National Parks* (writing that he and his fellow preservationists were "secular prophets, preaching a message of secular salvation.").
2. Nelson, *supra* n. 1.
3. See Katharine Hayhoe and Andrew Farley, *A Climate for Change: Global Warming Facts for Faith-Based Decisions.*
4. Nelson, *supra* n. 1.
5. See generally J. R. McNeil, *Something New Under the Sun: An Environmental History of the Twentieth-Century World.*
6. See Riazatt Butt, "Dr. Rowan Williams Says Climate Crisis a Chance to Become Human Again," *Guardian*; *e.g.*, Operation Noah, http://www.operationnoah.org/.
7. Emerson and Thoreau's earlier writings, in conjunction with those of the German writer, Johann von Goethe and English writers William Wordsworth and Samuel Taylor Coleridge helped inspire the Romantic movement of the nineteenth century, which "sought to make a case for nature as a prior sustaining context that humans need for the nurture of their soul." J.R. McNeill and Carolyn Merchant, *Encyclopedia of World Environmental History*, ed. Shepard Krech, III, 1:459. The notion of nature as central to the well-being of the human soul continues to be a defining feature in the United States, United Kingdom, and German environmental movements and is particularly engrained in Germanic notions of the value of nature.

8. Muir later carried on the Romantic-Transcendentalist movement in the United States, embedding concepts of nature protection within a larger moral framework.
9. Daryl Fisher-Ogden and Shelley Ross Saxer, "World Religions and Clean Water Laws," *Duke Environmental Law and Policy Forum*, 81.
10. See Troy L. Payne, "Comment: Cartesian Eco-Femdarkanism: She Comes from the Earth, Therefore We Are," *Environmental Law*, 201; Donald Worster, *Nature's Economy: A History of Ecological Ideas*, 28–29.
11. Christopher D. Stone, "Should Trees Have Standing? – Toward Legal Rights for Natural Objects," *Southern California Law Review*, 450.
12. Fisher-Ogden & Saxer, *supra* n. 9, at 98.
13. Bruce Yandle & Stuart Buck, "Bootleggers, Baptists, and the Global Warming Battle," *Harvard Environmental Law Review*, 190 (quoting Deepak Lal, *Unintended Consequences: The Impact of Factor Endowments, Culture, and Politics on Long-run Economic Performance*, 108–09.
14. Lucia A. Silecchia, "Environmental Ethics from the Perspectives of NEPA and Catholic Social Teaching: Ecological Guidance for the 21st Century," *William & Mary Environmental Law & Policy Review*, 667.
15. Ibid., 668–69.
16. Compare Lynn White, Jr., "The Historical Roots of our Present Ecologic Crisis," *Science* 155, 1203, with Jim Chen, "Essay: Legal Mythmaking in a Time of Mass Extinctions: Reconciling Stories of Origins with Human Destiny," *Harvard Environmental Law Review*, 279.
17. Fisher-Ogden and Saxer, *supra* n. 9, at 81.
18. Yandle and Buck, *supra* n. 13, at 189.
19. Ibid., 81.
20. Recently, an active debate has sprung up among prominent scientists and commentators over the wisdom of attempting to enlist religious leaders in efforts to address climate change. Compare Edward O. Wilson, *The Creation: An Appeal to Save Life on Earth*, 3, with Kevin Phillips, *American Theocracy: The Peril and Politics of Radical Religion, Oil, and Borrowed Money in the 21st Century*, 87–95.
21. Fisher-Ogden and Saxer, *supra* n. 9, at 68.
22. For example, rifts in the Christian community over notions of stewardship vs. dominion.
23. Cinnamon Carlarne, "Good Climate Governance: Only a Fragmented System of International Law Away?" *Law & Policy (Special Issue)*, 4; Michael Depledge and Cinnamon Carlarne, "Sick of the Weather: Climate Change, Human Health and International Law," *Environmental Law Review* 9, 231.
24. United States Conference of Catholic Bishops, "Global Climate Change: A Plea for Dialogue, Prudence, and the Common Good" http://www.usccb.org/sdwp/international/globalclimate.shtml.
25. Ibid., 5 ("As Catholic bishops, we make no independent judgment on the plausibility of 'global warming.' ").
26. Silecchia, *supra* n. 14, at 728.
27. U.S. Conference of Catholic Bishops, *supra* n. 24, at 1–2.
28. Ibid., 2.
29. R. Bruce Hall, "Evangelicals and Environmentalists United," *New Scientist*.
30. Phil McKenna, "Climate Change Unites Science and Religion," *New Scientist*.
31. Ibid., (quoting Eric Chivian, Director of Harvard's Center for Health and the Global Environment).
32. See The Traditional Values Coalition, "Interfaith Stewardship Alliance Officially Launched."
33. Evangelical Climate Initiative, *Climate Change: An Evangelical Call to Action*, 3.

34. Roy W. Spencer, Paul K. Driessen, and E. Calvin Beisner, *An Examination of the Scientific, Ethical and Theological Implications of Climate Change Policy.*
35. John Copeland Nagle, "The Evangelical Debate over Climate Change," *University of St. Thomas Law Journal,* 85.
36. Ibid., 55 (quoting Karen Breslau and Martha Brant, "God's Green Soldiers: A New Call to Combat Global Warming Triggers Soul-Searching and Controversy among Evangelicals," *Newsweek*, 49.
37. See generally Reinhard Henkel, "State–church relationships in Germany: past and present," *GeoJournal*, 307–16.
38. See Bernadette C. Hayes and Manussos Marangudakis, "Religion and Environmental Issues within Anglo-American Democracies," *Review of Religious Research*, 165.
39. See Church of England, articles on climate change.
40. Dr. Charles Reed, "Climate Change: Not Just a Green Issue, A Mission and Public Affairs Briefing Paper," Church of England.
41. Dr. Charles Reed, "Through the Glass Darkly – Europe and the Politics of Climate Change, a Mission and Public Affairs Briefing Paper," Church of England.
42. Ibid., 16–17.
43. Ibid., 17.
44. Dr. Charles Reed, "Towards a Post-Kyoto Climate Treaty for Climate Justice, A Mission and Public Affairs Briefing Paper," Church of England.
45. Ibid., 1.
46. Butt, *supra* n. 6.
47. Ibid.
48. Quakers in Britain, "Responding to Climate Change Articles."
49. Susan Seymour, Quakers in Britain, "A Quaker Response to the Crises of Climate Change."
50. Orientierungsgespraech in Deutschland vertretener Religionen zur Umweltpolitik unter besonderer Beruecksichtigung der Klimafrage.
51. Bishop Wolfgang Huber, "It is Not Too Late to Respond to Climate Change: An Appeal by the Chair of the Evangelical Church of Germany."
52. For a discussion of the phenomenon known as *Waldsterben*, see Lyn Jaggard, "The Reflexivity of Ideas in Climate Change Policy: German, European and International Politics," in *Europe and Global Climate Change*, 323, 328.
53. Christopher Landau, "Faith Leaders Urge Climate Curbs," *BBC News*.
54. Ibid.
55. Ibid.
56. Ibid.
57. For example, in October 2009, Penn State hosted a Conference entitled "Stewardship or Sacrifice? Religion and the Ethics of Climate Change," where one of the keynote speakers was Rev. Canon Sally Bingham, founder of Interfaith Power and Light, an initiative linking together over 5,000 congregations with affiliated programs in 29 states. http://www.stewardshiporsacrifice.com/. Similarly, in September 2007, the University of St. Thomas School of Law hosted a conference entitled *Peace with Creation: Catholic Perspectives on Environmental Law*, including discussions specific to questions of climate change.
58. Landau, *supra* n. 53.
59. Fisher-Ogden and Saxer, *supra* note 9, at 69 (2006) (citing Douglas L. Tookey, "Southeast Asian Environmentalism at its Crossroads: Learning Lessons From Thailand's Eclectic Approach to Environmental Law and Policy," *Georgetown International Environmental Law Review*, 350 (discussing how Buddhism "has played an important role in the protection of the environment in Thailand").
60. Ibid., 65.

B. Human Rights and Ethics

14

In Pursuit of a "New Secular": Human Rights and "A Common Word"

Nicholas Adams

This paper considers some questions in relation to how Christians and Muslims approach human rights, in the light of "A Common Word." My focus will be on how we (Muslims and Christians) reason about this topic, especially in the light of a widespread suspicion of the discourse of human rights—as it appears in secular or United Nations settings—among certain influential Christian theologians. The query I seek to address is, when Christians and Muslims consider questions of human rights, and their relation to religious teachings, how do we reason? What is the shape of our argumentation? My goal is to display some of the deep reasonings of my own Christian theological tradition, to notice some features of "A Common Word," and ask if those rationals of Christian theology evoke any answering thought in Muslim traditions.[1]

I assume that human rights are often viewed as claiming a universality that trumps the particularities of traditions. My argument is that they might be more fruitfully viewed as an attempt to establish a set of minimal rules, the purpose of which is to govern relations between traditions (rather than constituting a maximal framework for governing traditions themselves). This chapter investigates the meanings of "universal," "maximal," and "minimal" to elaborate this second view, and sets them in the context of certain notable features of "A Common Word," in pursuit of what I will call a "new secular." Our intellectual journey falls into three stages: first, the difference between unity and partnership; second, the Kantian aftermath; and third, "A Common Word" and its relationship to human rights.

My conclusion is that our task is to produce a political settlement analogous to those that were sought, but which failed, during the Reformation in Europe, leading up to the Peace of Westphalia. Like those settlements, they rest on a desire for the flourishing of communities which sustain long-term persistent theological internal differences. Like them, there is no expectation that these differences need to be overcome in order for persons to live peaceably together. Intense and unresolved theological disagreements do not have to be an obstacle in seeking the common good.

Unity and Partnership

It is helpful to begin with a distinction between two kinds of interfaith engagement involving Christians and Muslims. There are two competing tendencies currently playing out in Europe and North America regarding this engagement, and they have correspondingly different understandings of human rights. The first I will call a quest for "unity in diversity." The second is a quest for a "partnership of differences." I contrast these as follows.

The first tendency is a quest for unity in the midst of a diversity of religious traditions. The key category in this quest is agreement. The goal is consensus. In pursuit of this, such things as common ideals, hopes, and ground play an important role The quest itself is an importantly reparative move. It attempts to mend a widespread dominant idea that religious persons should seek neutral ground, language, goods. Set against this, the quest for common life represents a major and welcome advance. It seeks what is common, not what is neutral. Instead of insisting on neutral ground, it desires mutual ground.

The second tendency is a quest for a partnership of differences between members of dissimilar religious traditions. The key category in this quest is understanding. The goal of this quest is friendship or collegiality.[2] This quest is not so focused on common ideals, so much as on each other's ideals, and trying to understand them. It is not against agreement, of course, and it is certainly not against consensus. These are both precious goods that are highly prized and deeply valuable. But the marks of a partnership of differences are a valuing of understanding above agreement, and of collegiality above consensus.

"A Common Word" itself displays both tendencies. The quest for "unity in diversity" can be seen in the title of the document itself: "A *Common* Word between Us and You." *Sawa*, translated as "common," has strong connotations of things that are level, balanced, or equal. It expresses a vision of common ground or a level playing field. In section III of the "Common Word" document, this is worked out explicitly and repeatedly:

> "...it is clear that the Two Greatest Commandments are an area of common ground and a link between the Qur'an, the Torah, and the New Testament."[3]
>
> "Thus the Unity of God, love of Him, and love of the neighbour form a common ground upon which Islam and Christianity (and Judaism) are founded."[4]
>
> "...as Muslims, and in obedience to the Holy Qur'an, we ask Christians to come together with us on the common essentials of our two religions..."[5]
>
> "Let this common ground be the basis of all future interfaith dialogue between us..."[6]

The search for common ground and the recognition of common essentials are marks of the quest for a unity in diversity. This is, of course, not an attempt to create a synchretism, a new religion, or anything of this sort. It is the recognition of diversity, and the search for common ground within it.

The other tendency, a quest for a "partnership of differences," can be seen in the use of scriptures. The method of "A Common Word" in relation to scriptural texts is striking. Its mode is one of juxtaposition rather than comparison. It prefers to place texts next to each other and then withdraw, as it were, so that the reader has space to contemplate them—together—rather than to make strong claims about their identical meanings and then set about detailed comparative exegesis that backs up such claims.

The reader is encouraged to form judgements about the meaning of the unity of God, and the significance of love of the neighbour, in response to scripture. Section II of the "Common Word" document is instructively brief. The Qur'ānic passages are juxtaposed with texts from the Gospels of Matthew and Mark, and the relevant Leviticus intertext. There is no detailed exegesis or attempt to force a particular interpretation.

What the "Common Word" document refrains from doing is as important as what it does. It refrains from detailed exegetical argument, and instead places the magnetic sources—Qur'ān and Bible—near enough to each other for energy to be generated between them, in the reader's eyes. One can view "A Common Word" as a generator of electromagnetic force. It is when readers move the magnets of scripture that an electric field of interfaith engagement is produced that can do real work. The "Common Word" document does not itself move the magnets. Rather, it makes them available in a specific way, and it is for the readers to bring about their deeper interactions.

Finally, at the end of the "Common Word" document, the last word is not one of unity or agreement, but of peace and harmony in the face of differences. "So let our differences not cause hatred and strife between us. Let us vie with each other only in righteousness and good works."[7]

It is not that differences will be levelled, or that there is to be no more competition. It is rather that differences should not cause hatred, and that instead of strife, there should be the right kind of vying with one another. I cannot think of a better model for seeking understanding rather than agreement (signalled by "our differences") and collegiality rather than consensus (signalled by "let us vie with each other").

Summarizing, the "Common Word" document contains no talk of neutral ground or neutral language. It fully displays the repair that I call "unity in diversity." This is clear from its multiple references to common ground. But it also displays the second repair that I call a "partnership of differences." This is clear from its recognition that agreement is not a requirement for peace. Rather, the model for promoting peace is a recognition of each other's scriptural traditions, and the practice of interpreting them for each other.

We have, then, a contrast between seeking unity and seeking partnership, with corresponding contrasts between agreement and understanding, and friendship and consensus. I have also said, carefully, that it is not a matter of doing one *rather than the other.* An emphasis on partnership does not rule out unity; an emphasis on understanding and friendship also does not rule out agreement and consensus. It is a matter of the right kind of balance, and the right kind of relation between them.

We also have a description of the method of the "Common Word" document. This involves its practice of juxtaposing scripture, and encouraging energy to flow as a consequence of handling those scriptures together, of moving them, of creating force from their movement. "A Common Word" does not appeal to a common source, or a shared artefact. It appeals to two sources, in interaction with each other.

We can thus ask how "A Common Word" might aid us in thinking about the ethical implications of these two features. How might the relation of partnership and unity, and the method of scriptural juxtaposition, help us think about human rights?

The Kantian Aftermath

In this section I present a three-step argument. The first relates to Kant, especially in his *Metaphysics of Morals* and his *Religion Within the Boundaries of Mere*

Reason. The second relates to the Aristotelian repair of Kant, associated with Hegel and Marx in the Nineteenth Century, and then with Alasdair MacIntyre and Charles Taylor in our time. The third relates to the Christian scriptural repair of both Kantian and Hegelian understandings of ethics, associated with Stanley Hauerwas, Oliver O'Donovan, and John Milbank in our time. I will argue that "A Common Word" offers some instructive forms of repair in relation to this third kind, as it extends what is a largely Christian set of reflections into the interfaith sphere.

My concern here is to display some deep reasonings in contemporary Christian theology in relation to human rights, especially the commitment to responding to human suffering, but in the light of quite a widespread reluctance among Christian theologians to endorse the emphatically secular (United Nations–oriented) framework of the 1948 *Universal Declaration of Human Rights*.[8]

Step One: Kant

Kant's overwhelming genius was the articulation of rules.[9] The *Critique of Pure Reason* is a catalogue and defence of certain rules for making epistemological judgments. *The Critique of Judgement* represents one of the profoundest inquiries into the relationship between spontaneity and rules in human action. The *Metaphysics of Morals* displays Kant's mature thinking about rules in relation to law and ethics.[10] Kant viewed himself as a participant in an age that, more than any other, had discerned the rule-governed nature of human action in a law-governed natural world. He himself devoted his life to producing compendia of laws that express different kinds of order, and the rules that humans must follow as they participate in this order.

This vision of order, of laws, of rules has two striking features. First, Kant utterly rejected the notion that right action is rooted in self-interest, and the idea that the rightness of an action depends wholly on its actual outcomes. He rejected these perhaps because he was a well brought-up Christian. He insisted that we are human, not divine. We do not know how things will turn out: only God knows that. Instead, Kant promoted the idea of duty, and the pursuit of conformity to the moral law, in such a way that we might become worthy of happiness. In our age, when notions of duty seem baffling—especially to bankers and economists—and when the vast majority of people are utilitarians without conviction, Kant has much to teach us.

Second, Kant considered the rules governing human action to be universal and invariant. He consistently rejected the notion that rules are expressions of habits of action, and that habits are formed in locally particular ways. He refused to acknowledge that habits are products of particular histories, handed down in traditions, or embodied in institutions. Kant's vision is antitraditional, anti-institutional, and antihistorical. This is a profound problem. In our age, as we struggle to understand each other's traditions, each other's institutions, and each other's histories, Kant offers us too little encouragement.

I thus note a tension for Christian readers: Kant offers us a vision of order, and an encouragement to discern the rules that govern human action. One of the most arresting rules he articulates is that we should treat other agents as "ends in themselves," as having an intrinsic dignity independent of how they fit into our plans. He vigorously opposed the instrumentalization of others' lives and work. At the same time, Kant sets his face against any account that sees this vision of order, or the following of these rules, as the products of a tradition of worship. In a strange way, Kant did not think humans needed to be taught about this order or these rules: he thought they could simply be discerned through rational contemplation, unconnected with prayer and praise.

These tensions become acute for my Christian theological tradition when interpreting Kant's *Religion Within the Boundaries of Mere Reason,* which is also part of that same tradition.[11] On the one hand, the text is peppered with references to scripture. Indeed, of his great works, it contains more scriptural citations than any other. It is perhaps his most tradition-oriented piece of sustained thinking. On the other hand, it contains the starkest distortions of some of the most vitally important topics in Christian theology: it distorts Christology, and treats Jesus Christ as a mere example to be followed; it distorts grace, and treats sin as "radical evil"; it distorts ecclesiology, and treats the community almost as an accident.

Kant is the grandfather of human rights in many ways. Given the distortions of theological topics that lie at the heart of his philosophy, we should ask how these distortions came about. They were not the product of one thinker. The best way to make sense of them is to consider how Kant expresses a decisive cultural shift that had gradually come about after the Peace of Augsburg in the sixteenth century. It is important to understand these in order to see how significant "A Common Word" is in our contemporary context.

The Peace of Westphalia in 1648 established what one might call minimal rules for governing relations between religious communities. The failure of political and religious leaders to support the Peace of Augsburg of 1555 had contributed to the Thirty Years War. The minimal rules articulated at its end included two famous principles: That the ruler of a kingdom would determine the religion of his state (Catholic, Lutheran, Reformed) and that minority denominations in those states would be free to worship publicly without harassment. On the more philosophical side, the major thinkers of the period after the Peace of Westphalia—Descartes, Spinoza, Locke, and Leibniz—set themselves the task of formulating these minimal rules more precisely. They sought to discern how members of different traditions could all adopt a common set of rules for argumentation, for formulating and testing hypotheses, for interpreting scripture.

The vital thing to notice is that these rules presupposed the continuation of different traditions. These different traditions would continue to have their local customs, their particular practices, their distinctive theologies, their styles of worship. But they would be able to live together, in the same cities, in peace, because their relations with each other would be governed by a set of minimal rules.

These minimal rules were a response to massive suffering: entire economies had been bankrupted and entire regions had been destroyed by unpaid, desperate armies. Many of those who had survived armed assault were now picked off by the famine and disease caused by economic and agricultural collapses.

But the philosophers I mentioned, who are normally considered the fathers of modern philosophy, were not satisfied with minimal rules governing different traditions, as Stephen Toulmin has argued.[12] They began to call these rules Reason, and sought to extend its reach into all areas of life, including theology. When Diderot and d'Alembert published their *Encyclopédie* in the 1750s, they intended to organise *all* knowledge according to these now far-from-minimal rules. The *Encyclopédie* famously includes a most telling line, "Reason is to the philosopher what grace is to the Christian." Topics in theology would not merely be clarified but actively superseded by topics in philosophy.

Kant's *Religion Within the Boundaries of Mere Reason*, in 1793, continued this trend in a most intense fashion: He offered a complete view of religion, rendered in terms of these rules. What had started as minimal rules for the sake of peaceful relations between communities, had become what I will here term "maximal reason" for the sake of universal claims about everything. What had been conceived to regulate external interactions between communities were now extended to regulate meanings internal to those communities. Scripture was now subservient to these overarching rules, in the most comprehensive way imaginable. Instead of rules whose purpose was to govern the relations between traditions, they become—for Kant—rules for governing theology itself.

Step Two: Hegel

In his *Phenomenology of Spirit* and *Philosophy of Right* Hegel sought to correct Kant's antitraditional, anti-institutional, and antihistorical tendencies, while preserving his concern with articulating the rules that govern human action.[13] He recovered the Aristotelian concern with community, and treated concepts as products of historical processes. He paid attention to institutions, especially those which embodied theology and worship, law and learning. Following philosopher David Hume, he saw ethics as the life of a community articulated in norms and habits.

Various attempts to draw out the significance of these moves have been made in the last forty years in English-speaking scholarship on Hegel. The most significant of these are studies by Charles Taylor, Robert Pippin, Stephen Houlgate, and Terry Pinkard.[14] The focus of these studies is oriented to Hegel's willingness to confront, describe, and address problems arising from consciousness that we are "modern." Kant had offered a model of reasoning in which social memory played an insignificant role. Hegel, by contrast, understood "Reason" as the product of historical and social processes. Each era's claims represent answers to previous generations' questions; each era's practices represent settlements in the light of contradictions faced by previous generations, and so on. A Hegelian reading of Shakespeare's plays, for example, interprets them as dramatising and working through the questions and contradictions of his age.

Hegel's approach to moral life is similarly oriented to social and historical questions. Moral reasoning, for Hegel, displays one's sense of who one is, as part of a community of other moral reasoners. For Kant, one tests the degree to which one's maxims are universally applicable in order to discover whether one should act on them. For Hegel, by contrast, one learns moral habits because of who one is (and aspires to become), and because of the community to which one belongs.

The Hegelian repair of Kant took some time to play out in the English-speaking world, despite (or perhaps because of) the influence of Karl Marx. It took the publication of Gadamer's *Truth and Method* (translated in 1975), Charles Taylor's *Hegel* (1975), and Alasdair MacIntyre's *After Virtue* (1981) to propel Hegel's ideas into the mainstream of English-speaking thought, especially the idea that ethics is the product of historical communities, that communities promote particular virtues for their members, and that tradition is the bearer of all that is thinkable for us.[15]

It is a mistake to think that Hegel's thinking simply replaced Kant's. It did not. Kantian approaches—antitraditional, anti-institutional, antihistorical—did not die. They continued (and continue now) to cohabit with Hegelian approaches—traditional, institutional, and historical. Figures like John Rawls or Jürgen Habermas, who emphasise formal procedural aspects of moral reasoning and play down the significance of memory and local particularity, display this well. It is not a case of Kantian approaches being succeeded by Hegelian ones. We now have both, in dialogue with each other.

Hegel's emphasis on traditions, institutions, and histories is not the outcome of mere chance. Hegel was interested in the contradictions of his own time, principally those between a strong sense of tradition (especially, perhaps, in southern Germany at that time) and a sense that new possibilities faced European society (especially in the wake of the French Revolution). Hegel's life spanned the late Enlightenment and Romantic periods, including the Napoleonic wars, as the convulsive reordering of European affairs followed nationalistic rather than confessional lines. Different traditions from different communities struggled to make sense of each other; rival institutions—especially ecclesiastical and governmental—vied with one another for dominance. Local histories seemed not so readily to complement overarching histories of nationhood. These contradictions fascinated Hegel, and he saw no alternative to an insistence that reason means the processes by which such contradictions are resolved—generating new contradictions and new settlements in turn.

For a Kantian, such contradictions invite a more strenuous effort to discern the universal rules that govern the increasingly complex particularities. For a Hegelian, they invite a more strenuous effort to make sense of the histories and understand their relationship to each other. Whereas Kantian reason is identified with universal rules, Hegelian reason is identified with an understanding of relationships between locally particular forms of life.

Hegel did not go so far as to suggest that there is no overarching reason, however. On the contrary: his work displays a strong tendency to see local particularities in terms of a guiding spirit. Yet his willingness to think historically about such a spirit marks a significant correction of Kant's antihistoricism. The shift toward thinking about how we understand the relationships between local particularities also marks a significant correction of Kant's downplaying of the importance of such local particularities.

For members of religious communities Hegel's philosophy undoubtedly represents a welcome turn to traditions, to institutions, and to history. Instead of a method that resolves all disputes by turning to an antitraditional and antihistorical reason, the possibility is raised that it is precisely by attending to local particularities (rather than discounting them) that one can make sense of problems in modern life, and develop tools for addressing them.

Step Three: Scripture

Christian theologians in the 1980s responded very vigorously to Kantian (and perhaps more importantly, analytical-philosophical) tendencies to oppose tradition, institutions, and history. This can be seen in key Christian texts: Stanley Hauerwas' *A Community of Character* (1981), George Lindbeck's *The Nature of Doctrine* (1984), Oliver O'Donovan's *Resurrection and Moral Order* (1986), and John Milbank's *Theology and Social Theory* (1990).[16] Each, in different and sometimes opposing ways, insists upon the centrality of tradition, institutions, and history. But there is a key difference between this group and the Hegelians. Whereas figures like Gadamer, Taylor, and MacIntyre are oriented towards ancient Greece via the German tradition of the early nineteenth century, the Christian theologians are oriented to scripture via early twentieth century theologians such as Karl Barth and Dietrich Bonhoeffer, and to patristic theology via renewed attention to the theology of Saint Augustine. These theologians share the interest in Greek philosophy and German post-Kantian philosophy, to greater and lesser extents, but this interest is no longer the dominant focus.

It is not "tradition in general" that forms the center of these theologians' investigations. Rather, it is a sense that the particularities of Christian thought cannot be properly expounded, explained, or defended if they are translated into supposedly general categories. Each study, in different ways, attempts to generate an account of Christian thought out of the indigenous categories of that same thought. This marks a very significant move away from Hegel's historicism. Hegel had tried, in his *Lectures on the Philosophy of Religion*, to offer an overview of religious categories, and then make sense of different traditions in terms of the categories he developed. The theologians of the late twentieth century, however, variously refuse such an overview, and refuse to operate with any general set of categories. Jesus Christ is not an example of the general kind "human being," for them. Christian ethics is not a particular example of the general kind "ethics." Rather, Jesus Christ determines what "human being" means; and Christian ethics is itself a study of Christian categories and how they are taken to shape our understanding of the Christian life.

The key point in this step is that the simultaneous repairs of Kant and Hegel are undertaken through attention to Greek philosophy, Christian patristic theology, and—above all—an utter rootedness in scripture. It is the revelation of God, interpreted in a particular tradition, in particular ecclesial and university institutions and in communities' histories, and in practices of prayer, that makes sense of human action and its ethics.

The concern with rules, so magnificently displayed in Kant and Hegel, is now encompassed by the rule of rules, so to speak: scripture contains the deepest rules in the Christian tradition, the deepest patterns for interpreting human action, the deepest sources of repair for suffering in the world. Those rules are discerned through a long tradition of interpreting scripture within institutions.

The theologians introduce a significant shift, however. As Harkristuti Harkrisnowo perceptively notices in her chapter, the debates between Kant and Hegel often turn on understandings of law. It is a curious feature of the theological commentary that questions of law are not as prominent as one might expect. The theological accounts are more oriented to discerning the good in an ad hoc way in specific local situations. At a national level, when engaged in shaping legal frameworks—in the kind of important work undertaken by figures like Harkrisnowo herself—this inattentiveness to law must seem more than merely curious: it is a real lack. This reflects a genuine issue in theology. Modern society is a field of competing accounts of the good. Many Christian theologians see it as their vocation to make a strong case for their account; they show less interest in considering what kind of legal frameworks best serve such argumentation. This is compounded by a strong historical sense. Legal frameworks are the products of locally particular settlements and particular times. What works in England may not work in Scotland, let alone in Indonesia (although, of course, legal frameworks do travel; in pursuing the rule of law, former colonies often take over the legal frameworks of their former rulers). As I shall argue in due course, there is a good case for viewing human rights legislation as a possible framework for discussion between different religious traditions, with competing accounts of the good. But for that to be plausible, it needs to be understood in a certain way, and one that is not at all the dominant account of human rights.

"A Common Word" and Human Rights

These threads can now be drawn together. My claim is relatively simple: what started out as internal Christian tasks, during the period after the Reformation, have become shared interfaith tasks in the twenty-first century. I want to argue this twice: once in relation to minimal rules and reason, and once in relation to scriptural repair of philosophical traditions.

Minimal Rules and Reason

The Peace of Augsburg of 1555 was a Christian affair. So was the Peace of Westphalia of 1648. Its minimal rules were a Christian affair: to enable Catholics and Protestants to live in peace. They were a response to suffering, although not everyone's suffering was addressed by them. The minimal rules were not primarily oriented to enabling Christians and Jews to live in peace, for example. With the development of reason by Descartes, Spinoza, Locke, and Leibniz a strong Jewish intellectual voice becomes part of the picture, through Spinoza's *Tractatus Theologico-Politicus* (1670) and *Ethics* (1677), and this continued to be developed with the contributions made by Lessing (a Christian interested in Jewish and Islamic intellectual life), above all in *The Jews* (1749), *Nathan the Wise* (1779), Moses Mendelssohn's *Jerusalem* (1783), and *Morning Hours* (1785).

We see, however, the dominance of the idea of reason, no longer as a set of minimal rules, but now as maximal reason, among even the most religiously musical thinkers of the age. Locke had written *The Reasonableness of Christianity* in 1695 and Mendelssohn's *Jerusalem* (nearly a century later) included a similar argument that Judaism is a religion founded on reason. Both texts grapple with the question of how interpretations of scripture can be shown to be consonant with the dominant conceptions of reason in seventeenth century England and eighteenth century Germany. In each case, rather than scripture displaying what reason is, reason increasingly determines what scripture says.

The ballooning of Westphalia's minimal rules into the Enlightenment's maximal reason is now an interfaith matter in the twenty-first century. What we need is not an even further expanded maximal reason that can encompass Islam as well as Christianity and Judaism, but a recognition that there is no maximal reason that can encompass any of these traditions. Rather, these traditions are themselves generative of habits of *ratio*, of thinking, and one learns these rules by being a member of those traditions.

At the same time, we need minimal rules in 2010, just as communities did in 1555 and 1648. We need minimal rules to guide us in the public sphere of argumentation and legal challenges. We need minimal rules to safeguard the practice of religious worship in public. We need minimal rules to protect vulnerable minority groups.

We emphatically do not need attempts to "protect" tradition or scripture against reason, by retreats into antiphilosophical dogmatism. We need to find ways to reason together, without thinking we need to subscribe to maximal reason and without thinking we need to retreat from thinking. Our task is to formulate and promote such minimal rules together, in a kind of Peace of Westphalia, although a better peace, which will involve not just Protestants and Catholics, but now members of different religious traditions. If a slogan is needed: we are in search of a "new secular."

In relation to human rights, there are two urgent questions: What role should current discussions of human rights play in relation to such minimal rules? Is the notion of human rights inescapably an expression of maximal reason (meaning: secularly charged)?

Scriptural Repair of Philosophy

It was precisely the ballooning of minimal rules into maximal reason that led to the strong reassessment of the Enlightenment by Christian thinkers: Karl Barth, Dietrich Bonhoeffer, Hans Urs von Balthasar, in German, in the mid-twentieth century, and postliberal theologians, in English, in the late-twentieth century. Their overwhelming response is to insist that there are competing accounts of "reason." There are Kantian conceptions, which know nothing of tradition, institutions, and history, and which pursue a kind of secular, neutral reason. There are Hegelian conceptions embedded in traditions, utterly rooted in tradition, institutions, and history. And there are theological conceptions, explicitly rooted in scripture, patristic theology, and medieval engagements with Aristotle. Reason, for these thinkers, must be thought of as an utterly tradition-rooted set of habits of thinking.

Pope Benedict XVI set in motion a series of painful debates about the relation of reason to tradition in his Regensburg Address of 2006, when he contrasted what he took to be the view of the eleventh century Andalusian Ibn Hazm, that revelation is unconnected to reason, and the views of the fifth century North African Augustine and the thirteenth century Italian Thomas Aquinas, that there is a real analogy between divine *logos* and human *logos*.[17]

"A Common Word" is partly to be interpreted as a response to that Regensburg lecture. Just as the Pope's speech is rooted in scripture, while at the same time committed to a vision of a participation between God's reason and human reason, so "A Common Word" is rooted in scripture, but this time two scriptures. And instead of being committed to a single vision of anything, it practises a logic of juxtaposition. Above all, it emphatically refuses to pit faith against reason, or scripture against philosophy. It refuses such brute oppositions. Instead, it models a practice of reasoning from scripture, and invites Christians to participate.

"A Common Word" could be taken as arguing that because Muslims and Christians agree about the unity of God and the command to love the neighbor, they should agree about other things, too. In that case, when tackling the question of human rights, it might be tempting to think that the *Sawa* of "A Common Word" could be the basis for thinking about the equality of human beings in relation to international law.

I think this interpretation of "A Common Word" is flawed for two reasons, one negative and one positive. Negatively, Muslims and Christians actually may not agree about the unity of God and the command to love the neighbor. If the hope for peace expressed in "A Common Word" rests on agreement on these complex theological questions, its readers should brace themselves for disappointment. Positively, "A Common Word" does not say there is agreement on these issues; it says that there is common ground, and that is not at all the same thing.

A better interpretation, in my view, is that "A Common Word" itself argues from scriptures, but also presupposes that both Muslims and Christians argue from scriptures. It displays a practice, and reflects on such a display of a practice. It takes no view about how to interpret scriptures: It does not prescribe how narrowly or imaginatively one might undertake such interpretation. Nor does it take a view on how the particular passages cited are to be interpreted. Rather, it juxtaposes the scriptures and issues an astonishing invitation to their readers: *Let us interpret these scriptures together!* Such an invitation may expose all sorts of disagreement about how to understand the unity of God and love of the neighbor. Such disagreement is not a cause for fear. I suggested before that there are two tendencies in "A Common Word." Here, the first tendency is to say there is common ground: we both affirm the unity of God and love of neighbor. And the second tendency is to say we need to notice how differently we understand these, and to "vie with each other only in righteousness and good works."

In relation to reasoning about human rights, this is radical. If there is to be a Christian commitment to human rights, then I suggest there is a strong condition. Such a commitment must be to minimal rules, not to a maximal reason that sets itself against tradition and threatens to regulate it and even engulf it. While Kantian views assume that human rights are universal and indivisible, the Hegelian localised viewpoint contemplates their diversity. Minimal rules are nonetheless necessary to avoid the human rights trap of cultural relativism. I would like to know whether this proposal is attractive to my Muslim friends and colleagues.

It is worth amplifying this proposal a little. The idea that human rights are something universal, that supersede the particularities of tradition is itself an expression of a strong tendency in modern philosophy, which, I have argued, finds its culmination in Kant's late work. Yet it is not the only tendency. The Peace of Augsburg and the Peace of Westphalia were political and religious settlements, and were not driven by philosophical overconfidence. The problematic philosophical developments—from Descartes to Kant—took place in the century and a half that followed.

It is common in contemporary Christian theology to look to medieval and patristic theology for sources of repair when addressing problems of univocality or universality. The project of John Milbank is one of the more well-known attempts to bring Augustine and Aquinas into confrontation with thinkers like Hobbes and Kant, who are viewed as the heirs of Duns Scotus and William of Ockham.[18] This retrieval and reinterpretation of older sources marks one of the most generative trends in modern theology. It is, however, insufficient for dealing with questions of interfaith engagement. The medieval settlements in the West were theologically coherent and politically stable because they were resourced and policed by one single and authoritative Church. Different movements—most obviously the Franciscans—were incorporated into the Church, rather than treated as different entities with which the Church needed to maintain good relations. It was not until newer movements refused to be governed centrally that distinctively modern problems were generated, requiring distinctively modern solutions such as the Peace of Augsburg.

The challenges thrown up by damaged relations between Christians and Muslims perhaps more closely resemble the early modern difficulties associated with the Reformation than earlier disputations between Jews, Christians, and Muslims. The challenges are social and political more than they are theological. We need to find ways to live as neighbors, in the same cities, contributing to overlapping economies. There can be no appeal to a single authoritative body analogous to the Church. Appeals to medieval authorities work best within single traditions, and are least effective in addressing questions of relations between different traditions. International courts, or courts of human rights, cannot substitute for such an overarching authoritative body. Rather there will need to be appeals to multiple and particular religious bodies that have limited religious jurisdictions and whose judgments may themselves often be taken by their own religious communities as advisory rather than unconditionally binding.

It could be a significant contribution to our shared religious life in the coming years, if human rights can perform a task analogous to the Peace of Westphalia. It could begin by specifying minimal rules governing relations between different religious communities, and qualifying to some extent the authority of legislative religious bodies when they make judgments that affect communities that lie outside their jurisdiction. It is certainly worth trying this kind of "new secular."

"A Common Word" offers a generative first step. It suggests that the best way for Islam and Christianity—and Judaism, too, I would argue—to reason together about minimal rules, is to read scripture together. It may be that the conclusions of such reasonings might strongly resemble the articles in the Universal Declaration of Human Rights. But the actual reasonings leading to such conclusions may be quite different.

The problematic questions, however, need to be repeated. How far does the Universal Declaration of Human Rights, especially its claim to be universal, represent the expression of maximal reason? Maximal reason's role is to govern, and perhaps even replace, the traditional patterns of institutional and historical habits of thinking that guide the lives of Jews, Christians, and Muslims. Does the fact that the Universal Declaration of Human Rights is meant to be taken as a whole, and not separately, article by article, present positive opportunities for tradition that reason scripturally, or does it present yet one more obstacle to traditions more at home reasoning about these issues in a case-by-case fashion?

But there is also a third, more hopeful possibility. How far might the Universal Declaration of Human Rights be treated as the articulation of minimal rules, which might be reasoned through differently in different communities, by way of deep engagement with scripture and the long traditions of its interpretation? Such an approach would be an important step toward inaugurating a "new secular" of the kind I have described.

"A Common Word" offers us some encouragement and a fascinating model for thinking in this way. If we are able to learn from it, and reason together between traditions, the effects will be far-reaching.

Notes

1. For more explicit remarks about deep reasonings in connection with Scriptural Reasoning, see Nicholas Adams, *Habermas and Theology*, 234–55, and "Making Deep Reasonings Public," in *Modern Theology*, 385–401.
2. Readers familiar with literature on Scriptural Reasoning will observe here a shift from speech about friendship to speech about collegiality. This is in part a response to criticisms of scriptural reasoning. These criticisms rest on the assumption that friendship is primarily a feeling; it is in part also a response to developments in the Cambridge Inter-faith Programme, where forms of institutional collegiality play an important role parallel to friendships between persons. I assume here that collegiality can and often does involve friendship between persons.
3. *A Common Word Between Us and You*, 13.
4. Ibid.
5. Ibid., 15.

6. Ibid.
7. Ibid., 16.
8. United Nations. Communication No. 182/1984. *Universal Declaration of Human Rights*, G.A. Res. 217A, U.N. Doc. A/810 (Dec. 10, 1948).
9. For a more expanded discussion of these issues see Nicholas Adams, "Kant," in *The Blackwell Companion to Nineteenth Century Theologians.*
10. Immanuel Kant, *Critique of Pure Reason*; *Critique of the Power of Judgement*; and *Practical Philosophy* (includes *Groundwork to the Metaphysics of Morals*, *Critique of Practical Reason*, *The Metaphysics of Morals*).
11. Immanuel Kant, *Religion and Rational Theology* (includes *Religion within the boundaries of mere reason*).
12. Stephen Toulmin, *Cosmopolis.*
13. G. W. F. Hegel, *Phenomenology of Spirit* and *Elements of the Philosophy of Right.*
14. Charles Taylor, *Hegel*; Robert Pippin, *Hegel's Idealism*; Terry Pinkard, *Hegel's Phenomenology*; and Stephen Houlgate, *An Introduction to Hegel.* Taylor is himself a student of Isaiah Berlin, a champion of the recovery of late-eighteenth century thinkers like J.G. Hamann who sought to correct Kant's antihistoricism.
15. Hans Georg Gadamer, *Truth and Method*; Charles Taylor, *Hegel*; and Alasdair C. MacIntyre, *After Virtue.*
16. Stanley Hauerwas *A Community of Character*; George Lindbeck, *The Nature of Doctrine*; Oliver O'Donovan, *Resurrection and Moral Order*; and John Milbank, *Theology and Social Theory.*
17. Pope Benedict XVI, "Faith, Reason and the University.".
18. See especially, John Milbank, *Theology and Social Theory*, *supra* n. 16, and *Being Reconciled.*

15

Multiculturalism in Indonesia: Human Rights in Practice

Harkristuti Harkrisnowo

Nicholas Adams, as a theologian, covered human rights and issues of interfaith dialogue on a philosophical basis.[1] As a legal scholar, I shall explore the practical issues in the context of Indonesia's experience as the world's most populous Muslim country. I start with a review of how the philosophical issues parallel human rights discussions focused on universal values versus cultural relativism, followed by our Indonesian history of multiculturalism, the recent incidence of communal violence in Indonesia and our practical measures to oppose it, and finish with a review of the Indonesian human rights regime and the supporting institutions that implement it.

Islam and Democracy: Rights, Universalism, and Cultural Relativism

Indonesia is the world's most populous Muslim country (about 240 million inhabitants, of whom 86 percent are Muslim). As a developing country, we are now the world's third largest democracy. That is not to say that we, like any other country, could not improve our human rights performance. But I hope our successful democratic emergence from Indonesia's multidimensional (economic and political) crisis, post-1997 Asian financial meltdown has finally put to rest the canard that Islam as such is inconsistent with democracy. As in the case of India, itself with over 100 million Muslims in its population, things may not always look like classic Westminster parliamentary democracy, but democracy is not a purely Western value.

Like Turkey, Indonesia may have a Muslim majority, but it is not a sectarian state. Nonetheless, religious forces have consistently played a role in our political development. Our 1945 Constitution recognizes a special role for religion and religious freedom,[2] under which, in the traditional formulation, Indonesia and Indonesians believe in one God (*Tuhan yang maha esa*; understood in Indonesian as encompassing both the Christian Trinity and Muslim Allah), not unlike "A Common Word" before its time. So there is a shared recognition of (prior) revelations in religious terms, but the common recognition is a political compromise reaching back to the founding of the Republic, when it was feared that the Christian majority Eastern Islands would secede from what became the modern Indonesia if formal recognition were extended to Islam as majority religion.[3] On the political level reaching back to the late colonial period, however, we recognize three sometimes complementary, sometimes conflicting social movements or pillars of our independence movement and subsequent political development: Nationalists, Islamicists, and left-leaning Progressives (once upon a time, Socialists if not Communists).

Moving directly to human rights, Adams admirably presented the Hegelian versus Kantian philosophical framework for human rights. In the legal sphere, about 15 years ago we had in Asia an analogous broad public discussion concerning whether there was such a thing as specifically "Asian values" (in opposition presumably to "Western values," whatever that means). Within ASEAN, the discussion engaged in the pro-Asian values camp prominent Muslim politicians such as Dr. Mahatir Mohammed, then Prime Minister of Malaysia, but also non-Muslim proponents such as Lee Kuan Yew, then Prime Minister of Singapore. While discussed in terms of values, the heart of the matter was a disagreement about whether and how human rights should be realized in Asian societies, focused in a technical sense on the question of whether the group, in the form of the state, should take precedence over the individual.

From the human rights point of view, the Asian values discussion was couched in terms of universal interpretations of human rights (beginning with the United Nations 1948 Universal Declaration of Human Rights) versus interpretations rooted in cultural relativism. Without revisiting the entire complex legal topic, which was understood at the time as a hidden discussion about "soft" authoritarianism from the contra viewpoint, and in opposition to so-called Western hegemony from the pro viewpoint,[4] I would note that what one can glean from that debate may illuminate some hidden pitfalls also for Adams' philosophical approach.

The first is the hidden assumption that the universalist position is homogeneous. The full theoretical panoply of human rights doctrine is beyond the scope of this chapter. But at a very basic level, there are divisions also in the West concerning the relative emphasis placed upon civil and political rights versus economic and social rights (not to mention so-called third generation or group rights such as a formal right to development touched upon in David Linnan's chapter).[5] In a nutshell, for legal and political reasons based ultimately on views of the proper role of the state, and despite differing on specific details, virtually all countries embrace civil and political rights as legal rights in some form. The only tricky question is who determines what they are and when they have been violated. However, there are differing views concerning whether economic and social rights are legal rights versus political aspirations. The difference may not seem great to some theologians, but it is important in practice to the extent legal claims presumably are enforceable in this world, while moral claims perhaps only in the next. Similarly, Islamic legal scholars themselves would recognize in the form of *maqāṣid al-Sharīʿah* universal values as discussed in Waleed El-Ansary's chapter.[6]

The question of legal right versus political aspiration replays itself again at the level of collective or group rights. That split is based arguably on ideas about the international community as well as Kantian approaches. But how would religious scholars approach the issue of Kantian versus Hegelian concepts of human rights, if the putative conclusion might determine in parallel distributive justice-based claims of the developing world? For examples we could look either to the question of rights to development in terms of the developing world as a whole, or to the painful position of small island countries threatened by global warming (claiming their countries will disappear beneath the waves due to rising sea levels unless greenhouse gas targets are raised significantly above anything currently under discussion in the international community). So the distinction between legal and moral claims does matter. But in fairness, we must also ask whether claims about Kantian versus Hegelian approaches to human rights are subject to the same degree of political manipulation, sometimes involving authoritarian approaches, that seemed to lie behind the universalist versus cultural relativist approaches to human rights. And in the specific context of Islam, how shall we distinguish in practice between tribal or social versus religious views all encompassed within a very diverse worldwide community? Theoretically, the Muslim *ummah* (nation) may be a single worldwide community, but in practice there are enormous social, political, and human differences within and between various zones or areas within the Islamic world.[7]

So now we come to what may be the greatest practical assumption in a discussion of Hegelian versus Kantian approaches to human rights in a religious context. This is the assumption that a society has a single approach even to values within the same religion. We have some practical legal experience in Indonesia with a topic dear to many Muslims, even while concerning some Westerners, namely the introduction of *Sharīʻah* law principles (for example, the establishment of local provincial law in Aceh based upon *Sharīʻah* principles consistent with international human rights standards under the Helsinki Memorandum of Understanding, dated August 15, 2005, ending armed conflict in Aceh). The immensely practical problem is *whose* view of *Sharīʻah* the law should control.[8] In fact, the elephant in the room that arguably motivates "A Common Word" is the cacophony within Islam between competing viewpoints of traditionalist, modernist, and fundamentalist Islam.[9] The hidden assumption is that religious communities themselves are homogeneous. The breadth of signatories to "A Common Word" witnesses that this is not the case, but the devil is truly in the details once we shift from general principles to legal specifics.

I leave to distinguished Islamic scholars to debate the proper character of *Sharīʻah* (as a matter of *ijtihād* or interpretation, itself human rather than divine). But there are many different Islams or, more properly, differing interpretations of Islam, in Indonesia. Some Indonesian Muslims are textualists who embrace the Qur'ān very narrowly, in a manner somewhat reminiscent of those Christians who believe in a literal interpretation of the Bible. But, seriously, how many Muslims believe in stoning adulterers and cutting off the hands of thieves?[10] Others believe *Sharīʻah* requires only an ethical basis, which can be satisfied for some by an all-things-considered judgment, and for others by well-considered secular law. Whomever's viewpoint prevails makes a real, practical difference for anyone trying to implement the rule of law in the Islamic world.

So, from the lawyer's perspective, how should we reconcile Acehnese provincial law following *Sharīʻah*, but consistent with international human rights standards in the face of very diverse beliefs among Muslims? Acehnese provincial law, assumed to follow *Sharīʻah*, now requires all Muslim women to wear a headscarf (*ḥijāb*). In fact, traditional Islam would maintain that there should be no legal compulsion concerning wearing the *ḥijāb*, because it ultimately depends upon the woman. So now we face the perverse situation of law purporting to follow *Sharīʻah*, but that distinguished Islamic scholars would argue actually violates Islamic precepts.

What are sometimes presented publicly as Islamic views have also been rejected on occasion by a majority of Indonesian Muslims. The most extreme example probably involves the woeful misconception of violent *jihād* as understood by Indonesia's own Bali bombers in 2002 and 2005. They killed hundreds of victims, showed no misgivings or regrets after the fact, caused lasting economic hardship (due to the related fall off in tourism), and, probably not coincidentally, attacked national unity by staging their attacks in Bali, a majority Hindu area (sowing unrest also among ordinary Indonesians by rendering all Balinese suspicious of simple Muslim Indonesians present in Bali to work in the tourism industry). Meanwhile, the vast majority of Muslim Indonesians considered the bombings as crimes against humanity, separate and apart from the negative consequences for Indonesia as a whole. The Bali bombers' misconception has brought all Muslims, not only in Indonesia but all over the world, under the stigma of being people who accept violence as *jihād*.

Less obviously to the outside world, immediately prior to our current (male) President Susilo Bambang Yudhoyono (2004 to date), our (female) President was Megawati Sukarnoputri (2001–2004). When she was a presidential candidate, voices were raised, particularly by Islamic parties in Parliament (*Dewan Perwakilan Rakyat*, or the National People's Representative Assembly), that a woman could not become President of an Islamic (majority) country. This may have represented simple political maneuvering, to the extent Ibu Megawati was the leader of the largest nationalist party, hence a political opponent of the Islamic parties despite being a Muslim herself. Putting aside the question whether it is wise to use religious arguments this way in politics, that position was rejected by a majority of (Muslim) Indonesians and their political representatives insofar as Ibu Megawati did serve as President.

Similarly, wearing the headscarf or *ḥijāb*, much less heavy garments like the *burka* or *chador*, are not traditional customs of Indonesian Islam. In the last generation, female *kyai* (*'ulamā'* or Islamic scholars) and the wives of famous male *'ulamā'* often did not wear *ḥijāb* (typically only worn at Ramaḍān prayers, or on the *ḥajj* or pilgrimage to Mecca). Indonesian Muslim women take it as a personal affront if their character as good Muslims were to be determined by whether they do or do not wear the *ḥijāb* every day. Notwithstanding this, all Muslim women are required to wear a headscarf under provincial laws such as have recently been enacted in Aceh. In the eyes of distinguished Islamic scholars, however, a person's true character as a good Muslim is determined by what lies in his or her heart, rather than by attire.

The point for our purposes, captured more generally in the broad signatories to "A Common Word," is that Islam is a very broad and diverse religion. And within individual countries, practices may differ greatly, as with wearing the *ḥijāb* in Aceh versus Jakarta. It is probably not an accident that Islamic majority countries in South Asia (Pakistan) and Southeast Asia (Indonesia) have had female presidents, while no similar example comes to mind in the Middle East. But about 80 percent of Muslims now live outside the Middle East, even while society is changing there, too. In the presence of diversity within Islam, and across its many cultural zones, how should we evaluate the question of *whose* view of *Sharī'ah* might dominate under a Hegelian as opposed to Kantian human rights approach? To simply render everything a local matter tends in the direction of a least common denominator approach. Meanwhile, on the side of religion, I assume it desirable to achieve some higher level of agreement on human rights than the bare minimum. But this then functions as "universalism lite," so where is the gain in Hegelian terms?

Multiculturalism as Indonesian History

Not to say that I am more of a Hegelian rather than a Kantian, but I think we cannot ignore the importance of history in our personal and collective lives. As early as the eighth century of the Common Era, Indonesia already was visited regularly from abroad by many groups who brought their ideology, values, and, of course, customs and laws. We can see this in the depiction of the many kingdoms and empires that dot Indonesian history. Some visitors came to stay and live in Indonesia, producing new genres of communities in the 17,508 Indonesian islands. The fact is that the issue of diversity, hence also multiculturalism, is not a new experience for our country. This is one aspect of an already diverse population inhabiting Indonesia, from the Malay Northwest bordering on mainland Asia to our most Southeastern islands, a short distance from Australia and Oceana, where Polynesian, Caucasian, Negroid, and other races mingled and intermingled (as we would say, from Sabang to Merauke). Marriages among different races, different ethnic groups, and different religious beliefs have been practiced for a very long time.

During the eighth through the early eighteenth centuries, two forces drove the histories of most of the kingdoms and empires of the Indonesian archipelago. One was religion and the other was trade. The greatest religious influence probably began when three of the great world religions—Hinduism, Buddhism, and Islam—were introduced to Indonesia. Naturally, these religions were accompanied by their associated linguistic, scientific, legal, and administrative achievements and values in turn, which eventually came to have significant impact on Indonesian culture, with effects to the present day. Needless to say, due to the vastness of Indonesia, these new influences were spread unevenly across the archipelago. Even when and where they were influential, they were rarely adopted in their entirety. Instead, they were incorporated into the existing customs and culture, which then produced our unique social setting in the manner of a patchwork quilt. Indonesian society follows more the "salad bowl" than "melting pot" model of integrating foreign influences and people into society.

On the trade side, in the old days Indonesia attracted many traders from all over the world due to its rich spice resources. The many contemporaneous kingdoms of the Indonesian archipelago had flourished by trading as well, not only with foreign traders, but also with other kingdoms within the geographic boundaries of modern Indonesia, with people from different islands. Thus, this precolonial era witnessed the development of Asian trade networks across the South China and Arabian Seas, plus the Indian Ocean,[11] which enabled interaction among different people in different parts of modern Indonesia and its neighbors, interconnecting, intermingling, and exchanging not only goods, but also religion, science, ideas, values, and so on. We still find traces of the resulting rich cultural diversity in communities and islands throughout Indonesia.

Some may think of the colonial era as birthing modern Southeast Asia, but in hindsight, its chief significance may lie in creating the governmental mold in which the modern Indonesian state was cast. Despite varying influences in ideology, culture, science, and religion, today Indonesia remains one of the most ethnographically rich and diverse countries in the world. In terms of ethnicities, our own researchers maintain that we still have more than 400 ethnic and linguistic groups spread across the country. Many still embrace their own traditions and customary laws, and it is practically impossible for an Indonesian to interact only with people of similar ethnicity, religion, or related social characteristics. Hence, understanding and tolerance are important concepts for Indonesians to embrace outside the religious context. So to thrive in Indonesian society, the concept of pluralism must be inculcated early in life. Acknowledging differences and, at the same time, respecting the differing aspects of each individual become paramount. This is what "A Common Word" supports.

Conflict in a Heterogeneous Society

All Indonesians have a basic understanding that we are a heterogeneous society, that to be insulated or isolated merely within one's group would be impossible. Why? We all are faced with people of different belief or religious systems, or ethnic groups, or race, in our daily lives, in our neighbourhoods, in our workplaces, and in all of our communities and social groups. Society itself serves as an educational tool for this issue of pluralism. The majority of Indonesians have been brought up and nurtured in this very condition. That having been said, in this highly heterogeneous condition one cannot deny the existence of some communal conflicts.

Before 1998, for 30 plus years under the prior "soft" authoritarian government, Indonesia rarely saw communal conflict among differing ethnic, racial, or religious groups occurring, particularly those that erupted into violent conflict. This does not necessarily mean that we experienced no communal conflicts in the past. We did, but usually they were the result of pure political patronage or economic power struggles instead of a clash of cultural values, religious traditions, or other internalized values. In practical terms, the potential seeds of conflict were often sowed by then popular government relocation programs (*Transmigrasi*)[12] pre-1998, in which excess population from certain overpopulated islands was often relocated to less heavily settled islands. In practical terms, this meant that substantial ethnic communities were sometimes moved from one area of Indonesia to another, placing theretofore nonlocal ethnic groups in close proximity to local ethnic groups, directly competing for local resources. And differing ethnic groups often coincidentally were followers of different religions for purely historical reasons. Meanwhile, our precolonial history reveals that seldom were we presented with religion-based conflicts.

It is indeed unfortunate that communal conflicts seemingly increased as we entered the twenty-first century, and here "A Common Word" could help. Even more unfortunately, we also witnessed that some conflicts fanned the fires of (intra)religious issues, as well as issues between groups from different religious traditions. Following the global trend, religious fundamentalism appeared during the last decade of the twentieth century in Indonesia, too. While many would question the antecedents of such conflicts, the end of the twentieth century was marked by the deepening of religious fundamentalism across the world, where conflicts among religious groups seemingly became more and more frequent. Furthermore, a number of political groups seized upon this trend and related conditions. The practical problems often involved fundamentalist militias and organizations travelling within Indonesia under claims to defend their coreligionists. Under these circumstances, small personal or ethnic conflicts could and sometimes did spin out of local control as outside agents became involved for their own reasons. The government was often accused by extremists of taking sides when it simply attempted to maintain public order in opposition to escalating violence involving fundamentalist militias and similar vigilante organizations.

In larger Indonesian cities, conflicts were more often than not waged in the media and via public discussions and rallies protesting select statements from rival groups (often from within the same religion, although interreligious conflict typically receives greater international attention). Conditions were less peaceful in other regions of the country, particularly in rural areas and on distant islands (where nonlocal ethnic groups often had been moved during the prior thirty plus years of the *Transmigrasi* program). These regional conflicts naturally caused deep concern for many Indonesians, for such events often escalated into communal violence. The resulting losses were not only in material goods, but, tragically, involved the loss of thousands of lives. Conflicts in Sulawesi (Poso),[13] Maluku and Ambon,[14] and Kalimantan[15] were considered among the most violent communal conflicts in the history of Indonesia, with substantial loss of life, including among police and the military engaged in maintaining the peace (whose actions in defense of public safety often required justification to the broader Indonesian population, since religious fundamentalists in sectarian militias often claim the government is taking sides when it simply desires to keep the peace).[16]

Social analysts argue that the majority of conflicts were rooted initially in political and economic issues. However, because isolated initial conflicts often involved struggles between persons from differing ethnic groups, religious issues could and often did become part of the mix as tensions rose and religiously motivated militias became involved. Even though communal violence is almost absent now—due to the continuous hard work of the government and law enforcement—the trauma left from the tragedy is not as easy to deal with. Measures are still taken now to provide psycho-social help to the victims who may remain internally displaced persons in international law terms (refugees in ordinary English, though not as a matter of international law).

Yet I must say that, in spite of a limited number of high-profile conflicts occurring in a few regions, the vast majority of Indonesian people remain respectful of other individuals or groups professing a different faith from their own. In such a vast and populous country as Indonesia, where democracy thrives and freedom of speech and expression are exercised frequently, it is difficult to prevent some speech being considered offensive or improper, in particular by those of differing religious traditions (typically involving proselytizing efforts). Regrettably, sometimes these sparse events were exaggerated by some individuals or groups with a hidden agenda, which in turn provoked a hostile response from others.

As previously mentioned, religious conflicts or clashes have not been common in Indonesia in the past. While this is not to say that today religious conflict is a common occurrence, its frequency is slightly higher than in the past. Many conflicts are a result of misunderstanding of the concept of freedom of expression, which is a constitutional right (more often than not reflecting legal concerns about blasphemy and intrareligious disputes, for example, whether the Aḥmadiyyah heterodox Muslim sect may present their own version of Islam, which is considered heresy or apostasy by many conservative mainstream adherents of Islam in Indonesia).

To blame these conflicts on the teachings of individual religions is, of course, unfair, since all religions promote peace and harmony, even among those who do not profess the said religion. This is the ultimate message of "A Common Word' "s dual emphasis on love of God and love of neighbor. The question generally is, do interpretations of any scriptures really reflect their essence or do they reflect the ideology of the interpreters? To ask this question is simply a repetition in a broader sense of the question of *whose* views of *Sharī'ah* law should govern in the Islamic setting.

Practical Conflict Avoidance and Mitigation Measures

Confronted with potential conflicts, various measures have been tried in Indonesia to minimize the resulting danger. Interfaith dialogue is one general approach, where leaders from all religions were invited to speak openly in a collegial manner about the problems that concerned us all, to promote greater interfaith tolerance. The Indonesian Ministry of Justice and Human Rights has initiated such events, involving the Ministry of Religious Affairs, local government, and civil society.

Indonesia is a patriarchal and religious society. Indonesian people have high respect for their religious leaders. They do have significant influence, not only on the issues related to religious practices, but also on the daily conduct of people in society. As such, the conduct of religious leaders, either in their preaching or in their own daily lives, presents exemplary behavior to the community, particularly in terms of respecting other religious traditions and practices. Religious leaders can also warn others not to inflame their coreligionists against other religions. Such dialogues also revealed the beliefs of fundamentalist groups, which are alleged to create social barriers against other groups from different religions. This allowed for open discussion also of socially sensitive topics, such as broad claims by at least one such Muslim group of so-called attempts at "Christianization" (best understood probably as involving proselytization attempts).

In conjunction with this interfaith dialog, many called for social pressure to be applied to leaders of such groups, causing them to refrain from engendering animosity against others, which, in turn, might endanger the unity of the people. While this formulation perhaps sounds odd to foreigners, it captures deep themes in our political culture and belief systems, both the nationalists' focus on Indonesia as a united country and their abhorrence, born of history, of anything threatening Indonesia as unitary state. This is perhaps due to a combination of negative experiences with "divide and conquer" tactics during the colonial period and, more broadly, our multicultural heritage.

A number of civil society groups also have started to conduct live-in programs for young people, where they are encouraged to learn about other religions through living in the environment of those professing different religions. For example, Christian and Buddhist youngsters were placed in a *Pesantren* (an Islamic boarding school) and, similarly, Muslim, Buddhist, and Hindu youngsters were given opportunities to experience a Christian boarding school, where they closely interacted with their newly found friends, observing their ways, and trying to understand their ideas.

Open discussion among these youngsters, sometimes attended by elders from each religion, provides a forum for the exchange of views and perspectives on different topics, especially those related to the teaching and practices of each religion. Through this effort deploying Weber's *Verstehen* concept,[17] it is expected that by learning and knowing the values of peoples of other faiths, these young people would have a more comprehensive understanding concerning the "other." This kind of grassroots experience serves to eliminate any existing prejudices or misunderstandings. At the end of the day, each participant understood that basically each religion's tenets share the same values that place harmony and peace at its center, along the lines of "A Common Word" 's own dual emphasis on love of God paired with love of neighbor.

After experiencing this, the young people are requested in turn to share what they have learned with friends in their schools and neighborhoods or other gatherings, and how valuable it was. Such programs have been met with enthusiasm, and participants typically asserted their increased knowledge and understanding of each others' faiths. We believe society must educate children to work against intolerance, which otherwise could lead to repeated conflict in the next generation.

In another experimental program, experts on conflict resolution were invited and civil society groups were involved, since they are typically closest to grass roots society. During the following sessions, with the assistance of facilitators, participants probed the roots of conflict, to assess and understand the magnitude of its impact, to analyze, and finally to realize that actually there are amicable ways to address the differences among the conflicting groups, instead of resorting to violence. They were also exposed to the impact of conflict, be it violent or not, on the community involved, on society at large, and to the nation itself, whether in the short or long term. Victims of conflicts were invited and encouraged to share their experience and sufferings—physical and psychological—with participants.

More recently, the Ministry of Religious Affairs has also established an Interfaith Unit under its wing. This unit is responsible for promoting interfaith dialogue and restoring friendly relations among those with such problems. This is significant to the extent that, in Indonesia, the Minister of Religious Affairs is traditionally a leading Islamic party or mass organization politician, so that the Interfaith Unit is under the political leadership of a politician carrying substantial weight within the Islamic community.

Of course, whenever conflicts involve criminal acts, the police and the rest of the criminal justice system need to step in and take necessary measures to bring the perpetrators to justice without any discrimination. This is the lesson learned in conjunction with ending instances of serious communal violence previously mentioned (Central Sulawesi or Poso, Maluku and Ambon, and Kalimantan). Part of the lesson learned is that the government must also explain clearly to the public what it is doing and why, because there will be extremist voices claiming that the government is choosing sides in a religious dispute and seeking political advantage in arguing martyrdom for the casualties of government action. As for law enforcement officers, their presence is important to ensure that the rule of law is in place and that due process of law is implemented. All the while, their actions must be in accordance with human rights standards and norms. The nondiscriminatory nature of their acts alone would reflect how the state respects not only the law, but also human rights, as mandated by our 1945 Constitution.

Promotion and Securing of Human Rights

In Indonesia, human rights are constitutional rights, as stipulated mainly in Articles 28a to 28j of our 1945 Constitution, as amended. The struggle for human rights in Indonesia was a long time coming, reaching back pre-1998. It became more public in the 1970s, mostly in the civil and political sphere, particularly in terms of access to justice (often via legal aid attorneys bringing test or high-profile cases) and freedom of expression (particularly traditional press battles against censorship).

This occurred in opposition to the New Order, a term coined to depict the regime of President Suharto, who adopted a security-oriented approach during his 1966–1998 soft authoritarian control of Indonesian politics and society. Suppression of social movements deemed to endanger Suharto's power was rampant, and the press suffered from lack of freedom, which exacerbated human rights conditions during that entire era. Religious activities were also subject to substantial controls, due to concerns that they might become a focus of opposition to the regime.

Following the collapse of the New Order in the wake of economic and social turmoil triggered by the 1997 Asian financial crisis, Parliament enacted our Law on Human Rights (Law 39/1999). To make a long story short, the adoption of this law was the result of a long struggle by civil society to promote and protect human rights in Indonesia. In order to strengthen its legal basis, in 2001 a Second Amendment to the 1945 Constitution was adopted, introducing 10 new articles on human rights (basically, Articles 28a to 28j). In 1945, Indonesia had pledged nondiscrimination under its original Constitution, where the principles of humanity, unity, and social justice for all were emphasized. Yet there was no detailed enumeration of human rights in that document. Adoption of the 10 articles was a decision for a "bill of rights" approach to individual freedoms. However, state interpretation of the original principles and related constitutional rights had suffered under soft authoritarianism so that it departed from the authentic intention of our founding fathers. This is the political aspect of human rights, that just having a constitution or general philosophical principles is not enough, as witnessed in many countries around the world.

Allow me to step back into the past a little, for the benefit of the younger generation, to recapture how Indonesia came to be a modern democracy that respects human rights. In 1993, President Suharto's power was at its height. Times had already started to change, and even then he could not ignore international and local cries for human rights. The 1993 Vienna World Convention and related Declaration on Human Rights would soon appear. Attempting to be proactive, President Suharto established a new governmental institution, entitled the Indonesian National Human Rights Commission (KomnasHAM[18]), to deal with human rights issues in the country and to show the world that Indonesia did care about human rights. Due to the soft authoritarian political conditions, a number of candidates nominated to the Commission declined to join it. Their concern was that it would only serve as an extended hand of the government and that it would not have significant impact on human rights conditions in Indonesia.

Despite the reigning apathy and pessimism, the National Human Rights Commission started its embryonic work on human rights. By and by, the Commission gained credence through its work, so that people started to bring it allegations of human rights violations more often. Implicitly, the people chose the Human Rights Commission, an administrative public venue without formal enforcement powers, over the mostly nonpublic court system. Its leadership burden decreased after 1998, when new human rights and civil society groups were established. This provided more alternative avenues for people to resort to, should they experience problems related to human rights. It is still noteworthy that little resort was had to the judicial system in response to claimed human rights problems.

The 1998 social movement, which ousted Suharto, brought a totally new environment to the government and public. The most significant change was in the area of freedom of the press. Previously, during the Suharto era, the press was not allowed to publish news or opinions that would be considered threatening to the national security, unity, and establishment of the Indonesian state. Following the strengthening of the National Commission on Human Rights and in line with the 1993 Vienna Declaration and Program of Action, Indonesia adopted the First Five-Year National Action Plan on Human Rights in 1998, which was then followed by the second. This Action Plan also established National and Regional Human Rights Committees to implement it across the country. There are now four hundred forty committees nationwide, the largest human rights institutional network worldwide. To the best of my knowledge (although I write purely in my personal academic capacity as a law professor, acting as Director General for Human Rights in the Indonesian Ministry of Justice and Human Rights, I also represent my government in many international human rights institutions and assemblies such as the United Nations in Geneva), Indonesia—the world's most populous Muslim country—is the only country that has this kind of nationwide implementation structure.

After 1998, a flow of human rights instruments were ratified or acceded to, such as the *Convention Against Torture and Other Cruel, Inhuman or Degrading Treatment or Punishment* (ratified by Law 5/1998), the *Convention Against Racial Discrimination* (ratified by Law 29/1999), the *International Convention on Civil and Political Rights*, and the *International Convention on Economic, Social and Cultural Rights*. Hence, most of what people refer to as the international bill of rights has been adopted by Indonesia.

In addition, the national human rights legal regime was strengthened post-1998 by the enactment of various laws and the establishment of various state auxiliary institutions, to ensure not only human rights, but also good governance on the part of the government, all of which is intended to improve the state's accountability. In addition to the National Commission of Human Rights discussed, at present we have, for example, the Judicial Commission, a new Constitutional Court, our General Election Commission, the National Commission on Violence Against Women, a National Commission on Child Protection, our Commission Against Corruption, an Anti Monopoly Commission, our Anti Money Laundering Commission, and a Witness and Victim Protection Agency. They represent institutional watchdogs and a practical framework for the realization of human rights in Indonesia as the world's most populous Muslim country.

Finally, we should admit that Indonesia still faces a number of challenges to promoting and protecting human rights for all persons. The lack of comprehensive knowledge on human rights on the part of ordinary politicians (in both the executive and the legislative branches) is one major problem. The strain between secularism and a religious orientation, and a certain misperception of democracy among the people (stressing majority rule over minority rights), are other issues that need to be addressed. For this, collaboration among all parties involved, state and nonstate actors, secular and religious, is definitely needed. Herein may lie "A Common Word's"substantial potential contribution to the realization of human rights in Indonesia.

Notes

1. Nicholas Adams, chapter 14, this volume.
2. 1945 Constitution of the Republic of Indonesia Arts 28E, 29.
3. This is the historical problem of the Piagram Jakarta or Jakarta Charter, which provided in a preface to the draft 1945 Constitution that Islamic law would apply to Muslims, but which was dropped in tense negotiations surrounding the writing

of the Constitution as independence approached in the waning days of Japanese occupation. It returned as problem again in the 1950s Konstituente discussions, as well as post-1998 discussions of constitutional amendments. This agreement that the Muslim majority not seek special status or treatment in constitutional terms constituted both a foundational compromise in the Republic's creation, and a thorn in the side of those favoring an Indonesia of more distinctly Islamic character.

4. Amartya Kumar Sen, *Human Rights and Asian Values.*
5. David K. Linnan, chapter 18, this volume.
6. Waleed El-Ansary, chapter 12, this volume.
7. The six zones are: Arabic, Persian/Iranian, Turkish/Turkic, Indo-Pakistani-Bangladeshi, Black African, and Malay. Seyyed Hossein Nasr, *The Heart of Islam: Enduring Values for Humanity*, 87–100.
8. In technical Islamic usage one should distinguish between *fiqh,* or human interpretation, and *Sharī'ah* as God's law above human interpretation. But in practice secular lawmakers in Islamic countries speak of enacting law incorporating *Sharī'ah* principles, or enacting *Sharī'ah* law itself. The language of *fiqh* is the language of Islamic scholars, while using *Sharī'ah* to refer to Islamic law incorporated into actual legislation is the terminology of politicians acting as lawmakers in Indonesia. There is, of course, a broader argument in religious terms that *Sharī'ah* constitutes a moral rather than legal obligation, but our focus is the practical one of lawyers working in Islamic majority countries where politicians may desire for their own purposes, or in response to perceived constituent demands, to enact into secular law what they consider to be Islamic principles. The practical difficulty is that real Islamic scholars may tell such politicians more often than not that such enactments do not follow traditionalist Islamic principles. However, that does not stop them from undertaking such enactments as witnessed by the subsequently discussed obligation under provincial law in Aceh for all Muslim women to wear the *ḥijāb.*
9. See generally Seyyed Hossein Nasr, *Traditional Islam in the Modern World.*
10. Shaykh Ali Goma'a's *fatwā* contra for the contemporary environment: "As for the thief, both male and female, cut off their hands." (Q5: 38). See Shaykh Ali Goma'a, *al-Bayān* Goma'a's 70–75 (question 16).
11. See generally Philip D. Curtin, *Cross-Cultural Trade in World History*, 90–178.
12. Transmigration programs, http://en.wikipedia.org/wiki/Transmigration_program.
13. International Crisis Group, *Indonesia: Tackling Radicalism in Poso* (Jan. 22, 2008; International Crisis Group, *Indonesia Backgrounder: Jihad in Central Sulawesi*; Humanitarian Policy and Conflict Research International, *Sulawesi: The Conflict in Central Sulawesi.*
14. International Crisis Group, *Indonesia: Violence Erupts Again in Ambon* (May 17, 2004; International Crisis Group, *Indonesia: The Search for Peace in Maluku* (Feb. 8, 2008); International Crisis Group, *Indonesia: Overcoming Murder and Chaos in Maluku* (Dec. 19, 2000); Humanitarian Policy and Conflict Research International, *Maluku: The Conflict*, http://www.preventconflict.org/portal/main/maps_maluku_conflict.php.
15. Humanitarian Policy and Conflict Research International, *Kalimantan: The Conflict.*
16. International Crisis Group, *Jihadism in Indonesia: Poso on the Edge* (Jan. 24, 2007; International Crisis Group, *Weakening Indonesia's Mujahidin Networks: Lessons from Maluku and Poso* (Oct. 13, 2005).
17. See William T. Tucker, "Max Weber's *Verstehen*," *The Sociological Quarterly* 6 (1965): 157.
18. The Komnas HAM, http://www.komnasham.go.id/portal/en.

16

The "Common Word," Development, and Human Rights: African and Catholic Perspectives

Joseph M. Isanga

Religious beliefs carry important development and human rights implications. In a number of African countries, the lack of common understanding between the mainstream and fastest growing religions—Christianity and Islam in particular—has contributed to violent conflict and gross violations of human rights involving a small but potent minority of extremists.[1] Political and economic groups sometimes exploit religious diversity and differences.[2] Yet, the social impact of religion on Africa has not been entirely negative, as many religious groups have been, and continue to be, on the frontlines of the fight for social justice, respect for human rights, and development.[3]

Africa is the most conflict-ridden region of the world and has been since the end of the Cold War.[4] The Continent's performance in both development and human rights continues to lag behind other regions in the world. Such conditions can cause religious differences to escalate into conflict, particularly where religious polarity is susceptible to being exploited. The sheer scale of such conflicts underscores the urgency and significance of interreligious engagement and dialogue: "Quantitative and qualitative analysis based on a . . . database including 28 violent conflicts show that religion plays a role more frequently than is usually assumed."[5] This ambivalent character of religion[6]—its double potential for peace and its concomitant effects, such as socioeconomic development and human rights protection, but also for violent conflicts—is well understood and accepted.

Meanwhile, Christianity and Islam are outward-oriented religions that contain ideas for social action, engagement, and social justice. Pragmatically, in many African countries adherents of both religions live and work side by side in cooperative coexistence. In addition, the ubiquitous African traditional religiosity, with its proclivity to accommodation of diverse traditional spiritualities and expression, as well as practical integration of the secular and the sacred in all spheres of life—economic, social and political—prepares fertile ground for harmonious cooperation among the mainstream religions.

Religion and Armed Conflict in Africa

Interreligious dialogue is particularly important for Africa because a large portion of the African population is either Muslim or Christian. Muslims constitute about 45.1 percent of the African population or 371 million, and Christians constitute

Table 16.1 Religions in Africa, by regions

	Indigenous	*Muslim*	*Christian*	*Other*	*Total*
Eastern Africa	52,114,073	59,091,873	135,194,880	6,058,251	252,459,077
Middle Africa	21,001,056	13,528,373	61,821,241	437,688	96,788,358
Northern Africa	9,020,093	167,131,245	6,410,368	632,920	183,194,626
Southern Africa	14,089,672	871,722	34,202,095	1,087,807	50,251,296
Western Africa	41,617,613	130,835,929	66,685,296	1,601,876	240,740,714
Total	137,842,507	371,459,142	304,313,880	9,818,542	823,434,071
Percent	16.7%	45.1%	36.9%	1.2%	99.9%

Source: Amadu Jackay Kaba, "The Spread of Christianity and Islam in Africa: A Survey and Analysis of the Numbers and Percentages of Christians, Muslims and Those Who Practice Indigenous Religions," *Western Journal of Black Studies.*

36.9 percent or 304 million (Catholic population is circa 158 million and increasing), but the religious balance varies over regions.

Societies that are either highly fragmented or homogenous in terms of religious demography are relatively less prone to religious conflict.[7] This is because, compared to polarized societies, it is very difficult to organize or sustain a rebellion in either homogeneous or diverse societies.[8] The most trouble-ridden constellation is a polarized structure in which a religious majority faces a strong religious minority or in which two main groups, such as Christianity and Islam, are almost the same size.[9] Religious doctrinal differences themselves are not the pivotal factors.[10] More important are the religious structures, since they enable or inhibit mobilization on religious grounds, with polarized structures being especially dangerous in this respect.[11] Polarized religious structures exist in a number of African countries such as Nigeria, Sudan, Côte d'Ivoire, and Uganda.[12]

Studies document that religious polarization or any other measures of religious demography are not necessarily linked to the *onset* of civil war.[13] What is more, studies indicate that the existence or absence of natural resources is associated with a higher risk of war in Africa, to a much larger extent, than is religious plurality and difference of religious teachings.[14] From a theoretical standpoint, it is easy to find quotes that legitimize violence and intolerance, and vice versa, in every world religion.[15] Conversely, it is not difficult to find religious teachings common to these religions that promote love and peace. Both Islam and Christianity, for example, preach love (even for enemies), peace, and tolerance. Both have interpretations of their teachings that show that they strongly reject violence (for example, "Thou shalt not kill"). From a practical standpoint, however, the "dominant interpretation of the holy writings and the general discourse on religious ideas plays a decisive role."[16]

Monotheist religions in particular, such as Christianity and Islam, make claims of an exclusive theological truth, thus, they may not accept other religions as equal. Christians and Muslims also aim principally to proselytize. Violence may not be a measure of choice, but it is more likely that such religions will enter into conflict with other religious denominations or nonbelievers than those that do not practice proselytization. In fact, throughout history, the spread of Christianity and Islam has often, though not always, been accompanied by violence. Yet, it would be incomplete to characterize contemporary African conflicts as purely interreligious in nature. Therefore, it is important to understand the mediating role of exploitative economic and political interests separate and apart from development concerns. Invariably, religious organizations are more likely to play an escalating role if they are attached to one of the conflict parties.[17]

In a number of African conflicts, "warlords or other leading representatives of conflict parties made use of religious ideas and legitimized or called for violence with religion-inspired justifications."[18] Theoretically speaking, connections between political leaders, warring factions, and the overlap of religious boundaries with other social cleavages might make religions more vulnerable to manipulation by political actors.[19] Studies have found that connections between political leaders and religious organizations that exceed simple personal contacts are systematically linked to the use of religious ideas for conflict escalation.[20]

A survey of international jurisprudence also contains evidence of exploitation of differences between religions for political and economic objectives. Sudan and Nigeria exemplify this. In *Amnesty International and Others v. Sudan, African Commission on Human and Peoples' Rights*,[21] the African Commission on Human and Peoples' Rights held that the government of Sudan was liable for violations of human rights in southern Sudan. Not only were thousands of civilians killed in the course of the civil war, but the state had also oppressed southern Sudanese Christians and religious leaders, expelled all missionaries, arbitrarily arrested and detained priests, closed and destroyed church buildings, constantly harassed religious figures, and prevented non-Muslims from receiving aid.

Southern Sudan is predominantly Christian in contrast to northern Sudan, where the population consists mainly of Muslims.[22] The root cause of this civil war, however, is centered on the inequitable distribution of wealth derived from oil.[23] Religion was used as a wedge to divide the South from the North, but the distribution of resources and development issues were at stake as well.[24] This conflict spread to South Western Sudan (Darfur). There, Darfur's people rebelled against the government, complaining that Sudan had failed to develop the area.[25] In March 2005, the United Nations Security Council adopted resolution 1593, referring the Darfur situation to the International Criminal Court (ICC).[26] Pursuant to the resolution, the ICC now has issued an arrest warrant for President al-Bashir for crimes against humanity.[27]

In Nigeria, religious strife has often resulted in violence. Through decrees, Nigeria's military rulers appropriated mineral resources in the Niger Delta to the central government.[28] The people of the Niger Delta asserted that they had been denied a significant share of oil wealth.[29] They further maintained that the Nigerian Supreme Court, dominated by Muslim judges, who were appointed by Military Rulers from the Muslim North, inevitably ruled in favor of the Central government.[30] Predictably, most of the inhabitants of the Niger Delta are either Christians or adherents of traditional religion.[31] An issue similar to this one was argued before the African Commission on Human and Peoples' Rights. In *Social and Economic Rights Action Center for Economic and Social Rights v. Nigeria*,[32] it was alleged that the Nigerian government not only ignored the concerns of Ogoni communities in the Niger Delta regarding oil development, but that the government had responded to protests with massive violence and executions of Ogoni leaders. Seeing no solution in sight, people of the Niger Delta responded with armed struggle.[33]

Although many religious violent conflicts in Africa have an interdenominational dimension, some conflicts just feed off religious ideas in order to justify their recourse to violence. Somalia and northern Uganda are contemporary examples of this. In both situations, horrendous human rights violations have been perpetrated, partly in the name of religion. The Lord's Resistance Army (LRA) claimed that its campaign was aimed at restoring the Ten Commandments.[34] Now, the leaders of the LRA stand charged by the ICC for, *inter alia*, crimes against humanity.[35] A mix of religion and politics is at the root of the violence and human rights violations in Somalia, where the Union of Islamic Courts is trying to establish stability in the beleaguered Horn of Africa, beset by persistent violence and lawlessness on land and at sea.[36]

Some of the internal African conflicts that have had a religious dimension at their base metamorphosed and dispersed to neighbouring countries with disastrous regional economic and human rights consequences. These conflicts may begin on the basis of religious difference but have at times evolved along ethnic lines. For example, the conflict in Southern Sudan first dispersed to Western and South Western Sudan (Darfur) and then spilled over into Chad.[37] The conflicts in Southern Sudan spilled over into Uganda, and those in Uganda spilled over into the Democratic Republic of Congo (DRC), which in turn pulled in several other African nations—Angola, Zimbabwe, Burundi, and Rwanda.[38]

The DRC conflict involved gross violations of human rights. In the *Case Concerning Armed Activities on the Territory of the Congo (Democratic Republic of the Congo v. Uganda)*,[39] DRC claimed, inter alia, that Uganda engaged in the illegal exploitation of Congolese natural resources and violated international human rights law by killing, injuring, and abducting Congolese nationals or robbing them of their property. The International Court of Justice (ICJ) held that "whenever members of the UPDF [Uganda Peoples' Defense Forces] were involved in the looting, plundering and exploitation of natural resources in the territory of the DRC, they acted in violation of the *jus in bello*, which prohibits the commission of such acts by a foreign army in the territory where it is present."[40] This armed incursion led also to gross violations of human rights in its wake. The ICJ found "credible evidence sufficient to conclude that the UPDF troops committed acts of killing, torture and other forms of inhumane treatment of the civilian population, destroyed villages and civilian buildings...incited ethnic conflict...and did not take measures to ensure respect for human rights...in the occupied territories."[41]

Another example of interstate violence involving resources, although initiated by a country with a history of interreligious violence, is the war between Nigeria, Chad, and Cameroon. Recourse to the use of armed violence in order to have access to oil did not stop in the Niger Delta. The Nigerian military also went on to occupy an area of Chad along with the Cameroonian Peninsula of Bakassi. Adjudicated before the ICJ, in *Cameroon v. Nigeria* (The Land and Maritime Judgment),[42] Nigeria contended, inter alia, that "Cameroon's claim to a maritime boundary should have taken into account the wells and other installations on each side of the line established by the oil practice and should not change the status quo in this respect." Whatever their source or cause, conflicts tend not only to result in human rights violations, but also push the affected persons (refugees) further into poverty.[43]

With most of these conflicts, violations of human rights and wastage of resources had an immediate or mediate religious dimension, either in their inception or execution and dispersion. Thus, it is particularly important that states and religious communities understand this and work for "A Common Word" or understanding among them. Since the population of the African continent is mostly Muslim and Christian, it is crucial that the two religions work to promote common understanding among them. During his recent visit to Africa, Pope Benedict XVI maintained that religion "rejects all forms of violence and totalitarianism: not only on principles of faith, but also of right reason."[44] Furthermore, he expressed the hope that the "enthusiastic cooperation of Muslims, Catholics and other Christians in Cameroon, be a beacon to other African nations of the enormous potential of an interreligious commitment to peace, justice and the common good," adding, "religion and reason mutually reinforce one another."[45] The most effective use of development resources would presuppose cooperation rather than competition.

African and Catholic Church Perspectives

If potential involvement of religion in armed conflict represents the downside, potential involvement of religion in development is the upside. In Africa, there are reasons to hope that common religious understanding can take place. Such perspectives are primarily religious in nature. Traditional religions and spirituality that predisposed Africans to Christianity and Islam have not entirely been displaced from African consciousness and worldview. Traditional religion is ubiquitous—as it is integrated in every aspect of life—economic, social, and political.[46] Africans integrate the secular and the sacred. Religion and reason—the basis for religion's commitment to this world—are thus not alien to the African worldview. African traditional religion is paradigmatic in regard to the promotion of cooperative coexistence and integration of development in every aspect of life.[47]

In general, most Africans are still very religious people for whom the proposition that religion and reason should coexist has resonance. According to Professor John Mbiti:

> Africans are notoriously religious...Religion permeates into all the departments of life so fully that it is not easy or possible always to isolate it. ...Because traditional religions permeate all the departments of life, there is no formal distinction between the sacred and the secular, between the religious and nonreligious, between the spiritual and the material areas of life. Wherever the African is, there is his religion: he carries it in the fields where he is sowing seeds or harvesting a new crop; he takes it with him to the beer party or to attend a funeral ceremony; and if he is educated, he takes religion with him to the examination room at school or in the university; if he is a politician he takes it to the house of parliament.[48]

Africa's traditional religions were not highly competitive among themselves.[49] This is because traditional religions had (and have) no universalistic ambitions; they were ethnic or national in character.[50] Any such religion would be bound to the people among whom it evolved. One traditional religion would not seek to propagate itself among another ethnic group.[51] Traditional religions had and have no missionaries to propagate them. Indeed, there is no conversion from one traditional religion to another, therefore, social tension that often accompanies proselytization is absent.[52] This process of accommodation has been extended in some countries to the relations between Christianity and Islam, although, the competition for African hearts and minds (evangelization and *dakwah*) that

Christianity and Islam exhibit has sometimes been exploited to disastrous ends. In many African countries, however, it is possible to find Christians and Muslims in the same family or workplace.[53]

Except in situations where religion is politicized, usually for economic or social advantages, most African countries understand the need for Christianity and Islam to coexist.[54] Due to economic development needs in many African countries, Christian and Islamic groups have a genuine opportunity to obtain the cooperation of the state, which would welcome religious actors as legitimate development partners.[55] Thus, religion, far from being the source of discord, violence, and underdevelopment, could be deployed as a tool to propel African development.

So where might religion, society, and development overlap in a positive sense? First, Africa's development and human rights challenges cannot be analyzed purely through the prism of religion. Primarily due to globalization, the Continent is increasingly engaged in modern life. This too, however, can be an opportunity for promoting "Common Word" approaches in Africa. Further, in an increasingly globalized world, characterized among other things by faster and easier means of communication, there are considerable chances for greater understanding of diverse cultures and religions. Many Africans, for instance, now use mobile phones and the Internet.[56] The more interaction that takes place, the more the significance attached to the different cultural expressions of common values will diminish.

Moreover, African states themselves, although with some setbacks, have expressed firm resolutions to put an end to the past marked by strife and conflict, including religious conflict. The Preamble of The Constitutive Act of the African Union recognizes that the "scourge of conflicts in Africa constitutes a major impediment to the socio-economic development of the continent and of the need to promote peace, security and stability as a prerequisite for the implementation of our development."[57] It also acknowledges the link between development on the one hand and democracy and human rights on the other. The principles of this Union include "respect for democratic principles, human rights, the rule of law and good governance" and the "promotion of social justice to ensure balanced economic development."[58] Importantly, African countries, such as South Africa, Botswana, Ghana, Senegal, Ethiopia, and Tanzania are providing examples to others regarding good governance, democracy and respect for human rights.[59]

Lastly, there are signs of hope that the international community is changing its attitude towards Africa, and consequently that the African Union is changing its view of the world. Africa cannot help but remember the legacy of colonization and the attitudes on which it was premised. Western colonization was premised on the assertion that Western values were superior to all others.[60] The Assembly of the African Union has expressed confidence that a new paradigm is underway with the election of President Obama (who coincidentally has Kenyan relatives). They stated that "under the dynamic and wise leadership of President Obama and with his reaffirmed commitment to the promotion of dialogue on all strategic issues of interest to the future of humanity and his sensitivity to the global challenges confronting the world, a new hope for change in the world would be created."[61] Change of attitude is particularly important with regard to how developed countries and international financial institutions, or organizations dominated by them, have crafted solutions to African development challenges. The IMF Managing Director Dominique Strauss-Kahn recently said, "[w]e understand that we need to change the way we work with Africa."[62] The paradigm of development assistance has not developed Africa. Instead, it has discouraged entrepreneurship and encouraged corruption and dictatorships/presidents for life (clinging to power), which tend toward violent internal or interstate conflict and human rights violations.[63] Trade and investment would be the solution for African development issues, and by extension, the antidote to human rights challenges. Particular attention should be given to the technical cooperation between developed and developing countries, where multinationals engaged in the exploitation of African natural resources generally pay host governments only a small percentage of profits after costs have been recouped.[64]

The ongoing global economic challenges will probably exacerbate the African challenges, because most countries are now becoming increasingly protectionist.[65] Africa's small share of international trade is likely to be impacted the most. African heads of state have expressed the view that "the current fall in consumer demand, particularly in developed countries, resulting in job losses do not result in protectionism that would exclude products, particularly from Africa and the developing world" and that the Doha Development Round needs to be completed to ensure that the developing countries have access to the markets of the developed world.[66] There has been little progress recently in reducing the barriers to exports from developing countries to developed countries. In December 2005, the developed country members of the World Trade Organization vowed that by 2008 they would make at least 97 percent of their tariff lines duty-free and quota-free for imports originating from the least developed countries.[67] "Excluding arms and oil, the proportion of developing countries' exports that have duty-free access to developed countries' markets has remained largely unchanged since 2004; it even fell slightly in the case of least developed countries."[68]

The African holistic view of reality was shared by Pope Paul VI's concept of integral and authentic development. Development cannot be conceived in purely material terms. Thus, in his encyclical, *Populorum Progressio,* Pope Paul VI stated that:

> The development we speak of here cannot be restricted to economic growth alone. To be authentic, it must be well rounded; it must foster the development of each man and of the whole man. As an eminent specialist on this question has rightly said: "We cannot allow economics to be separated from human realities, nor development from the civilization in which it takes place. What counts for us is man—each individual man, each human group, and humanity as a whole."[69]

In Africa, basic education is desperately needed. Development is a multifaceted issue, and education is the most fundamental approach to resolving development challenges. The poor are often caught in a vicious cycle. The United Nations acknowledges that "[t]he poor are not only those with the lowest incomes but also those who are the most deprived of health, education and other aspects of human well-being."[70] To break that cycle a multipronged approach and an array of simultaneous interventions are required, beginning with education. Indeed, the second goal of the Millennium Declaration concerned the achievement of Universal Primary Education. To this end Pope Paul VI proposed some concrete steps to achieve authentic development—basic education:

> [E]conomic growth is dependent on social progress...and...basic education is the first objective for any nation seeking to develop itself. Lack of education is as serious as lack of food; the illiterate is a starved spirit. When someone

learns how to read and write, he is equipped to do a job and to shoulder a profession, to develop self-confidence and realize that he can progress along with others. ...[L]iteracy is the "first and most basic tool for personal enrichment and social integration; and it is society's most valuable tool for furthering development and economic progress."[71]

In order for African children to reach their full potential and for countries to develop, the gains made in universal primary education must be replicated at the secondary level. "At present, 54 per cent of children of the appropriate age in developing countries attend secondary school."[72] There are some who think that focusing on basic health care and primary education is halting African development. They believe that investment in higher education is tantamount and that "Africa needs its own science and technology skills base to become an equal partner in the global economy."[73]

Pope Benedict XVI, speaking to Cameroonians in 2009, noted that:

Christians and Muslims...often live, work and worship in the same neighbourhood. Both believe in one, merciful God who on the last day will judge mankind (cf. *Lumen Gentium*, 16). Together they bear witness to the fundamental values of family, social responsibility, obedience to God's law and loving concern for the sick and suffering. By patterning their lives on these virtues and teaching them to the young, Christians and Muslims not only show how they foster the full development of the human person, but also how they forge bonds of solidarity with one's neighbours and advance the common good.[74]

The holistic worldviews of the different religious traditions should and can inform understanding of human rights. The Cold War's dichotomy in human rights conceptions (which is more important: civil and political versus economic and social rights)[75] seems to have been replaced by the so-called Clash of Civilizations.[76] Categories of West and East are categories of inclusion and exclusion. It is wrong to conceive Western culture and Christianity, Islam, or both, or even African cultures, in terms of confrontation instead of cooperation and mutual respect. "Each civilization or culture contains competing values that correspond to similar values existing within other cultures."[77] But, looking to the holistic worldviews of these religious traditions, as well as to the increasing globalization, there is a lesson for a holistic conception of human rights as this has implications for development. The dichotomy between civil-political and economic-social-cultural rights has transformed most development initiatives. Behind this divide is socialist-capitalist opposition.[78] Many people in the West and East, to this day, are still thinking in terms of the opposition. However, none of these is perfect. The truth is in the middle. That truth it seems requires a holistic approach, a rapprochement of the dialectical oppositions. Pope John Paul II seemed to support that approach. He stated the "Church's social doctrine adopts a critical attitude toward both liberal capitalism and Marxist collectivism."[79]

Pope John Paul II often talked about solidarity as a virtue.[80] One way to promote that solidarity today, over 60 years from the start of the United Nations and adoption of the United Nations Declaration of Human Rights, is to really be united. The International Covenant on Economic, Social and Cultural Rights provides that "each State Party to the present Covenant undertakes to take steps, individually and through international assistance and co-operation, especially economic and technical, to the maximum of its available resources, with a view to achieving progressively the full realization of the rights recognized in the present Covenant by all appropriate means."[81] The interpretation of this Article by the Committee on Economic, Social and Cultural Rights is that "international cooperation for development...for the realization of economic, social and cultural rights is an obligation of all States. It is particularly incumbent upon those States which are in a position to assist others in this regard."[82]

The United Nations Charter also calls for international economic and social cooperation. The Charter provides that the United Nations shall promote "higher standards of living...and conditions for economic and social progress and development," "solutions of international economic, social, health, and related problems; and international cultural and educational cooperation" and that "[a]ll Members pledge themselves to take joint and separate action in co-operation with the [UN] for the achievement of the purposes set forth in Article 55."[83] The Declaration on the Right to Development is anchored on precisely this Charter obligation. The Preamble of the Declaration provides that "[b]earing in mind the purposes and principles of the Charter of the United Nations relating to the achievement of international co-operation in solving international problems of an economic, social, cultural or humanitarian nature."[84] Article 3(3) of the Declaration provides that "[s]tates have the duty to co-operate with each other in ensuring development and eliminating obstacles to development. States should realize their rights and fulfill their duties in such a manner as to promote a new international economic order based on sovereign equality, interdependence, mutual interest and co-operation among all States." Inevitably though, the developed nations that are in a position to influence international financial institutions are not keen to adopt this human rights-based approach.[85]

The practice of taking economic, social, and cultural rights as seriously as civil and political rights is witnessed by the increasing justiciability accorded to those rights across many jurisdictions and legal instruments—whether directly or indirectly. Many constitutions of African countries,[86] international and regional human rights instruments, and jurisprudence, regard these rights as properly belonging to state responsibility. The African Commission on Human and Peoples' Rights held in *Social and Economic Rights Action Center and Center for Economic and Social Rights v. Nigeria*,[87] that Nigeria violated the rights to health, a clean environment, and property. The South African case of *Minister of Health v. Treatment Action Campaign* (TAC)[88] concerned an alleged violation of the right to public health care services. The Constitutional Court held that there was a state obligation to "take reasonable legislative and other measures, within its available resources, to achieve the progressive realisation of this right." In addition, that same court, in *Minister of Public Works v. Kyalami Ridge Environmental Association* ,[89] found that there was a constitutional obligation of government to provide access to adequate housing.

Looking to the developed world, the European Court of Human Rights has been able indirectly to find positive obligations of the state with respect to economic rights. For example, in *Airey v. Ireland*,[90] the Court noted that many civil and political rights had social and economic implications involving positive obligations. In *Chapman v. The United Kingdom*,[91] the Court held that Article 8 of the European Convention on Human and Fundamental Rights implied positive state obligations to facilitate the Gypsy way of life. In addition, the European Committee on Social Rights held in *European Roma Rights Centre v. Greece*,[92] that the implementation of Article 16 of the European Convention on Human and Fundamental Rights with regard to nomadic groups, including itinerant Roma, implies that adequate stopping places should be provided. In *International Association Autism Europe v. France*,[93] Autism Europe claimed that France had failed to provide sufficient education to adults and children with autism. Moreover, they claimed that social rights can be progressively realized when they are very complex and expensive, but this realization must occur within a reasonable time with the maximum use of available resources. This Committee held that lack of overall progress by France constituted a violation. In *F. H. Zwaan-de Vries v. The Netherlands*,[94] the applicant claimed that legislation that granted unemployment benefits to married men, but not married women, was discriminatory. The United Nations Human Rights Committee held that discriminatory legislation in the field of economic, social, and cultural rights can violate the right to equality in International Covenant of Civil and Political Rights. In the *Case of the "Five Pensioners" v. Perú*,[95] the Inter-American Court of Human Rights held that Peru had violated the rights to private property and judicial protection by arbitrarily modifying the pension amounts. In the *Case of the "Street Children" (Villagrán-Morales et al.) v. Guatemala*,[96] that Court held that the right to life comprises of not only the right of all persons to not be deprived of life arbitrarily, but also the right to have access to the conditions needed to lead a dignified life. In the *Case of the Yean and Bosico Children v. The Dominican Republic*,[97] that Court requested that the State guarantee access to free elementary education for all children, regardless of their background or origin.

In spite of the above instruments and jurisprudence, very few developed countries recognize in these international instruments serious international obligations as reaching social and economic rights. Many of these nations regard economic, social, and cultural rights as political aspirations rather than true legal rights. As a result of this prevalent mind-set, more than strictly legal approaches are needed. It could mean a rethinking of traditional human rights instruments with a view toward social and global responsibility. It could also mean strengthening global development approaches. The Millennium Development Goals (MDGs) are a step in the rights direction. In adopting the Millennium Declaration in the year 2000, the international community pledged to "spare no effort to free our fellow men, women and children from the abject and dehumanizing conditions of extreme poverty."[98] But these are not only development objectives; they encompass universally accepted human values and rights, such as freedom from hunger, the right to basic education, and the right to health. These goals are now challenged by a global economic downturn, with the possibility of unraveling even the few gains made on that front.[99] Perhaps the greatest threat to world peace is not so much interstate war and absolute state sovereignty, but internal conflicts feeding off extreme conditions of poverty.

African and Global Challenges and Opportunities

Social teachings of religious groups are particularly instructive. In his Encyclical, *Sollicitudo Rei Socialis*, Pope John Paul II identified important obstacles faced by developing nations, focusing the solution:

> [O]ne must denounce the existence of economic, financial and social mechanisms which, although they are manipulated by people, often function almost automatically, thus accentuating the situation of wealth for some and poverty

> for the rest. These mechanisms, which are maneuvered directly or indirectly by the more developed countries, by their very functioning favor the interests of the people manipulating them at [and] in the end they suffocate or condition the economies of the less developed countries.[100]

John Paul II proposed that "[s]urmounting every type of imperialism and determination to preserve their own hegemony, the stronger and richer nations must have a sense of moral responsibility for the other nations, so that a real international system may be established which will rest on the foundation of the equality of all peoples."[101] The Holy See's membership at the United Nations could be utilized by working with Islamic countries on matters of common concern, such as international development.

African nations also must make their contribution regarding change of attitudes. Instead of a definitive embrace of genuine and irreversible democratic governance, personal rule shrouded in a facade of democratic elections continues to be the norm in many countries of Africa. Violations of human rights and *coup d'états* continue to take place in Africa, in spite of the provision in the Constitutive Act of the African Union for the "right of the Union to intervene in a Member State...in respect of grave circumstances, namely war crimes, genocide and crimes against humanity."[102] Not only did the African Union fail to intervene in the Darfur situation, but when the International Criminal Court (ICC) indicted the President of Sudan for human rights atrocities, the Union urged the "United Nations Security Council...to defer the process initiated by the ICC."[103] In addition, the African Union called for a moratorium on the use of universal jurisdiction—a fairly effective instrument in fighting impunity. The African Union called on "all United Nations Member States, in particular the EU States, to suspend the execution of warrants issued by individual European States."[104] The AU responded in similar fashion to the latest crisis in Zimbabwe and recent coup d'états, but must do better than this.

Capital exporting states are understandably reluctant to invest in African states characterized by political instability.[105] And yet, for all their rhetoric and promises in the Constitutive Act of the African Union—to promote democracy, human rights, and intervene in countries that violate human rights on a gross scale[106]—African conflicts continue, as unstable countries and coup d'états litter the landscape. Indeed, the Protocol to the African Charter on Human and Peoples' Rights on the establishment of an African Court of Human and Peoples' Rights,[107] which preconditions individual petitions of the Court on a permissive prior and optional grant by their state parties, is yet another example of leadership that is reluctant to embrace full human rights protection.

But there are hopeful signs too. In Madagascar, after the recent coup d'état, weeks of political unrest devastated the economy and worried foreign investors.[108] The fact that the African Union suspended Madagascar after the coup seems to be an important first step to self-criticism. Perhaps, we can hope to build on that and urge African states to act consistently wherever respect for democracy and human rights are threatened or nonexistent, such as Guinea, Zimbabwe, Kenya, Sudan, Algeria, Somalia, Algeria, Morocco, and Tunisia.

Making Progress on Religion and Development

So, what concrete steps on the development side might resonate with the "Common Word" approach? First, there is a need to identify and overcome attitudinal obstacles. Pope John Paul II identified important structural obstacles faced by developing nations in his Encyclical *Sollicitudo Rei Socialis*, stressing the moral responsibility of other nations.[109]

Second, in a more globalized world, we must take advantage of modern means of communication in the promotion of the common word or action—media and the Internet—to promote common understanding as part of social awareness and outreach. The one who controls and shapes the word (message)—usually the media—matters more than ever. Is there a significant Internet presence regarding interreligious dialogue?

Third, a pragmatic approach requires development and advocacy for the virtue of solidarity. Christianity and Islam seemingly share views of social responsibility. As President Obama noted, it is possible to promote common understanding while collaborating for development through service projects that bring together people of diverse religious affiliations.[110] Since religious competition often frustrates such initiatives, it is imperative that governments give priority to collaboration-based projects. That way, as Obama noted, "we can turn dialogue into interfaith service, so bridges between peoples lead to action—whether it is combating malaria in Africa, or providing relief after a natural disaster."[111]

Fourth, we need to adopt the strategy of optimistic recognition of and emphasis on positive developments. A journey of a thousand miles famously begins with taking the first step, and continues one step at a time. The international community, the Catholic Church, the World Council of Churches, and Islamic countries taking an active part could recognize and work closely with individual African countries and the African Union in the promotion of positive and incremental developments. We may, for instance, point to the fact that Africans are committed to ending conflicts, whether interreligious or otherwise.

Fifth, while recognizing the contribution of globalization, it is also important to use local, more familiar strategies—focusing on African solutions and best practices. As President Obama noted, "There need not be contradictions between development and tradition. Countries like Japan and South Korea grew their economies enormously while maintaining distinct cultures."[112] The Constitutive Act of the African Union also binds the African Union to: "[r]espect for democratic principles, human rights, the rule of law and good governance" and the "[p]romotion of social justice to ensure balanced economic development."[113] These principles have begun to be lived out by the African Union and individual countries, which provides local best practices.[114] Christianity and Islam can most effectively solve tensions by each taking advantage of the best local practices: Africans solutions to African problems. This could be done by emphasizing best practices (beacons of hope) in countries with significant populations of Muslims, Christians, and other religions such as Senegal, Tanzania, and South Africa.

Sixth, religious actors could pursue joint efforts of engagement with international financial institutions, such as the IMF and World Bank. International actors, such as the Catholic Church, World Council of Churches, and Organization of Islamic Conference, could lead the way in engaging such institutions. These exchanges could change current attitudes in developed countries regarding developing countries, especially those in Africa. After many years of struggling with IMF and World Bank policies, perhaps these institutions are ready to listen more than ever because development assistance largely has not succeeded in Africa.

Seventh, while official or public sector development assistance has made some dents in African poverty, it has not really led to significant economic breakthrough. Development assistance has tended to discourage entrepreneurship, encourage corruption, and leaderships' clinging to power (dictatorships/presidents for life), which commonly engender internal or interstate conflict and human rights violations. Private sector trade and investment is the way to express respectful solidarity with Africa. I admit to not understanding enough about the specifics of Islamic views of economics and development. Are Islamic and traditional academic (Western) economic concepts of investment the same or different? What can we learn from and share with our Muslim brothers and sisters?

Finally, within the public sector, Africa needs investment in education. As President Obama noted, "[A]ll of us must recognize that education and innovation will be the currency of the twenty-first century."[115] This education must include molding new attitudes or paradigms in the present and future generations of people toward religious coexistence and partnership based on common ground and mutual interest. It means underscoring the contribution of social entrepreneurship and capital to the overall development of society. There is a role for religion in development, too.

Notes

1. See Heike Behrend, "Is Alice Lakwena a Witch? The Holy Spirit Movement and Its Fight against Evil in the North," in *Changing Uganda: The Dilemmas of Structural Adjustment and Revolutionary Change*, 164–65. The author notes that the violent conflict in the Northern Uganda had a religious dimension. See also U.S. Department of State, *International Religious Freedom Report* regarding the interreligious violent conflict in Northern Nigeria. Shamsul Bari—a United Nations Independent Expert on the Situation of Human Rights in Somalia—also noted that the public stonings, floggings, and summary executions carried out by Islamist armed groups in central and southern Somalia highlighted the "deteriorating" human rights situation in the strife-torn nation. See UN News Center, *Somalia: UN Expert Urges End to Inhuman Practices After Recent Stonings*.
2. Pope Benedict XVI notes that, "some assert that religion is necessarily a cause of division in our world; and so they argue that the less attention given to religion in the public sphere the better. Certainly, the contradiction of tensions and divisions between the followers of different religious traditions, sadly, cannot be denied. However, is it not also the case that often it is the ideological manipulation of religion, sometimes for political ends, that is the real catalyst for tension and division, and at times even violence in society?" Pope Benedict XVI, "Meeting with Muslim Religious Leaders, Members of the Diplomatic Corps and Rectors of Universities in Jordan."
3. Pope Benedict XVI, *Caritas in Veritas* (2009).
4. Kofi Annan, *The Causes of Conflict and the Promotion of Durable Peace and Sustainable Development in Africa*. Annan noted that in 1996 alone, 14 of the 53 countries of Africa were afflicted by armed conflicts, accounting for more than half of all war-related deaths worldwide.
5. Matthias Basedau and Alexander De Juan, "The 'Ambivalence of the Sacred' in Africa: The Impact of Religion on Peace and Conflict in Sub-Saharan Africa."
6. See R. Scott Appleby, *The Ambivalence of the Sacred: Religion, Violence, and Reconciliation*.
7. Paul Collier and Anke Hoeffler, "Greed and Grievance in Civil War," 587. See also James D. Fearon and David Laitin, "Ethnicity, Insurgency, and Civil War," *American Political Science Review*, 75–90.

8. Ibrahim Elbadawi and Nicholas Sambanis, "Why Are There So Many Civil Wars in Africa? Understanding and Preventing Violent Conflict," *Journal of African Economies*, 254.
9. Marta Reynal-Querol, "Ethnicity, Political Systems, and Civil Wars," *Journal of Conflict Resolution*, 32–33.
10. Basedau and De Juan, "The 'Ambivalence of the Sacred' in Africa," 8.
11. Ibid.
12. Ibid.
13. Elbadawi and Sambanis, "Why Are There So Many Civil Wars in Africa?" See also Basedau and De Juan, "The 'Ambivalence of the Sacred' in Africa," 8.
14. Ibid., 245.
15. For a general discussion, see Appleby, *The Ambivalence of the Sacred.* Mark Juergensmeyer, *Terror in the Mind of God: The Global Rise of Religious Violence.* See also, David Little, "Religious Militancy," in *Turbulent Peace: The Challenges of Managing International Conflict*, 79–91.
16. Basedau and De Juan, "The 'Ambivalence of the Sacred' in Africa," *supra* n. 5, 10.
17. Ibid., 11.
18. Ibid., 16. The cases between 1990 and 2007 include: Angola, Central African Republic, Chad, Congo Republic, Côte d'Ivoire, DR Congo, Ethiopia, Guinea, Liberia, Nigeria, Rwanda, Senegal, Sierra Leone, Somalia, South Africa, Sudan, and Uganda. Ibid., 17, tbl. 3.
19. Andreas Hasenclever and Volker Rittberger, "Does Religion Make a Difference? Theoretical Approaches to the Impact of Faith on Political Conflict," in *Religion in International Relations: The Return from Exile*, ed. Fabio Petito and Pavlos Hatzopoulos, 107. See also, Jonathan Fox, *Religion, Civilization, and Civil War: 1945 Through the New Millennium.*
20. This was the case in Central African Republic, Congo Republic, Côte d'Ivoire, Nigeria, Senegal, South Africa, Sudan, and Uganda. See Basedau and De Juan, "The 'Ambivalence of the Sacred' in Africa," *supra* n. 5, 22, tbl. 6.
21. Amnesty International, Comité Loosli Bachelard, Lawyers Committee for Human Rights, Association of Members of the Episcopal Conference of East Africa v. Sudan, Africa.
22. Ibid., ¶ 19.
23. See Amnesty International, *Sudan: The Human Price of Oil.* Benjamin Bock argues that "the war has never been merely a north-south or Muslim-Christian conflict…Sudan's intractable civil war is fundamentally a struggle over resources and how the country's wealth should be shared." Benjamin Bock, "Sudan: Mixing Oil and Blood," in *Amnesty Magazine.*
24. In *The Presbyterian Church of Sudan v. Talisman Energy Inc.*, the Court acknowledged that there was "evidence that southern Sudanese were subjected to attacks by the Government, that those attacks facilitated the oil enterprise."
25. Amnesty International USA, *Darfur: 'When Will They Protect Us?.'*
26. S.C. Res. 1593, U.N. Doc. S/RES/1593 (March 31, 2005), http://daccess-dds-ny.un.org/doc/UNDOC/GEN/N05/292/73/PDF/N0529273.pdf?OpenElement.
27. Prosecutor v. Omar Hassan Ahmad Al Bashir.
28. See the Preamble of Nigeria's Petroleum Act, Chapter P10 of the Laws of the Federation of Nigeria.
29. Africa Recovery: United Nations, *Delta Communities Protest Neglect.*
30. Section 162(2) of the 1999 Constitution guarantees that 13 percent of the revenue from natural resources be paid as derivation to oil-producing states from the Federation Account. The above right was upheld by the Supreme Court in the landmark case of *A.G. Federation v. A. G. Abia State.*
31. Peter Pham, *Islamism Comes to the Niger Delta.*

32. The Soc. & Econ. Rights Action Ctr. for Econ. & Soc. Rights v. Nigeria, African Comm. Hum. & Peoples' Rights.
33. On June 8, 2009, however, the parties in *Wiwa v. Shell*, 1:02-cv-07618-KMW-HBP (S.D.N.Y. Mar. 18, 2009), agreed to settle human rights claims charging the Royal Dutch/Shell company, its Nigerian subsidiary, Shell Petroleum Development Company (SPDC or Shell Nigeria), and the former head of its Nigerian operation, Brian Anderson, with complicity in the torture, killing, and other abuses of Ogoni leader Ken Saro-Wiwa and other nonviolent Nigerian activists in the mid-1990s in the Ogoni region of the Niger Delta. Documents relating to the settlement are available at http://wiwavshell.org/documents/Wiwa_v_Shell_SETTLEMENT_AGREEMENT.Signed.pdf.
34. It is difficult to assess the degree and character of the religious dimension of the LRA. According to the Human Rights Watch, the LRA, like its predecessor, Alice Lakwena's Holy Spirit Movement, initially believed that they could confront government troops' bullets armed with nothing more than stones and Shea butter oil smeared on their chests to protect them. Joseph Kony, generally understood to be the leader of the LRA, performed an eclectic mix of rituals, some drawn from Christianity, some from the indigenous Acholi traditional religion, and, increasingly, some from Islam. The fighters were told that those who obeyed the Holy Spirit would not be killed in battle: those who obeyed would be protected, while only those who offended the Holy Spirit would die. See Rosa Ehrenreich, "The Scars of Death: Children Abducted by the Lord's Resistance Army" in *Uganda*, ed. Yodon Thonden and Lois Whitman. See also Behrend, *Is Alice Lakwena a Witch?*, *supra* n. 1, 164–65; Ayebare Adonia, "Bullets Puncture the Faith of Ugandan Rebels," *Ottawa Citizen.*
35. *Prosecutor v. Kony*, Case No. ICC-02/04-01/05.
36. U.N. News Center, *Somalia: UN Expert Urges End to Inhuman Practices After Recent Stonings.*
37. "Eastern Chad is temporary home to about 300,000 refugees who have fled Sudan's Darfur conflict." Rebels, reportedly supported by the Sudanese government, have been trying to overthrow the Chadian government for three years. See Danny Padire, "Chad: 125 Rebels Killed in Battle," *World News Network*, May 8, 2009.
38. Yoweri K. Museveni, *Sowing the Mustard Seed: The Struggle for Freedom and Democracy in Uganda*, 177.
39. Case Concerning Armed Activities on the Territory of the Congo (Democratic Republic of the Congo v. Uganda), ¶ 245.
40. Ibid., ¶ 245.
41. Ibid., ¶ 211.
42. Land and Maritime Boundary Between Cameroon and Nigeria (Cameroon v. Nigeria) 2002 I.C.J. Reports 303, ¶ 256.
43. Department of Economic and Social Affairs of the U.N. Secretariat (DESA), U.N. Development Programme, The Millennium Development Goals Report 2008 (Aug. 2008), 7.
44. Pope Benedict XVI, "Meeting With Representatives of the Muslim Community of Cameroon."
45. Ibid.
46. John S. Mbiti, *African Religions and Philosophy* (London: Heinemann, 1971), 1–2.
47. Ibid.
48. Ibid.
49. Ibid., 4.
50. Ibid.
51. Ibid.
52. Ibid.
53. Pope Benedict XVI, "Meeting With Representatives of the Muslim Community of Cameroon."

54. Constitutions of many African countries provide for the separation of religion and state as a condition for social harmony and religious coexistence. For example, Angola Constitution, Arts. 8, 18, Constitution of The Republic of the Gambia, Art. 100(2)(b), Constitution of the Republic of Liberia, Art. 14., Constitution of the Federal Republic of Nigeria, Art. 10, Constitution of the Republic of Senegal, Arts. 1, 4, Constitution of the Republic of Uganda, Arts. 7, 71(b)
55. For example, Article 15(2) of the Constitution of the Republic of South Africa provides that "Religious observances may be conducted at state or state-aided institutions." In some countries, "state-aided institutions" include schools or health care facilities belonging to specific religious organizations.
56. Sharon LaFraniere, "Cell phones Catapult Rural Africa to 21st Century," *N. Y. Times*.
57. Constitutive Act of the African Union, 11 July 2000.
58. Ibid., Article 4.
59. Kaufmann D., A. Kraay, M. Mastruzzi 2009, *Governance Matters VIII: Governance Indicators for 1996–2008*.
60. Article VI of The Berlin Conference: The General Act of Feb. 26, 1885 refers to colonizers "bringing home to them [colonial territories] the blessings of civilization."
61. See H.E. Jean Ping, *Message of Congratulations to Mr. Barack Obama, President of the United States of America*.
62. Int'l Monetary Fund, "Africa Conference Debates Way Forward Amid Crisis," *IMF Survey Magazine: Countries and Regions, Tanzanian Conference*.
63. Thus, Professor Neil Turok (Chair of Mathematical Physics, University of Cambridge and founder of the African Institute for Mathematical Sciences or AIMS) argues, "One trillion dollars has been given in aid to Africa over the last 40 years, but that money has not reduced the need for aid in Africa, you have to ask yourself was it invested wisely? I would say it has done more harm than good. It has been used to create dependency, I think it's time for a rethink and at a very minimum I think a fraction of a percent of all the aid going to Africa must be dedicated to creating skilled people in Africa." Julian Siddle, "Africa Aid 'Needs Science,'" *BBC News*.
64. John Ghazvinian, *Untapped: The Scramble for Africa's Oil*, 286.
65. Mark Landler, "Trade Barriers Rise as Slump Tightens Grip," *N.Y. Times*, March 23, 2009, A1.
66. See *Addis Ababa Declaration on the International Financial Crisis*, (Assembly/AU/Decl.2 (XII). Investment creates jobs. See Raymond Baguma, "New Investments to Create 13,000 Jobs," *The New Vision*.
67. World Trade Organization, *Ministerial Declarations, Annexes*, WT/MIN(05)/DEC (December 22, 2005) ¶ 36.
68. Millennium Development Goals, *supra* n. 44, 46.
69. Pope Paul VI, *Populorum Progressio*, citing Louis Joseph Lebret, *Dynamique concrète du développement Paris: Economie et Humanisme*, 28.
70. Millennium Development Goals, *supra* n. 43, 5.
71. Pope Paul VI, *Populorum Progressio*, *supra* n. 70.
72. Millennium Development Goals, *supra* n. 44, 14.
73. Siddle, "Africa Aid 'Needs Science.'"
74. Pope Benedict XVI, "Meeting With Representatives of the Muslim Community of Cameroon."
75. Professor Oloka-Onyango argues that the "Cold War stalemate…caused both western and eastern mentors to turn a blind eye to the human rights violations of their client states…both categories of human rights—economic, social and cultural and civil and political—suffered as a consequence." J. Oloka-Onyango, "Beyond the Rhetoric: Reinvigorating the Struggle for Economic and Social Rights in Africa," *California Western International Law Journal* 26 (1995): 4. Some African scholars even argued

that the protection of civil and political rights should await the implementation of economic and social rights.

76. See Samuel P. Huntington, "The Clash of Civilizations?" *Foreign Affairs* 72 (Summer 1993), 22–50.
77. Abdullahi Ahmed An-Na'im, "Globalization and Jurisprudence: An Islamic Law Perspective," *Emory Law Journal*, 28.
78. Because of an ideological impasse, instead of adopting a unitary International Bill of Human Rights, the United Nations adopted two separate bills—the International Covenant on Civil and Political Rights and the International Covenant on Economic, Social and Cultural Rights. United Nations General Assembly, Resolution 217 (III): International Bill of Human Rights, A/RES/3/217.
79. Pope John Paul II, "Sollicitudo Rei Socialis" (address to the Bishops, Priests Religious Families, sons and daughters of the Church and all people of good will for the twentieth anniversary of "Populorum Progressio," December 30, 1987).
80. Ibid.
81. United Nations. International Covenant on Economic, Social and Political Rights, U.N. Doc. A/6316 (1966), 993 U.N.T.S. 3, entered into force Jan. 3, 1976.
82. Committee on Economic, Social and Cultural Rights, General Comment 3, *The Nature of States Parties' Obligations.*
83. U.N. Charter arts. 55 and 56.
84. C.H.R. res. 1997/72, ESCOR Supp. (No. 3) at 235, U.N. Doc. E/CN.4/1997/72 (1997.
85. According to Oloka-Onyango, the explanation for this is that "despite assertions that the administration of development assistance is an apolitical exercise, it is quite clearly linked to specific national interests . . . and the perpetuation of structures of dependency and control." Evidence of linkage can be located in the conditionality attached to such assistance, such as the stipulation that all raw materials, spare parts, equipment, etc., be purchased from the donor country irrespective of cost or the possibility of cheaper procurement elsewhere, and that technical assistance be expatriate (normally from the donor country) regardless of local availability of personnel. Oloka-Onyango, 20.
86. Algeria Const. Art. LIII (right to education); Art. LIV (right to health); Art. LV (right to work). Republic of the Congo Const. Art. XXXIV, §1 (public health); Art. XXXVII, §1 (right to education); Art. XLVI (right to healthy environment); Art. XLIII (right to development). Ethiopia Const. Art. XLIII(1) (right to improved living standards and to sustainable development). Namibia Const. ch. 3 Art. XX (right to education). Angola Const. Art. XXIX, §3 (right to education); Art. XXXI (creation of conditions for fulfillment of the economic, social and cultural rights of youth); Art. XLVII (medical and health care). Benin Const. Arts. XII & XIII (education of children). Burkina Faso Const. Art. XVIII (right to education, social security, health, etc). Chad Const. Art. XXXV (right to education). Equatorial Guinea Const. Art. XXIII (right to primary education). Rep. of Guinea Const. Art. XV (right to health).
87. The Soc. & Econ. Rights Action Ctr. & the Ctr. for Econ. & Soc. Rights v. Nigeria, Afr. C.H.R., Comm. No. 155/96.
88. Minister of Health v. Treatment Action Campaign 2002 (5) SA 721 (CC) (S. Afr.).
89. Minister of Pub. Works v. Kyalami Ridge Envt'l. Ass'n (CCT 55/00) [2001] ZACC 19; 2001 (3) SA 1151 (CC); 2001 (7) BCLR 652 (CC) (29 May 2001).
90. Airey v Ireland, 2 E.C.H.R. 305, 319 (1979).
91. Chapman v. United Kingdom, 33 E.H.R.R. 18, ¶ 96 (2001).
92. European Roma Rights Centre v. Greece, 41 E.H.R.R. SE14, ¶ 25 (2004).
93. Int'l Ass'n Autism-Europe v. France, 38 E.H.R.R. CD265 (2004).
94. U.N. Human Rights Committee, Communication No. 182/1984 (9 April 1987), U.N. Doc. Supp. No. 40 (A/42/40) (1987): 160–69.
95. "Five Pensioners" Case, Case No. 12,034, Inter-Am. C.H.R. (Feb. 28, 2003).

96. "Street Children" Case, Case No. 11,383, Inter-Am. C.H.R. (Nov. 19, 1999).
97. The Yean and Bosico Children v. Dominican Republic, Case No. 12,189, Inter-Am. C.H.R., ¶ 244 (Sep. 8, 2005).
98. United Nations Millennium Declaration, A/Res/55/2 (2000).
99. "In all but two regions, primary school enrollment is at least 90 percent." Millennium Development Goals, *supra* n. 43, 4. "In almost all regions, the net enrollment ratio in 2006 exceeded 90 percent, and many countries were close to achieving universal primary enrollment. In sub-Saharan Africa, however, the net enrollment ratio has only recently reached 71 percent, even after a significant jump in enrollment that began in 2000." Ibid., 13.
100. Pope John Paul II, 16, http://www.vatican.va/edocs/ENG0223/__P4.HTM.
101. Ibid., 39, http://www.vatican.va/edocs/ENG0223/__P6.HTM.
102. Constitutive Act of the African Union, Art. 4(h)(providing for the "right of the Union to intervene in a Member State pursuant to a decision of the Assembly in respect of grave circumstances, namely: war crimes, genocide and crimes against humanity").
103. See Decision on the Application by the International Criminal Court (ICC) Prosecutor for the Indictment of the President of the Republic of the Sudan, Assembly/AU/Dec. 221(XIII).
104. Decision on the Implementation of the Assembly Decision on the Abuse of the Principle of Universal Jurisdiction, Assembly/AU/Dec. 213(XII) (2002).
105. Michael Fleshman, "Laying Africa's Roads to Prosperity," in *Africa Renewal.*
106. Constitutive Act of the African Union, Art. 4.
107. Protocol to the African Charter on Human and Peoples' Rights on the Establishment of An African Court of Human and Peoples' Rights, Arts. 5 & 34(6), OAU Doc. OAU/LEG/EXP/AFCHPR/PROT (III) (June 9, 1998).
108. "AU Suspends Madagascar Over 'Coup'," ABC News.
109. Pope John Paul II, 39.
110. As President Obama put it, "human history has often been a record of nations and tribes—and, yes, religions—subjugating one another in pursuit of their own interests." Barack Hussein Obama, U.S. President, "Remarks by the President on a New Beginning."
111. Ibid.
112. Ibid.
113. Constitutive Act of the African Union, Art. 4.
114. Daniel Kaufmann, Aart Kraay, Massimo Mastruzzi, *Governance Matters VIII: Governance Indicators for 1996–2008.*
115. Obama, *supra* n. 110.

C. Development

17

An Islamic Perspective on Economic Development

Zamir Iqbal and Abbas Mirakhor

Islam has provided a blueprint of how a society is to be organized, and how the affairs of its members are to be conducted in accordance with its prescriptions. The system itself has not been applied in its entirety, with the exception of a brief period at the inception of Islam. Only in recent decades have Muslims become interested in society-wide implementation of Islamic teachings, with all this implies for development. What differentiates Islam from many other systems of thought is its unitary perspective, which refuses to distinguish between the sacred and the profane, and which insists that all of its elements must constitute an organic whole. Consequently one cannot study a particular aspect or part of an Islamic system, say its economics, in isolation without a knowledge of the conceptual framework that gives rise to that part or aspect anymore than one can study a part of a circle without conceptualizing the circle itself. Moreover, Islam formulates a particular relationship between *Allāh*, man, society, and the Divine Law. This relationship directly affects the workings of the economic system and implies an integral approach to human development. In this regard, "A Common Word" highlights the foundation for an Islamic theology of development with analogues to Christian teachings discussed in David Linnan's chapter in a historical context.

Within the dominant Western economic tradition, the history of the idea of development has a rich pedigree. It dates back at least to the Scottish Enlightenment.[1] Recently, Martha Nussbaum,[2] and to some extent Amartya Sen,[3] have drawn implications for contemporary thinking on development from an Aristotelian analysis of human flourishing in which humans are regarded as the final end of development, rather than a means to social order and progress. The recent sharp focus of dominant thinking on human development has been necessitated by the alarming growth of poverty across the globe. The World Bank estimates that nearly 80 percent of the world's population (5.3 billion) lives in low- or middle-income countries.[4] Of this number, 20 percent (1.1 billion) live on incomes below the international poverty line (less than a dollar a day), many of them inescapably trapped in perpetual poverty.[5]

In the course of its colorful history, the question of how economies change and grow has received a wide spectrum of responses, each containing a set of policy prescriptions based on assumptions regarding human behavior, institutional structure, the role of state and markets, and distributive justice. Each response by one generation of thinkers was found wanting by the next, as we shall see in the following section. The primary purpose of this chapter is, therefore, to provide an outline of essential elements of Islam's conception of development in the context of "A Common Word" and to help locate this conception within the spectrum of currently dominant ideas. It is thought that such an overview is important not only to provide a basis for comparison and contrast between Islamic and other conceptions of development, but also because heretofore these other conceptions have been the foundation of development policies and their implementation in Muslim countries. Although the paper's body focuses chiefly on the Islamic world, it concludes by relating this to the rest of the world.

Outline of Contemporary Approaches to Development

Thinking about development has evolved over many years producing a galaxy of definitions and meanings of the concept. Discourse regarding the various lines of thought and the empirical results of their application has become intense during the last three decades, and a consensus view of what development should mean and how to achieve it has yet to emerge. Before the Great Depression, much faith was placed in the unhindered workings of markets to achieve material development. After World War II, however, development thinking went through a fundamental change primarily influenced by the experience of the Great Depression. Markets were no longer trusted to generate automatically full employment of resources. This was particularly the case in policy prescriptions to developing countries. The basic idea was that the low-income countries could duplicate the material growth performance of rich countries. To do this, governments of these countries should take a leadership role in directing the development process. This period coincided with the ideological Cold War period. The rich countries in the West undertook to help the governments of low-income countries through development aid, provided that their politics would align with those of the West. The disappointing results of this model and lower availability of development aid soon paved the way for development models in the 1980s and 1990s that focused on structural reform. Toward the end of the last century, development professionals had to admit that structural reforms had not fully succeeded in reducing the gap between the rich and the poor either internationally or internally in many developing countries. In fact, the gap had increased. Even in countries where the structural reform policies had achieved some measure of success, income and wealth distribution had worsened. Overall, poverty rates had grown at an alarming rate, and the burden of debt of developing countries to the rich countries, and to their "international institutions," had increased dramatically threatening widespread default.

During the closing decades of the last century, development thinking went through another historic twist and turn as development specialists, intellectuals, and professionals began questioning the basic premise of the then dominant thinking that saw development as material growth and, facing the failure of the leading model, looked to at least prevent poverty from spreading. Professionals such as Mahbub ul Haq urged changing focus to "human development."[6] These efforts culminated in the closing years of the twentieth century in the work of Amartya Sen on *Development as Freedom*, arguing that the focus of development should be expanding the capabilities of people to empower them to do things they value.[7] Concurrent with the efforts of Mahbub ul Haq, Amartya Sen, and others, the New Institutional Economics (NIE) came into prominence with policy implications for development.[8] The NIE argued that in order to make economic progress, developing countries had to reform their institutional structure (i.e., the rules of the game). In short, high transactions costs—that is search and information costs, bargaining and decision costs, contract negotiation, and enforcement costs—render a market dysfunctional. Therefore, the collection of devices that organizes and supports transactions—channels for the flow of information; laws and regulations that define property rights and enforce contracts; and the informal rule, norms, and codes that help markets to self regulate—must provide a workable market design that keeps transaction costs low.[9]

This conclusion was reached as a result of empirical enquiries addressed to the question of why countries differed so widely in their economic performance. While differences in capital per worker, investment in human capital, and technology explain *some* differences in the level of per capita income among countries, none of these can be considered the fundamental reason for the underdevelopment of many countries, especially when capital and technology are mobile. The result of these studies confirmed that better performing economies had better institutions. The poorer performing economies not only suffered from deficient institutions but also from a "path dependency" that created an inertia, making change and reform difficult. The following sections, therefore, provide a rudimentary sketch of the contours of Islam's conception of development. In this regard, we shall see that Islam provides a strong platform of "devices and procedures to enable markets to work smoothly."[10]

Before proceeding, it is important to differentiate between "rules" and "norms." Both terms are used in the NIE literature. For example, institutions are defined as formal rules and informal norms and their enforcement characteristics. In what follows, we avoid using the term "norm," agreeing with Elinor Ostrom who says: "By norms, I mean shared prescriptions known and accepted by most of the participants themselves involving intrinsic costs and benefits rather than material sanctions or inducements."[11] She distinguishes between norms and rules by the fact of enforceability and sanctions. An example of a norm, according to Ostrom, is the precept: "put charity before justice." Such precepts "are part of the generally accepted moral fabric of a community. I refer to these cultural prescriptions as norms."[12] Rules, on the other hand, are "enforced prescriptions about what action or states of the world are required, prohibited, or permitted."[13] Since all of the prescribed precepts discussed in an Islamic development context are those that are ordained by the Creator from the Islamic point of view, they are rules not norms. In this sense, Islam is a rules-based system, and its conception of how humans and their collectivities can achieve material and nonmaterial progress is grounded on a scaffolding of rule-compliance, which assures such progress.

Islamic Conception of Development

Islam legislates for man according to his real nature and the possibilities inherent in the human state, as addressed in the previous chapters on comparative theology, mysticism, and metaphysics. Without in any way overlooking the limited and weak aspects of human nature, Islam envisages man in light of his primordial nature as a theomorphic being, the vicegerent of the Creator on earth, and a theophany of *Allāh*'s attributes with all the possibilities that this implies. It considers man as having the possibility of being perfect but with a tendency of neglecting his potentialities by remaining only at a level of sense perception. It asks, therefore, that in turn for all the blessings with which man is provided, he remembers his real nature, keep in mind his terrestrial journey, seek to realize the full potential of his being, and remove all obstacles that bar the correct functioning of his intelligence. To order human life into a pattern intended for by its Creator, man is provided with a network of injunctions, attitudes, and rules that represent the concrete embodiment of the Divine Will in terms of specific codes of behavior by virtue of acceptance—through the exercise of one's free choice—a person becomes a Muslim and according to which one lives one's private and social life. This network of rules is called the *Sharī'ah*, etymologically derived from the root meaning "the road," or that which leads to a harmonious life here and felicity hereafter.

The emphasis on the Islamic axiological principle of Unity forms the basis for the fundamental belief that Islam knows no distinction between the spiritual and temporal, between the sacred and the profane, or between the religious and the secular realms. Yet, only in the last three decades of the twentieth century did professionals look at broader conceptions of development than just growth of physical-material-producing capacity, as the preceding outline suggests. The idea that economic growth is only an element of the overall progress of human beings, and that humans should be the end rather than means of development is a relatively recent idea in mainstream development literature. Even in the most sophisticated of conceptions—that of Sen's development as freedom—the imperative of self-development as a prerequisite for cognizance of the substantive meaning of freedom receives little attention.[14] If development should mean freedom and functioning, an exercise of capabilities, what guarantee is there that capabilities and functioning—doing what one values—will not lead to a fully self-centered, selfish outcome that has produced massive poverty and misery for a large part of the humanity side-by-side with such astonishing opulence and colossal wealth accumulation for a few? Without a doubt some minimum level of income is necessary to avoid destitution and absolute poverty before one is able to think, reflect, and meditate upon one's action-decision choices. But beyond that, embarking on a phenomenological process of self-development becomes an imperative for humans to cognize the responsibilities of the human state from an Islamic point of view.

The Islamic concept of development, therefore, contains three organically interrelated dimensions:

1. Individual self-development called *rushd*;
2. Physical development of the earth called *'imārah*;[15] and
3. Development of the human collectivity, which includes both.[16]

The first dimension specifies a dynamic process of the growth of the human person toward the realization of *Allāh*-given potentiality,[17] alluded to in previous chapters in the context of theological anthropology.[18] The second dimension specifies the utilization of natural resources to develop the earth to provide for the material needs of the human individual and collectivity. The third dimension refers to progress of the collectivity towards full integration and unity. Self-development is the all-important anchor, for without it, progress in the other two dimensions is not possible in a balanced and appropriate manner; any forward movement in them without self-development leads to harmful distortions, such as the environmental crisis discussed in preceding chapters. All three dimensions must therefore proceed in tandem to achieve the desired balance (i.e., progress must be accompanied by justice both in its general [*'adl*] and interpersonal [*qisṭ*] conceptions).

The Qur'ān describes the metaframework for this development in that specific objectives are articulated and achieved with the adoption and implementation of institutions—rules of behavior and their enforcement characteristics—specified by the Qur'ān. The traditions of the Prophet, who implemented the institutional structure specified by the Qur'ān in Medina, are also essential in this regard. The framework thus implemented is referred to as the "Archetype Model." It is the ultimate frame of reference for implementation of the metaframework, and in principle, involves the application and implementation of it by the human being who best understood its meaning, substance, and objectives, namely, the Prophet of Islam.

This is not exclusive to Muslims, however. As a plural state, Medinan society was organized under a social contract, entered into between the Prophet and the multifaith inhabitants of Medina shortly after Muslims migrated from Mecca to Medina in 622.[19] This social contract, which came to be known as the Constitution of Medina, was composed of a series of documents and contained about 50 clauses of a practical set of agreed procedures. The documents that constitute the agreement between the Prophet and representatives of all inhabitants of Medina came into being at a time when many of the verses of the Qur'ān relating to socioeconomic-political issues were yet to be revealed. Nevertheless, the Constitution of Medina demonstrates how a multifaith, plural society led by the Prophet protected private property and its citizens rights by establishing equality and an infrastructural framework, along with an appeal process, that protected their rights. The Constitution of Medina affirmed that while the social contract was the ruling constitutional mechanism, members of each faith had the right to be judged according to the rulings of their own faith, with all this implies for "A Common Word." The Constitution created social solidarity, particularly in defense of the embryonic state in the making. It is important to note here that Medina in this context symbolizes the whole of Muslim society with a global perspective, not simply a city-state. The Archetype Model is therefore relevant not only to religious minorities living within the Islamic world, but to the Western world itself, to which we shall return in the conclusion.

In this sense, the Archetype Model operationalized and, to an extent, localized the conditions necessary for development as specified by the Qur'ān. The metaframework specifies rules (institutions) that are, to a degree, abstract, while the Archetype Model articulates the operational form of these rules. The core economic objectives of these rules include reducing uncertainty in economic transactions, allowing mutual sharing of economic risks, and permitting consumption smoothing for all members of the society, as we shall see in the following sections.

One of the foundational concepts to the justification of an Islamic view of development is *walāyah*, *Allāh*'s love-bond with His creation in general and humanity in particular.[20] *Walāyah* of the Creator for His creation is manifested through the act of creation and provisioning of its sustenance. For humans, as part of creation, this means provision of sufficient resources for sustaining human life. It also means provision of rules to sustain and flourish on this plane of existence. Humans reciprocate this love by extending it to their neighbors, both human and nonhuman, as "A Common Word" demonstrates. *Walāyah* is thus among the richest and most comprehensive words in the Arabic vocabulary. It is also a gerund denoting a relational activity between two things, most fundamentally of working towards intimate proximity.

Before describing Islamic development's institutional structure, it is helpful to situate the Islamic conception of development with respect to the constants of other conceptions (i.e., the roles of scarcity, rationality, state, and markets). All conventional conceptions of development without exception have assumed that scarcity is a general constraint posing a serious challenge for individuals and societies throughout human history. All these conceptions have also assumed a type of rationality first formulated during the Enlightenment in terms of the independence of reason, then refined in the twentieth century, with some modification in the form of "bounded-rationality" in mid-century. All conceptions also relied, to various degrees, on the role of the state and the role of the market, with some conceptions taking polar views on either total reliance on the state (such as communism or national socialism) or total reliance on the market (such as pure market capitalism of the neoclassical type) as instruments of solving the scarcity problem and creating social order and harmony. Associated with each conception were also institutional structures.

With respect to the role of scarcity, the Islamic view would suggest that the Benevolent, Merciful, Cherisher-Lord would not leave humans without sufficient natural-material resources to perform the duties expected of them. Consequently, the assumption that at a macro and general level humanity faces scarcity would be untenable.[21] This is not the case from a microperspective, however. Individuals, groups, and subsections of humanity do experience conditions of plenty as well as scarcity as one of the important tests of human experience on this plane of existence.[22] There is also a third type of scarcity that may be referred to as physical, temporal, or existential[23] scarcity, of which the Qur'ān repeatedly reminds mankind. This arises from the fact of the finite conditions of humanity on this plane of existence; the physical conditions of man impose a set of finite constraints. This particular notion receives considerable attention in the Qur'ān, which repeatedly reminds mankind of the shortage of time they are allowed on this earth, the rapidity of its passage, and the speed with which man's physical abilities erode over that short timeframe. This is illustrated by the question humans are asked after their transition to the next plane of existence: "How long have you tarried [on the earth]?" The answer to which is "a day, or part of a day" (Q 18:19). Thus, this temporal or existential scarcity of time, physical, and mental abilities forces humans to face the problem of allocating scarce means to alternative ends. "The resources that are ultimately scarce are life, time, and energy because of human finitude, aging, and mortality."[24] So there are three types of scarcity: macro, micro, and existential. The Qur'ān does not accept macroscarcity as a real problem; microscarcity is an issue that involves the twin pursuits of socioeconomic justice (*qisṭ*) and patience with the test of individual lack of resources; finally, existential and physical scarcity is an essential feature of the human condition on this plane of existence. When discussing the problem of scarcity, the firm distinction between these three types must be kept in mind.

With respect to the role of rationality, the Enlightenment notion that reason is self-sufficient and the sole arbiter of affairs, what Nicholas Adams, in his chapter, calls "maximal reason" is incorrect from an Islamic point of view. Since Ibrahim Kalin's chapter critiques this position in detail, suffice it to say here that the Qur'ān makes clear not only the importance of knowledge (*'ilm*) but its unlimited expanse to the point that it exhorts the Prophet to pray: *Say (O Messenger): My Cherisher-Lord, increase me in knowledge* (Q 20:114).

Substantive as well as instrumental rationality is possible according to this view, since *Allāh* has endowed humans with the faculty of *'aql* to allow a process of meditative-reflective reasoning.[25]

Regarding the role of the state and the market, the Islamic view of development conceives of these institutions differently from conventional approaches. In contrast to the notion of nation-states in the latter, there is no recognition given to an entity that can come close to the idea of a sovereign nation-state in the former. The Qur'ān makes references to people (*qawm*) identified with the prophets and messengers sent to them, such as the people of Noah (Q 7:69), Moses (Q 7:148), Abraham (Q 9:70), Jonah (Q 10:98), and of the other prophets. There is also identification of a people by their temporal leaders like the Pharah (Q 7:109) or with their behavior pattern such as the believing (Q 27:86), unbelieving (Q 23:44), ignorant (Q 27:55), unjust (Q 23:28), wrongdoers (Q 21:74), and the like. From all these verses, it becomes clear that a group of humans that share certain values are recognized as having a corporate identity. Thus the individual members of the group as well as the whole people in the group can be held accountable. As detailed as the Qur'ān is in describing the taxonomy of various groupings of humans in terms of their value systems, beliefs, and behavior, no recognition is given to nation-states as such. Of course, there are references in the Qur'ān to geographic entities such as the Byzantine Empire (*al-Rūm*), after which a chapter of the Qur'ān was named (chapter 30), or Sheba, a country with 12 townships after which another chapter (34) was named. However, the Qur'ān does not identify these and others as nation-states, but as groupings of people with their shared values and belief system. We outline the economic role of the state in greater detail in the following sections. Suffice it to say here that no authority has any legitimate basis for creating rules that contradict those that are specified in the metaframework and operationalized in the Archetypal model.

Turning to the concept of the market, the Qur'ān explicitly acknowledges its existence (Q 25:7, 20) and places great emphasis on contracts of exchange (*bay'*) and trade (*tijārah*). Since a contract of exchange is needed for trade of goods and services as well as other economic transactions, the former is more general than the latter. In another verse (Q 4:29), the Qur'ān commands that trade must be based on mutual consent. These and other verses make clear that prescribed rules require that economic transactions be based on freedom of choice and freedom of contract, which in turn require property rights over possessions to be exchanged. (It is also clear that political allegiance is based on a contract of exchange [*mubāya'ah*], requiring freedom of choice.) The Archetypal Model operationalized the conception of exchange and trade and the use of the market as the mechanism for this purpose. While the historical evidence strongly suggests that markets existed in Arabia before, even in Medina, it was the Prophet himself who created the first market structured in accordance with the prescribed rules of conduct specified by the Metaframework such that justice would prevail in exchange and trade. The Prophet himself specified these rules and encouraged their internalization by prospective participants before entering the market. The history of the evolution, operation, and growth of the market that the Prophet created in Medina underlines the importance and centrality of the market and rules related to its operation in an Islamic economy, to which we now turn.

Institutional Structure

The development of exchange on the basis of the legal institution of "contractus" rather than "status" is considered an essential antecedent of the development of markets.[26] In a recent book, *Reinventing the Bazaar*, John McMillan asserts that:

> Any successful economy has an array of devices and procedures to enable markets to work smoothly. A workable platform has five elements: information flows smoothly; property rights are protected; people can be trusted to live up to their promises; side effects on third parties are curtailed; and competitions are fostered.[27]

Two elements on which McMillan focuses as key to workable market design are free flow of information and trust, both of which, when they have a strong market presence, lower transaction costs. McMillan refers to a study of the bazaar in Morocco by Clifford Geertz who concludes that, in the bazaar he studied,

> [information] is poor, scarce, mal-distributed, and intensely valued. The level of ignorance about everything from product quality and going prices to market possibilities and production costs is very high, and much of the way in which the bazaar functions can be interpreted as an attempt to reduce such ignorance for someone, increase it for the someone, or defend someone against it.[28]
>
> McMillan adds:
>
> Prices are not posted for items beyond the most inexpensive. Trademarks do not exist. There is no advertising. Experienced buyers search extensively to try to protect themselves against being overcharged or being sold shady goods. The shoppers spend time comparing what various merchants are offering, and the merchants spend time trying to persuade shoppers to buy from them.[29]

These observations and assessments are not restricted to the bazaar in Morocco. Such a study can be replicated in the bazaars of all Muslim countries with generally the same conclusions. This is incredibly paradoxical, for the rules prescribed by the Qur'ān and explicated and implemented by the Prophet were addressed precisely to reduce transactions costs. In the market of Medinah, for example, the Prophet ensured, through propagation of rules of market behavior, that there would be no interference with the free flow of information regarding the quantity, quality, and prices of goods and services in the market to the point that he forbade a previous common practice of middleman meeting trade caravans outside the city and purchasing their supplies before entering the market. The market supervisors, appointed by the Prophet, ensured that there was no fraud, cheating, withholding of information, or other practices that lead to the malfunctioning of the price mechanism. His Archetypal Model was replicated in the centuries that followed in all the countries that had accepted Islam. Beginning early in their history and continuing well through the first millennium, Muslims structured their markets in the form of bazaars, which looked almost the same all over the then Islamic world. They were so structured even physically to possess characteristics that promoted rule compliance. Each physical segment of the market was specialized with respect to products. This allowed agglomeration economies resulting from physical concentration of similar traders in the same location. Prices were thus determined by fierce competition among suppliers, and every market was intensely supervised by a person called *muḥtasib* (person in charge of holding participants to accountability). This practice was started by the Prophet who appointed the first market supervisor. During the second and third centuries, market supervision was supplemented by self-regulation of each profession and trade by guilds.[30] Both supervisory devices were based on the rule-enforcement mechanism of "commanding the good and forbidding evil" in urging compliance with rules. These enforcement devices were fortified by the physical architecture of the bazaars that were constructed such that a grand mosque was located at the center of the bazaar with respect to all its segments. Every market participant, particularly the sellers, had an opportunity to attend at least two of the five daily prayers, noon and afternoon, congregationally in the mosque. This was an opportunity for the market participants to be reminded of their Creator, of their obligations to Him and to other humans, and of the accountability in the Last Day. Although the bazaars worked efficiently with these rules and devices, unfortunately, they did not have the opportunity to evolve in order to meet the requirements of an expanding economy or the growing complexity in economic relations. While presently physical remnants of bazaars exist in a number of Muslim countries, as Geertz has observed, they are highly underdeveloped, and the Islamic rules of market behavior are distinguished by their absence.

Regarding contract rights, it is worth noting that throughout the legal history of Islam, a body of rules has been formulated constituting a general theory of contracts based on the Qur'ān and the tradition of the Prophet. This body of rules covering all contracts has established the principle that any agreement not specifically prohibited by the Divine Law was valid and binding on parties and must be enforced by the courts, which are to treat the parties to a contract as complete equals. The command of faithfulness to the terms of contracts constitutes an important rule of social interaction.

There is a strong interdependence between contract and trust; without the latter, contracts become difficult to negotiate and conclude and costly to monitor and enforce. When and where trust is weak, complex and expensive administrative devices are needed to enforce contracts. Moreover, by now it is well known that complete contracts—ones that foresee all contingencies—do not exist, since not all contingencies can be foreseen. When and where property rights are poorly defined and protected, the cost of gathering and analyzing information is high, and trust is weak, it is difficult to specify clearly the terms of contracts and enforce them. In these cases, transaction costs are high. Where and when transaction costs are high, there is less trade, fewer market participants, less long-term investment, lower productivity, and slower economic growth. As North has pointed out, when and where there is rule-compliance and enforcement, certainty that property rights will be protected and contracts honored increases. In this case, individuals are more willing to specialize, invest in long-term projects, undertake complex transactions, and accumulate and share useful technical knowledge. Keefer and Knack argue that:

> In fact, substantial evidence demonstrates that social norms prescribing cooperation or trustworthy behavior have significant impact on whether societies can

overcome obstacles to contracting and collective action that would otherwise hinder their development.[31]

Beginning in the last decades of the twentieth century, there has emerged considerable interest in the importance of trust and cooperation.[32] It was noted earlier that trust is essential for the proper functioning of the market. More than that, however, trust is necessary for social solidarity. In fact, Uslander equates social with generalized trust in the society.[33] Among the conclusions Keefer and Knack draw from a survey of published empirical cross-country research on trust is that: (1) the levels of trust and trustworthiness vary significantly across countries, and (2) both trust and trustworthiness "have significant effect on economic outcomes and development." Moreover, they assert that "social norms that produce trust and trustworthiness can solve the problem of credible commitment" which, where and when exists, causes disruption in economic, political, and social interactions among humans. The problem of credible commitment arises when parties to an exchange cannot commit themselves or believe others cannot commit themselves to carry out contractual obligations. Where this problem exists, long-term contracting will not be widespread and parties to exchange will opt for spot-market transactions. In a cross-country study, Knack and Keefer find that per capita economic growth increases nearly by 1 percent per year for every 10 percent increase in the number of people who express trusting attitudes. They conclude that "evidence is fairly clear that income equality and education are linked to trust and other development-promoting norms."[34]

Social Justice and Development

The Qur'ān makes clear that all property belongs to the Creator, who has made all the created resources available for humans to empower them to perform what their Creator expects of them. This ultimate ownership will remain preserved for the Creator, with all this implies for social justice. Humans are allowed to combine their physical labor with the created resources to produce the means of sustenance for themselves and others of mankind. This right of access to resources created by the Cherisher Lord belongs universally to all of mankind (Q 2:29). There are only two ways in which individuals can gain legitimate property rights in the limited sense of the previous two rules governing property. Individuals can gain property rights through a combination of their own creative labor and other resources or through transfer—via exchange, contracts, grants, or inheritance—from others who have gained property right title to an asset through their own labor. Fundamentally, therefore, work is the basis of acquiring rights to property. Work is considered a duty; its importance is reflected in the fact that it is mentioned in a large number of verses in the Qur'ān. Work is a foundation of "belief." "Indeed there is nothing for the human other than (what is achieved through) effort and that (the results of) his effort will be seen and then he will be repaid fullest payment" (Q 53:39–41). The next rule governing property forbids gaining instantaneous property rights claim without commensurate work. The exception is transfer via gifts from others who have gained legitimate property rights claim on the asset transferred. The prohibition covers theft, bribery, gambling, interest from money lent, or, generally, income from unlawful sources.

Resources are created for all of mankind; therefore, if a person is unable to access these resources, her/his claim to resources (as an extension of the invariant ownership of the Creator) cannot be violated. All individuals have property right claims in resources even if they are unable to partake in the act of production. These rights must be redeemed, in kind or in monetary equivalence. In short, the Qur'ān considers the more able as trustee-agents in using these resources on behalf of the less able. In this view, property is not a means of exclusion but inclusion in which the rights of those less able in the income and wealth of the more able are redeemed. The result would be a balanced economy without extremes of wealth and poverty. The operational mechanism for redeeming the right of the less able in the income and wealth of the more able are the network of mandatory and voluntary payments such as *zakāt* (2.5 percent on wealth), *khums* (20 percent of income), and payments referred to as *ṣadaqāt*. This is the foundation of the rule of sharing ordained by the Creator, who also threatens those who shirk in meeting this obligation and violate the rule of sharing (Q 24:33; 3:180; 4:36–37; 92:5–11).

The next rule governing property imposes limitations on disposing a property over which legitimate rights are claimed. Property owners have a severely mandated obligation not to waste, squander, or destroy (*itlāf* and *isrāf*), use property opulently (*iṭrāf*), or as means of attaining unlawful (*ḥarām*) purposes. Once the rules governing property right claims are observed and related obligations, including sharing, are discharged, property rights on the remaining part of income, wealth, and assets are held sacred and no one has the right to force appropriations or expropriation.

Finally, distribution takes place postproduction and sale when all factors of production are given what is due to them commensurate with their contribution to production, exchange, and sale of goods and services. Redistribution refers to the postdistribution phase when the charge due to the less able are levied. Followers of all religions must remain fully conscious of their partnership with those who are less fortunate throughout the process of wealth creation and the fact that they must redeem the rights of others in the created income and wealth. Being unable to access resources to which they have the right does not negate the share of the poor in income and wealth of the more able. Moreover, even after these rights are redeemed, the remaining wealth is not to be accumulated, since wealth is considered as the lifeblood of the economy. Accordingly, Islam incorporates other donative institutions such as *awqāf*, or endowments, to play a key role in fostering all three dimensions of development.

Concluding Remarks

Although Muslims and Christians share the commandments to love God and love the neighbor, severe imbalances in the three organically interrelated dimensions of self-development, physical-material development, and societal development suggest a collective failure to realize these commandments. As Pope Benedict XVI argues in his recent encyclical on unbridled capitalism, "without truth, without trust and love for what is true, there is no social conscience and responsibility, and social action ends up serving private interests and the logic of power, resulting in social fragmentation, especially in a globalized society at difficult times like the present."[35] Indeed, secular approaches to economic development based on a fragmented view of man and nature have led to the current socioeconomic equilibrium. Accordingly, a shared religious response is necessary. It is here that an Islamic approach to development, in which the problem has been a lack of application rather than theory, is relevant to the West. As Seyyed Hossein Nasr asks in his chapter:

> Why can we not sit together and devise a new economic philosophy based on our mutual understanding of human nature in its full reality and our sense of justice that is a reflection of a Divine Quality in human life? Why simply be passive observers to the attempt now being made to infuse new life by artificial means into the cadaver of that greedy and selfish capitalism that has already done all of us, or should we say almost all of us, so much harm?

It is hoped that "A Common Word" can be a catalyst for a shared theology of development between the Abrahamic traditions to realize the supreme commandments of love of God and love of neighbor.

Notes

The authors wish to thank the editors for their valuable comments and suggestions. Views expressed in the article do not reflect views of the World Bank Group or INCEIF.

1. Jerry Z. Muller, *The Mind and the Market: Capitalism in Western Thought.*
2. Martha C. Nussbaum, *Frontiers of Justice.*
3. Amartya Sen, *Development as Freedom.*
4. *World Development Indicators 2009.*
5. Ibid.
6. Mahbub ul Haq, *Reflections on Human Development.*
7. Sen, *Development as Freedom,* supra n. 3.
8. See for instance Douglas North, *Understanding the Process of Economic Change.*
9. John McMillan, *Reinventing the Bazaar: A Natural History of Markets.*
10. Ibid., ix.
11. Elinor Ostrom, "Doing Institutional Analysis: Digging Deeper Than Markets and Hierarchies," in *Handbook of New Institutional Economics,* 824.
12. Ibid., 831.
13. Ibid.
14. For example, Giri suggests that Sen's idea of development as freedom lacks a treatment of the self that is necessary for human freedom and well-being and needs to be improved in several areas to make it a more complete view of freedom. Ananta Kumar Giri, "Rethinking Human Well-being: A Dialogue with Amartya Sen," *Journal of International Development,* 1003–18.
15. See for instance (Q 11:61). For an in-depth analysis, see Abbas Mirakhor and Idris Samawi Hamid, *Islam and Development: The Institutional Framework*, ch. 5.
16. For a detailed analysis of each dimension, see Abbas Mirakhor and Idris Samawi Hamid, *Islam and Development*, ch. 4.
17. One who is making progress on the path to perfection is called *rashīd*. The opposite of self-development is *ghayy*, meaning deep ignorance (Q 2:256).
18. See especially the chapters 3 and 5 respectively by Seyyed Hossein Nasr and Ibrahim Kalin, this volume.
19. See for instance S.K. Sadr, *The Economy of the Earliest Islamic Period.*
20. For a fuller discussion of *walāyah* and related concepts, see *Islam and Development*, supra n. 15, ch. 4.
21. See for instance Q 15:21. For a fuller discussion, see *Islam and Development*, supra n. 15, section 5.1.1.
22. See for instance Q 89:15-20; Q 30:37-38.

23. Walter Weisskopf, *Alienation and Economics*, 22.
24. Ibid., 22–23.
25. For a detailed analysis, see *Islam and Development*, supra n. 15, ch. 4.
26. Karl Polanyi, *Primitive, Archaic, and Modern Economics.*
27. McMillan, *Reinventing the Bazaar*, supra n. 9, ix.
28. Clifford Geertz, "The Bazaar Economy: Information and Search in Peasant Marketing," *American Economic Review*, 28–32.
29. McMillan, *Reinventing the Bazaar*, supra n. 9, 41.
30. See for instance Adam Mez, *The Renaissance of Islam*, ch. 26; M.J. Kister, "The Market of the Prophet," *Journal of the Economic and Social History of the Orient*; and Hussein Shihata, *Market Competition in Light of the Islamic Shari'ah.*
31. Philip Keefer and Stanley Knack, "Social Capital, Social Norms and the New Institutional Economics," in *Handbook of New Institutional Economics*, 700.
32. See for instance Edward Lorenz, "Trust, Contract and Economic Cooperation," *Cambridge Journal of Economics*, 301–15; Keiron O'Hara, *Trust from Socrates to Spin*; and Eric M. Uslaner, *The Moral Foundation of Trust.*
33. E.M. Uslander, *The Moral Foundation of Trust.*
34. Philip Keefer and Stanley Knack, "Social Capital, Social Norms and the New Institutional Economics," 721.
35. Pope Benedict XVI. *Caritas in Veritate.* Encyclical Letter, 2009, paragraph 5.

18

A Common View of Development: Richer Versus Better, and Who Decides?

David K. Linnan

The religious anchor of "development" is love of neighbor, where it fits directly under the umbrella of "A Common Word." Beyond that foundation, however, there is considerable ambiguity. Most religious treatments of development presumably focus on social justice claims at the retail level (amelioration of poverty, tied often to charity and linked indirectly to Christian scriptural authority for the special place of the poor) versus broader distributional justice claims at the wholesale level (North-South divide, or differentiated and special treatment for developing countries, and now also concerns like global climate change's anticipated disproportionate impact on developing countries). But poverty alleviation does not equate directly to development because, despite its prominent place in documents such as the United Nations Millennium Development Goals (MDG), the wholesale or governmental level of development is still more often understood as some form of society-wide modernization, whether institutional, technological, or otherwise.

That is seemingly the crux of the whole North-South conflict minus dependency rhetoric, so what shall we make of development ordinarily? If viewed as an exercise among independent states, from a modern international law perspective one could treat development as a priority among states as independent actors, or as taking place within a unitary international community (with claims in the alternative to rights to development at the level of member states in the community, or human rights of the disadvantaged at an individual level). The conceptual "trick" in traditional secular rights analysis is to find a sovereign, whether a state or a hypothetical community, against which to assert such "rights" claims in terms of individual worth or distributive justice at the societal or individual level. The traditional approach in the religious context has been to seek an external anchor in some order of the universe preordained by God. The essence of such a preordained order is commonly referred to as "natural law." For purposes of our own applications analysis, we are focused more on development in action. For discussion purposes, we need not choose a single intellectual frame of reference. Intellectual frameworks are always close to the surface, however, especially under current circumstances in areas of common challenges like climate change. The challenge in a diverse environment is in recognizing the balancing of interests going on even while the dialogue is conducted typically in terms of differing justifications. Who owes what to whom, and why?

Concerning international public health, the good news is that people in most of the developing world, including its children in particular, are healthier and live substantially longer than even 50 years ago. This results from general advances in maternal health and child survival, plus extended life expectancy. This is not the case in sub-Saharan Africa, however, raising problems of how to address health differentials within the developing world, including appropriate technology issues.

The balance of this chapter first examines the general orientation of secular development policy, which has been premised at least since the 1970s on neoclassical economic approaches (the Washington Consensus). We then move from economic development to health as broader social indicator before examining specific Catholic and Protestant views of development. We finish with a review of recent World Bank development approaches, including sustainability concerns.

Historical and Social Background

Ordinary concepts of development present definitional problems of their own. Initial issues include what actually constitutes development (material, spiritual, technological, or whatever), how to measure it (via per capita gross domestic product, or GDP; employing social or public health indicators like educational attainment or life expectancy;[1] or more recently pursuing environmental ideals like sustainability), how best to achieve it (via what combination of economic and social policies, plus under what form of government: state or society), and the political exercise of explaining where and why things go wrong or right (implying causality after the fact).

On a political level, however, the ordinary definitions hide more issues than they clarify. Development takes place at the collective or state rather than individual level at which Christianity focuses (given God's relationship to man, linked with individual salvation). It happens largely in a non-Western setting, often where there may be serious doubt about whether there even is a modern state, as opposed to an aggregation of tribes (or even a failed state suffering from endemic armed conflict). Development or foreign assistance is also a major industry with its own multilateral (World Bank, UNDP, ADB, etc.) and bilateral (USAID, CIDA, GTZ, etc.) bureaucracies. I have yet to meet any person in any country who does not believe that things would be better if only they (and their society) were wealthier. This is the easy aspect—everyone desires to be richer. That is not to praise consumerism as such, since many people would devote such greater wealth to serving others, gaining knowledge, or pursuing other selfless activities. So there is an openness and even eagerness among all to pursue economic development cooperatively on an international basis.

By the same token, if the discussion goes beyond economic aspects to governance and political questions like democratization or human rights on the gender level, especially if local practices are considered by foreigners to impede development, foreign participation often meets resistance rather than acceptance. So in local eyes, foreign involvement in development may oscillate between being regarded as a help on the economic side, and a hindrance or impermissible interference on the social side. The problem is that, over the past 30 years, the focus of development on an operational level typically has shifted away from simple physical infrastructure like building roads or dams in the nature of hardware, and instead focus has shifted to the nonphysical or software side to embrace ideas like governance or capacity building (indirectly embracing ideas like human capital).[2] This is the problem of who decides what *better* means, once you move beyond economic performance as such? But, as recognized by Joseph Isanga, cultural practices can negatively affect even economic development.

Ultimately, the issue becomes whether it makes sense to register claims of right to support when outsiders think local views impede development. By way of concrete example, the accepted view among development professionals is that the single best investment from an economic point of view in the early stages of development of traditional societies is in the education of women. The consistently observed payback comes from increased attention to health and nutrition in the home, healthier children, and economically more secure families. But what is the proper response if this observed economically advantageous approach were rejected by some for social reasons? What happens when the conservative social claim is rooted in religious interpretation? Whose responsibility are the resulting negative effects (opportunity costs in economic terms)?

Posing questions about "richer" versus "better" today is different compared to the same exercise 30–40 years ago. What used to be considered the undifferentiated developing world is now recognized as containing post-World War II, postindependence great success stories (typically in East Asia[3]), as well as dismal failures (typically in sub-Saharan Africa), and a wide spectrum of outcomes in between (often in Central and South America). Once upon a time, the issue was whether development should be equated to modernization, and modernization to Westernization.[4] Success stories involving non-Western societies complicate that (Japan going back to the nineteenth century, more recently countries like Korea, Singapore, and China). Meanwhile, current inquiries into development's failure in individual countries often focus on factors rooted in social and cultural aspects. Success stories also challenge coincidentally politically expedient explanations for underdevelopment like dependency theory, even while theoretical justifications for development's support have ranged from claims that there is a human right to development (entailing enforceable claims on resources from wealthier countries) to the idea that economic and other support is offered freely by wealthier nations to developing countries simply because it is in the wealthier nations' own political and economic interest.

Meanwhile, the formal role of religion in development is visible in the modern Western setting typically via charities with a recognized religious link (e.g., Save the Children[5] or World Vision[6]). Many Protestant Churches in particular have adopted under various approaches to the social gospel ideas of secular development targets like the United Nation's Millennium Development Goals (MDGs),[7] and the Catholic Church's longstanding social doctrine which has incorporated development prominently via Papal encyclicals beginning with Pope Paul VI's *Populorum Progressio* (1967)[8] and most recently in Pope Benedict XVI's *Caritas in Veritate* (2009).[9]

The ground is also currently shifting on the basis of questions rooted in distributional justice concerns within or between countries in the form of issues about unequal income distribution (development producing winners and losers), migration (rural to urban or between countries, pursuing employment and a better life), access to amenities with economic or public health effects (e.g., education, electrification, and clean water), sharing technology (representative for broader issues revolving around claims to special and differential treatment for developing countries in any number of settings), and rising expectations, which may lead to social unrest if they remain unsatisfied. So development is at one level a technical challenge, but its failure presents political problems. And hearkening back to our introduction conceptualizing development, arguments about independent states versus secular rights-based claims in a unitary international community, versus more religiously oriented natural law-based claims are best understood at the level of justification.

Economic Management and Development

Economic development as topic of academic focus is most commonly tied to the wave of newly independent colonies post-World War II, and indirectly to the activities of international economic institutions. These were initially the World Bank and International Monetary Fund, which by the late 1950s turned from rebuilding Europe to development work in the newly independent colonies (referred to generically as the Bretton Woods institutions, and later the Bretton Woods system). The related 1947 General Agreement on Tariffs and Trade (GATT) was followed by the 1994 World Trade Organization (WTO), and trade liberalization mounted in importance in conjunction with development strategies such as export-led economic growth. The still ongoing Doha Development Round is the latest evidence of the connection between understandings of the international economic system and the concept of development. As a result, (secular) understandings of development have changed over time even as economic circumstances and theories have changed. And while Socialist countries and much of the Islamic world stayed outside the GATT/WTO system initially, since the 1990s country membership is increasingly universal. But membership is traditionally understood as an election for certain market-oriented economic approaches in managing national economies, rather than as political act per se, even while broader membership has increased pressure for changing the Bretton Woods system itself.

Meanwhile, technical economic understandings behind development policies have changed, but continue to reflect a certain lack of consensus in the (development) economics profession concerning the proper explanation of, and approach to, mysteries like differentials in economic growth rates (e.g., why is China growing so fast since circa 1990 and Latin America at a moderate pace, even while the economies of some African countries have shrunk post-1960s independence?). So the 1950s–1960s view of development is best understood as balanced between political views focused on modernization (originally looking backwards to the question of how Western countries developed) and economic growth in the form of industrialization.

The 1950s–1960s development era simply assumed the role of the secular state in leading development, and founded the original understanding of modernization in trying to emulate the development of European states. The political background included an orientation toward social democracy (arguably as legacy of Fabian socialism to which the market typically took a back seat; more recently, the discussion is phrased in terms of a "social market" under labor party policies as intellectual inheritors). Newly independent countries still focused necessarily on primary industries as the typical inherited economic bulwark of late colonial era economies. They were often greatly dependent upon commodities prices as a result, and well-trained indigenous human resources were exceedingly rare. At the height of the Cold War, the newly independent states might stress central planning for ideological reasons, but coming as often from (Western) Fabian socialist as

Eastern Block sources. This was an era of economic ideas bordering on autarky, like import-substitution policies and infant industry protection to accelerate industrialization.

On the level of international politics, beyond the Cold War, the 1970s became the era of the New International Economic Order (NIEO), gaining its name from the Declaration for the Establishment of a New International Economic Order, adopted by the United Nations General Assembly in 1974, which referred to a wide range of trade, financial, commodity, and debt-related issues in the original North-South context.[10] The NIEO was intended to be a revision of the international economic system in favor of developing countries, replacing the Bretton Woods system. Newly independent states focused on primary industries claimed sovereignty over their natural resource-based economies in opposition to multinational enterprises. They sought at the same time to decrease the influence of private sector enterprises, often tied to their former metropolitan states, in emphasizing state-owned enterprises. Separately, the development of international environmental concerns also dates to the 1970s, with the 1972 United Nations Conference on Human Environment and the resulting 1972 Stockholm Declaration[11] as sources, followed in a separate development line by the 1992 Rio Declaration on the Environment and Development,[12] the 2002 Johannesburg Declaration on Sustainable Development,[13] and ultimately the 2009 United Nations Climate Change Conference in Copenhagen (to be addressed separately in conjunction with sustainability concerns).

The 1970s created external economic problems for developing countries generally in the form of the first oil price shock, but which coincidentally benefited oil-producing states in the Islamic world. The attendant recycling of petrodollars gained through oil price hikes into sovereign loans by the international banking system is often tagged as the source of the early 1980s Latin American debt crisis. We recall the Latin American debt crisis mostly as the background of the economic policy prescription referred to generally as the "Washington Consensus."[14] The Washington Consensus is shorthand for a policy emphasis at the government level on elimination of fiscal deficits for stability purposes, moving public expenditure priorities from consumption to investment, raising revenues via tax reform, financial sector reform in terms of market-determined, positive real interest rates to avoid misallocation of funds and discourage capital flight, trade liberalization, encouragement of foreign direct investment, privatization, deregulation and the clear establishment of property rights to enable the market mechanism. The Washington Consensus as relatively pure neoclassical economics approach reflected political and economic currents in place then (and largely still).[15] It was implemented in development practice by means of IMF conditionality, via a focus on macroeconomic policy and institutions (for example, establishment of politically independent, technically competent central banks for monetary policy, or government agencies responsible for competition policy). This was linked theoretically with the adoption of a rule-of-law framework to provide enforceable contract and property rights. Reform of many of the same institutions (courts and judiciary, etc.) were involved as with a separate push for democratization and human rights, but the legal changes were specifically oriented toward economic development.[16]

The 1980s development emphasis shifted toward open markets and trade liberalization, linked with export-oriented development particularly in Asia's case, and correspondingly away from state-led development. Financial sector liberalization as part of deregulation also played a part to the extent the push to create banking and capital markets for economic management purposes resulted in the entire emerging markets phenomenon (and so portfolio investment took its place as means to mobilize domestic and foreign investment funds for development purposes).

The economic orientation visible in the Washington Consensus also changed IFI policy more broadly and rendered developing countries much more reliant on private sector investment flows in parallel. Portfolio and direct foreign investment became part of the standard development playbook. This liberal market orientation assumed an even higher profile at the end of the 1980s with the fall of the Berlin wall, following which formerly socialist countries shifted toward a market orientation and privatized state-controlled economies on a massive basis. The 1994 WTO creation and the 1999 accession of China, alongside former socialist countries joined also by countries from the Islamic world, has resulted in a world where the economic direction within the international community comes more at the level of the G-20 countries, including from the Islamic world Turkey, Saudi Arabia, and Indonesia, rather than from the G-7 as the traditional core group of industrialized countries.

The private sector has reorganized production and supply chains internationally in conjunction with innovations such as free trade areas (FTAs, permissible under Gatt/WTO Article XXIV), also pursuing services liberalization in both multilateral and FTA fora. Beyond traditional multinational enterprises, an entirely new generation of multilateral enterprises headquartered in the developing world (mostly, but not exclusively, in Asia) are now pursuing business internationally. Striking differences are visible within the present and former developing countries in terms of newer South-South cooperation, for example the market oriented Asian private sector dealings in entering still statist Africa, or within South America, the 2006 Bolivian hydrocarbon nationalizations having the greatest effects on Petrobras as Brazilian energy concern and Spanish-Argentinean Repsol (so *not* on traditional, Western multinationals).

On the whole, the economic prospects of the developing world have changed radically since the 1960s, albeit unevenly. The practical question is the extent to which it makes sense to talk about developing countries as a whole versus traditional societies, returning to the modernization question, precisely because of the noted changes. If there are successful models of how to modernize, what does it mean if a society chooses not to pursue them? But equally, what does it mean if problems like climate change render traditional development strategies like industrialization much more difficult?

International Health and Development

Public health is another area of general interest for international development.[17] It is an integral part of social-based measures of development, separate from GDP-based measures of economic development, and so is of direct interest to us in trying to determine to what extent substantial development progress has been made. On a statistical level, the focus and chief objective measures involved include maternal and child survival (infant mortality as well as child mortality through age five), as well as life expectancy generally. The hidden question is the extent to which medical science and public health approaches have produced very significant advances also in low- and middle-income countries during the past 50 years;

comparable to what occurred perhaps 100 years ago in the industrialized world. This would be a welcome development, but on a policy level the issue should be understood in terms of whether an epidemiologic transition has occurred, and what would be the proper response if the predominant causes of mortality have shifted from infection to chronic disease and injury as in the developed countries. In practical terms, the problem is whether developing countries have advanced to a public health stage where their problems are not that different from public health challenges in high-income countries, including obesity, diabetes, cancer, etc. For development purposes, it also carries over into questions about human rights approaches to health, as well as prospective international health policy.

At the middle of the last century, there was little doubt that infectious diseases were the major killers of children in low- and middle-income countries. Child mortality was known to be high in a qualitative sense, but quantitative data at national and regional levels were practically nonexistent. Most deaths were not reported to any level of the health system, had no medically established cause and occurred within the community.[18] As a result, the only national mortality information came from census data, which measured deaths from all causes, without any way to categorize them by type. The census data did allow for the determination of infant mortality rates and life expectancy at birth. The figure below shows that the period between the late 1970s through the 1990s was characterized by very rapidly declining infant mortality in various regions of the developing world (United States and Bangladesh are included for specific comparisons as high-income Western and relatively low-income Islamic majority countries).

The trend has continued and a new pattern of childhood mortality is emerging in the developing world. From 1960 to 1990, the infant mortality rate in developing countries typically dropped from a range of 140–160 to below 100 per 1,000 births.

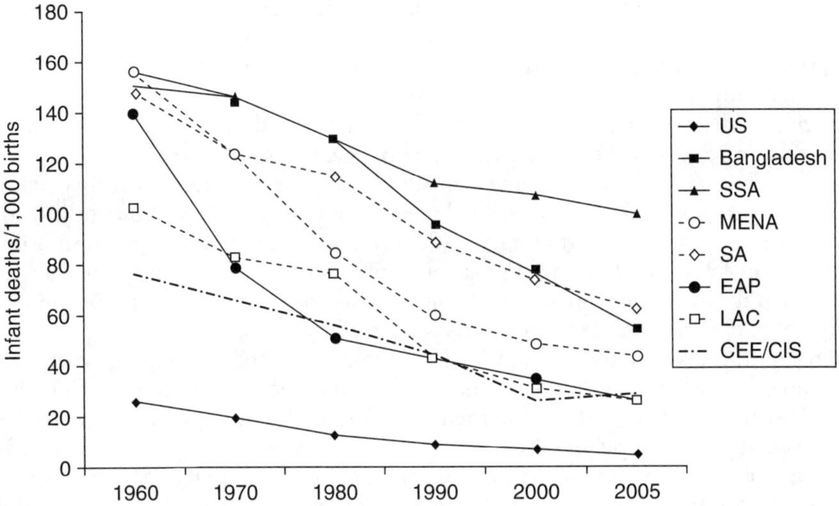

Figure 18.1 Decrease in Infant Mortality Rate since 1960 by Country/Region. World Bank regional indices are: Subsaharan Africa (SSA), Middle East and North Africa (MENA), South Asia (SA), East Asia and Pacific (EAP), Latin America and Caribbean (LAC), and Central and Eastern Europe/CIS (CEE/CIS).

Source: World Bank, UNICEF.

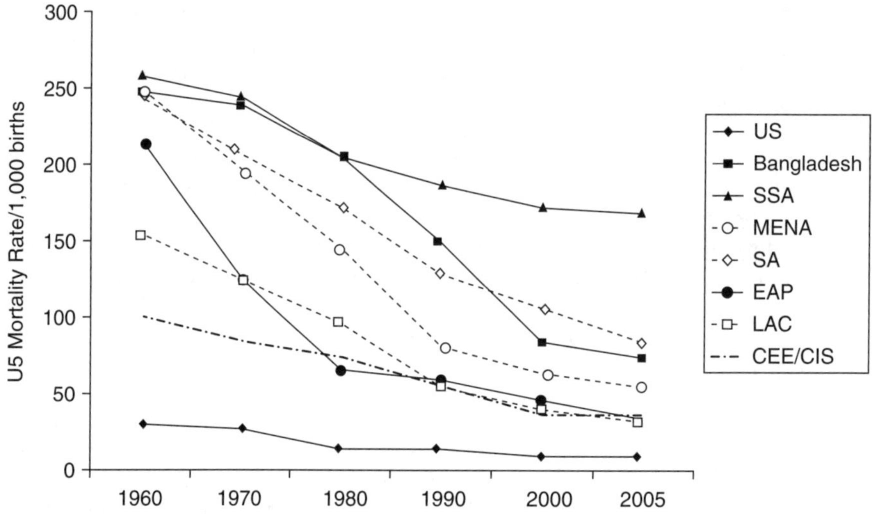

Figure 18.2 Decrease in Under Five Mortality Rate since 1960 by Country/Region. World Bank regional indices are: Subsaharan Africa (SSA), Middle East and North Africa (MENA), South Asia (SA), East Asia and Pacific (EAP), Latin America and Caribbean (LAC), and Central and Eastern Europe/CIS (CEE/CIS).

Source: World Bank, UNICEF.

Between 1990 and 2005 the infant mortality rate fell by up to 50 percent again. By World Bank regional categories, in the Middle East and North Africa (MENA) the rate dropped from 59 to 43, in South Asia (SA) from 89 to 63, in East Asia and the Pacific (EAP) from 43 to 26, in Latin America and the Caribbean (LAC) from 43 to 26, in Central and Eastern Europe/CIS (CEE/CIS) from 44 to 29. The only notable exception was in sub-Saharan Africa (SSA), where between 1990 and 2005 the rate dropped only from 112 to 101 (starting from a relatively high level).[19] Figure 18.2 provides a clear picture of how in early child mortality decreased, measured as the mortality rate for children under five years of age, per 1,000 live births.

The picture of a relative decline is much the same as for infant mortality (which the under-five mortality statistics includes), showing higher child mortality than in the United States as representative Western country, but evincing real improvement from 1960 to 1990 and thereafter. The rate of death in children under five years old declines primarily through the elimination of measles, tetanus, and the control of diarrhea and pneumonia, as witnessed by the case of Bangladesh. These were the targets of international health programs in the developing world that promoted early and exclusive breast-feeding, focused on mothers getting their children immunized, and taught them to bring children in for treatment when they showed signs of pneumonia, etc.

Here the examination needs to focus more closely on Bangladesh as a (Islamic majority) country for international health purposes with relatively rare child mortality statistics including cause of death. With the rapid decrease in many traditional causes of death (by over two-thirds) there was a proportional increase in drowning as a cause of death as shown in the figure 18.4.

Drowning has been the leading injury killer in early childhood in Matlab, Bangladesh, from the inception of record keeping. It has not changed, as noted by

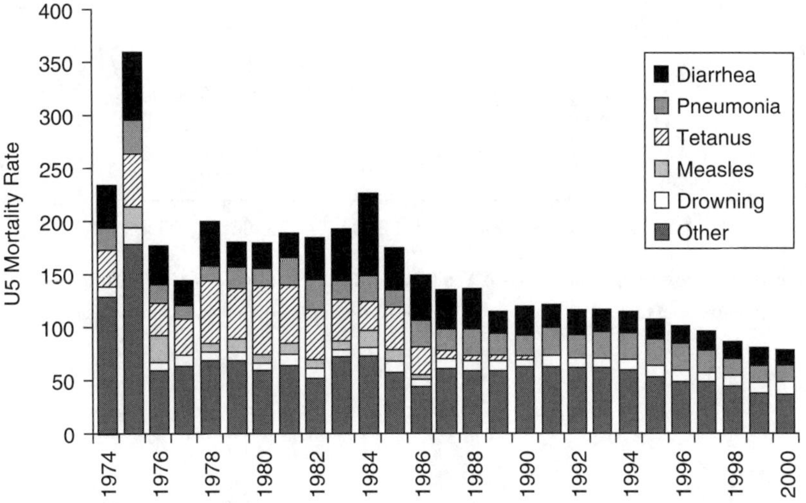

Figure 18.3 Decrease in Under Five Mortality, Matlab Bangladesh 1974–2000.
Source: Reports from International Centre of Diarrheal Disease Research, Dhaka Bangladesh 2003.

the middle gray line in figure 18.3, which shows the death rates from drowning. As the other causes of mortality—primarily infectious causes such as diarrhea and pneumonia—have decreased due to effective interventions, the relative proportion of drowning mortality has increased as shown by the light gray line. While it was responsible for less than 10 percent of 1–4 year olds' deaths in 1983, it claimed 57 percent of 1–4 year olds' deaths in 2000. This change of predominant cause of mortality from communicable causes to injury and non-communicable causes represents the epidemiologic transition where developing countries begin to resemble wealthy countries.[20] Figure 18.5, from a national household health survey conducted in Bangladesh in 2003, shows that the leading causes of injury death now are substantially the same as what is seen in the OECD countries.[21]

For infants, suffocation and drowning were the leading causes of death from injury. For toddlers, aged 1–4 years, the overwhelming cause of injury death was drowning (up to 90 percent). Drowning remained the leading injury cause of death in the 5–9 age group, although at a diminished rate. In subsequent age groups, drowning was overtaken by transportation, mainly road traffic accidents, which became the leading unintentional cause of death for children in late adolescence. The single leading cause of death in late adolescents was suicide. Like the dog that did not bark, what is missing is the traditional infectious killers of the 1960s as the modern development era commenced. These are statistics from a South Asian developing country reckoned as part of the Islamic world, and mortality may still be higher than in the richer industrialized countries for which the United States serves as proxy. The Bangladesh data represent the idea that most of the developing world, including some of the relatively disadvantaged parts of the Islamic world, has already undergone the epidemiologic transition, representing success in health development terms, but presenting questions about future directions.

In Figure 18.6 we examine the increase in life expectancy since 1960 by World Bank regions in the developing world, including Bangladesh and the

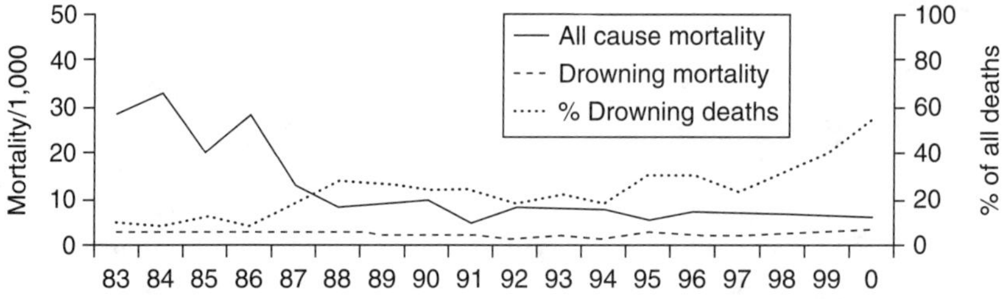

Figure 18.4 Drowning Deaths in 1–4 Year Olds, Matlab Bangladesh 1983–2000.
Source: Reports from International Centre of Diarrheal Disease Research, Dhaka Bangladesh 2003.

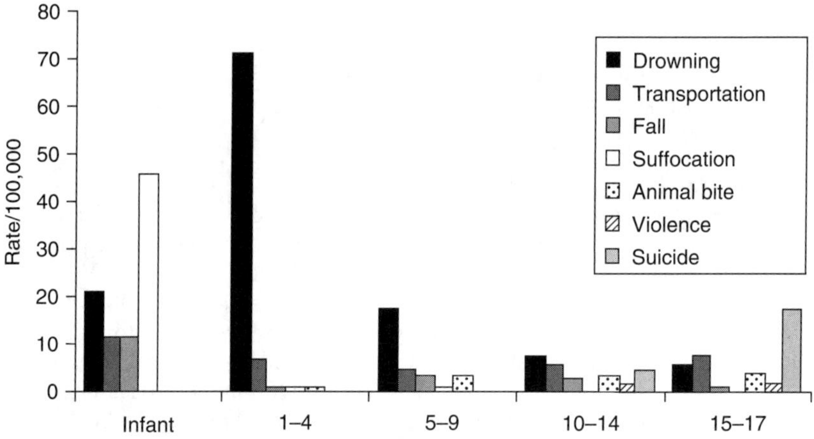

Figure 18.5 Leading Causes of Fatal Child Injury in Bangladesh 2003.
Source: Bangladesh Health and Injury Survey, Report on Children.

United States for comparison purposes. The picture tends toward the converse of child survival, namely that, except for sub-Saharan Africa, life expectancy in the developing world has increased essentially on a linear basis since 1960, rising particularly in much of the Islamic world (understood as captured in the Middle East and North Africa together with South Asia) from a range of 40–50 years in 1960, to the mid-to-high 60s by 2005 (an increase of approximately one-third). Meanwhile, viewing the United States as proxy for the richer industrialized countries, life expectancy rose from 70 in 1960 to 78 in 2005 (an increase of circa 10 percent, albeit from a higher base).

To interpret all of the above public health data correctly, the real question behind the above child mortality and life expectancy data is what has been happening since the 1980s in sub-Saharan Africa (northern parts of which coincidentally belong to the Islamic world), by comparison to other developing countries? Without going into a deeper statistical analysis, the general problem is the recognized issue of HIV/AIDS infection rates in Africa.[22] The high rate of infection for

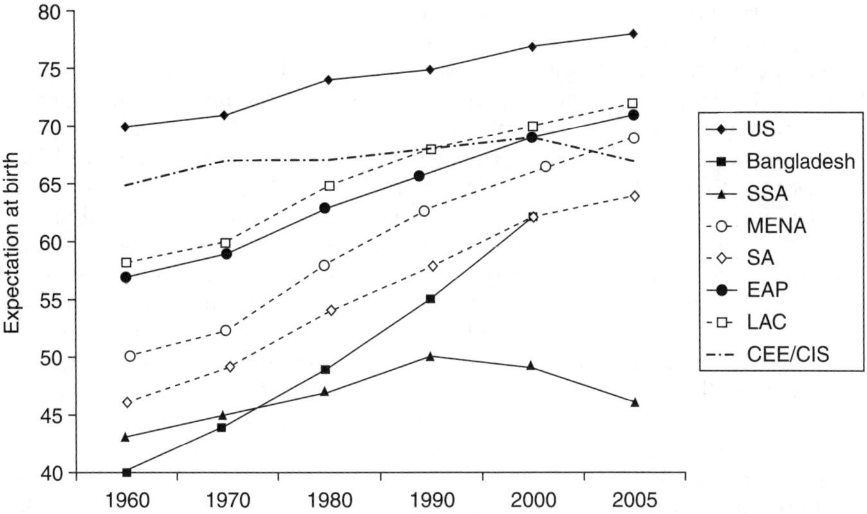

Figure 18.6 Increase in Life Expectancy since 1960 by Country/Region. World Bank regional indices are: Subsaharan Africa (SSA), Middle East and North Africa (MENA), South Asia (SA), East Asia and Pacific (EAP), Latin America and Caribbean (LAC), and Central and Eastern Europe/CIS (CEE/CIS).

Source: World Bank, UNICEF.

HIV/AIDS entails that sub-Saharan Africa is apparently the only major area of the developing world not to make the epidemiologic transition. Depending upon how one characterizes the data, this means that sub-Saharan Africa exists, in public health terms, somewhere in the 1970s to 1980s, and so still suffers from many of the same infectious disease and similar public health problems that predominated when most developing countries originally achieved independence.

The problem for our purposes is how to reconcile the state of public health affairs in sub-Saharan Africa with the evidence of epidemiologic transition visible in Bangladesh and the balance of the developing world? There are three issues to consider for those thinking about public health and development among application aspects of "A Common Word." First, the good news is that people in most of the developing world, including its children in particular, are healthier and live substantially longer than even fifty years ago. This is probably best understood in terms of technology transfer on the level of public health and medicine from the wealthier part of the international community, which those favoring distributive justice should recognize as a success.

Second, it would seem that the developing world, in public health terms, now really contains two distinct divisions, the majority of countries like Bangladesh where improved public health means that the epidemiologic transition has already occurred, versus sub-Saharan Africa where high incidence of HIV/AIDS and infectious disease mean that public health may be no better than in the 1970s. And public health in sub-Saharan Africa is arguably worse than 40 years ago, to the extent claims are made that HIV/AIDS is hollowing out whole populations of working age adults in some sub-Saharan African countries, leaving behind children and the old (although relatively high child mortality itself may reflect maternal HIV/AIDS infection transmission to infants).

Third, the problem is how to deal with the two distinct divisions of the developing world in terms of application of resources, which is ultimately a religious or ethical question, on a policy level? There are several different aspects to this problem, but the underlying issue is inherent in population numbers. Using standard population figures, the world's 2008 population is estimated at 6,692,030,277 persons, of whom 27 percent or approximately 1,807 million are under the age of 15.[23] The comparable 2008 figures by region are: (1) East Asia and Pacific (EAP), 1,931,175,566 persons, of whom 23 percent or approximately 444 million are under the age of 15; (2) (Eastern) Europe and Central Asia (ECA), 441,347,675 persons, of whom 19 percent or approximately 84 million are under the age of 15; (3) Latin America and the Caribbean (LAC), 565,294,000 persons, of whom 29 percent or approximately 164 million are under the age of 15; (4) Middle East and North Africa (MENA), 324,785,110 persons, of whom 31 percent or approximately 94 million are under the age of 15; (5) South Asia (SA), 1,542,945,433 persons, of whom 33 percent or approximately 509 million are under the age of 15; and (6) sub-Saharan Africa (SSA), 817,956,997 persons, of whom 43 percent or approximately 353 million are under the age of 15. So within what arguably would traditionally be considered the developing world, the balance is sub-Saharan Africa with a total population of 818 million (352 million under the age of 15) against all others (EAP + ECA + LAC + MENA + SA) with a total population of 4,806 million (1,295 million under the age of 15). So, depending upon which measure you wish to employ, the population comparison between sub-Saharan Africa and the balance of the developing world is approximately 5.9 persons living elsewhere in the developing world for every one living in sub-Saharan Africa (or approximately 3.7 times as many children under the age of 15).

Distributive justice is normally considered a problem between the rich and the poor in terms of the international community, but the above comparison is essentially between low- and middle-income countries. Where and why should available international public health resources be allocated within the developing world? Characterizing health as a human right, as commonly heard in the international health circles, would indicate that all needs of all people should be met. But in a practical sense, resources are limited. So what does "A Common Word" tell us about resolving this dilemma of application in the world of politics and governments?

At one level, given that sub-Saharan Africa contains a relatively small portion of the developing world's population, there is a hidden distributive justice question about priorities. Maternal health and child survival, alongside life expectancy, have improved markedly over the past 50 years in the developing world ex–sub-Saharan Africa. But there is still a further distance to travel to achieve full parity with the developed world. Should the public health focus now differ within the developing world based upon the epidemiologic transition achieved in most areas, even while they remain low- to middle-income countries economically speaking? Should a disproportionate share of the available resources be concentrated in sub-Saharan Africa as that geographic area where the greatest need arguably exists? How does the Islamic world understand this question, given that sub-Saharan Africa is a conflict prone, often mixed, religious area?

Finally, there is what might be considered an appropriate technology question inherent in the large investments in international public health by substantial private donors like the Gates Foundation. Their generosity is unquestioned, but they are large enough in an absolute sense also to influence public policy, so that they have an agenda-setting effect in developing country public health. They tend to be focused on sub-Saharan Africa and stress technologically based solutions, for example funding malaria vaccine research over the distribution of insecticide soaked mosquito nets at the village level. Part of the problem is the potential diversion of resources in the larger setting already referred to, if the public health problems of the developing world ex–Sub-Saharan Africa are no longer infectious diseases, but rather accidents and chronic diseases. A technologically sophisticated solution like a successful malaria vaccine or similar response to remaining infectious disease would be laudable, but may represent an inefficient use of resources. It underplays simpler, less technologically oriented approaches that might be appropriate to address issues like drowning as the leading killer of small children in Bangladesh (or traffic accidents as leading killer of their teenage siblings).

Building fences around bodies of water, or teaching small children to swim, or making teenagers wear motorcycle helmets are not sexy in a technological sense. So there is probably a greater readiness to pursue high science approaches like advanced pharmacological research in the Western world. However, the root of the problem is in understanding what is the appropriate technology for solving public health challenges in most of the developing world, given epidemiologic transition and simple idea that the most substantial public health gains arguably are already available simply via low-tech measures like providing clean water and educating women through the primary, if not secondary school level.

Catholic and Protestant Views of Development

There has been a longstanding effort to address modern social and moral issues within the framework of Catholic social magisterium (social doctrine) as enunciated by Papal encyclicals, beginning with Pope Leo XIII's *Rerum Novarum* (*On Capital and Labor*, 1891)[24] extending in a more or less unbroken line through Pope Benedict XVI's *Caritas in Veritate* (*Charity in Truth*, 2009).[25] The ultimate direction of both was to articulate the Catholic Church's view of the proper response to changing social conditions. Meanwhile the Catholic Church recognizes a missionary aspect (evangelization) to social doctrine post-Vatican II,[26] but seemingly on an entirely different scale compared to Protestantism.[27]

The late-nineteenth century problem in the West was how to react to the industrial revolution and wretched conditions for the working man versus the wealth of the robber baron era that conjured the specter of socialism within the national state. The nineteenth century Catholic response was to articulate a special place for the working man and a mutual frame of reference for capital and labor, intermediated by unions and under the regulatory aegis of the state. This was offered in conjunction with ideas about the working man being entitled to a fair or living wage (and all parties involved to a modicum of social peace). The early twenty-first century problem is how to address development understood in a global North-South context, most forcefully treated by Pope Paul VI's *Populorum Progressio* (*Progress of Peoples*, 1967) articulated in the 1960s, still in the context of the single national state, within the international community, now in the context of increasing globalization clearly reaching beyond the national state. This encyclical coincidentally embraces the concept of "integral" development, meaning reaching beyond mere economic development to other aspects such as spiritual and cultural development.

Charity is at the heart of the Catholic Church's social doctrine, and is considered under Jesus' teachings a synthesis of the law as equivalent to "A Common Word" 's focus on love of God and neighbor. The formal doctrinal response of Pope Benedict XVI to development under circumstances of globalization in 2009's *Caritas in Veritate* has been to stress the continuity of Catholic social doctrine in elucidating a humanism in the form of "authentic human development" informed by religion, coupled with opposition to purely technological interpretations of development and materialism as such, grounded theologically in true charity understood as the practical implementation of the love of neighbor.[28] This is linked in a practical sense to an emphasis on nonprofit oriented economic undertakings society-wide, in conjunction with the concept of justice and the common good, linked to authentic human development as concerning the whole of an individual. So there seems to be a clear conflict with the neoclassical economic emphasis visible in the Washington Consensus.

Caritas in Veritate alludes to concepts like a duty to preserve creation paralleling environmental concepts such as sustainability, although the terminology may differ. It criticizes what it would regard as unrestrained capitalism, but distances itself equally from ideologies denying in toto the value of development. Similarly, it acknowledges that the Catholic Church may also engage in the development process with ethical nonbelievers, as well as representatives of other religions, the role of nongovernmental organizations (NGOs), and of a now democratic state. The surprising character of *Caritas in Veritate*, for those familiar professionally with the economics and practical side of international development, is the extent to which it attempts to articulate social theory conscious of social science–based development debates, even while maintaining its distance in not employing directly the development professional's terminology (perhaps because that would incorporate its social science frame of reference).

One result is that *Caritas in Veritate* is more of a theoretical survey document, seemingly lacking *Populorum Progressio's* direct moral impact dating back to the early 1960s era of postcolonial independence and the New Economic Order at the UN level. It is addressed perhaps more to intellectual development issues in the midst of current globalization (and in the context of a global recession), rather than articulating detailed moral guidance in an accessible framework for ordinary Catholics in the nineteenth century tradition of *Rerum Novarum*. That having been said, there is no formal checklist of topics constituting the heart of Catholic social doctrine for development or other purposes, although there seem to be at least seven thematic areas at the core of Catholic social doctrine: (1) sanctity of human life and dignity of the person; (2) call to family, community, and participation: (3) a balance of rights and responsibilities; (4) preference for the poor and vulnerable; (5) dignity of work and the rights of workers; (6) solidarity, and (7) care for God's creation (and integral development, although that arguably is encompassed in the foregoing list). In stressing continuity, *Caritas in Veritate* seemingly embraces the full pallet of concerns.

Caritas in Veritate celebrates continuity in Pope Paul VI's *Populorum Progressio* vision of development even while it tends to underplay Pope John XXIII's preceding emphasis around the time of the Second Vatican Council on expanding Catholic social doctrine from relations within society to the level of relations between rich and poor nations, with a duty of the rich to aid the poor (under *Mater et Magistra* or *Christianity and Social Progress*, 1961[29]), and his link of world peace to the laying of a foundation consisting of proper rights and responsibilities between individuals, social groups, and states at the local as well as international levels, including criticism of the Cold War era's nuclear arms race and a desire to expand the UN's role (under *Pacem in Terris* or *Peace on Earth*, 1963[30]). As a doctrinal matter, these concerns are anchored theologically speaking in *Gaudiam et Spes*, or the *Church's Pastoral Constitution in the Modern World* (1965),[31] promulgated by Pope Paul VI as one of the Apostolic Constitutions as outputs of Vatican II, which has served within Catholicism ever since as a means of engaging the modern world.

Caritas in Veritate is similarly largely silent on the contribution of Pope John Paul II, who engaged the then Socialist block from the perspective of a former Polish cardinal who had cohabited in Eastern Europe with an actual Socialist (Communist) government in the late Soviet era. Meanwhile, he is perhaps best remembered in conjunction with development for his worldwide travels, including through much of the developing world. In this area, John Paul II reflected on the problem of a growing recognition of theoretical individual human value in the public sphere, even while it remained under attack in practice (under *Laborem Exercens* or *Human Work*, 1981,[32] tying directly into the nineteenth-century tradition on the 90th anniversary of *Rerum Novarum*, reinforced on its 100th anniversary under *Centesimus Annus* or *One Hundred Years*, 1991,[33] as well as articulating the formal link as a matter of social teaching between *Rerum Novarum* and *Populorum Progression* under *Sollicitudo Rei Socialis* or *On Social Concerns*, 1987,[34] on *Populorum Progressio's* 20th anniversary as social and political change gripped Eastern Europe). To that extent, Pope John Paul II's perspective on remaking society in Eastern Europe after the fall of communism was perhaps as striking as that of Pope John XXIII contemplating the North-South divide at the time of colonial independence. In its place, *Caritas in Veritate* stresses the world's changed nature because of globalization and that inequality has been growing within countries following economic policies in line with the Washington Consensus. This has in turn lowered social protections problematically in the search to expand direct investment for economic growth purposes. So here we see again a seeming conflict in terms of what are typically argued to be disproportionate effects on the poor under the Washington Consensus.

Doctrinal niceties aside, the problematic tension by the time of Pope Benedict XVI may be captured in the idea that, while *Rerum Novarum* was written to benefit the (Western) working man, more recently globalization and development strategies—like export-oriented development—led to rich countries moving manufacturing overseas, to the practical benefit of the (developing country's) working man. So what is the theological equivalent of trade adjustment assistance for displaced (developed country) workers, even while social theory at a country level posits that rich countries should aid poor ones? And further, how to reflect changes from a traditional Eurocentric to a global Catholic Church (due to the rapid increase of Christians in the developing world, coupled with increased secularization in Europe)? The problem is that traditional approaches to distributive justice within individual states, well-suited for nineteenth century society, no longer work as patterns of economic production have changed, even while the composition of the Catholic Church is changing. *Caritas in Veritate* opines that the focus of international aid must now support rule of law efforts under another name (state of law), emphasizing human rights and democratic institutions at the state level.

Strikingly from "A Common Word's" perspective, *Caritas in Veritate* opines that both secularism and religious fundamentalism are harmful to public life in general and human development in particular. They hinder the combination of reason and religious faith necessary to developmental and fraternal collaboration between believers and nonbelievers reaching back to *Gaudium et Spes*. But there remains intellectual tension between articulating a view of *truth in charity* at a relatively high doctrinal level, coupled with a pronounced suspicion of capitalistic excesses, while contemplating development's material successes in majority non-Christian and non-Islamic areas like East Asia (meanwhile considering the preservation of creation in terms also of environmentally conscious development). The practical problem is whether you can have it all in development terms, and, if the answer is no, what are the proper choices from the religious and moral viewpoint? This choice problem becomes particularly acute in the current context of conflicting pictures of development based upon widely differing goals such as rapid economic growth via a more traditional export-oriented industrialization strategy, versus internally focused human development downplaying economic growth per se in favor perhaps of rural development to counter the urban migration phenomenon, versus a sustainability focus.

Protestant views of development are distinguishable from papal articulation of Catholic social doctrine, even while they may be harder to trace in detail because of decentralized Protestant organizational structures. Protestant views of development, rather, grew organically from a long (evangelical) missionary tradition, but accepted already in the early 1960s the idea of mixing secular development with evangelism, while the Catholic Church accepted such secular elements separately as a result of Vatican II.[35] Here one must distinguish also between Protestant denominational organizations at the level of annual conventions or national churches, relief[36] or long-term development efforts also at the level of individual church congregations, and a multitude of Christian relief and development NGOs often with evangelical roots—such as World Vision International (discussed subsequently as a well-documented example).[37] What they tend to share is an emphasis on biblical scripture, conscience, and individual salvation, linked with a willingness to remake society. Their evangelical element renders them, in the modern setting, a coalition of ideas and institutions for development, in opposition to the Catholic Church's unitary hierarchy with consistently developed social doctrine reaching back to the nineteenth century.[38]

World Vision International, well known for sponsorship of children and activities in almost 100 countries,[39] grew out of the 1940s American "new evangelism" movement, as ecumenical or interdenominational undertaking. Its development activities are best understood as continuing the spirit of the nineteenth century American network of Protestant evangelical voluntary societies guided by a vision of moral and spiritual progress, which engaged at various times in political and social action—including prison reform, temperance, and the abolition of slavery. But such NGOs are not alone in their activism, since also at the mainline denomination level there have been some adoptions in particular of the United Nations' MDGs as part of individual denominations' designated social gospels,[40] plus the current custom of individual church congregations undertaking to build schools or sponsor small-group, short-term medical missions to developing countries (typically involving three to five medical personnel from the congregation going overseas for one to two weeks to staff specialized clinics, such as for eye care).

World Vision's evangelical roots are evident in its own approaches to development in which material (development) and spiritual (mission) elements are not clearly separate. In the world of Christian development, evangelized and unevangelized areas equate to developed/undeveloped areas, subject to an analysis of spiritual and material needs. There may be a general sense in Protestant theology that weak or vulnerable groups may generate their own theologies (e.g., theologies of development, women, or the poor),[41] but, on an anthropological level, activities of World Vision's staff in the field have been characterized as engaging in holistic development. Theirs is a strategy of emulating Christ in paying attention to both material and spiritual poverty (as opposed to secular development institutions, which are focused on material well-being only).[42] This ties into an extensive body of missionary literature[43] and, at the individual World Vision staff level, is characterized as "lifestyle evangelism," understood as working on material development tasks with the proper motivation, attitude, and approach in which the Christian organization would become part of the community at the village level.

That having been said, such development assistance was not conditioned on local people being Christians. Instead, the concept was that by working visibly at the village level as members of the community, the villagers themselves would observe the commitment to material and spiritual well-being. At the same time, World Vision managed links back at the retail level to Western donors supporting individual children or communities. However, in fact, funds solicited for the support of individual children were commonly invested in community level development projects (building a school, drilling a well, etc.).

This level of local engagement and building bridges to individual donors represents a specific form of Christian development. At the same time, albeit more often in conjunction with relief than development work, faith-based development NGOs more recently may work with government funding for specific secular tasks (for example, administering humanitarian assistance following natural disasters, a relief task, but also administering urban-based efforts against human trafficking and in support of rural agricultural development programs like drilling wells, development tasks).[44] This relatively recent approach represents a broader practice encompassing both faith-based and secular NGOs engaged particularly in humanitarian relief based upon secular funding, rather than favoritism as such, toward Christian organizations. It may, however, lead to the anomaly of Christian faith-based development organizations working on secular development tasks in Muslim majority countries under stringent conditions.[45] This may place the Christian faith-based development organizations performing secular development tasks in an ambiguous position analogous to late colonial-era churches, which were often interpoised between the metropolitan country and indigenous populations, with the problem being their support of native welfare within the colonial frame of reference. But in practical terms, substantial secular funding flowing to Christian faith-based development institutions probably reflects rather the issue of how both secular and faith-based NGOs fund their operations generally in pursuing projects seriatim.

IFI Technical and Newer Views of Development (Sustainability)

The technical issue is how have the IFIs approached development since the 1980s in this market-oriented environment? The market orientation in general terms is a function of economic policy views dating back to the Washington Consensus of the 1980s. But at the technical level of implementation, approaches have changed in particular as the focus of development has shifted from building roads, etc. to "software" in terms of creating institutions and building capacity. Broadly speaking, the IFIs seemingly have embraced the new institutional economics referred in Zamar Iqbal and Abbas Mirakhor's[46] treatment of specifically Islamic development approaches. Changes in IFI approaches are visible over time via an abbreviated content review of the World Bank's flagship annual development report, the World Development Report since the late 1980s (WDR, published since 1978 with each report focused on a particular aspect of development). Our focus will be on seven WDR themes, then we end with a quick examination of sustainability and climate change concerns, which are normally associated more with the United Nations Environmental or Development Programs (UNEP and UNDP) than with the IFIs as traditional development leadership.

The first WDR thematic point is *inequality*. The WDRs identify two areas of inequality: inequality within countries (WDR coverage in mid to late 2000s) and inequality between developing and developed countries (WDR coverage in the late 1990s). The World Bank seems to believe policies that promote the well-being of a few in the population at the expense of the poor, women, ethnic, and racial minorities are to blame for inequality within countries. To that end, the World Bank identified equity as all citizens having roughly equal opportunities in politics and economics to succeed depending on ability. A knowledge boom in the late 1990s was identified as a potential cause of inequality between developing and developed countries (also known as the digital divide). To that end, developing countries were advised to invest in education and technical training, and actively seek knowledge in developed countries.

The second WDR thematic point is *poverty*. Poverty was discussed almost every year, with two WDRs (1990 and 2000/2001) having poverty as their specific focus. Lack of opportunity and lack of ability to take advantage of available opportunities are consistently cited as reasons why the poor stay poor. Lack of opportunity in 1990 meant a lack of jobs, and the World Bank recommended that governments focus on promoting jobs to match the (typically unskilled) labor force. Lack of ability to take advantage of opportunities was identified in the early 1990s as lack of access to health care and education. In the mid 2000s, the World Bank still identified illiteracy and ill health as two of the main reasons the poor remain poor. The World Bank has long advocated giving the poor access to jobs and a political voice as well as social services (education and health care). Reduction of poverty was finally identified in the 2000 WDR as the main goal of development, matching timing of the United Nations' MDGs.

The third WDR thematic point is *education*. Virtually every WDR of the past 20 years mentions education. WDRs identify primary education as a service to be provided by the state, and a survey of developing countries in the 2007 WDR indicated that a significant number of countries believed poor primary education was the most important barrier to the younger generation's economic productivity. Commencing in the early 1990s, specific mention was made that primary education was especially important for girls. During the early 2000s, this discussion was expanded to encompass racial and ethnic minorities. The issue of education was linked to the issue of health care by stating in the early 1990s that increased education made people better able to apply scientific knowledge to their lives and take care of themselves. In WDR 2000/2001, illiteracy was identified as one of two main problems that keep the poor in developing countries impoverished. By the late 2000s, WDRs acknowledge that educating a single generation directly affects the educational prospects of the next. The hidden question behind education may be leadership, however, given that the modernization theorists of the 1960s focused on higher education and technology as the pathway from a traditional to a modern society. So primary education may be necessary to increase human capacity on average, but what is the proper balance between resources for primary, secondary and tertiary education in an increasingly complex world?

The fourth WDR thematic point is *health care*. Like education, health care is mentioned in virtually every WDR during the past 20 years. Health care is identified as a public service that should be provided, especially to the poor, by the state. In the early 1990s key components of health care were identified as mass immunizations, nutrition, and family planning. Birth control as religiously sensitive topic was not mentioned, although population growth is and remains a concern in development.

The fifth WDR thematic point involves *rural to urban migration*. In 1988, the WDR discussed the importance of financial spending in both the rural and urban sectors. Through the late 1990s, however, the World Bank engaged in benign neglect of the rural sector and focused on urban areas as the focal points of development and industry (presumably due to a focus on industrialization). Three-quarters of the population in developing countries remains in rural areas, which seemingly forced a shift in focus since the late 2000s to agriculture's role in development. The 2008 WDR, focused on agriculture, reflects the recent acknowledgment that increase in agricultural productivity serves development. From an economic growth perspective, however, GDP contribution benefits more from industrialization than from farming. Meanwhile, industrialization normally draws significant rural to urban migration as collateral effect, contributing indirectly to modernization insofar as urban migration tends to remove migrants from traditional society, but also creates the problem of the developing world's megacities that place large demands on government and the environment.

The sixth WDR thematic point involves *governance*. Governance is a relatively neutral term for government performance, including civil society. The 1997 WDR advised governments to work within their capabilities. To be stable and trusted, governments were advised to set and play by their own rules. By staying within functional limits, governments would remain stable and could gradually expand capacity over time. The 1997 WDR also took a strong stance against government corruption. The single major shift within WDRs during the past 20 years regards the role of the state. Pre-1997, WDRs contemplated leaving everything possible to markets (following the Washington Consensus view that government control of any economy would fail). Since 1997, the WDRs recognize that strong and stable governments must work within their capabilities (rather than extolling minimal government on an unreserved basis). Starting in the early 1990s, WDRs made some acknowledgement that governments needed to step in where markets failed and correct market failures. From such time to the present, WDRs extol pursuit of the rule of law, or at least the establishment of a stable legal system, as a goal serving multiple purposes.

The seventh and final WDR thematic point involves the *environment*. The effects of development on the environment first surfaced in the 1992 WDR. In 1992, the focus was on policies promoting overconsumption of natural resources recognized as limited commodities. The early 1990s view seemed to follow the idea that inefficient use of resources could negatively impact development by offering future generations fewer development opportunities. Cost/benefit analysis was advocated as the way to determine how to implement environmental policies in developing countries, whenever such policies competed with economic development. By contrast, the 2003 WDR refers to the issue of sustainable development, and adopts a more serious tone. Since the early 2000s, WDRs shift the focus to a discussion of pollution, and how pollution and other environmental problems would lead to health problems as well as lowered economic productivity. While early 1990s WDRs contemplate environmental policies as a decision for each individual country, the 2003 WDR embraces sustainable development as a global issue requiring management of resources by developing countries and technology sharing by developed countries (paralleling the 2002 Johannesburg Declaration on Sustainable Development contemporaneously in the UN System, recalling that the WDR is a publication of an IFI, although Johannesburg's roots are in the 1992 Rio Declaration on the Environment and Development).

We have previously reviewed the idea that the environment has been a concern in development reaching all the way back to the 1972 Stockholm Declaration. However, parallel environmental developments since 1992 have focused on climate change and greenhouse gas emissions. The preferred approach to economic development since the 1960s has been industrialization, on which basis, via export-led development, Asia realized its development successes (with the WTO contributing to trade liberalization). Industrialization, however, traditionally increases greenhouse gas emissions, which has been the point of contention between the industrialized countries and the developing world since climate change became a concern. Human-induced climate change itself is the subject of continuing political dispute, although considered opinion in the scientific community seems to accept climate change as a fact, even while debates continue concerning its full dimensions. Sustainability itself as highlighted at Johannesburg is still a more theoretical concept than detailed policy prescription, however, so at the current stage of discussion there is concern about the future direction of development efforts. There are still only the glimmerings of an understanding concerning how to address climate change's effects specifically on development. So we close on the previously voiced question about the eye of the needle, namely what does "A Common Word" have to say if industrialization as customary means to raise incomes and pursue development more broadly becomes increasingly problematic due to the limited capacity of the environment?

Notes

1. Here one would think in practice of the United Nations' human development indicators or HDI, which are published in annual UN Human Development Reports and are used to generate annual league tables for all countries. The HDI actually combines subindicators for economic growth (GDP), public health, and education levels in a single figure. The problem in practice is that it is very difficult for a relatively poor country to finance superior public health or universal public education, with the result that country income levels largely predetermine performance on social indicators in most low- and middle-income countries.
2. This is, however, something of a sleight of hand reflecting the adoption of language by multilateral development institutions like the World Bank to cast governance and problems like corruption as a technical management challenge rather than political problem (because the IFIs are nominally prohibited from undertaking political activity in aid-recipient countries under their charters, lest they interfere in internal affairs).

3. The bloom was a bit off the rose following the 1997 Asian financial crisis, but development professionals would recall here the era of the "East Asian Miracle" promulgated by the eponymous World Bank publication. See *The East Asian Miracle: Economic Growth and Public Policy.*
4. Concerning the broader modernization concept, see David Linnan, "The New, New Legal Development Model," in *Legitimacy, Legal Development and Change: Law and Modernization Reconsidered* (forthcoming 2011).
5. See Save the Children, http://www.savethechildren.org.
6. See World Vision, http://www.worldvision.org.
7. For example, in 2006 the Episcopal Church in the United States adopted the MDGs as its top mission priority at its General Convention. See The Episcopal Church, "ONE Episcopalian Campaign."
8. Pope Paul VI, "Populorum Progressio."
9. Pope Benedict XVI, "Caritas in Veritate."
10. See 1 May 1974, A/RES/S-6/3201.
11. See United Nations Environment Program, "Declaration of the United Nations Conference on the Human Environment"; Louis Sohn, "The Stockholm on the Human Environment," *Harvard International Law Journal.*
12. See 12 August 1992, A/CONF.151/26 (Vol. I).
13. Johannesburg Declaration on Sustainable Development, A/CONF.199/20, Chapter 1, Resolution 1, Johannesburg, September 2002.
14. The "Washington Consensus" was a liberal economic policy approach of the IFIs or Bretton Woods institutions, meaning the IMF and World Bank, rather than the United States government. However, it is fair to say that the U.S. government basically agreed with the Washington Consensus.
15. On a technical level, however, it has been criticized for contributing to income inequality within countries, even while it may be raising average incomes.
16. See T. Ginsburg, "Does Law Matter for Economic Development? Evidence from East Asia."
17. Concerning the entire topic of international public health work, I acknowledge the material contribution of Dr. Michael J. Linnan, a former Center for Disease Control and Prevention epidemiologist and current medical director of The Alliance for Safe Children (see http://www.tasc-gcipf.org, active Asia wide). Opinions expressed remain the author's own responsibility.
18. Kenneth Hill et al., *Trends in Child Mortality in the Developing World: 1960 to 1996.*
19. "State of the World's Children 2008," in the UNICEF digital library (accessed March 26, 2010).
20. A. R. Omran, "The Epidemiologic Transition: a Theory of the Epidemiology of Population Change," *Milbank Memorial Fund Quarterly* 29.
21. "A League Table of Child Deaths by Injury in Rich Nations," *Innocenti Report Card Issue No. 2,* in the UNICEF digital library, http://www.unicef-irc.org/publications/pdf/repcard2e.pdf (accessed March 26, 2010).
22. See joint United Nations Programme on HIV/AIDS (UNAIDS) and World Health Organization, *AIDS epidemic update.*
23. All figures in this paragraph are as of 2008 from the World Bank's WDI Online (World Development Indicators), estimated to the nearest million in the text for discussion purposes.
24. Http://www.vatican.va/holy_father/leo_xiii/encyclicals/documents/hf_l-xiii_enc_15051891_rerum-novarum_en.html.
25. Http://www.vatican.va/holy_father/benedict_xvi/encyclicals/documents/hf_ben-xvi_enc_20090629_caritas-in-veritate_en.html.

26. Perhaps because of its status as oftentimes the sole countervailing social institution in authoritarian states, in areas of the developing world such as South and Central America, as well as Africa, the Catholic Church since Vatican II has been involved frequently asserting human rights on behalf of the poor against authoritarian governments, keeping uncomfortable company sometimes with left-leaning secular social movements (for example, in opposition to apartheid in South Africa, where the South African Communist Party was a prominent ally of the African National Congress). See Ian Linden, *Global Catholicism: Diversity and Change since Vatican II*, 91–198.
27. Understood in the sense of classic "missions," the technical concept of shared missiology between Catholics and Protestants is itself a post-Vatican II creation. See F.J. Versdtaelen, "The Genesis of a Common Missiology: A Case Study of Protestant and Catholic Mission Studies in the Netherlands, 1877–1988," in A. Camps, L.A. Hoedemaker, M.R. Spindler & F.J. Verstraelen, eds, *Missiology, An Ecumenical Introduction: Texts and Contexts of Global Christianity*, 423–37. But on the Protestant side mission grows organically from evangelism. See Gerald H. Anderson, "American Protestants in Pursuit of Mission: 1886–1986," in A. Camps, et al, *Missiology, An Ecumenical Introduction: Texts and Contexts of Global Christianity*, 374.
28. Some commentators from inside the Catholic Church see a more direct link between the approach evident in *Caritas in Veritate* and Benedict VI's attitude before being elevated to the Papacy toward issues of inculturation, understood as the issue of the localization of Christianity, since Catholic bishops in Asia and Africa are much more conscious of interfaith relations than the Vatican, although prior popes arguably had a more open stance than the current pope, which may have carried indirectly into "A Common Word" via the Pope's Regensburg address which triggered the process. Ian Linden, *Global Catholicism: Diversity and Change since Vatican II*, 237–60.
29. http://www.vatican.va/holy_father/john_xxiii/encyclicals/documents/hf_j-xxiii_enc_15051961_mater_en.html.
30. http://www.vatican.va/holy_father/john_xxiii/encyclicals/documents/hf_j-xxiii_enc_11041963_pacem_en.html.
31. http://www.vatican.va/archive/hist_councils/ii_vatican_council/documents/vat-ii_cons_19651207_gaudium-et-spes_en.html.
32. http://www.vatican.va/holy_father/john_paul_ii/encyclicals/documents/hf_jp-ii_enc_14091981_laborem-exercens_en.html.
33. http://www.vatican.va/holy_father/john_paul_ii/encyclicals/documents/hf_jp-ii_enc_01051991_centesimus-annus_en.html.
34. http://www.vatican.va/holy_father/john_paul_ii/encyclicals/documents/hf_jp-ii_enc_30121987_sollicitudo-rei-socialis_en.html.
35. J.A.B. Jongeneel & J.M. van Engelen, "Contemporary Currents in Missiology," in *Missiology, An Ecumenical Introduction*, supra note 27 at 438, 439. Concerning the history and development of Catholic and Protestant ideas of mission, see generally A. Camps, "The Catholic Missionary Movement from 1492 to 1789," in *Missiology, An Ecumenical Introduction*, supra note 27 at 213; J.A.B. Jongeneel, "The Protestant Missionary Movement up to 1789," id. at 222; A. Camps, "The Catholic Missionary Movement from 1789 to 1962," in *Missiology, An Ecumenical Introduction,* supra note 27 at 229; A.Wind, "The Protestant Missionary Movement from 1789 to 1963," in *Missiology, An Ecumenical Introduction*, supra note 27 at 237; G.M. Verstaelen-Guilhuis, "The History of the Missionary Movement from the Perspective of the Third World," in *Missiology, An Ecumenical Introduction*, supra note 27 at 253; Gerald H. Anderson, "American Protestants in Pursuit of Mission: 1886–1986," in *Missiology, An Ecumenical Introduction*, supra note 27 at 374. While early Islam spread across broad geographic areas, modern dakwah as the closest Islamic equivalent to evangelism simply does not have a similar recent history.

36. This may occur in response to domestic as well as international catastrophes, whether Hurricane Katrina's 2005 strike of New Orleans or the 2010 Haitian earthquake, which destroyed much of Port au Prince, so that relief activity as charitable undertaking may be as often domestic as international, while longer-term development activity is more characteristically internationally oriented.
37. Such denominational activities are not invariably evangelical, defined as attempts to establish churches in new locations. See Fred Kniss & David Todd Campbell, "The Effect of Religious Orientation on International Relief and Development Organizations," *Journal for the Scientific Study of Religion*, 93.
38. Erica Bornstein, *The Spirit of Development: Protestant NGOs, Morality and Economics in Zimbabwe*, 17–22.
39. http://www.worldvision.org/content.nsf/learn/our-international-work?OpenDocument&lpos=top_drp_OurWork_International. The scope of its activities and nature of present efforts are captured in the idea that in 2009 World Vision International had revenues of U$1.2 billion, which consisted of 34% government grants, 37% private cash contributions, and 28% gifts in kind, coupled with its approach to soliciting private support as under its "gift catalog" soliciting donations to serve a wide variety of relief and development purposes. See http://donate.worldvision.org/OA_HTML/xxwv2ibeCCtpSctDspRte.jsp?lpos=top_drp_WaysToGive_Gift Catalog&go=gift&&section=10389.
40. For example, http://www.e4gr.org/ (Episcopal Church).
41. This probably represents the view of Protestantism in the developed world, with the issue increasingly being what are the theologies that come out of developing countries themselves under the influence of non-Western cultures? See *Missiology, An Ecumenical Introduction*, supra note 27 at 263–420.
42. Tetsunao Yamamori, Introduction to T. Yamamori, Bryant L. Myers & D. Connor, eds, *Serving the Poor in Asia*, 1; *Id.* at 105–48, 169–210.
43. See Erica Bornstein, supra note 38 at 46–48.
44. In 2009, World View International received 34% of its U$1.2 billion budget from government grants, http://www.worldvision.org/content.nsf/about/ar-financials?Open&lpos=lft_txt_2009-Annual-Review#FinancialHighlights, so at U$400+ million the amounts are not insignificant.
45. The example that comes to mind is USAID running efforts against human trafficking in Indonesia via the International Catholic Migration Commission. Similar tensions may exist also with faith-based development organizations operating in countries with a left-leaning government. See Tomas Valoi, "Holistic ministry in large-scale relief, Mozambique," in *Serving with the Poor in Africa*, ed., Tetsunao Yamamori, 105.
46. See Iqbal & Mikrahor, chapter 17, this volume.

Bibliography

"AU Suspends Madagascar Over 'Coup'." ABC News (Mar. 20, 2009). http://www.abc.net.au/news/stories/2009/03/20/2522364.htm.

A Common Word and Future Muslim-Christian Engagement. Cambridge, October 12–15, 2008.

"A Common Word Between Us and You." The Official Web site of "A Common Word." http://www.acommonword.com.

A Common Word Between Us and You. Jordan: The Royal Aal al-Bayt Institute for Islamic Thought, 2009.

"A Common Word Between Us and You." *Sophia: The Journal of Traditional Studies* 14, no. 2 (Winter 2008–2009): 16–38.

Abdul-Rahman, Muhammad Saed. *The Meaning and Explanation of the Glorious Qur'an*. London: MSA Publications Limited, 2007.

Adams, Nicholas. *Habermas and Theology*. Cambridge: Cambridge University Press, 2006.

______. "Kant" in *The Blackwell Companion to Nineteenth Century Theologians*. Edited by David Fergusson. Oxford: Blackwell, forthcoming.

______. "Making Deep Reasonings Public." *Modern Theology* 22 (July 2006): 385–401.

Adang, Camilla. *Muslim Writers on Judaism and the Hebrew Bible from Ibn Rabban to Ibn Hazm*. Leiden, The Netherlands: E. J. Brill, 1996.

Addis Ababa Declaration on the International Financial Crisis, Assembly/AU/Decl.2 (XII).

Adonia, Ayebare. "Bullets Puncture the Faith of Ugandan Rebels." *Ottawa Citizen*, October 18, 1988. http://www.refugeelawproject.org/working_papers/RLP.WP11.pdf.

A. G. Federation v. A. G. Abia State (Nigeria), 96 LRCN 559, 595–97 (2002), http://www.nigeria-law.org/Attorney-General%20of%20the%20Federation%20%20V%20%20Attorney-General%20of%20Abia%20State%20&%2035%20Ors.htm.

______. *The Revival of Religious Sciences*. http://www.ghazali.org/site/ihya.htm.

Ahmad, Ali. "Nigeria." In *Environmentalism in the Muslim World*, edited by Richard C. Foltz. New York: Nova Science Publishers, 2005.

Africa Recovery: United Nations. *Delta Communities Protest Neglect*. http://www.un.org/ecosocdev/geninfo/afrec/subjindx/131nigr6.htm.

Airey v Ireland, 2 E.C.H.R. 305, 319 (1979).

Ali, Abdullah bin Hamid. "The Speech and Word of Allah (Kalām): In Light of Traditional Discussions." http://www.masud.co.uk/ISLAM/ust_abd/speech_word.htm.

Algeria Constitution (1996).

Allen, Michael. "Mysticism Panel." Commentator at *Theory and Application of A Common Word*, Rudolph C. Barnes Sr. Symposium, University of South Carolina, Columbia, S.C. March 26–27, 2009. http://www.lfip.org/barnes/2009/videopage.htm.

The Alliance for Safe Children. http://www.tasc-gcipf.org.

Alliance of Religions and Conservation. "Madinah in Saudi Arabia to Become Islamic Eco City: Windsor Announcement." News release. November 2, 2009, http://www.arcworld.org/news.asp?pageID=359.

Alvaro. "Indiculus Luminosus." *Medieval Islam* by Gustva von Grunebaum. Chicago/London: The University of Chicago Press, 1946.

Amman Message, http://ammanmessage.com/media/openLetter/english.pdf.

Amnesty International, Comité Loosli Bachelard, Lawyers Committee for Human Rights, Association of Members of the Episcopal Conference of East Africa v. Sudan, Afr. C.H.R., Comm. No. 48/90, 50/91, 52/91, 89/93 (1999). http://www1.umn.edu/humanrts/africa/comcases/48-90_50-91_52-91_89-93.html.

Amnesty International. *Sudan: The Human Price of Oil*. http://www.amnesty.org/en/library/asset/AFR54/001/2000/en/82ee4ed1-dfc5–11dd-8e17-69926d493233/afr540012000en.pdf.

Amnesty International USA. *Darfur: "When Will They Protect Us?"* http://www.amnestyusa.org/document.php?id=ENGAFR540432007.

"The Anaphora." Online Novgorod. http://www.novgorod.ru/english/read/information/orthodox-hymnody/hymn/.

Anderson, Gerald H. "American Protestants in Pursuit of Mission: 1886–1986." *Missiology, An Ecumenical Introduction: Texts and Contexts of Global Christianity*, edited by A. Camps, L.A. Hoedemaker, M.R. Spindler, and F.J. Verstraelen, 374–420. Grand Rapids: William Eerdmans Publishing, 1995.

Andrae, Tor. *Les origins de l'Islam et le christianisme*. Translated by Jules Roche. Paris: Adrien-Maisonneuve, 1955.

Angola Constitution (1992).

An-Na'im, Abdullahi Ahmed. "Globalization and Jurisprudence: An Islamic Law Perspective." *Emory Law Journal* 54 (2005): 25–51.

Annan, Kofi. *The Causes of Conflict and the Promotion of Durable Peace and Sustainable Development in Africa*. http://www.un.org/ecosocdev/geninfo/afrec/sgreport/report.htm.

Anselm, Saint. *Proslogion: With the Replies of Gaunilo and Anselm*. Translated by Thomas Williams. Indianapolis/Cambridge: Hackett Publishing Company, Inc., 1995.

Appleby, R. Scott. *The Ambivalence of the Sacred: Religion, Violence, and Reconciliation*. Lanham: MD: Rowman and Littlefield Publishers, Inc., 2000.

Appleby, R. Scott, and Martin Marty. "Fundamentalism." *Foreign Policy* 128 (January-February, 2002): 16–22.

Aquinas, Thomas. *Summa Theologica*. New York: Benziger Brothers, Inc., 1947.

Asad, Talal. *Formations of the Secular*. Stanford, CA: Stanford University Press, 2003.

Āshtīyānī, Sayyid Jalāl al-Dīn. editor. *Sharḥ Risālat al-Mashā'ir*. Tehran: Mu'assasa-yi Intishārat-i Amīr Kabīr, 1376.

Assmann, Jan. "The Mosaic Distinction: Israel, Egypt, and the Invention of Paganism." *Representations* 56 (1996): 48–67.

Ayoub, Mahmoud M. *The Qur'an and Its Interpreters*. Vol. 2. Albany, New York: State University of New York Press, 1992.

Baguma, Raymond. "New Investments to Create 13,000 Jobs." *The New Vision*, April 6, 2009, http://www.newvision.co.ug/D/8/12/677206.

Barnes Symposium. *Theory and Application of A Common Word*. March 26–27, 2009, http://www.lfip.org/barnes/2009/videopage.htm.

Bartholomew, Patriarch. *Encountering the Mystery: Understanding Orthodox Christianity Today*. New York: Doubleday, 2008.

Basedau, Matthias and Alexander De Juan. "The 'Ambivalence of the Sacred' in Africa: The Impact of Religion on Peace and Conflict in Sub-Saharan Africa." German Inst. of

Global and Area Studies, Working Paper No. 70 (2008). http://www.giga-hamburg.de/dl/download.php?d=/content/publikationen/pdf/wp70_basedau-juan.pdf.

Bauer, Walter. *Orthodoxy and Heresy in Earliest Christianity*. Translated by a team from the Philadelphia Seminar on Christian Origins. Edited by Robert A. Kraft and Gerhard Krodel. Philadelphia: Fortress Press, 1971.

Beaumont, Mark. "Muslim Readings of John's Gospel in the 'Abbasid Period." *Islam and Christian—Muslim Relations* 19, no. 2 (April 2008): 179–97.

Bebbington, David W., *Evangelicalism in Modern Britain: A History from the 1730s to the 1980s*. London: Unwin Hyman Ltd., 1989.

"Behind the Violence: Causes, Consequences and the Search for Solutions to the War in Northern Uganda." Refugee Law Project Working Paper No. 11, 2004. http://www.refugeelawproject.org/working_papers/RLP.WP11.pdf.

Behrend, Heike. "Is Alice Lakwena a Witch? The Holy Spirit Movement and Its Fight Against Evil in the North." *Changing Uganda: The Dilemmas of Structural Adjustment and Revolutionary Change*. Edited by Holger Berndt Hansen and Michael Twaddle. London: James Curry, 1991.

Benin Constitution (1990).

Bentham, Jeremy. *Introduction to the Principles of Morals and Legislation*. Oxford: Clarendon Press, 1823.

Berger, Peter L., Bridget Berger, and Hansfried Kellner. *The Homeless Mind*. New York: Vintage Books, 1974.

Berger, Rose Marie. "Radical Possibility." *Sojourners Magazine* 38, no. 2 (2009): 12.

Berlin Conference: The General Act of Feb. 26, 1885.

Bock, Benjamin. "Sudan: Mixing Oil and Blood." *Amnesty Magazine*, Amnesty International USA. http://www.amnestyusa.org/amnestynow/sudan.html.

Bornstein, Erica. *The Spirit of Development: Protestant NGOs, Morality and Economics in Zimbabwe*. Stanford: Stanford Univ. Press, 2005.

Boyarin, Daniel. *Border Lines: The Partition of Judeo-Christianity*. Philadelphia: University of Pennsylvania Press, 2004.

"The Bosporus Declaration: Joint Declaration of the Conference on Peace and Tolerance." The Ecumenical Patriarch of Constantinople. http://www.patriarchate.org/documents/joint-declaration.

Breslau, Karen, and Martha Brant. "God's Green Soldiers: A New Call to Combat Global Warming Triggers Soul-Searching and Controversy Among Evangelicals." *Newsweek* (February 13, 2006).

Brown, Thomas C. and Robin Gregory. "Survey: Why the WTA-WTP Disparity Matters." *Ecological Economics* 28 (1999): 323–35.

Bukhārī, Muḥammad. *Ṣaḥīḥ Bukhārī*. Edited by The Thesaurus Islamicus Foundation. Stuttgart: *Jamī'at al-Maktab al-Islāmī*, 1421AH/2001 CE.

Bulliet, Richard W. *The Case for Islamo-Christian Civilization*. New York: Columbia University Press, 2004.

Burdeau, Cain, "Orthodox Patriarch Pleads for Environmental Action." *USA Today* (October 21, 2009). http://content.usatoday.net/dist/custom/gci/InsidePage.aspx?cId=thenewsstar&sParam=31867547.story.

Burke, Edmund. *Reflections on the Revolution in France*. Cambridge, MA: Harvard University Press, 1790.

Burkina Faso Constitution (1991).

Butt, Riazatt. "Dr. Rowan Williams Says Climate Crisis a Chance to Become Human Again," *Guardian* (October 14, 2009). http://www.guardian.co.uk/uk/2009/oct/13/rowan-williams-climate-crisis.

Camps, A. "The Catholic Missionary Movement from 1492 to 1789." *Missiology, An Ecumenical Introduction: Texts and Contexts of Global Christianity*, edited by A.

Camps, L.A. Hoedemaker, M.R. Spindler & F.J. Verstraelen, 213–21. Grand Rapids: William Eerdmans Publishing, 1995.

Carlarne, Cinnamon. "Good Climate Governance: Only a Fragmented System of International Law Away?" *Law and Policy (Special Issue)* 30, no. 4 (2008): 450–80.

Case Concerning Armed Activities on the Territory of the Congo (Democratic Republic of the Congo v. Uganda), 2005 I.C.J. 116 (Dec. 19), ¶ 245, http://www.icj-cij.org/docket/files/116/10455.pdf.

Cerchio, Salvatore, Jeff K. Jacobsen, and Thomas F. Norris, "Temporal and Geographical Variation in Songs of Humpback Whales *Megaptera novaeangliae*: Synchronous Change in Hawaiian and Mexican Breeding Assemblages." *Animal Behavior* 62 (2001): 313–29.

Chad Constitution (1996).

Chapman v. United Kingdom, 33 E.H.R.R. 18, ¶ 96 (2001).

Chen, Jim. "Essay: Legal Mythmaking in a Time of Mass Extinctions: Reconciling Stories of Origins with Human Destiny." *Harvard Environmental Law Review* 29 (2005): 279–320.

Chittick, William C. *Science of the Cosmos, Science of the Soul: The Pertinence of Islamic Cosmology in the Modern World.* Oxford: Oneworld, 2007.

______. *The Self-Disclosure of God: Principles of Ibn al-'Arabī's Cosmology.* Albany: State University of New York Press, 1998.

______. *The Sufi Path of Knowledge: Ibn al-'Arabi's Metaphysics of Imagination.* Albany: State University of New York Press, 1989.

Church of England. Briefing Papers on Climate Change, http://www.cofe.anglican.org/info/socialpublic/international/climatechange/.

Clement, Saint. *Against Heresies.* Catholic Encyclopedia. http://www.newadvent.org/fathers/0103.htm.

Coase, R. H. "The Problem of Social Cost." *The Journal of Law and Economics* III (1960): 1–44.

Colby, Michael E. "Environmental Management in Development: The Evolution of Paradigms." *Ecological Economics* 3 (1991): 193–213.

Collier, Paul and Anke Hoeffler. "Greed and Grievance in Civil War." Oxford Economic Papers 56 (2004): 563–95.

Committee on Economic, Social and Cultural Rights, General Comment 3. *The Nature of States Parties' Obligations.* (Fifth session, 1990) U.N. Doc. E/1991/23, annex III at 86 (1991). http://www.unhchr.ch/tbs/doc.nsf/0/94bdbaf59b43a424c12563ed0052b664?Opendocument.

"Congress Bestows Medal on Orthodox Christian Leader." *LA Times* (October 22, 1997) http://articles.latimes.com/1997/oct/22/news/mn-45441.

Constitutive Act of the African Union. 11 July 2000. OAU Doc. CAB/LEG/23.15 (entered into force May 26, 2001), http://www.africa-union.org/root/au/AboutAu/Constitutive_Act_en.htm.

Curtin, Philip D. *Cross-Cultural Trade in World History.* Cambridge: Cambridge Univ. Press, 1984.

Cutsinger, James S. "*Hesychia*: An Orthodox Opening to Esoteric Ecumenism." *Paths to the Heart: Sufism and the Christian East.* Bloomington, Indiana: World Wisdom, 2002. Http://www.cutsinger.net/pdf/hesychia_an_orthodox_opening.pdf.

______. editor. *Paths to the Heart: Sufism and the Christian East.* Bloomington, Indiana: World Wisdom, 2002.

______. editor. *Reclaiming the Great Tradition: Evangelicals, Catholics, and Orthodox in Dialogue.* Downers Grove, Illinois: InterVarsity Press, 1997.

______. "That Man Might Become God: Lectures on Christian Theology." University of South Carolina. http://www.cutsinger.net/pdf/that_man_might_become_god.pdf.

Dagli, Caner. *Jihad and the Islamic Law of War*. Amman, Jordan: Royal Aal al-Bayt Institute for Islamic Thought, 2007. http://www.haqqani.org.es/Contenidos/jihad.pdf.

Das Internationale Netzwerk Engagierter Buddhisten. "Orientierungsgespräch in Deutschland vertretener Religionen zur Umweltpolitik unter besonderer Berücksichtigung der Klimafrage." Das Internationale Netzwerk Engagierter Buddhisten (May 6–7, 2002). http://www.buddhanetz.org/aktuell/goettingen.htm.

al-Dārimī, ʿ Uthmān b. Saʿīd. *al-Radd ʿalā al-Jahmiyyah*. Kuwait: Dār al-ʿIlm, 1970.

______., *Sunan al-Dārimī*. Edited by The Thesaurus Islamicus Foundation. Stuttgart: *Jamīʿat al-Maktab al-Islāmī*, 1421AH/2001 CE.

Decision on the Application by the International Criminal Court (ICC) Prosecutor for the Indictment of the President of the Republic of the Sudan, Assembly/AU/Dec. 221(XIII). http://www.africaunion.org/root/UA/Conferences/2009/Jan/Summit_Jan_2009/doc/CONFERENCE/ASSEMBLY%20AU%20DEC%20%20208-240%20(XII).pdf.

Department of Economic and Social Affairs of the U.N. Secretariat (DESA), U.N. Development Programme. The Millennium Development Goals Report 2008 (Aug. 2008). http://www.un.org/millenniumgoals/pdf/The%20Millennium%20Development%20Goals%20Report%202008.pdf.

Depledge, Michael and Cinnamon Carlarne. "Sick of the Weather: Climate Change, Human Health and International Law." *Environmental Law Review* 9 (2007): 231–40.

Dickinson, Daniel. "Eco-Islam hits Zanzibar fishermen." *BBC News* (February 17, 2005). http://news.bbc.co.uk/go/pr/fr/-/2/hi/africa/4271519.stm.

Dien, Mawil Izzi Dien. *The Environmental Dimensions of Islam*. Cambridge, England: Lutterworth Press, 2000.

Dryden, John. Preface to *Religio Laici*, by John Dryden (1682). "Deism." In *Encyclopedia of Religion*, 2nd edition, 15 vols. New York: Macmillan Reference, 2005.

Dupré, Louis. *The Enlightenment and the Intellectual Foundations of Modern Culture*. New Haven, CT, and London: Yale University Press, 2004.

Ehrenreich, Rosa. "The Scars of Death: Children Abducted by the Lord's Resistance Army." *Uganda*, edited by Yodon Thonden and Lois Whitman. Human Rights Watch, 1997.

El-Ansary, Waleed. "The Spiritual Significance of *Jihād* in the Islamic Approach to Markets and the Environment." PhD dissertation. George Washington University, 2006.

El Cheikh, Nadia Maria. *Byzantium Viewed by the Arabs*. Cambridge, MA: Harvard University Press, 2004.

Elbadawi, Ibrahim and Nicholas Sambanis. "Why Are There So Many Civil Wars in Africa? Understanding and Preventing Violent Conflict." *Journal of African Economies* 9 (2000): 244–69.

Episcopalians for Global Reconciliation. http://www.e4gr.org/.

The Episcopal Church. "ONE Episcopalian Campaign." http://www.episcopalchurch.org/109618_ENG_HTM.htm.

The Epistle of Mathetes to Diognetus (Trans. Roberts-Donaldson) Chapter VII. http://www.earlychristianwritings.com/text/diognetus-roberts.html.

Equatorial Guinea Constitution (1995).

Esposito, John and Dalia Mogahed. *Who Speaks for Islam: What Over a Billion Muslims Really Think*. New York, NY: Gallup Press, 2007.

Ethiopia Constitution (1994).

European Roma Rights Centre v. Greece, 41 E.H.R.R. SE14, ¶ 25 (2004). http://www.escr-net.org/caselaw/caselaw_show.htm?doc_id=401086.

Evangelical Climate Initiative. "*Climate Change: An Evangelical Call to Action*." Christians and Climate, 2006. http://pub.christiansandclimate.org/pub/statement-booklet.pdf.

Fearon, James D. and David Laitin. "Ethnicity, Insurgency, and Civil War." *American Political Science Review* 97 (2003): 75–90.

"Final Declaration of the Catholic-Muslim Forum." Presented at The Catholic-Muslim Forum, Rome, Italy, November 4–6, 2008.

Finnis, John. "Natural Law and Legal Reasoning." *Cleveland State Law Review* 38:1 (1990): 1–13.

Fisher-Ogden, Daryl, and Shelley Ross Saxer. "World Religions and Clean Water Laws." *Duke Environmental Law and Policy Forum* 17 (2006): 63–118.

"Five Pensioners" Case, Case No. 12,034, Inter-Am. C.H.R. (Feb. 28, 2003). http://www1.umn.edu/humanrts/iachr/C/98-ing.html.

Fleshman, Michael. "Laying Africa's Roads to Prosperity." *Africa Renewal*, 22 #4 (January 2009): 12–15. http://www.un.org/ecosocdev/geninfo/afrec/vol22no4/224-infrastructure.html.

Fogel, Robert William. *The Fourth Great Awakening and the Future of Egalitarianism*, Chicago: University of Chicago Press, 2000.

Fox, Jonathan. *Religion, Civilization, and Civil War: 1945 Through the New Millennium*. Lanham, MD: Lexington Books, 2004.

Frank, Philipp. *Modern Science and its Philosophy*. Cambridge: Harvard University Press, 1949.

Gadamer, Hans Georg. *Truth and Method*. Edited by Joel Weinsheimer and Donald G. Marshall. London: Continuum Publishing Group, 1975.

Gambia Constitution (1997).

Geertz, Clifford. "The Bazaar Economy: Information and Search in Peasant Marketing." *American Economic Review* 68 (May 1978): 28–32.

Georgescu-Roegen, Nicholas. *Analytical Economics*. Cambridge: Harvard University Press, 1966.

______. "Utility and Value in Economic Thought." *Dictionary of the History of Ideas*. Edited by Philip P. Weiner, vol. 4. New York: Charles Scribner & Sons, 1973: 450–57.

al Ghazālī, Abū Ḥāmid. *Qawā'id al-'Aqā'id fī l-Tawḥīd* in *Rasā'il al-Ghazālī*. Beirut: Dār al-Fikr, 1996.

Ghazvinian, John. *Untapped: The Scramble for Africa's Oil*. Orlando, FL: Harcourt, Inc. 2007.

Ginsburg, T. "Does Law Matter for Economic Development? Evidence from East Asia" 34 Law & Society Review (2000): 829–56.

Giri, Ananta Kumar. "Rethinking Human Well-being: A Dialogue with Amartya Sen." *Journal of International Development* 12 (2000):1003–18.

Goddard, Hugh. *A History of Christian-Muslim Relations*. Chicago: New Amsterdam Books, 2000.

Goma'a, Ali. *al-Bayān*. Cairo: al-Muqaṭṭam, 2005.

______. *al-Ṭarīq ilā al-Turāth al-Islāmī*. al-Muhandisīn, al-Jīzah: Nahḍat Miṣr lil-Ṭibā'ah wa-al-Nashr wa-al-Tawzī', 2004.

Gray, John. *Al Qaeda and What It Means to Be Modern*. New York: The New Press, 2003.

Gray, Louise. "Medina To Go green." *Telegraph* (November 3, 2009). http://www.telegraph.co.uk/earth/earthnews/6487910/Medina-to-go-green.html.

Gregg, Robert C., translated, *Athanasius: The Life of Antony and the Letter to Marcellinus*. New York: Paulist Press, 1980.

Gregory, Saint. *Theological Orations*. http://www.newadvent.org/fathers/3102.htm.

Griffith, Sidney. *The Church in the Shadow of the Mosque: Christians and Muslims in the World of Islam*. Princeton: Princeton University Press, 2008.

______. "Syriacisms in the 'Arabic Qur'ān': Who were those who said 'Allāh is third of three' according to *al-Mā'idah* 73." In *A Word Fitly Spoken: Studies in Mediaeval Exegesis of the Hebrew Bible and the Qur'ān Presented to Haggai Ben-Shamma*.

Edited by Simon Hopkins, Sarah Stroumsa, and Bruno Chiesa. 83–110. Jerusalem: Ben-Zvi, 2007.

Gülen, M. Fethullah. *M. Fethullah Gülen: Essays, Perspectives, Opinions.* Somerset, NJ: The Light Inc., 2002.

Habermas, Jurgen. *The Divided West*, edited and translated by Ciaran Cronin. Cambridge: Polity Press, 2008.

ul Haq, Mahbub. *Reflections on Human Development.* New York: Oxford University Press, 1995.

Haddad, Yvonne Yazbeck and Wadi Z. Haddad, editors. *Christian-Muslim Encounters.* Gainesville, FL: University Press of Florida, 1995.

Halkin, A. S. "The Hashwiyya." *Journal of the American Oriental Society* 54, no. 1 (1934): 1–28.

Hall, R. Bruce. "Evangelicals and Environmentalists United," *New Scientist* (April 1, 2006). http://www.newscientist.com/article/mg19025454.700.

al-Ḥārith b. Abī Asama. *Musnad al-Ḥārith (Zawā'id al-Haythamī).* Madina: Markaz Khidmat al-Sunnah, 1992.

Hasenclever, Andreas and Volker Rittberger. "Does Religion Make a Difference? Theoretical Approaches to the Impact of Faith on Political Conflict," *Religion in International Relations: The Return from Exile.* edited by Fabio Petito and Pavlos Hatzopoulos, 107–14. New York, NY: Palgrave Macmillan, 2003.

Hauerwas, Stanley. *A Community of Character: Toward a Constructive Christian Social Ethic.* South Bend, IN: University of Notre Dame Press, 1981.

Hayes, Bernadette C. and Manussos Marangudakis. "Religion and Environmental Issues Within Anglo-American Democracies." *Review of Religious Research* 42, no. 2 (2000): 159–74.

Hayhoe, Katherine, and Andrew Farley. *A Climate for Change: Global Warming Facts for Faith-Based Decisions.* New York: Faith Words, 2000.

Heap, Shaun Hargreaves, Martin Hollis, Bruce Lyons, Robert Sugden, and Albert Weale. *The Theory of Choice: A Critical Guide.* Oxford: Blackwell Publishers, 1994.

Hegel, G. W. F. *Elements of the Philosophy of Right.* Edited by Allen W. Wood. Cambridge: Cambridge University Press, 1991.

______. *Phenomenology of Spirit.* Oxford: Oxford University Press, 1979.

______. *The Philosophy of History*, translated by J. Sibree. Buffalo, NY: Prometheus Books, 1991.

Henkel, Reinhard. "State–Church Relationships in Germany: Past and Present," *GeoJournal* 67 (2006): 307–16.

Hick, John. "Islam and Christian Monotheism." *Islam in a World of Diverse Faiths.* Edited by Dan Cohn-Sherbok, 1–17. New York: St. Martin's Press, 1991.

Hill, Kenneth, et al. *Trends in Child Mortality in the Developing World: 1960 to 1996.* New York: UNICEF, 1999.

Himmelfarb, Gertrude. *The Roads to Modernity: The British, French and American Enlightenments.* London: Vintage Books, 2004.

Hobson, J. A. *Work and Wealth.* New York: The Macmillan Company, 1922.

Houlgate, Stephen. *An Introduction to Hegel: Freedom, Truth and History.* Oxford: Wiley Blackwell, 2005.

Huber, Bishop Wolfgang. "It Is Not Too Late to Respond to Climate Change: An Appeal by the Chair of the Evangelical Church of Germany." Evangelical Church in Germany, EKD-Text 89, June 2007, http://www.ekd.de/download/ekd_texte__89_engl(1).pdf.

Huber, Bishop Wolfgang. "The Judeo-Christian Tradition." *The Cultural Values of Europe.* edited by Hans Joas and Klaus Wiegandt. 43–58. Liverpool: Liverpool University Press, 2008.

Hull, R. Bruce. "God's Will and the Climate: as Evangelicals Join the Fight Against Climate Change, Are We at a Turning Point in Bringing Religion and Environmentalism Together." *New Scientist* 190, no. 2545 (2006): 23.

Humanitarian Policy and Conflict Research International. *Kalimantan: The Conflict*, http://www.preventconflict.org/portal/main/maps_kalimantan_conflict.php.

______. *Maluku: The Conflict.* http://www.preventconflict.org/portal/main/maps_maluku_conflict.php.

______. *Sulawesi: The Conflict in Central Sulawesi*, http://www.preventconflict.org/portal/main/maps_sulawesi_conflict.php.

Huntington, Samuel P., "The Clash of Civilizations?" *Foreign Affairs* 72 (Summer 1993): 22–50. http://www.foreignaffairs.com/articles/48950/samuel-p-huntington/the-clash-of-civilizations.

Ibn Hishām. *al-sīrat al-Nabawiyyah.* Beirut: Dār al-Kutub al-'Ilmiyyah, 2004.

Ibn Isḥāq. *Sīrat Rasūl Allah.* In *The Life of Muhammad.* Translated by A. Guillaume. 79–81. Oxford: Oxford University Press, 1955.

Ibn Kathīr. *Tafsīr.* Beirut: Dār al-Ma'rifah, 2006.

Int'l Ass'n Autism-Europe v. France, 38 E.H.R.R. CD265 (2004).

International Crisis Group. *Indonesia Backgrounder: Jihad in Central Sulawesi* (Feb. 3, 2004). Asia Reporter No. 74, http://www.crisisgroup.org/home/index.cfm?id=2500&l=1.

———. *Indonesia: Overcoming Murder and Chaos in Maluku* (Dec. 19, 2000). Asia Report No. 10.

______. *Indonesia: The Search for Peace in Maluku* (Feb. 8, 2008). Asia Report No. 31. http://www.crisisgroup.org/home/index.cfm?id=1454&l=1

______. *Indonesia: Tackling Radicalism in Poso* (Jan. 22, 2008). Asia Briefing No. 75. http://www.crisisgroup.org/home/index.cfm?id=5266&l=1.

______. *Indonesia: Violence Erupts Again in Ambon* (May 17, 2004). Asia Briefing No. 32, http://www.crisisgroup.org/home/index.cfm?id=2754&l=1.

International Crisis Group. *Jihadism in Indonesia: Poso on the Edge* (Jan. 24, 2007), Asia Report No. 127. http://www.crisisgroup.org/home/index.cfm?id=4624&l=1.

______. *Weakening Indonesia's Mujahidin Networks: Lessons from Maluku and Poso* (Oct. 13, 2005). Asia Report No. 103, http://www.crisisgroup.org/home/index.cfm?id=3751&l=1.

International Monetary Fund. "Africa Conference Debates Way Forward Amid Crisis." *IMF Survey Magazine: Countries and Regions, Tanzanian Conference.* March 13, 2009. http://imf.org/external/pubs/ft/survey/so/2009/CAR031309A.htm.

Israel, Jonathan I. *Enlightenment Contested: Philosophy, Modernity and the Emancipation of Man. 1670–1752.* Oxford: Oxford University Press, 2006.

Jaggard, Lyn. "The Reflexivity of Ideas in Climate Change Policy: German, European and International Politics." In *Europe and Global Climate Change.* Edited by Paul G. Harris. Edward Elgar Publishing, 2007.

al-Jāḥiẓ, Abū 'Uthmān. *al-Radd 'ala'l-Naṣārā* in *Rasā'il al-Jāḥiẓ al-Rasa'il al-Kalamiyyah.* Edited by 'Ali Bu-Malham. Beirut: Dār wa-Maktabat al-Hilāl and Dār al-Biḥār, 2004.

Jastrow, Robert. *God and the Astronomers.* New York: W. W. Norton & Co., 2000.

Johannesburg Declaration on Sustainable Development, A/CONF.199/20, Chapter 1, Resolution 1, Johannesburg, September 2002.

Jongeneel, J.A.B. "The Protestant Missionary Movement up to 1789." *Missiology, An Ecumenical Introduction: Texts and Contexts of Global Christianity.* Edited by A. Camps, L.A. Hoedemaker, M.R. Spindler & F.J. Verstraelen, 222–28. Grand Rapids: William Eerdmans Publishing, 1995.

Jongeneel, J.A.B. & J.M. van Engelen. "Contemporary Currents in Missiology." *Missiology, An Ecumenical Introduction: Texts and Contexts of Global Christianity.* Edited by A.

Camps, L.A. Hoedemaker, M.R. Spindler & F.J. Verstraelen, 438–57. Grand Rapids: William Eerdmans Publishing, 1995.

al-Juday', 'Abd Allāh Yūsuf. *al-'Aqīdah al-Salafiyyah fī Kalām Rabb al-Bariyyah*. Riyāḍ: Dār al-Imām Mālik, 1995.

Juergensmeyer, Mark. *Terror in the Mind of God: The Global Rise of Religious Violence*. Berkeley, CA: University of California Press, 2003.

Kahneman, Daniel and Amos Tversky. "Prospect Theory: An Analysis of Decision Under Risk." *Econometrica* 47, no. 2 (1979): 263–92.

Kaba, Amadu Jackay. "The Spread of Christianity and Islam in Africa: A Survey and Analysis of the Numbers and Percentages of Christians, Muslims and Those Who Practice Indigenous Religions." *Western Journal of Black Studies* 29 (2005): 553–70, tbl 1.

Kalin, Ibrahim. "Islam and Peace: A Survey of the Sources of Peace in the Islamic Tradition." *Islamic Studies* 44 (2005): 327–62.

______. "Knowing the Self and the Non-Self: Towards a Philosophy of Non-Subjectivism." *Journal of Muhyiddin Ibn 'Arabi Society* 43 (2008): 93–106.

______. *Knowledge in Later Islamic Philosophy: Mullā Ṣadrā On Existence, Intellect and Intuition*. Oxford: Oxford University Press, 2010.

______. "Roots of Misconception: Euro-American Perceptions of Islam Before and After September 11th." *Islam, Fundamentalism, and the Betrayal of Tradition*. Edited by Joseph Lumbard, 149–85. Bloomington, IN: World Wisdom Inc., 2004.

______. "Seeking Common Ground Between Muslims and Christians." Paper presented at *A Common Word and the Future of Muslim-Christian Relations*. Georgetown University, Washington DC, 2009.

______. "Sources of Tolerance and Intolerance in Islam: The Case of the People of the Book." *Religious Tolerance in World Religions*. Edited by Jacob Neusner and Bruce Chilton, 239–73. West Conshohocken, PA: Templeton Foundation Press, 2008.

Kant, Immanuel. *Critique of the Power of Judgement*. Edited by Paul Guyer and Eric Matthews. Cambridge: Cambridge University Press, 2000.

______. *Critique of Pure Reason*. Edited by Paul Guyer and Allen Wood. Cambridge: Cambridge University Press, 1998.

______. *Practical Philosophy*. Edited by Mary Gregor. Cambridge: Cambridge University Press, 1996.

______. *Religion and Rational Theology*. Edited by Allen Wood and George Di Giovanni. Cambridge: Cambridge University Press, 2001.

Kaufmann D., A. Kraay, & M. Mastruzzi. *Governance Matters VIII: Governance Indicators for 1996–2008* (2009). http://info.worldbank.org/governance/wgi/mc_chart.asp.

Keefer, Philip and Stanley Knack. "Social Capital, Social Norms and the New Institutional Economics." *Handbook of New Institutional Economics*. Edited by Claude Menard and Mary M. Shirley. Dordrecht, the Netherlands: Springer, 2005.

Kister, M.J. "The Market of the Prophet." *Journal of the Economic and Social History of the Orient* (January 1965): 272–76.

Kniss, Fred & David Todd Campbell, "The Effect of Religious Orientation on International Relief and Development Organizations." *Journal for the Scientific Study of Religion* 36 (1997): 93–103.

Kolb, David. *The Critique of Pure Modernity: Hegel, Heidegger and After*. Chicago: The University of Chicago Press, 1986.

Krech III, Shepard, J. R. McNeill and Carolyn Merchant, editors. *Encyclopedia of World Environmental History*. Vol. 1. New York: Routledge, 2003.

Küng, Hans. *Christianity and the World Religions*. London: Fount, 1987.

LaFraniere, Sharon. "Cell phones Catapult Rural Africa to 21st Century," *The New York Times* (August 25, 2005) http://www.nytimes.com/2005/08/25/international/africa/25africa.html.

Lal, Deepak. *Unintended Consequences: The Impact of Factor Endowments, Culture, and Politics on Long-Run Economic Performance.* Cambridge: The MIT Press, 1998.

Land and Maritime Boundary Between Cameroon and Nigeria (Cameroon v. Nigeria) 2002 I.C.J. Reports 303, ¶ 256 (Oct. 10), http://www.icj-cij.org/docket/files/94/7453.pdf.

Landau, Christopher. "Faith Leaders Urge Climate Curbs," *BBC News* (November 28, 2008). http://news.bbc.co.uk/2/hi/europe/7753784.stm (accessed March 26, 2010).

Landler, Mark. "Trade Barriers Rise as Slump Tightens Grip." *The New York Times* (March 23, 2009) A1, http://www.nytimes.com/2009/03/23/world/23trade.html?scp=1&sq=Trade%20Barriers%20Rise%20as%20Slump%20Tightens%20Grip,%20&st=cse.

Lash, Nicholas. *Believing Three Ways in One God: A Reading of the Apostle's Creed.* South Bend, IN: University of Notre Dame Press, 1993.

"Latest Major Action: 9/23/2008." The Official Web site of "A Common Word." http://www.acommonword.com/index.php?page=newcontent&item=3.

Lawson, Sister Penelope, trans., *On the Incarnation: The Treatise De Incarnatione Verbi Dei by St. Athanasius.* New York: Macmillan Publishing Company, 1946.

Lawson, Todd. *The Crucifixion and the Qur'ān.* Oxford: Oneworld Publications, 2009.

Lebret, L.J., O.P. *Dynamique concrète du développement Paris: Economie et Humanisme.* Les editions ouvrierès, 1961.

Lesser, Jonathan A., Daniel E. Dobbs, and Richard O. Zerbe, Jr. *Environmental Economics and Policy.* Reading, MA: Addison-Wesley Longman, 1997.

Liberia Constitution (1986).

Lindbeck, George A. *The Nature of Doctrine: Religion and Theology in a Postliberal Age.* Louisville, KY: Westminster John Knox Press 1984.

Linden, Ian. *Global Catholicism: Diversity and Change Since Vatican II.* New York: Columbia University Press, 2009.

Lings, Martin. *Muhammad: His Life Based on the Earliest Sources.* Cambridge: The Islamic Texts Society, 1991.

Linnan, David. "The New, New Legal Development Model." In *Legitimacy, Legal Development & Change: Law & Modernization Reconsidered, edited by David Linnan.* Forthcoming 2011.

Little, David. "Religious Militancy," in *Turbulent Peace: The Challenges of Managing International Conflict*, edited by Chester A. Crocker, Fen Osler Hampson, and Pamela Aall, 79–91. United States Institute of Peace Press, 2001.

Llewellyn, Othman Abd-ar-Rahman. "The Basis for a Discipline of Islamic Environmental Law." In *Islam and Ecology: A Bestowed Trust*, edited by Richard C. Foltz, Frederick M. Denny, and Azizan Baharuddin. Cambridge: Harvard University Press, 2003.

Lorenz, Edward. "Trust, Contract and Economic Cooperation." *Cambridge Journal of Economics* 23 (1999): 301–15.

Lossky, Vladimir. *Orthodox Theology: An Introduction.* New York: St. Vladimir's Seminary Press, 1989.

Lumbard, Joseph. editor. *Islam, Fundamentalism, and the Betrayal of Tradition: Essays by Western Muslim Scholars.* Bloomington, Ind.: World Wisdom, 2004.

______. "Koranic Inclusivism in an Age of Globalization." *Iqbal Review* 46, no. 2 (April 2005): 95–104. http://www.allamaiqbal.com/publications/journals/review/oct05/index.htm.

______. "The Uncommonality of 'A Common Word.'" *Crown Paper.* Brandeis University Crown Center for Middle East Studies 3 (October 2009). http://www.brandeis.edu/crown/publications/cp/CP3.pdf.

Lutz, Mark and Kenneth Lux. *Humanistic Economics: The New Challenge.* New York: The Bootstrap Press, 1988.

Macdonald-Radcliff, Alistair and Roland Schatz, editors. *C1 Annual Dialogue Report on Religion and Values: 2009*. Beirut: InnoVatio Ltd., 2009. http://www.yale.edu/faith/downloads/070809%20C-1%20World%20Dialogue%202009%20Report.pdf.

MacIntyre, Alasdair C. *After Virtue: A Study in Moral Theory*. London: Duckworth, 1981.

Macquarrie, John. "Christ and the Saviour Figures." *Jesus Christ in Modern Thought*. London: SCM Press and Philadelphia: Trinity Press International, 1990.

______. *Principles of Christian Theology*, 2nd edition. New York: Macmillan, 1997.

Madelung, Wilferd. "The Origins of the Controversy Regarding the Creation of the Qur'ān." In *Religious Schools and Sects in Medieval Islam*, 504–25. London: Variorum Reprints, 1985.

Madigan, Daniel A. "Gottes Botschaft an die Welt: Christen und Muslime, Jesus und der Koran." *Communio* 32.1 (2003): 100–12.

______. "Mary and Muhammad: Bearers of the Word." *Australasian Catholic Record* 80 (2003): 417–27.

______. "*Nostra Aetate* and the Questions It Chose to Leave Open." *Gregorianum* 87.4 (2006): 781–96.

______. "People of the Word: Reading John's Prologue with a Muslim." *Review and Expositor* 104.1 (2007): 81–95.

al-Maghnīsāwī, Abū 'l-Muntahā. *Imām Abū Ḥanīfa's Al-Fiqh al-Akbar Explained*. Translated by Abdur-Rahman ibn Yusuf. Santa Barbara: White Thread Press, 2007.

Malherbe, Abraham J. and Everett Ferguson, translated. *Gregory of Nyssa: The Life of Moses*. New York: Paulist Press, 1978.

Mbiti, John S. *African Religions and Philosophy*. London: Heinemann, 1971.

McAuliffe, Jane Dammen. *Qur'anic Christians: An Analysis of Classical and Modern Exegesis*. Cambridge: Cambridge University Press, 1991.

McCarthy, A. J. *The Theology of al-Ash'arī*. Beirut: Imprimerie Catholique, 1953.

McDermott, Martin J. *The Theology of al-Shaikh al-Mufid (413–1022)*. Beirut: Dar El-Machreq, 1978.

McKenna, Phil. "Climate Change Unites Science and Religion." *New Scientist* (January 17, 2007). http://www.newscientist.com/article/dn10975-climate-change-unites-science-and-religion.html.

McMillan, John. *Reinventing the Bazaar: A Natural History of Markets*. New York: W.W. Norton & Company Inc., 2002.

McNeil, J. R. *Something New Under the Sun: An Environmental History of the Twentieth-Century World*. New York: W.W. Norton & Co., 2001.

Menocal, Maria Rosa. *The Ornament of the World: How Muslims, Jews, and Christians Created a Culture of Tolerance in Medieval Islam*. Boston: Little, Brown and Company, 2002.

Meyendorff, John. *Byzantine Theology: Historical Trends and Doctrinal Themes*. New York: Fordham University Press, 1974.

______. *Grégoire Palamas: Défense des saints hésychastes*. Vol. 2. Louvain: Spicilegium Sacrum Lovaniense, 1959.

______. editor. *Gregory Palamas: The Triads*. New York: Paulist Press, 1982.

Mez, Adam. *Islamic Civilization in the Fourth Century of Hijrah*. Translated by Salahuddin Khuda Bukhsh and D.S. Margoliouth. London: Luzac & Co., Inc., 1937.

______. *The Renaissance of Islam*. New York: AMS Press, 1975.

Mill, John Stuart. *System of Logic*. New York: Harpers and Brothers, 1884.

Milbank, John. *Being Reconciled: Ontology and Pardon*. London: Routledge, 2003.

Mill, John Stuart. *Theology and Social Theory: Beyond Secular Reason*. Oxford: Blackwell, 1990.

Minister of Health v. Treatment Action Campaign 2002 (5) SA 721 (CC) (S. Afr.) (2002). http://www.saflii.org/za/cases/ZACC/2002/15.pdf.

Minister of Pub. Works v. Kyalami Ridge Envtl. Ass'n (CCT 55/00) [2001] ZACC 19; 2001 (3) SA 1151 (CC); 2001 (7) BCLR 652 (CC) (29 May 2001). http://www.saflii.org/za/cases/ZACC/2001/19.pdf.

Mirakhor, Abbas and Idris Samawi Hamid. *Islam and Development: The Institutional Framework*. New York: Global Scholarly Publications, 2010, Ch. 5.

Mishan, Ezra J. *Economic Myths and the Mythology of Economics*. Atlantic Highlands, N.J.: Humanities Press International, 1986.

"Morning Prayers." Orthodox Church in America, http://yya.oca.org/TheHub/Prayers/VariousPrayers/morning_prayers.htm.

Muhaiyaddeen, M.R. Bawa. *Asmā'ul-Ḥusnā: The 99 Beautiful Names of Allah*. Philadelphia: Fellowship Press, 1979.

bin Muhammad, H.R.H. Prince Ghazi. "*A Common Word Between Us and You*: Theological Motives and Expectations." Eugen Biser Award Ceremony Speech, Munich Germany (November 22, 2008). http://www.acommonword.com//en/Ghazi-Biser-Speech.pdf.

______. *The Crisis of the Islamic World*. London: Islamic World Library, 1996.

Muller, Jerry Z. *The Mind and the Market: Capitalism in Western Thought*. New York: Anchor Books, 2002.

Murata, Sachiko and William C. Chittick. *The Vision of Islam*. New York: Paragon House, 1994.

al-Mūsawī al-Khū'ī, Al-Sayyid Abū al-Qāsim. *The Prolegomena to the Qur'ān*. Translated by Abdulaziz A. Sachedina. New York: Oxford University Press, 1998.

Museveni, Yoweri. *Sowing the Mustard Seed: The Struggle for Freedom and Democracy in Uganda*, (Oxford: Macmillan, 1997).

Musgrave, Alan. " 'Unrealistic Assumptions' in Economic Theory: The F-twist Untwisted." *Kyklos* 34 (1981): 377–87.

Muslim, Sahīh . *Kitāb al-Dhikr wa'l-Du'ah wa al-tawbah*. 15 (*Hadīth* 7054).

Nagel, Thomas. *Mortal Questions*. Cambridge: Cambridge University Press, 1979.

______. *The View From Nowhere*. New York: Oxford University Press, 1986.

Nagle, John Copeland. "The Evangelical Debate Over Climate Change." *University of St. Thomas Law Journal* 5 (2008): 53–86.

______. "Playing Noah." *Minnesota Law Review* 82 (1998): 1171–260.

Namibia Constitution (1992).

Nasr, Seyyed Hossein. "Comments on a Few Theological Issues in Islamic-Christian Dialogue." In *Christian-Muslim Encounters*, edited by Yvonne Yazbeck Haddad and Wadi Zaidan Haddad, 457–67. Florida: Florida University Press, 1995.

______. *The Encounter of Man and Nature: The Spiritual Crisis of Modern Man*. London: Allen & Unwin, 1968.

______. *The Heart of Islam: Enduring Values for Humanity*. San Francisco: Harper San Francisco, 2002.

______. *Ideals and Realities of Islam*. London: George Allen and Unwin, 1966.

______. "Islam and the Environment." Lecture delivered at Georgetown University School of Foreign Service in Doha, Qatar, January 26, 2009. http://cirs.georgetown.edu/63063.html.

______. *Islam and the Plight of Modern Man*. Chicago: Kazi Publications, 2001.

______. "Islamic-Christian Dialogues: Problems and Obstacles to be Pondered and Overcome." *Muslim World*, July-October, 1998: 457–67.

______. *Islamic Life and Thought*. Chicago: Kazi Publications 2001.

______. *Islamic Philosophy from its Origin to the Present: Philosophy in the Land of Prophecy*. New York: State University of New York Press, 2006.

______. *Knowledge and the Sacred*. Albany, New York: State University of New York Press, 1989.

______. *Man and Nature: The Spiritual Crisis in Modern Man.* Chicago: Kazi Publications, 2007.

______. "Perennial Ontology and Quantum Mechanics: A Review Essay of Wolfgang Smith's *The Quantum Enigma: Finding the Hidden Key.*" *Sophia* (Summer 1997): 137.

______. *The Need for a Sacred Science.* Albany, New York: State University of New York Press, 1993.

______. *Religion and the Order of Nature.* New York: Oxford University Press, 1996.

______. *Science and Civilization in Islam.* Cambridge: Harvard University Press, 1968.

______. *Traditional Islam in the Modern World.* London and New York: KPI Limited, 1987.

______. *We and You: Let Us Meet in God's Love.* Speech given at First Catholic-Muslim Forum Conference, Vatican City, November 4–6, 2008. http://acommonword.com/en/attachments/107_Nasr-speech-to-Pope.pdf.

Nelson, Robert H. "Environmental Religion: A Theological Critique." *Case Western Reserve Law Review* 55 (2004): 51–80.

______. "The Judeo-Christian Roots of Eco-Theology" in *Taking the Environment Seriously.* Edited by Roger E. Meiners and Bruce Yandle, Lanham, Md.: Rowan and Littlefield, 1993.

Newman, N. A., translated. *The Early Christian-Muslim Dialogue Dialogue: A Collection of Documents From the First Three Islamic Centuries.* Hatfield, PA: Interdisciplinary Bible Research Institute, 1993.

"The Nicene Creed." Center for Reformed Theology and Apologetics, http://www.reformed.org/documents/index.html?mainframe=http://www.reformed.org/documents/nicene.html.

"The Nicene Creed." Orthodox Wiki, http://orthodoxwiki.org/Nicene-Constantinopolitan_Creed.

Nigeria Constitution (1999).

Norris, Frederick W. *Faith Gives Fullness to Reasoning: The Five Theological Orations of Gregory of Nazianzen.* Translation by Lionel Wickham and Frederick Williams. New York: E.J. Brill, 1991.

North, Douglas. *Understanding the Process of Economic Change.* Princeton, New Jersey: Princeton University Press, 2005.

Nussbaum, Martha C. *Frontiers of Justice.* New York: The Belknap Press, 2006.

Nyazee, Imran Ahsan Khan. *Theories of Islamic Law.* Islamabad: International Institute of Islamic Thought and Islamic Research Institute, 1994.

Obama, Barack Hussein. "Remarks by the President on a New Beginning." Address before Cairo University, June 4, 2009. http://i2.cdn.turner.com/cnn/2009/images/06/04/obama.anewbeginning.pdf.

O'Donovan, Oliver. *Resurrection and Moral Order: An Outline for Evangelical Ethics.* Leicester: Inter-Varsity Press, 1986.

O'Hara, K. *Trust from Socrates to Spin.* Duxford, UK: Icon Books, Ltd., 2004.

Oloka-Onyango, J. "Beyond the Rhetoric: Reinvigorating the Struggle for Economic and Social Rights in Africa." *California Western International Law Journal* 26 (1995): 1–71.

Omran, A. R. "The Epidemiologic Transition: a Theory of the Epidemiology of Population Change," *Milbank Memorial Fund Quarterly* 29 (1971): 509–38.

Operation Noah. http://www.operationnoah.org/.

Orthodox Peace Fellowship. "The Hevesy of Racism." http://incommunion.org/?p=263.

Ostrom, Elinor. "Doing Institutional Analysis: Digging Deeper Than Markets and Hierarchies." In *Handbook of New Institutional Economics*, edited by Claude Menard and Mary M. Shirley, 819–48. Dordrecht, the Netherlands: Springer, 2005.

Padire, Dany. "Chad: 125 Rebels Killed in Battle." *World News Network*, May 8, 2009, http://www.iol.co.za/index.php?click_id=68&art_id=nw20090508164252196C560893&set_id=.

Patton, Walter Melville. *Ahmed ibn Hanbal and the Mihna*. Leiden: E. J. Brill, 1897.

Payne, Troy L. "Comment: Cartesian Eco-Femdarkanism: She Comes from the Earth, Therefore We Are." *Environmental Law* 37 (2007): 201–40.

Pera, Marcello. *Perché Dobbiamo Dirci Cristiani*. Segrate, Italy: Mondadori, 2008.

Peters, J.R.T.M. *God's Created Speech*. Leiden: E.J. Brill, 1976.

Petroleum Act, Chapter P10 of the Laws of the Federation of Nigeria, http://www.nigeria-law.org/Petroleum%20Act.htm.

Pham, Peter, *Islamism Comes to the Niger Delta*, http://worlddefensereview.com/pham113006.shtml.

Phillips, Kevin. *American Theocracy: The Peril and Politics of Radical Religion, Oil, and Borrowed Money in the 21st Century*. New York: Viking Press, 2006.

Ping, H.E. Jean. *Message of Congratulations to Mr. Barack Obama, President of the United States of America* (Assembly/AU/Message (XII) (Nov. 5, 2008).

Pinkard, Terry. *Hegel's Phenomenology: The Sociality of Reason*. Cambridge: Cambridge University Press, 1996.

Piper, John, video response to "A Common Word." http://www.desiringgod.org/Blog/1032_a_common_word_between_us/.

Pippin, Robert. *Hegel's Idealism: The Satisfactions of Self-Consciousness*. Cambridge: Cambridge University Press, 1989.

Polanyi, Karl. *Primitive, Archaic, and Modern Economics*. Boston: Beacon Press, 1971.

Pope Benedict XVI. *Caritas in Veritate*. Encyclical Letter, 2009. http://www.vatican.va/holy_father/benedict_xvi/encyclicals/documents/hf_ben-xvi_enc_20090629_caritas-in-veritate_en.html.

______. "Faith, Reason, and the University." Address given at the University of Regensburg, Regensburg, Germany, September 12, 2006, http://www.ewtn.com/library/papaldoc/b16bavaria11.htm.

______. Homily given at the Mass for the Inauguration of the Pontificate of Pope Benedict XVI, Vatican City, April 24, 2005. http://www.vatican.va/holy_father/benedict_xvi/homilies/documents/hf_ben-xvi_hom_20050424_inizio-pontificato_en.html.

______. "Meeting With Muslim Religious Leaders, Members of the Diplomatic Corps and Rectors of Universities in Jordan." Address before Mosque al-Hussein bin Talal – Amman, Jordan, May 9, 2009. http://www.vatican.va/holy_father/benedict_xvi/speeches/2009/may/documents/hf_ben-xvi_spe_20090509_capi-musulmani_en.html.

______. "Meeting With Representatives of the Muslim Community of Cameroon." March 19, 2009. http://www.vatican.va/holy_father/benedict_xvi/speeches/2009/march/documents/hf_ben-xvi_spe_20090319_comunita-musulmana_en.html.

Pope John XXIII. *Mater et Magistra*. http://www.vatican.va/holy_father/john_xxiii/encyclicals/documents/hf_j-xxiii_enc_15051961_mater_en.html.

______. *Pacem in Terris*. http://www.vatican.va/holy_father/john_xxiii/encyclicals/documents/hf_j-xxiii_enc_11041963_pacem_en.html.

Pope John Paul II. *Laborem exercens*. http://www.vatican.va/holy_father/john_paul_ii/encyclicals/documents/hf_jp-ii_enc_14091981_laborem-exercens_en.html.

______. "Sollicitudo Rei Socialis." December 30, 1987. http://www.vatican.va/edocs/ENG0223/_INDEX.HTM.

Pope Paul VI, *Ecclesiam Suam*, encyclical letter, August 6, 1964. http://www.vatican.va/holy_father/paul_vi/encyclicals/documents/hf_p-vi_enc_06081964_ecclesiam_en.html.

______. *Gaudium et Spes*. http://www.vatican.va/archive/hist_councils/ii_vatican_council/documents/vat-ii_cons_19651207_gaudium-et-spes_en.html.

______. "Lumen Gentium." In *Vatican Council II: Constitutions, Decrees, Declarations*, edited by Austin Flannery. Northport, NY: Costello Publishing Co., 1996.

http://www.vatican.va/archive/hist_councils/ii_vatican_council/documents/vat-ii_const_19641121_lumen-gentium_en.html.

______."Nostra Aetate." Declaration, October 28, 1965. http://www.vatican.va/archive/hist_councils/ii_vatican_council/documents/vat-ii_decl_19651028_nostra-aetate_en.html.

______."Populorum Progressio." Encyclical of Pope Paul VI, no. 35, March 26, 1967. http://www.vatican.va/holy_father/paul_vi/encyclicals/documents/hf_p-vi_enc_26031967_populorum_en.html (accessed March 26, 2010).

Presbyterian Church of Sudan v. Talisman Energy Inc., 582 F.3d 244 (2nd Cir. 2009).

Prosecutor v. Kony, Case No. ICC-02/04-01/05 (Feb. 23, 2009). http://www.icc-cpi.int/iccdocs/doc/doc635577.pdf .

Prosecutor v. Omar Hassan Ahmad Al Bashir, Ref. No. ICC-02/05-01/09 (Mar. 4, 2009). http://www.icc-cpi.int/iccdocs/doc/doc639078.pdf.

Protocol to the African Charter on Human and Peoples' Rights on the Establishment of An African Court of Human and Peoples' Rights, Arts. 5 & 34(6), OAU Doc. OAU/LEG/EXP/AFCHPR/PROT (III) (June 9, 1998). http://www.achpr.org/english/_info/court_en.html.

Qayyim al-Jawziyyah, Ibn. *Zad al-Masir fi 'Ilm al-Tafsīr.* Beirut: al-Maktab al-Islāmī, 2002.

Quakers in Britain. "Responding to Climate Change." http://www.quaker.org.uk/responding-climate-change.

al-Qurṭubī, Abū 'Abdullah Muḥammad ibn Aḥmad al-Anṣārī. *al-Jāmi' li-Aḥkām al-Qur'ān* (10 vols.). Cairo: Dār al-Ḥadīth, 2002.

Radhakrishnan, S. *The Principal Upanisads.* London: George Allen and Unwin Ltd., 1969.

Rahner, Karl. "The Oneness and Threefoldness of God in Discussion with Islam." In *Theological Investigations, Vol. XVIII: God and Revelation*, 105–21. New York: Crossroads, 1983.

Ratzinger, Cardinal. *Church, Ecumenism and Politics: New Essays in Ecclesiology.* New York: Crossroad, 1988.

______. *Truth and Tolerance: Christian Belief and World Religions.* Translated by Henry Taylor. San Francisco: Ignatius Press, 2004.

al-Rāzī, Fakhr al-Dīn. *al-Tafsīr al-Kabīr* (32 vols.). Cairo: al-Maṭba'ah al-Bahiyyah al-Miṣriyyah, 1934–1962.

Reed, Dr. Charles. "Climate Change: Not Just a Green Issue: A Mission and Public Affairs Briefing Paper." Church of England, http://www.cofe.anglican.org/info/socialpublic/international/climatechange/climatechange.pdf.

______. "Through the Glass Darkly—Europe and the Politics of Climate Change, a Mission and Public Affairs Briefing Paper." Church of England, (Oct. 2007). http://www.cofe.anglican.org/info/socialpublic/international/climatechange/glass.pdf.

______. "Towards a Post-Kyoto Climate Treaty for Climate Justice: A Mission and Public Affairs Briefing Paper." Church of England. http://www.cofe.anglican.org/info/socialpublic/international/climatechange/postkyoto.pdf.

Republic of the Congo Constitution (1992).

Republic of Guinea Constitution (1990).

"Responses from Christian Leaders," The Official Web site of "A Common Word." http://www.acommonword.com/index.php?lang=en&page=responses.

Reynal-Querol, Marta. "Ethnicity, Political Systems, and Civil Wars." *Journal of Conflict Resolution* 46 (2002): 29–54.

Rissanen, Seppo. *Theological Encounter of Oriental Christians with Islam During Early Abbasid Rule.* Abo: Abo Akademis Förlag, 1993.

Robinson, Neil. *Christ in Islam and Christianity.* Albany: State University of New York Press, 1991.

Rūmī, Jālāl al-Dīn. *Masnavī-i ma`navī*. Tehran: Nashr-i Sāles, 2004.

_____. *The Mathnāwī of Jalálu'ddín Rúmí*. London: Luzac, 1982.

Rubin, Michael. "'Dialog of Civilizations'—A First-Hand Account," *Middle Eastern Quarterly* 7:1 (2000). http://www.meforum.org/39/irans-dialogue-of-civilizations-a-first-hand.

Sadr, S.K. *The Economy of the Earliest Islamic Period*. Tehran: Shahīd Beheshti University Publishing, 1996.

Sagoff, Mark. *Price, Principle, and the Environment*. New York City: Cambridge University Press, 2004.

Saint Maximos the Confessor. "Two Hundred Texts on Theology and the Incarnate Dispensation of the Son of God." *The Philokalia*, vol. 2 translated by Palmer, G.E.H., Philip Sherrard, and Kallistos Ware. London: Faber and Faber, 1981.

Samir, Samir K. and Jorgen S. Nielson, editors. *Christian Arabic Apologetics During the Abbasid Period, 750–1258*. Leiden: E.J. Brill, 1994.

Save the Children. http://www.savethechildren.org.

Sax, Joseph L. *Mountains Without Handrails: Reflections on the National Parks*. Ann Arbor: University of Michigan Press, 1980.

Schrodinger, Erwin. *Science and Humanism*. Cambridge: Cambridge University Press, 1951.

Schumacher, E.F. *Guide for the Perplexed*, New York: Harper Perennial, 1977.

_____. *Not by Bread Alone: Lectures by E. F. Schumacher*. Bloomington: World Wisdom Books, forthcoming.

Sen, Amartya. *Development as Freedom*. New York: Anchor Books, 1999.

_____. *Human Rights and Asian Values*. Carnegie Council on Ethics and International Affairs: New York, 1997 (Sixteenth Morgenthau Memorial Lecture on Ethics & Foreign Policy).

Senegal Constitution (2001).

Seymour, Susan. "A Quaker Response to the Crises of Climate Change." Quakers in Britain, http://www.quaker.org.uk/quaker-response-crisis-climate-change.

Shboul, Ahmad M. H. "Byzantium and the Arabs: The Image of the Byzantines as Mirrored in Arabic Literature." *Arab-Byzantine Relations in Early Islamic Times*. Edited by Michael Bonner, 235–60. Aldershot, Hants; Burlington, VT: Ashgate/Variorum, 2004.

Shah-Kazemi, Reza. "God as 'The Loving' in Islam." *Sophia: The Journal of Traditional Studies* 14, no. 2 (Winter 2008–2009): 74–104.

Shihata, H. H. *Market Competition in Light of the Islamic Sharī'ah*. Department of Commerce, Al-Azhar University, 1977.

Siddle, Julian. "African Aid 'Needs Science.'" *BBC News*, April 18, 2009. http://news.bbc.co.uk/2/hi/science/nature/7998169.stm.

Silber, John. "Patriarch Bartholomew—A Passion for Peace," The Ecumenical Patriarch of Constantinople, http://www.patriarchate.org/patriarch/passion-for-peace.

Silecchia, Lucia A. "Environmental Ethics from the Perspectives of NEPA and Catholic Social Teaching: Ecological Guidance for the 21st Century." *William and Mary Environmental Law and Policy Review* 28 (2004): 659–798.

Smith, Huston. *Beyond the Post-Modern Mind*. New York: Quest Books, 2003.

Smith, Wolfgang. *Cosmos and Transcendence: Breaking Through the Barrier of Scientistic Belief*. Peru, Illinois: Sherwood Sugden & Co., 1984.

_____. *The Quantum Enigma: Finding the Hidden Key*. Peru, Illinois: Sherwood Sugden, 1995.

Stone, Daniel. "The Green Pope." *Newsweek* (April 17, 2008). http://www.newsweek.com/id/132523

Soc. & Econ. Rights Action Ctr. for Econ. & Soc. Rights v. Nigeria, African Comm. Hum. & Peoples' Rights. Afr. C.H.R., Comm. No. 155/96 (2001). http://www1.umn.edu/humanrts/africa/comcases/155-96.html.

Sohn, Louis. "The Stockholm on the Human Environment." *Harvard International Law Journal* 14 (1973): 423–515.
South Africa Constitution (1996).
Spencer, Roy W., Paul K. Driessen, and E. Calvin Beisner. "An Examination of the Scientific, Ethical and Theological Implications of Climate Change Policy." Interfaith Stewardship Alliance (2005). http://www.cornwallalliance.org/docs/an-examination-of-the-scientific-ethical-and-theological-implications-of-climate-change-policy.pdf.
Stone, Christopher D. "Should Trees Have Standing? - Toward Legal Rights for Natural Objects." *Southern California Law Review* 45 (1972): 450–501.
"Street Children" Case, No. 11,383, Inter-Am. C.H.R. (Nov. 19, 1999). http://www1.umn.edu/humanrts/iachr/C/63-ing.html.
al-Tabarānī, Sulaymān Ahmad. *al-Mu'jam al-Kabīr*. Mosul: al-Jumhūrīyah al-ʿIraqīyah, 1983.
Ṭabarī, 'Alī ibn Sahl Rabbān. *Tārīkh al-Umam wa-al-Mulūk*. Amman: Dār al-Afkār al-Duwaliyyah.
______. "Treatise." In *The Early Christian-Muslim Dialogue: A Collection of Documents from the First Three Islamic Centuries*, edited by N. A. Newman, 568–657. Hatfield, PA: Interdisciplinary Biblical Research Institute, 1993.
al-Tamīmī, Abū Yaʿlā. *Musnad Aiī Yaʿlā*. Damascus, 1984.
Taylor, Charles. *Hegel*. Cambridge: Cambridge University Press, 1975.
______."Lichtung or Lebensform: Parallels Between Heidegger and Wittgenstein." In *Philosophical Arguments*. Cambridge, MA: Harvard University Press, 1995.
______. "What is Human Agency?" In *Human Agency and Language: Philosophical Papers 1*. Cambridge: Cambridge University Press, 1999.
Taymiyyah, Ibn. *al-Jawāb al-Sahīh li-man Baddala Dīn al-Masīh*. Vol. I. Edited by 'Alī b. Hasan b. Nāsir al-Almā'i. Riyadh: Dār al-Fadīlah, 2004.
The Traditional Values Coalition. "Interfaith Stewardship Alliance Officially Launched," Dec. 1, 2005, http://www.traditionalvalues.org/read/2512/interfaith-stewardship-alliance-officially-launched/.
"There's a Wideness in God's Mercy." *The Hymnal 1982*. New York: The Church Hymnal Corporation, 1982.
Thomas, David. *Anti-Christian Polemic in Early Islam: Abū 'Īsā al-Warrāq's "Against the Trinity."* Cambridge: Cambridge University Press, 1992.
______. *Early Muslim Polemic Against Christianity: Abu `Isa al-Warraq's "Against the Incarnation."* Cambridge: Cambridge University Press, 2002.
______. "The Doctrine of the Trinity in the Early Abbassid Era." *Islamic Interpretations of Christianity*, edited by Lloyd Ridgeon, 78–98. New York: St. Martin's Press, 2001.
Thurman, Howard. *Meditations from the Heart*. Boston: Beacon Press, 1999.
al-Tirmidhī, Sunan. *Kitāb Fadā'il al-Qur'ān*. Edited by The Thesaurus Islamicus Foundation. Stuttgart: Jamī'at al-Maktab al-Islāmī, 1421AH–2001 CE).
Tookey, Douglas L. "Southeast Asian Environmentalism at its Crossroads: Learning Lessons From Thailand's Eclectic Approach to Environmental Law and Policy." *Georgetown International Environmental Law Review* 11 (1999): 307–62.
Toulmin, Stephen. *Cosmopolis*. Chicago: University of Chicago Press, 1992.
Tucker, William T. "Max Weber's *Verstehen*." *The Sociological Quarterly* 6 (1965): 157. http://www.jstor.org/stable/4105245
Uganda Constitution (1995).
UNICEF. "A League Table of Child Deaths by Injury in Rich Nations," *Innocenti Report Card Issue No. 2*. http://www.unicef-irc.org/publications/pdf/repcard2e.pdf.
UNICEF digital library. "State of the World's Children 2008." http://www.unicef.org/sowc08/docs/sowc08.pdf (accessed March 26, 2010).
United Nations. Communication No. 182/1984 (9 April 1987), in *Report of the Human Rights Committee*, U.N. Doc. Supp. No. 40 (A/42/40) (1987): 160–69.

United Nations. *International Covenant on Economic, Social and Political Rights.* U.N. Doc. A/6316 (1966), 993 U.N.T.S. 3, entered into force Jan. 3, 1976. http://www2.ohchr.org/english/law/cescr.htm.

______. *Johannesburg Declaration on Sustainable Development.* A/CONF.151/26 (Vol. I) (12 August 1992). http://www.un.org/esa/sustdev/documents/WSSD_POI_PD/English/POI_PD.pdf.

______. *Millennium Declaration*, A/Res/55/2 (2000). http://www.un.org/millennium/declaration/ares552e.htm.

______. *Universal Declaration of Human Rights*, G.A. Res. 217A, U.N. Doc. A/810 (Dec. 10, 1948).

United Nations Charter arts. 55 and 56. http://www.un.org/en/documents/charter/chapter9.shtml.

United Nations Commission on Human Rights. *Report on the Status of the International Covenants on Human Rights.* 1997/72, ESCOR Supp. (No. 3) at 235, U.N. Doc. E/CN.4/1997/72 (1997). http://daccessdds.un.org/doc/UNDOC/GEN/G96/144/32/PDF/G9614432.pdf?OpenElement

United Nations Environment Program. "Declaration of the United Nations Conference on the Human Environment." http://www.unep.org/Documents.Multilingual/Default.asp?DocumentID=97&ArticleID=1503.

United Nations General Assembly. Declaration for the Establishment of a New International Economic Order. 1 May 1974, A/RES/S-6/3201.

______. Resolution 217 (III): International Bill of Human Rights, A/RES/3/217, http://www.un-documents.net/a3r217.htm.

United Nations News Center. *Somalia: UN Expert Urges End to Inhuman Practices After Recent Stonings,* http://www.un.org/apps/news/story.asp?NewsID=33079.

United Nations Security Council, S/Res/1593(2005), http://daccess-dds-ny.un.org/doc/UNDOC/GEN/N05/292/73/PDF/N0529273.pdf?OpenElement.

United Nations Program and World Health Organization program on HIV/AIDS (UNAIDS). "AIDS epidemic update." November 2009. WHO Geneva, 2009, 11 (UNAIDS/09.36E / JC1700E). http://data.unaids.org/pub/Report/2009/JC1700_Epi_Update_2009_en.pdf.

United States Conference of Catholic Bishops. "Global Climate Change: A Plea for Dialogue, Prudence, and the Common Good." United States Conference of Catholic Bishops http://www.usccb.org/sdwp/international/globalclimate.shtml.

U.S. Congress. *Congressional Record.* 110th Cong., 2d sess., 2008. Vol. 154, no. 151, H 8655–57.

U.S. Department of State. *International Religious Freedom Report* (2005), http://www.state.gov/g/drl/rls/irf/2005/51489.htm.

Uslander, E.M. *The Moral Foundation of Trust.* New York: Cambridge University Press, 2002.

Valoi, Tomas. "Holistic Ministry in Large-Scale Relief, Mozambique." *Serving with the Poor in Africa*, edited by Tetsunao Yamamori, 105. Monrovia, CA : MARC, 1996.

van Bruinessen, Martin and Julia Day Howell, *Sufism and the "Modern" in Islam.* New York: I.B. Tauris, Ltd., 2007.

Van Ess, Josef. *The Flowering of Muslim Theology.* Cambridge MA: Harvard University Press, 2006.

Veatch, Henry B. *For an Ontology of Morals: A Critique of Contemporary Ethical Theory.* Evanston: Northwestern University Press, 1971.

Versdtaelen, F. J. "The Genesis of a Common Missiology: A Case Study of Protestant and Catholic Mission Studies in the Netherlands, 1877–1988." *Missiology, An Ecumenical Introduction: Texts and Contexts of Global Christianity.* Edited by A. Camps, L.A. Hoedemaker, M.R. Spindler & F.J. Verstraelen, 423–37. Grand Rapids: William Eerdmans Publishing, 1995.

Verstaelen-Guilhuis, G.M. "The History of the Missionary Movement from the Perspective of the Third World," in *Missiology, An Ecumenical Introduction: Texts and Contexts of Global Christianity*. Edited by A. Camps, L.A. Hoedemaker, M.R. Spindler & F.J. Verstraelen, 253–62. Grand Rapids: William Eerdmans Publishing, 1995.

Vlachos, Heirotheos. *A Night in the Desert of the Holy Mountain: Discussion With a Hermit on the Jesus prayer*. Translated by Effie Mavromichali. Levadia, Greece: Birth of the Theotokos Monastery, 1991.

Volf, Miroslav, Ghazi bin Muhammad and Melissa Yarrington, editors. *A Common Word: Muslims and Christians on Loving God and Neighbor*. Cambridge, UK: William B. Eerdmans Publishing Co., 2010.

Waardenburg, Jacques. *Muslims and Others: Relations in Context*. Berlin: Walter de Gruyter, 2003.

Wamp-Ellison Resolution. *Concurrent Resolution Supporting Christian, Jewish, and Muslim Interfaith Dialogue that Promotes Peace, Understanding, Unity, and Religious Freedom*, HR Res. 374, 110th Cong., 2nd sess., *Congressional, Record* 154, no. 151, daily ed. (Sept. 23, 2008): H 8655–57.

Ware, Bishop Kallistos. *The Orthodox Way*. Crestwood, New York: St Vladimir's Seminary Press, 1995.

Weisskopf, Walter. *Alienation and Economics*. New York: Dutton, 1971.Wind, A. "The Protestant Missionary Movement from 1789 to 1963. *Missiology, An Ecumenical Introduction: Texts and Contexts of Global Christianity*. Edited by A. Camps, L.A. Hoedemaker, M.R. Spindler & F.J. Verstraelen, 237–52. Grand Rapids: William Eerdmans Publishing, 1995.

Whale Trust, "Humpback Whale Song." http://www.whaletrust.org/whales/whale_song.shtml.

White, Jr., Lyn. "The Historical Roots of Our Present Ecologic Crisis," *Science* 155, no. 3767 (1967): 1203–07.

Wicksteed, Philip. *Common Sense of Political Economy*. London: Macmillan and Co., Limited, 1910.

Williams, Archbishop of Canterbury, Rowan. "A Common Word for the Common Good." In *A Common Word Between Us and You*. Jordan: The Royal Aal al-Bayt Institute for Islamic Thought, 2009. http://www.acommonword.com/lib/downloads/Common-Good-Canterbury-FINAL-as-sent-14-7-08-1.pdf.

Williams, Rowan. "A Common Word for the Common Good," *Sophia: The Journal of Traditional Studies* 14, no. 2 (Winter 2008–2009): 39–65.

Wilson, Edward O. *The Creation: An Appeal to Save Life on Earth*. New York: W.W. Norton, 2006.

Wiwa v. Shell, 1:02-cv-07618-KMW-HBP (S.D.N.Y. Mar. 18, 2009). http://wiwavshell.org/documents/Wiwa_v_Shell_SETTLEMENT_AGREEMENT.Signed.pdf.

Wolfson, Harry Austryn. *The Philosophy of the Kalam*. Cambridge: Harvard University Press, 1976.

Wood, Barbara. *Alias Papa: A Life of Fritz Schumacher*. Oxford: Oxford University Press, 1985.

World Bank. *The East Asian Miracle: Economic Growth and Public Policy*. New York: Oxford University Press, 1993.

World Council of Churches. "Learning to Explore Love Together." Oikoumene. http://www.oikoumene.org/fileadmin/files/wcc- main/documents/p6/Learning_to_Explore_Love_Together.pdf.

World Development Indicators 2009. Washington, D.C.: World Bank Publications, 2009. World Trade Organization, *Ministerial Declarations, Annexes*, WT/MIN(05)/DEC (December 22, 2005) ¶ 36. http://www.wto.org/english/thewto_e/minist_e/min05_e/final_annex_e.htm#annexf36.

World Vision. http://www.worldvision.org.

______. http://www.worldvision.org/content.nsf/learn/our-international-work? Open Document&lpos=top_drp_OurWork_International.

______. http://www.worldvision.org/content.nsf/about/ar-financials?Open&lpos=lft_txt_2009-Annual-Review#FinancialHighlights.

Worster, Donald. *Nature's Economy: A History of Ecological Ideas.* Cambridge: Cambridge University Press, 1994.

Yamamori, Tetsunao. Introduction to *Serving the Poor in Asia, edited by* T. Yamamori, Bryant L. Myers & D. Connor. Monrovia, CA: MARC, A Division of World Vision International. 1995.

Yandle, Bruce, and Stuart Buck. "Bootleggers, Baptists, and the Global Warming Battle." *Harvard Environmental Law Review* 26 (2002): 177–230.

Yean and Bosico Children v. Dominican Republic, Case No. 12,189, Inter-Am. C.H.R., ¶ 244.

Contributors

Nicholas Adams is the Academic Director of the Cambridge Inter-Faith Programme at the University of Cambridge, UK. He studied music and then theology at Cambridge, gaining a doctorate for his work on Jürgen Habermas. His principal scholarly focus is religious argumentation in the public sphere, pursued through engagements with German Idealism (in relation to Christian theology) and Scriptural Reasoning as a model for handling multiple sets of categories simultaneously. He is the author of *Habermas and Theology* (Cambridge University Press, 2006). Having held a research fellowship at Trinity Hall, Cambridge, he is currently on the permanent faculty of the School of Divinity at the University of Edinburgh, where he teaches theology and ethics.

Cinnamon P. Carlarne is an environmental lawyer working principally on evolving systems of domestic and international environmental law and policy in the School of Law and the School of the Environment, University of South Carolina. She studied environment science at Baylor University (BA 1998) and the University of Oxford (MS 2002) and law at UC-Berkeley (JD 2001) and University of Oxford (BCL 2003). Her current work focuses on comparative climate change law and policy-making, and fragmentation in international environmental law. She is the author of *Climate Change Laws & Policy: EU & US Perspectives* (Oxford University Press, 2010) as well as of various articles in the areas of domestic and international environmental law.

Rev. Dr. John Chryssavgis was born in Australia, where he matriculated from the Scots College (1975). He received his degree in Theology from the University of Athens (1980), a diploma in Byzantine Music from the Greek Conservatory of Music (1979), and was awarded a research scholarship to St. Vladimir's Theological Seminary (1982). He completed his doctoral studies in Patristics at the University of Oxford (1983). After several months in silent retreat on Mt. Athos, he served as personal assistant to the Greek Orthodox Primate in Australia (1984–94) and was co-founder of St. Andrew's Theological College in Sydney (1985), where he was Sub-Dean and taught Patristics and Church History (1986–95). He was also Lecturer in the Divinity School (1986–90) and the School of Studies in Religion (1990–95) at the University of Sydney. In 1995, he moved to Boston, where he was appointed Professor of Theology at Holy Cross School of Theology and directed the Religious Studies Program at Hellenic College until 2002. Currently, he serves as theological advisor to the Ecumenical Patriarch on environmental issues.

James S. Cutsinger teaches theology and religious thought at the University of South Carolina at Columbia. He studied political theory and Russian at Cornell College (BA 1975) and theology at Harvard University (PhD 1980). A widely recognized writer on the *sophia perennis* and the perennialist school, he is also an authority on the theology and spirituality of the Christian East. His publications include *Advice to the Serious Seeker: Meditations on the Teaching of Frithjof Schuon* (SUNY, 1997), *Not of This World: A Treasury of Christian*

Mysticism (World Wisdom, 2003), *Reclaiming the Great Tradition: Evangelicals, Catholics, and Orthodox in Dialogue* (InterVarsity, 1997), and *Paths to the Heart: Sufism and the Christian East* (Fons Vitae, 2002).

Caner Dagli teaches in the Department of Religious Studies at College of the Holy Cross. He studied religion at George Washington (MA) and Near Eastern Studies at Cornell (BA) and Princeton (PhD). In 2006–7 he served as Interfaith Affairs Consultant in the Royal Hashemite Court of Jordan, where he participated in such projects as *An Open Letter to the Pope* (in response to the Regensburg lecture) and *A Common Word Between Us and You*. He is the author of *The Ringstones of Wisdom* (Kazi Publications, 2004), a study and translation of Ibn al-Arabi's *Fuṣūṣ al-Ḥikam*, and has published in the fields of Islamic philosophy and Sufism. He is an associate editor for the forthcoming *Study Qur'ān* from Harper Collins under chief editor Seyyed Hossein Nasr.

Maria M. Dakake teaches courses on Islam and other Near Eastern religious traditions, as well as on women in religion in the Department of Religious Studies at George Mason University. She is one of the founding faculty members of the interdisciplinary Islamic Studies Program recently established at George Mason University. She studied government at Cornell (BA 1990) and Near Eastern Studies at Princeton (MA 1998; PhD 2000). Her research interests lie in the fields of Islamic theology, philosophy, and mysticism, with a particular interest in Shī'ite and Sufi traditions and in women's issues. She has published articles and presented papers on early Shī'ism, Islamic philosophy, and Sufism. She most recently completed a book entitled *The Charismatic Community: Shi'ite Identity in Early Islam* (SUNY, 2008) and is working on an edited volume on women and Sufism.

Waleed El-Ansary is Assistant Professor of Religious Studies at the University of South Carolina, where he teaches comparative religion, Islamic studies, and Islamic economics. He studied economics at George Washington University (BA 1986) and the University of Maryland (MA 1998), and religious and Islamic studies at George Washington University (MPhil 2005; PhD 2006). He is a consultant to the Grand Mufti of Egypt and is involved in interfaith dialog. He has authored numerous publications in the areas of religion, science, and economics.

HE Shaykh Ali Goma'a is a leading signatory of *A Common Word Between Us and You* and holds one of the highest positions in Sunni Islam as Grand Mufti of Egypt, Dār al Iftā', Cairo. He is a master of both the Islamic intellectual (*'aqlī*) and transmitted (*naqlī*) sciences, and author of over 50 books as well as scores of articles. He has supervised more than 70 theses in different universities. He specializes in the science of the foundations of Islamic law (*uṣūl al-fiqh*), and studied Islamic law at al-Azhar University, Cairo (BA 1979; MA 1985; PhD 1988). There he taught in the Faculty of Islamic and Arabic Studies from the time he received his MA until his appointment as Grand Mufti of Egypt in 2003. Via Dār al Iftā', personally and through Islamic jurists working under his supervision, is responsible for the issuance of numerous significant *fatwas* or religious opinions guiding Muslims in religious questions.

The Right Reverend William O. Gregg is Assistant Bishop of the Episcopal Diocese of North Carolina-Charlotte Office. He was ordained and consecrated VI Bishop of Eastern Oregon in 2000 before coming to the Charlotte Office of the Episcopal Diocese of North Carolina in 2007. He studied at Richmond (BA 1973) and Boston University (MA 1980) as well as theology at Episcopal Divinity School in Cambridge, MA (MDiv 1977) and Notre Dame (PhD 1993). Bishop Gregg served 2001–6 as Chair of the Standing Commission on Ecumenical Relations of the General Convention of the Episcopal Church (a policy and strategy body), and serves currently as an Anglican member of the International Anglican-Orthodox Theological Dialog, and as a member of the Episcopal House of Bishops Theology Committee. He has also taught theology at St. Mary of the Woods College, a Roman Catholic women's college, and served as parish priest or chaplain in New London, CT, Charlottesville, VA, Abingdon, VA, Terra Haute, IN, and the Diocese of Northern Indiana.

Harkristuti Harkrisnowo is a widely known criminologist and public commentator, as well as human and women's rights activist in Indonesia, the world's most populous Islamic country. She studied law at the University of Indonesia (SH, LLM) and criminology at Sam Houston State University (MA, PhD). She teaches at the University of Indonesia where she leads its Center for the Study of Human Rights and serves simultaneously as Director General for Human Rights in the Indonesian Ministry of Justice. Since 1999, she has been a member of the Indonesian National Law Commission, a reform body. She is also a senior advisor to the Indonesian National Human Rights Commission and has worked within government at the deputy secretary level in the short-lived Ministry of Human Rights. She has visited at the University of South Carolina School of Law to teach in an intensive course titled "*Women's & Human Rights Under Islam.*"

Zamir Iqbal is a lead investment officer with the Quantitative Strategies, Risk and Analytics (QRA) Department of the World Bank Treasury. He earned his BBA in business, MS in computer science, and PhD in international finance from the George Washington University, where he also serves as adjunct faculty of international finance. He has written extensively in the area of Islamic finance in leading academic journals and has presented at several international forums. His research interests include Islamic finance, financial engineering, and risk management. He has co-authored several books on Islamic finance on diverse topics such as theory and practice of Islamic finance, globalization of Islamic finance, risk analysis, and stability of an Islamic financial system.

Joseph M. Isanga is a faculty member at Ave Maria School of Law in Naples, Florida and former postdoctoral research associate at the University of Notre Dame's Center for Civil and Human Rights. He is a widely published scholar on human rights in Africa and has expertise in international law, jurisprudence, law, ethics, and public policy. He is a priest from the Diocese of Jinja, Uganda. He received a BPhil from the Pontifical Urban University in Rome; a BD and LLB from Makerere University in Kampala, Uganda; a Diploma in Legal Practice from Law Development Center in Kampala, Uganda; and an LLM and JSD from the University of Notre Dame, Indiana.

Ibrahim Kalin is a faculty member at the Prince Alwaleed Bin Talal Center for Muslim-Christian Understanding, Georgetown University. He is a signatory of *A Common Word Between Us and You,* acting as its Official Spokesperson. He received his BA in history from the University of Istanbul, MA in Islamic philosophy from the International Institute of Islamic Thought and Civilization (ISTAC), and PhD in religious and Islamic studies from George Washington University. His broad interests reach into Islamic culture and history, and he is the author of *Knowledge in Later Islamic Philosophy: Mulla Ṣādrā on Existence, Intellect, and Intuition* (Oxford University Press, 2010). Prior to coming to Georgetown, he taught in the Department of Religious Studies at the College of the Holy Cross and was founding director for the SETA Foundation for Political, Economic and Social Research based in Ankara, Turkey.

David K. Linnan is a scholar of comparative, economic, and public international law with a special interest in Asian law. He studied humanities at Emory University (BA 1976) and law at the University of Chicago (JD 1979) and the University of Freiburg i.Br., Germany. He has held research or teaching appointments at the University of South Carolina-Columbia (currently in the School of Law & School of the Environment), the University of Washington-Seattle, the Australian National University in Canberra (RSPAS & Faculty of Law), the University of Melbourne, the University of Indonesia Faculty of Law and Graduate Law Program in Jakarta (separately), and the Max-Planck-Institut (Strafrecht), Freiburg i.Br.,

Germany. Since 2000 he has been the program director for the Law & Finance Institutional Partnership (http://www.lfip.org), a legal and financial sector reform project run from Jakarta now as an academic consortium of Indonesian and foreign universities.

Joseph Lumbard is Chair of the Islamic and Middle Eastern Studies Program at Brandeis University and a former adviser on interfaith affairs to King Abdullah II of Jordan. He received his PhD and MPhil in Islamic Studies from Yale University, and MA in Religious Studies and BA from George Washington University. His research focuses upon Islamic intellectual traditions with an emphasis on Sufism and Islamic philosophy. He is an associate editor for the forthcoming Harper Collins *Study Qur'ān*, and the editor of *Islam, Fundamentalism, and the Betrayal of Tradition* (World Wisdom, 2009), a collection of essays that examines the religious, political, and historical factors that have led to the rise of Islamic fundamentalism.

Daniel A. Madigan is an Australian Jesuit priest who teaches in Georgetown University's Department of Theology as the Jeanette W. and Otto J. Ruesch Family Associate Professor and Director of Graduate Studies. He studied history at Monash University (BA 1st Hons 1977), Christian religion at the Jesuit Theological College and Melbourne College of Divinity (BD 1983), and Islamic religion at Columbia University (MPhil 1993; PhD 1997). He is a Consultor of the Vatican's Commission for Religious Relations with Muslims, and a Senior Fellow of Georgetown's Prince Alwaleed Bin Talal Center for Muslim-Christian Understanding, and of the Woodstock Theological Center at Georgetown, where he directs a project on Christian theologies that are responsive to Islam. Before moving to Georgetown he taught in Rome, where he was the founder and director (2002–7) of the Institute for the Study of Religions and Cultures at the Pontifical Gregorian University. His main fields of teaching and research are Qur'ānic Studies, Interreligious Dialogue, and particularly Muslim-Christian relations. He has also taught as a visiting professor at Columbia University, Ankara University, Boston College, and Central European University.

Abbas Mirakhor is the Distinguished Scholar and First Holder of the Chair of Islamic Finance in the International Centre for Education in Islamic Finance, Kuala Lumpur, Malaysia. He attended Kansas State University, where he received his BA, MA, and PhD in economics in 1969. From 1969 to 1984, he taught in various universities in the United States and Iran. From 1984 until 1990, he served on the staff of the IMF, and from 1990 to 2008, he was the Executive Director for Afghanistan, Algeria, Ghana, Islamic Republic of Iran, Morocco, Pakistan, and Tunisia. Dr. Mirakhor is the co-author of several books on Islamic economics and finance. Some of his noteworthy works are *Islam and Development: The Institutional Framework* (with Idris Hamid, Global Scholarly Publications, 2010), *Globalization and Islamic Finance* (with Zamir Iqbal and Hossein Askari, Wiley, 2009), *Stability of Islamic Finance* (with Zamir Iqbal, Noureddine Krichenne, and Hossein Askari, Wiley, 2009), and *Essays on Iqtisad: The Islamic Approach to Economic Problems* (with Baqir al-Hasani, Nur, 1989). He has received several awards including Order of Companion of Volta for service to Ghana, conferred by the President of Ghana in 2005; Islamic Development Bank Annual Prize for Research in Islamic economics, shared with Mohsin Khan in 2003; and Quaid-e Azam Star for service to Pakistan, conferred by the President of Pakistan in 1997.

Seyyed Hossein Nasr is University Professor of Islamic Studies at the George Washington University, and is one of the world's leading experts on Islamic thought and spirituality. He has authored more than 50 books and 500 articles. Born in Tehran, raised in the United States, and graduate of the Massachusetts Institute of Technology (MIT) and Harvard, Professor Nasr is a well known and highly respected intellectual figure in both the West and the Islamic world. He is the chief editor of the forthcoming Harper Collins *Study Qur'ān*.

Index